Countering the Financing of Terrorism

Groups committing acts of terrorism have adapted their means of financing to elude detection since the 9/11 attacks in the United States. Surveying the global community's multi-year effort to cut off terrorist funding, this volume offers a much-needed analysis of a complex, widely discussed, yet poorly understood subject. While books on terrorism have touched upon the topic, this is the first comprehensive, balanced, and scholarly overview of terrorist financing, its methods, and efforts to counter it. Bringing together leading analysts of terrorism, international relations, global finance, law, and criminology, this book provides a critical assessment of the international effort to restrict terrorist financing. It evaluates the costs and benefits and offers recommendations for more effective policies for the future.

Thomas J. Biersteker is Curt Gasteyger Professor of International Security and Conflict Studies at the Graduate Institute of International Studies, Geneva and Olive C. Watson Professor at the Watson Institute for International Studies and Department of Political Science, Brown University.

Sue E. Eckert is Senior Fellow at the Watson Institute for International Studies, Brown University. She previously served as Assistant Secretary of Commerce responsible for regulating dual-use commodities, and as senior staff on the House International Relations Committee dealing with sanctions and export controls.

Contributions: Zachary Abuza; Donald deKieffer; Douglas Farah; Rohan Gunaratna; Jeroen Gunning; Michael Levi; Samuel Munzele Maimbo; Amit Modi; Nikos Passas; Peter Romaniuk; Jessica Stern and Phil Williams.

Countering the Financing of Terrorism

Edited by Thomas J. Biersteker and
Sue E. Eckert

Routledge
Taylor & Francis Group

LONDON AND NEW YORK

First published 2008
by Routledge
2 Park Square, Milton Park, Abingdon, Oxon OX14 4RN

Simultaneously published in the US and Canada
by Routledge
270 Madison Ave, New York, NY 10016

Routledge is an imprint of the Taylor & Francis Group, an informa business

© 2008 Thomas J. Biersteker and Sue E. Eckert, editorial matter and selection;
the contributors, their own chapters

Typeset in Times New Roman by
RefineCatch Limited, Bungay, Suffolk
Printed and bound in Great Britain by
Antony Rowe Ltd, Chippenham

British Library Cataloguing in Publication Data
A catalogue record for this book is available from the British Library

Library of Congress Cataloging in Publication Data
A catalog record for this book has been requested

ISBN10: 0–415–39642–5 (hbk)
ISBN10: 0–415–39643–3 (pbk)
ISBN10: 0–203–94463–1 (ebk)

ISBN13: 978–0–415–39642–4 (hbk)
ISBN13: 978–0–415–39643–1 (pbk)
ISBN13: 978–0–203–94463–9 (ebk)

Contents

Illustrations

Contributors

Zachary Abuza is Professor and Chair of the Department of Political Science and International Relations at Simmons College and is the author of *Militant Islam in Southeast Asia: Crucible of Terror* (Lynne Rienner, 2003).

Thomas J. Biersteker is Curt Gasteyger Professor of International Security and Conflict Studies at the Graduate Institute of International Studies, Geneva and Olive C. Watson Professor at the Watson Institute for International Studies and Department of Political Science, Brown University.

Donald E. deKieffer is a principal in the Washington, DC law firm of deKieffer & Horgan, specializing in international trade regulation with emphasis on international anti-counterfeiting and antidiversion.

Sue E. Eckert is Senior Fellow at the Watson Institute for International Studies, Brown University. She previously served as Assistant Secretary of Commerce responsible for regulating dual-use commodities, and as senior staff on the House International Relations Committee dealing with sanctions and export controls.

Douglas Farah was formerly an investigative reporter for the *Washington Post*. He is the author of the recent book, *Blood from Stones: The Secret Financial Network of Terror* (Broadway Publishers, 2004).

Rohan Gunaratna is Head of the International Centre for Political Violence and Terrorism Research at Nanyang Technological University's Rajaratnam School of International Studies in Singapore, and author of *Inside Al-Qaeda: Global Network of Terror* (Columbia University Press, 2002).

Jeroen Gunning is lecturer in the Department of International Politics at the University of Wales, Aberystwyth, and author of *Hamas in Politics: Democracy, Religion, Violence* (Hurst, 2005). He is a specialist on fund raising from diaspora communities.

Michael Levi is Professor of Criminology at the University of Cardiff, Wales, and writes on organized crime and money laundering. He is author of

Drugs and Money: Managing the Drug Trade and Crime Money in Europe (Routledge, 2005).

Samuel Munzele Maimbo is Financial Sector Specialist, South Asia Finance and Private Sector Unit at the World Bank and is the author of "Informal Funds transfer Systems: An Analysis of the Informal *Hawala* System," a paper jointly published by the World Bank and the IMF.

Amit Modi is a graduate student at Harvard University's Department of Government.

Nikos Passas is Professor at the College of Criminal Justice, Northeastern University, and an expert on informal value transfer systems and transnational crime. He is the author of *Organized Crime* (Variorum Press, 2003) and the Editor in Chief of *Crime, Law and Social Change: an International Journal*.

Peter Romaniuk is Assistant Professor at John Jay College of Criminal Justice, City University of New York, and previously was Senior Research Assistant with the Watson Institute's Targeting Terrorist Finances Project.

Jessica Stern is Lecturer in Public Policy at the Kennedy School of Government, Harvard University and author of *Terror in the Name of God: Why Religious Militants Kill* (Ecco, 2003).

Phil Williams is Professor of Public and International Affairs, University of Pittsburgh, where he directs the Ridgeway Center's Program on Terrorism and Transnational Crime. He is author of *Combating Transnational Crime: Concepts, Activities and Responses* (Frank Cass Publishers, 2001).

Preface and acknowledgements

In the immediate aftermath of the attacks of 11 September, each of us reflected on our research and the ways in which it might prove relevant to the emerging counter-terrorism agenda. We were already actively working on the multilateral tool of targeted financial sanctions, but the instrument of financial controls took on new salience as it became the cornerstone of international efforts to combat terrorist financing. This book reflects our joint effort to take stock of what we know and what we have learned about the financing of terrorism and about global efforts to counter it.

There were relatively few experts on the financing of terrorism or ways to counter it at the time of the attacks. Intelligence officers, treasury and finance officials, and national security staff were actively engaged with the subject, but there was virtually no research activity underway within the academy. Most of the traditional terrorism experts – leading scholars like Martha Crenshaw, Bruce Hoffman, or Brian Jenkins – were focused on broader aspects of the motivations behind groups using terrorism and on effective ways to counter them. The financing of terrorism was a relatively arcane subject, and we began this project with scant literature from the wider scholarly community to inform our analysis.

We were motivated to produce this book because we were dissatisfied with much of the public discourse about the financing of terrorism and efforts to curtail it. We also wanted to publish a volume that included the best minds working on the subject drawn from throughout the world today. Too much of the published work by self-proclaimed "experts" on terrorist financing is little more than semi-informed speculation about possible channels for raising and moving funds at best, and hyperbole and exaggeration at worst. There is a growing literature, but much of it is based on over-generalizations from a single illustration or case study of terrorist financing, without regard to the differences that exist among groups committing acts of terrorism or important changes that have taken place in financing and financial regulation over time. We have worked closely with our authors on their contributions to this volume, but the views expressed are, of course, those of the individual authors of each chapter. We thank each and every one of them for their intellectual contributions and patience in bringing this volume to fruition.

This project began as a joint initiative of Brown University's Watson Institute for International Studies and Harvard University's Transnational Dynamics project, located at the Kennedy School of Government. We owe a significant debt of gratitude to Sanjeev Khagram, director of the Harvard project, for his leadership and participation in the first of the two conferences we organized on the subject. He and his Kennedy School colleagues, Jessica Stern and Sarah Alvord, were instrumental in the initial planning and financial support of a conference co-hosted by the Watson Institute that launched the project in fall 2003. It was at this initial conference that we first conceptualized this volume, out of which we selected many of the authors included in this compilation. Following directly from the conversations and discussion at the conference, particularly with insights from our friend and key collaborator from Northeastern University's College of Criminal Justice, Nikos Passas, we also realized that there were important new arenas of research that were not adequately covered by our initial formulation.

We were fortunate to receive financial support from the United States Institute of Peace to convene a second workshop, again at the Watson Institute, this time to bring together prospective authors with more developed chapter proposals. We had the good fortune to work with USIP program officer Taylor Seybolt, and we convened an expanded group during the fall of 2004. The structure of this book is a direct reflection of that meeting. We began with a premise drawn from Jessica Stern's research that the social organization of groups committing acts of terrorism matter for a variety of different things, which we extended to include the financing of terrorism. That is, different groups engaging in acts of terrorism vary in their organizational form, and accordingly, in the ways they raise and move funds. Hierarchically organized groups would differ from decentralized, networked groups. Territorially based groups with discrete territorial goals would differ from millenarian groups with global ambitions. We proceeded to explore different vehicles for the raising and moving of funds, considering charities, links to crime, trade diversion, the use of informal value transfer systems (or *hawalas*), and the use of high-value commodities like diamonds. We assessed the financial regulatory responses both in the US and as they were extended throughout the rest of the world, with an eye toward policy effectiveness and lessons to be learned from previous "wars" on drugs and organized crime.

None of this could have been accomplished without the extraordinary support of our Brown University student research assistants. Their research ingenuity, scholarly tenacity, and good humor were essential for keeping the project going. We wish to extend our thanks and gratitude to Elizabeth Goodfriend, Jesse Finkelstein, Aaron Halegua, Jonathan Liu, Justin Ouimette, Suzanne Smith, and Barron Youngsmith. For their excellent research and editorial assistance, Kate Roll, Craig Kennedy, and Michael Boyce deserve special recognition and thanks. Kimberly Jones of the Northeastern University provided important assistance on issues related to informal value transfer systems and commodities. Special thanks for his assistance also go to our long-term colleague and collaborator in every sense of the word, Peter Romaniuk, now on the faculty of the City University of New York. The conference support staff of the Watson Institute, Ellen Carney White in particular, deserve a special word of praise and thanks for their ever-efficient and good natured organizational support.

Finally, an effort of this nature is not possible without the support of understanding families. We wish to thank in particular our spouses, Nancy Biersteker and Mark Sawoski, for their endless patience and interest during the many times we were preoccupied with terrorist financing. And a special thanks to two little people, Matthew and Catherine Sawoski, who have grown much during the course of this exercise, but who make it all worthwhile.

Thomas J. Biersteker and Sue E. Eckert

Abbreviations

AML	Anti-Money Laundering
AML/CFT	Anti-Money Laundering/Combating the Financing of Terrorism
APEC	Asia/Pacific Economic Cooperation
ARS	Alternative Remittance System
ASG	Abu Sayyaf Group
AUSTRAC	Australian Transaction Reports and Analysis Center
BSA	Bank Secrecy Act
CFT	Countering the Financing of Terrorism
CICTE	Inter-American Committee against Terrorism
CTAG	Counter-Terrorism Action Group
CTAP	Counter-Terrorism Action Plan
CTC	Counter-Terrorism Committee
CTED	Counter-Terrorism Executive Directorate
CTR	Currency Transaction Report
DDII	Dewan Dakwah Islam Indonesia, Islamic Propagation Council of Indonesia
ECHR	European Convention on Human Rights
ETA	Euskadi Ta Askatasuna, Basque Homeland and Freedom
FARC	Las Fuerzas Armadas Revolucionarias de Colombia, Revolutionary Armed Forces of Colombia
FASP	Financial Sector Assessment Program
FATF	Financial Action Task Force
FinCEN	Financial Crimes Enforcement Network (US)
FinTRAC	Financial Transactions Reports Analysis Center (Canada)
FIU	Financial Intelligence Unit
FSRB	FATF-Style Regional Body
FTO	Foreign Terrorist Organization
GCC	Gulf Cooperation Council
GIA	Armed Islamic Group (Algeria)
GICM	Moroccan Islamic Combatant Group
GSPC	Salafist Group for Prayer/Call and Combat
HT	Hizb-ut Tahrir, Islamic Party of Liberation

IEEPA	International Emergency Economic Powers Act
IFTS	Informal Funds Transfer Systems
IIRO	International Islamic Relief Organization
IMF	International Monetary Fund
IMU	Islamic Movement of Uzbekistan
INCSR	*International Narcotics Control Strategy Report*
IRA	Irish Republican Army
IRSO	Islamic Resistance Support Organization
ISI	Inter-Services Intelligence (Pakistan)
IVTS	Informal Value Transfer Systems
JI	Jemaah Islamiyah
JUI	Jamiat Ulema-e-Islam, Assembly of Islamic Clergy (Pakistan)
KMM	Kumpulan Mujahidin Malaysia
KOMPAK	Komite Penanggulangan Krisis, Indonesian Committee for the Creative Education for Child Labour Foundation
KYC	Know Your Customer
LeT	Lashkar-e-Taiba, Army of the Pure (Pakistan)
LJ	Lashkar-e-Jhangvi, Army of Jhang (Pakistan)
LTTE	Liberation Tigers of Tamil Eelam
MAB	Muslim Association of Britain
MAK	Maktab-il Khidamat, Afghan Service Bureau
MENAFATF	Middle East and North Africa Financial Action Task Force
MERC	Medical Emergency Relief Charity
MILF	Moro Islamic Liberation Front (Philippines)
MMI	Mujahidin Council of Indonesia
MSB	Money Services Business
MVT	Money or Value Transfer
NCCT	Non-Cooperative Countries and Territories
NCIS	National Criminal Intelligence Services (UK)
NIF	National Islamic Front (Sudan)
OASIS	Operational and Administrative System for Import Support
OCC	Office of the Comptroller of the Currency (US)
OECD	Organization for Economic Cooperation and Development
OFAC	Office of Foreign Assets Control
OGBS	Offshore Group of Banking Supervisors
PAN	Partai Amanat Nasional, National Mandate Party (Indonesia)
PFLP	Popular Front for the Liberation of Palestine
PIERS	Port Import Export Reporting Service (Hong Kong)
PIRA	Provisional Irish Republican Army
PUPJI	*Pedoman Umum Perjuangan al-Jama'ah al-Islamiyyah, The General Guidebook for the Struggle of Jemaah Islamayah*
QK	Quality King
RICO	Racketeer Influenced and Corrupt Organizations Act

ROSC	Report of the Observance of Standards and Codes
RUF	Revolutionary United Front (Sierra Leone)
SAR	Suspicious Activity Report
SDGT	Specially Designated Global Terrorist
SDN	Specially Designated National
SDT	Specially Designated Terrorist
SSP	Sipah-e-Sahaba Pakistan
TBBs	Trade Bulletin Boards
TWH	Takfir wal-Hijra
UNODC	United Nations Office on Drugs and Crime
UNSCR	United Nations Security Council Resolution
UTM	University of Technology of Malaysia
WB	World Bank

1 Introduction

The challenge of terrorist financing

*Thomas J. Biersteker and
Sue E. Eckert*

In the immediate aftermath of the attacks of 11 September 2001, the Bush Administration told the American public that it would not mount a traditional effort in its "war on terrorism." The campaign would be a protracted affair, invoking non-traditional methods, institutions, and resources, including an effort to suppress both the raising and the movement of funds that could be used to support the acts of global terrorists. As President George W. Bush declared on 24 September 2001:

> We will direct every resource at our command to win the war against terrorists, every means of diplomacy, every tool of intelligence, every instrument of law enforcement, every financial influence. We will starve the terrorists of funding, turn them against each other, rout them out of their safe hiding places, and bring them to justice.[1]

The logic underlying this strategy is profoundly a state-centered one. States are the centerpiece of the strategy and are to be held accountable for actions emanating from their territories. States are expected to increase their coercive capacity to deal with the challenges of global terrorism by strengthening intelligence gathering, law enforcement, and imposing new financial controls to counter the financing of terrorism (CFT).

National level financial controls are central to countering the financing of global terrorism. Indeed, military actions notwithstanding, new financial measures have been among the most powerful tools deployed by the United States and the international community. There is little doubt that such controls can have important effects. To begin with, limiting the resources available to groups engaged in terrorism may prevent some attacks from taking place, or at least can reduce the impact of attacks that cannot be prevented. For example, former FBI director Louis J. Freeh noted how the 1993 attack on the World Trade Center took place earlier than planned and was less devastating than intended by Ramzi Yousef, the convicted mastermind of the attack, because of the group's limited financial resources.[2]

The imposition of effective financial controls can also have a positive deterrent effect. Once the provision of financial resources to groups utilizing terrorism has been criminalized, contributors to charitable organizations become increasingly cognizant of the potential for the diversion of their funds. Given the evidence that charitable contributions have been diverted in the past, and given the passage of legislation that criminalizes charitable funds' diversion, individual contributors have a strong incentive to ensure that the proceeds of their contributions do not end up being used for terrorist purposes.

Financial controls can provide invaluable assistance in reconstructing events after a terrorist attack, identifying additional members and supporters of the group committing the act of terrorism, and gaining a better understanding of the group's modus operandi and internal organization. Financial intelligence is typically more reliable than other forms of intelligence. It was financial information that helped law enforcement establish the first links between the hijackers and other conspirators after 11 September.[3] In theory, therefore, financial controls can perform preventive, deterrent, investigative, and analytical functions, all of which are vital for curtailing acts of terrorism. Finally, financial controls also have political utility, as they demonstrate concrete policy measures that governments can take in a multi-faceted effort to counter future acts of terrorism.

Once the goal of "starving the terrorists of funding" was proclaimed, national government agencies and international organizations faced the question of how best to achieve the objective. There were already a number of policy instruments or measures that different agencies had at their disposal prior to 11 September, and in most institutional settings, these constituted their initial response to the problem. Within the United States, for example, institutions and procedures existed within the Treasury Department's Office of Foreign Assets Control (OFAC) and the Financial Crimes Enforcement Network (FinCEN) – relating to the enforcement of international sanctions targeting terrorist finances and the control of money laundering activities. OFAC, in particular, already maintained extensive lists of "Specially Designated Terrorists" (SDTs) and terrorist groups and routinely issued notices to banks and other financial institutions to block their transactions. FinCEN engaged in financial intelligence gathering and assisted with the regulation of anti-money laundering activities directed toward disrupting the activities of drug traffickers. The National Security Council had specialists devoted to the analysis of transnational terrorist threats. The Federal Bureau of Investigations and the Central Intelligence Agency also had financial intelligence gathering activities underway, but as *The 9/11 Commission Report: Final Report of the National Commission on Terrorist Attacks Upon the United States* ("9/11 Commission Report") indicated, the coordination of these different activities was woefully inadequate.

Internationally, the United Nations Convention for the Suppression of the Financing of Terrorism had been adopted in December 1999, although at the time of the 11 September attacks, only four countries had ratified the convention. The Financial Action Task Force, created by the G7 in 1989, encouraged states to establish due diligence and "know your customer" provisions in international banking regulations in an effort to curb the money laundering activities associated with the proceeds of the illegal drug trade globally, provisions that were widely viewed as directly relevant to countering terrorist financing. The United Nations Security Council passed Resolution 1267 in October 1999, imposing economic sanctions and establishing a Sanctions Committee to monitor and enforce targeted financial sanctions against the Taliban regime in Afghanistan. The resolution specifically named Osama bin Laden and called upon the Taliban to turn him over "without further delay" because of his indictment in the United States for the bombings of the US embassies in Kenya and Tanzania in 1998.

There were also dramatic, and in some instances, sweeping new policy initiatives undertaken immediately following the attacks of 11 September – the passage of the USA PATRIOT Act ("Patriot Act") in the United States and the unanimous adoption of UN Security Council Resolution 1373 – that built on these institutional foundations and established procedures to define and shape the course of countering terrorist financing in a very changed security environment. The Patriot Act strengthened anti-money laundering statutes and provided law enforcement agencies with powerful new tools and authority geared toward the prevention, as well as the investigation, of terrorist activities. Executive Order 13224 froze the US-based assets and blocked all transactions of designated individuals and organizations supporting terrorist activities.

With the passage of UN Security Council Resolution (UNSCR) 1373 on 28 September 2001, the Security Council expressed its clear intention to do something significant to stem terrorists' access to financial support. The resolution called for criminalizing active or passive support for terrorists, the expeditious freezing of funds, the sharing of operational information by Member States, and the provision of technical assistance to enhance multilateral cooperation in this area. The resolution also called upon Member States to sign the UN Convention for the Suppression of the Financing of Terrorism and established an innovative process to implement the terms of the resolutions under the guidance of the Counter-Terrorism Committee (CTC). In October 2001, the Financial Action Task Force (FATF) moved beyond its focus on money laundering and adopted Eight Special Recommendations on Terrorist Financing to supplement its 40 recommendations on anti-money laundering activities.

Most of these initial policy responses focused on formal sector financial controls, harmonizing governmental policy, and improving financial regulatory capacity throughout the world. They were essentially attempts to strengthen the financial capacity of the state, parallel to efforts to strengthen the state's intelligence gathering, intelligence sharing, and surveillance capabilities. In the case of the Patriot Act, informal value transfer systems (IVTS or *hawalas*) were added to the list of traditional financial service institutions as possible sources of terrorist funds transfer. Subsequently, interest grew in the potential use by terrorist groups and supporting organizations of high value commodities (diamonds, gold), trade diversion, and petty crime (credit card fraud, cigarette smuggling, and other criminal schemes associated with largely self-sufficient terrorist cells). Charities and NGOs also came under intensified scrutiny, several of which were placed on lists leading to asset freezes and closure in different parts of the world.

The central purpose of this book is to examine whether these efforts to regulate formal sector financial transactions are appropriate to, or adequate for, the objective of countering the financing of terrorism, especially related to al Qaeda. Enhancing financial regulation was a logical response to the attacks of 11 September, given that the formal financial sector was used to transfer most of the operational funds used to support the operation. It was also something regulators knew how to do, and it provided an opportunity to advance ideas they had been developing for years. Derived, as they were, from existing regulatory approaches, they embody a number of assumptions. We intend to interrogate these assumptions in the pages that follow, based on an analysis of the actions taken, the variety of different mechanisms used for raising and moving of funds, and changes in the organizational structure and strategies of terrorist groups during the more than five years that have passed since the attacks of 11 September.

Assumptions embedded in the regulatory approach to countering terrorist financing

The regulatory response to countering terrorist financing is based on five core assumptions. First, it is assumed that all groups or organizations engaged in acts of terrorism are essentially the same. Accordingly, the regulatory measures designed to disrupt the financing of hierarchically organized groups are applied similarly and assumed to be equally effective against groups with varying organizational forms (from decentralized cells to virtual networks). Similarly, the mechanisms used against organizations with relatively limited goals of self-determination in a given territory like the IRA, ETA, or the Red Brigades are assumed to be effective against a transnational network like al Qaeda and its affiliates. Yet, groups engaged in committing acts of terrorism differ dramatically in their organizational structure, goals, and form (see Chapters 2 and 5 by Jessica Stern and Amit Modi, and by Jeroen Gunning), and it is now apparent that al Qaeda itself has undergone a substantial metamorphosis since 11 September 2001 (see especially Chapter 3 by Rohan Gunaratna).

Second, it is assumed that formal sector financial institutions are or can be principal sources of terrorist funds transfer. While there is substantial evidence that the US banking system was used for the transfer of up to $300,000 prior to the attacks of 11 September,[4] there is less evidence that formal sector financial institutions have been used extensively since that time. There is widespread speculation that transfers of funds have been driven underground into the informal sector, and growing evidence that groups committing acts of terrorism are increasingly reliant on smuggling and crime (see Chapters 6, 7 and 12 by Phil Williams, Donald E. deKieffer, and Michael Levi).

Third, it is assumed that the regulation of formal financial institutions can be extended to the operations of informal financial networks and other potential sources of financial transfers. The United States and other countries increasingly require the registration of informal value transfer systems. There have been similar initiatives with regard to charitable giving in the United States and the United Kingdom, a move that has created both disruption and growing concern in the private and religious foundation world. Whether registration and reporting requirements are the best or most effective means to address these concerns remains to be seen (see Chapters 5 and 8 by Jeroen Gunning, and Nikos Passas and Samuel Maimbo).

Fourth, it is assumed, that the *hawala* system and similar informal value transfer systems operating in other parts of the world play an important role in the financing of terrorism. The record-keeping practices of these institutions can be difficult to decipher and monitor, and al Qaeda used them to transfer funds prior to 11 September. It is certainly possible for IVTS to be used for the transfer of the relatively small amounts of funds needed for committing acts of terrorism; however, it is striking to note the limited extent to which there is concrete evidence of the use of these systems in recent cases of terrorism (see Chapter 8 by Nikos Passas and Samuel Maimbo).

Fifth and finally, it is assumed that there is an emergent "nexus" between organized crime and terrorism. While there are examples of links between drug smuggling and the generation of revenue for groups using terrorism – from the FARC in Colombia to the Taliban in Afghanistan – there is relatively little evidence of sustained connections between large-scale organized crime and groups committing acts of terrorism. As Phil Williams and Michael Levi point out in their separate contributions to this volume, most of the contacts appear to be discrete opportunistic transactions, rather than a sustained "nexus" and there are serious questions about the conditions under which organized criminal organizations are willing to take on the state as directly as groups using terrorism.

These five assumptions upon which much of the US and global regulatory response has been based, may not be entirely correct or fully warranted, and it is our intention in this book to engage in a critical examination of them. The volume will focus on what we believe is potentially wrong, missing, or misleading with the approach taken to date. The extent to which al Qaeda has changed will be addressed, as well as whether the response to terrorist financing has kept pace with the changes. Finally, we will consider the potential counter-productive effects of continuation of the current approach without adaptation.

We begin by positing that the nature of the groups utilizing terrorism as a tactic varies dramatically across the globe and that knowledge of the social organization of different groups using terror will tell us something about how they raise, move, and use funds across territorial settings. In addition, groups using terror as a tactic are social organizations who learn and adapt their methods in response to regulatory and enforcement efforts. Thus, there appears to be movement of their activity from the formal financial sector to the informal and underground economies or to more sophisticated, trade-facilitated channels. We will also assess critically the effectiveness and consequences (both intended and unintended) of the global regulatory effort to control terrorist financing.

The financing of terrorism

The World Bank and International Monetary Fund define the financing of terrorism as "the financial support, in any form, of terrorism or of those who encourage, plan, or engage in it."[5] This rather broad definition, of course, begs the question of what an act of terrorism actually is, although elements of a definition contained in existing international conventions include *the deliberate use of violence against civilian targets, with the intention of instilling terror in a population for some political goal or purpose*. What then do we really know about the financing of terrorism? Beyond a general description of the complexity and variety of different measures used to finance acts of terrorism, it is possible to begin with a brief sketch of the state of knowledge about the subject.

First, and most important, it does not take a large amount of funds to commit an act of terrorism. According to the 9/11 Commission's *Monograph on Terrorist Financing*, the attacks of 11 September cost al Qaeda somewhere in the range of $400,000 to $500,000, of which approximately $300,000 passed through the hijackers' bank accounts in the United States.[6] According to US sources, the Bali bombings in 2002 cost somewhere in the range of $20,000 to $35,000, paid for out of transfers of about $130,000 from al Qaeda to Jemaah Islamiyah, the Indonesian-based group.[7] The Istanbul bombings in 2003 are estimated to have cost less than $40,000.[8]

The 1998 Africa Embassy bombings are estimated to have cost less than $50,000,[9] while the first World Trade Center bombing in 1993 cost only $18,000.[10] It is reported that the conspirators were able to fund the operation themselves from criminal activities, including check and credit card fraud, and through donations raised from a local charity. The operational costs of the devastating March 2004 Madrid attacks were initially estimated to have been only $10,000, though Spanish government officials subsequently concluded they were above $60,000.[11] In this instance, the perpetrators allegedly raised money by peddling hashish and ecstasy and through the fraudulent sale of holy water purportedly from Mecca. The dynamite and shrapnel stuffed into the backpacks used in the attacks were stolen from mines in northern Spain. Costs were further minimized by preparing materials at a decrepit rural cottage with no electricity or running water. The official Home Office inquiry into the London subway bombings in 2005 put the total cost of overseas trips, bomb-making equipment, rent, car hire, and internal UK travel at about $15,000, financed through defaulted loans, account overdrafts, and bounced checks.[12]

The relatively low cost of operations has prompted some observers to argue that because terrorist acts are so inexpensive, finding, freezing, and seizing assets is absolutely critical. Essentially, "every dollar matters. Disrupting the flow of funds (even in small amounts) can stop or postpone an imminent attack."[13] Others use the same evidence to conclude that the low cost of operations means that effectively freezing terrorist financing is an impossibly hopeless task. While it is clear that a focus on terrorist financing alone is insufficient and cannot be counted on to stop the commitment of future acts of terrorism, as we argue elsewhere and in the conclusion of this volume, there are good reasons to pursue the effort, however difficult the challenges involved. As previously noted, we know that the 1993 attack on the World Trade Center illustrated just how important money can be at an operational level. In 1995 Ramzi Yousef, the confessed organizer of the operation, admitted that the perpetrators had wanted to build a bigger bomb but were not able to, due to lack of funds. In addition, a key break in the investigation came because the terrorists attempted to recover a deposit fee they paid on a rented truck used to facilitate the attack.

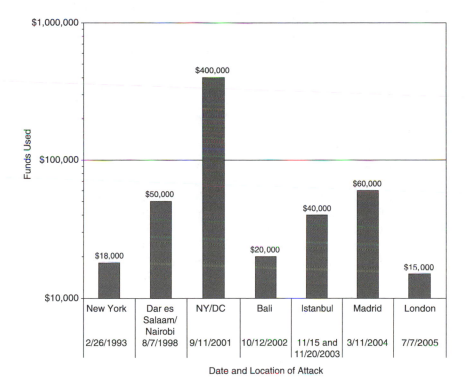

Figure 1.1 Cost of terrorist attacks.

In spite of the relatively low operational cost of committing acts of terrorism, actual terrorist operations use only a small portion of the funds that terrorist organizations require for their support infrastructure. This broader infrastructure includes the costs of recruitment, indoctrination, training, logistical support, the dissemination of propaganda, political activities, and other material support.[14] Australian Commonwealth Director of Public Prosecutions, Damian Bugg, estimated in 2003 that:

> al Qaeda spends about 10% of its income on operational costs. The other 90% goes on the cost of administering and maintaining the organization, including the cost of operating training camps and maintaining an international network of cells. So called "sleepers" must also cost significant sums to establish and maintain.[15]

In the final analysis, while the operational costs of terrorism may be low (from $15,000 for multiple bomb attacks on the transportation system in London to $500,000 for the destruction of two skyscrapers in New York), the total cost of a terrorist attack is probably much higher, due to the requirements of recruiting, training, indoctrination, living expenses, and disseminating information. Even if we accept these estimates, as former US Defense Secretary Donald Rumsfeld lamented, "The cost–benefit ratio is against us! Our cost is billions against the terrorists' costs of millions."[16]

The second thing we know about the financing of terrorism is that there are a wide variety of methods for the raising, moving, and storing of funds and that it is important analytically to distinguish between these different aspects of terrorist financing. In many ways, al Qaeda poses a relatively new kind of security threat. It is not a threat emanating from another state or from a terrorist organization located within a state. It is a threat from a non-state actor, a transnational organization or movement, using tactics of terrorism and operating on a global scale. It is probably most similar historically to the international anarchist movement of the late nineteenth and early twentieth century.[17] Although there are some similarities, the threat from al Qaeda is qualitatively different from either state terrorism or terrorism emanating from within, directed against, and largely contained within, a single state (such as the LTTE in Sri Lanka or the FARC in Colombia). Al Qaeda is a global, complex, transnational, networked phenomenon, with a capacity to inflict harm and impose costs on people and institutions across the planet. Efforts to counter it effectively will require a networked, multilateral response. It is an extremely complex and difficult project. It is not an impossible one, however, and the technology, if not always the political will to employ it, is available.

According to the Council on Foreign Relations Task Force on Terrorist Financing, al Qaeda was notably and deliberately decentralized, compartmentalized, flexible and diverse in all of its operations, including its financial operations.[18] It was not based largely on Osama bin Laden's personal wealth, although his wealth was apparently significant at earlier phases of the operation of the organization, during the early and middle 1990s. His wealth appears to have been largely depleted since that time and was no longer a major source of financing for the organization at the time of the 11 September attacks.

The financial network of pre-11 September al Qaeda has been characterized by layers and redundancies. Al Qaeda has raised funds from a variety of sources and moved these funds in a variety of different ways. It has changed its structure, recruitment, and operating modalities, over time – in ways that have significance for the raising, moving, storing, and utilizing of financial resources. With regard to the raising of funds, al Qaeda has often operated under a cloak of legitimacy – managing legitimate businesses, such as Osama bin Laden's enterprises in the Sudan or honey traders in Yemen. In these instances, the profits from legitimate businesses were channeled to terrorist ends. Al Qaeda has also operated criminal enterprises – some large, and some small. Cells of the organization are reputed to be self-supporting, and engage in smuggling, small-scale fraud, petty crime, and outright theft.

The most important source of financial support – at least up to and immediately following the attacks of 11 September – came from continuous fundraising efforts that date back to the methods established to support the mujahideen in the 1980s: charities, NGOs, mosques, special fundraisers, intermediaries, facilitators, and direct solicitations of wealthy individuals.[19] *Zakat* (the Islamic concept of tithing and alms obliging Muslims to contribute to charitable causes) contributions are largely unregulated, seldom audited, have been co-mingled with other funds, and can be skimmed off for other purposes, including the commitment of acts of terrorism. Some of the charitable giving to al Qaeda has apparently been willful (such as that allegedly raised by the Afghan Support Committee, the Pakistani Al Rashid Trust, the Wafa Humanitarian Organization, and the Kuwaiti Revival of Islamic Heritage. Some of the charitable giving has not been willful, however, and funds can be diverted without the knowledge of donors. Most of the charitable fundraising that has been diverted to terrorism has been collected in the wealthier Islamic countries, and Saudi Arabia has had a very special relationship with al Qaeda (its funding, recruitment, and issue definition). In recent years, however, al Qaeda has expanded its relationships with organizations like Jemaah Islamiyah (JI), that have their own financial support networks, and following the March 2003 US-led invasion, with groups operating in Iraq. In late 2006, al Qaeda is reported to have joined forces with the Algerian group, the Salafist Group for Preaching and Combat, known by its French initials as GSPC, operating throughout North Africa.[20]

State sponsorship, or the provision of direct financial support to non-state armed groups, has historically been a significant source of the financing of terrorism. Both the United States and the former Soviet Union supported proxy groups engaged in committing acts of terrorism during the Cold War, and the practice of state support of terrorism has continued in the post Cold

War era, particularly in the contemporary Middle East and South Asia.[21] Al Qaeda received significant forms of state support from the Taliban regime in Afghanistan, before that regime was toppled in 2001, but there is little evidence that it has relied on state sponsorship since that time. Although we acknowledge the significance of state sponsorship of terrorism, our primary focus in this book is on al Qaeda and affiliated groups engaged in the commitment of transnational acts of terrorism (in contrast to groups focused on securing self-determination for a fixed territorial space), and hence we have chosen not to devote a separate chapter to state sponsorship.

With regard to the moving of funds, there is evidence that the global, formal sector financial system has historically been used extensively. As the 9/11 Commission Report indicated, $300,000 of the funds used for the operation passed directly through the US banking system. By making extensive use of correspondent banking relationships, and by moving funds through off-shore tax havens, formal sector institutions located in under-regulated territories have had access to virtually any location on the globe. In addition, under or unregulated havens with limited bank supervision and lax anti-money laundering laws, ineffective law enforcement, and/or a culture of bank secrecy – historically, places such as Dubai and the Cayman Islands – have been used. Furthermore, funds have been moved in and out of virtually unregulated locations such as Afghanistan under the Taliban regime. The Islamic banking and financial system has also been used and generally tends to be less well regulated than the rest of the global financial system. There tends to be a good deal of mystification of the Islamic banking system, however, and the extent to which it should be singled out for criticism and potential scrutiny tends to be exaggerated.[22]

Another vehicle for the potential transfer or movement of funds is the extensive IVTS or *hawala* system that plays an important role in transfers of funds for guest workers across the globe. Like the Islamic banking system, the vast majority of *hawala* transfers are perfectly legitimate, and as described in Chapter 8 by Nikos Passas and Samuel Maimbo, the system performs an important social function, particularly for guest workers attempting to transfer small amounts of remittances home. *Hawala* means "trust" in Hindi, and there are variants of the system operating throughout the Islamic world and China, in addition to India. In many parts of the developing world, this is the only effective and cost-effective way to transfer funds. Until recently, however, the system has fallen largely outside of the formal regulatory system, and because of this, it is suspected as being a likely vehicle for the movement of funds supporting acts of terrorism.

Other potential vehicles for the movement of funds used for terrorist purposes include transfer pricing mechanisms – long utilized by transnational corporations interested in getting funds out of countries with restrictive currency controls. Chapter 7 by Donald deKieffer considers some of the trade diversion mechanisms that could be used for the disguised transfers of funds.

Finally, there is growing evidence that traditional methods of smuggling – of cash, of precious metals, and of gemstones – using the same routes and methods employed by drug traffickers, arms dealers, and transnational criminal organizations may also have been used by groups committing acts of terrorism. In Chapter 9, Douglas Farah explores the use of diamonds by al Qaeda during a period when formal sector transactions appear to have been closed down.

With regard to the storing of funds, there are again a variety of mechanisms used by different organizations, and by the same organization over time. The holding of cash is one of the most widespread methods. Like most groups committing acts of terrorism historically, there is also evidence that al Qaeda has relied extensively on family members, friends and close allies as safe havens and locations for the storage of capital. *Sunday Times* correspondent Nicholas Fielding has stressed the importance of family networks in the origins and sustenance of the organization.[23] Douglas Farah has written extensively about the role of diamonds for both the movement and the holding of value for al Qaeda after the United States first froze the organization's funds in US financial institutions following the embassy bombings in 1998.[24] There is also the possibility, discussed briefly by Phil Williams in Chapter 6, that ad hoc arrangements with other terrorist organizations and possibly with transnational criminal organizations could also provide a channel for the movement and storage of funds used to commit acts of terrorism.

The third thing we know about the financing of terrorism is that the social organization of different groups using terrorism can have important implications for how they raise, move, and use funds. As explored more generally by Jessica Stern and Amit Modi in Chapter 2, different organizational forms of terrorism – ranging from hierarchical, commander-cadre terrorist organizations to virtual, networked, decentralized groups (like radical anti-abortionists or the Aryan Nations in the US) – have significant implications for the internal workings of terrorist groups. Organizational structure has implications for the mission, decision-making procedures, recruitment strategies, and the financing of groups using terrorism. Hierarchical organizations tend to have separate divisions responsible for the raising and moving of funds, and draw on diversified sources to secure their operations, ranging from the diversion of funds from charitable giving to diversion from legitimate businesses. Virtual, decentralized networks tend to rely more heavily on individual contributions made through the Internet – an increasingly conducive vehicle for fund-raising – and on criminal activities.[25]

There is now widespread sentiment – reflected in Rohan Gunaratna's Chapter 3 – that al Qaeda has been transformed from more of a hierarchical organization into a networked movement since the attacks of 11 September. In between these two extremes are a variety of different organizational forms associated with national self-determination movements interested in control over a discrete territorial space. Those groups that have succeeded in forcing the state out of major portions of territory – the Tamils in Sri Lanka or the FARC in Colombia – sometimes operate like quasi-states and obtain much of their financing from forms of taxation, either on trade transactions, from kidnapping, or from extortion of those seeking protection from potential kidnappings.

Fourth, and finally, we know that groups using terrorism have changed their methods of raising and of moving funds over time, and in the particular case of al Qaeda, there is good evidence that the organization has increasingly moved out of formal sector institutions and into a variety of different forms of illicit activities and the gray economy. As we will discuss in the conclusion of this volume, this is probably at least in part in response to the global effort to regulate and limit the use by terrorists of formal sector financial institutions since 2001. There is greater reliance today on the use of decentralized petty crime (or a variety of different "self-help" systems) to support the operations of semi-autonomous cells within what increasingly appears to be more of a dispersed social movement, than a formal organization. This eliminates the need both to move and to store large amounts of funds.

Credit card fraud has been one way for cells operating in Europe and the US to finance their activities. As we learned from the Madrid bombings, small-scale drug trafficking, and the fraudulent sale of petty goods were also used as sources of local financing for the operation. As formal sector channels have increasingly been closed down, groups using terrorism have increasingly moved their assets out of formal sector financial institutions. Some are suspected to have used informal value transfer systems like the *hawalas* for transfers of funds, while others have resorted to traditional cash smuggling. Still others have speculated that there has been an increasing propensity for groups using terrorism to establish linkages with organized crime, something British investigators charged following arrests made in London in August of 2004.

Since 11 September 2001, US Department of the Treasury officials claim that $147 million worth of terrorist assets have been blocked or frozen worldwide.[26] Given the relatively small amount of funds that are needed to commit devastating acts of terrorism, this might be viewed as an impressive achievement. There are questions, however, about the reliability and significance of these figures. It is not clear whether they include the funds frozen prior to 11 September 2001, particularly those funds of al Qaeda and of the Taliban regime frozen under UNSCR 1267 dating from October 1999, some of which have been released. If they do, the $147 million figure is a somewhat more modest achievement. The figure also appears to be a cumulative amount, rather than the current amount of funds frozen.

There is also some question as to the percentage of total funds frozen that is associated with al Qaeda. According to the 2005 Terrorist Assets Report produced by the US Treasury Department's Office of Foreign Assets Control, a total of \$13.8 million in assets of international terrorist organizations were blocked in the US as of the end of that year. Of that total, only \$7.5 million was associated directly with al Qaeda, with most of the remainder associated with Hamas (\$6.2 million of the \$13.8 million total).[27] Thus, most of the recent increase in the total amount of funds frozen may be coming from the ongoing addition of groups associated with acts of terrorism in the Israeli–Palestinian conflict, particularly from the listing of Hamas and Hezbollah. The continuing increase in total funds frozen may therefore have more to do with the addition of new groups and their affiliated front organizations, than it does with the increased effectiveness of a global regulatory effort against al Qaeda. In the final analysis, however, we agree with US Treasury department officials who argue that the most appropriate measures of the effectiveness of efforts to counter the financing of terrorism are not the total amounts frozen or the number of people added to the lists, but the degree of isolation and difficulty experienced by the targets of the measures. Unfortunately, degree of isolation and difficulty in financing operations are far more difficult to quantify, and since our analysis is not based on classified sources of information, it is difficult for us to measure success (or failure) on these criteria impartially and objectively.

Structure of the book

The book is organized into three parts: (I) the social organization of groups committing acts of terrorism; (II) the financial organization of terrorism, including assessments of both fundraising and the movement of funds; and (III) the policy responses to the terrorist financing challenge at the national and international levels.

Part I of the volume describes different organizational forms of terrorism, ranging from hierarchical, commander-cadre terrorist organizations to virtual, de-centered terrorist groups/networks. It analyzes the internal workings of terrorist organizations – including their mission, decision-making procedures, and recruitment strategies – and evaluates the effects of exogenous factors, such as government policy responses, on such organizations. Specific attention is focused on several cases: al Qaeda (particularly how the organization has changed since 11 September), Jemaah Islamiyah (JI) in Southeast Asia, and Hezbollah.

Part II discusses how patterns of terrorist financing vary according to the different social organization of terrorist groups. Experts explore the means by which different types of terrorist organizations raise money through charities, trade diversion, and criminal activities. The mechanisms for movement of such funds are then examined – from use of the formal banking sector to informal value transfer systems and the use of commodities and other resources.

Part III addresses policy responses of governments and international organizations to the challenge of countering the financing of terrorism. Progress in the so-called "war" on terrorist financing is presented – including the challenges of coping with the vast volume of material generated by new reporting requirements – along with a discussion of international institutional initiatives to confront the issue. The effectiveness of such efforts to deny terrorists the ability to raise and move funds is assessed, exploring the adequacy of existing regulatory policy responses focused largely on formal sector mechanisms and the prospects of new approaches to state regulatory policy.

A concluding chapter synthesizes the findings, draws out broader implications, and offers recommendations for new approaches to counter the financing of terrorism.

Notes

1 "President Freezes Terrorists' Assets," Remarks by the President, Secretary of the Treasury O'Neill and Secretary of State Powell on Executive Order, 24 September 24, 2001 Online. Available http://www.whitehouse.gov/news/releases/2001/09/20010924–4.html> (accessed 6 September 2006).
2 L. J. Freeh, Statement Before the United States Senate Committee on Appropriations, Subcommittee for the Departments of Commerce, Justice, and State, the Judiciary, and Related Agencies, 4 February 1999. Online. Available HTTP: <http://www.fas.org/irp/congress/1999_hr/990204-freehct2.htm> (accessed 5 September 2006).
3 D. Lormel, Testimony before the Senate Judiciary Committee, Subcommittee on Technology, Terrorism, and Government Information, 9 October 2002. Online. Available HTTP:<http://corprisk.timberlakepublishing.com/files/10–9.pdf#search=%22Lormel%202002%20testimony%22> (accessed 6 September 2006).
4 J. Roth, D. Greenberg, and S. Wille, *Monograph on Terrorist Financing* (Staff Report to the Commission), National Commission on Terrorist Attacks Upon the United States, 2004, p. 3. Online. Available HTTP: <http://www.9–11commission. gov/staff_statements/911_Terr   Fin_Monograph.pdf#search=%229%2F11%20commission%20monograph%22> (accessed 7 September 2006).
5 *Comprehensive Reference Guide to Anti-Money Laundering and Combating the Financing of Terrorism*, 2nd edition (Washington, DC: The World Bank and the International Monetary Fund, 2003) pp. I–1. Online. Available HTTP: <http://www1.worldbank.org/finance/html/amlcft/referenceguide.htm> (accessed 24 April 2007).
6 Roth et al., *Monograph on Terrorist Financing*, p. 3.
7 C. Realuyo and S. Stapleton, "Response to Bali: An International Success Story," *eJournal USA*, US State Department, September 2004. Online. Available HTTP: <http://usinfo.state.gov/journals/ites/0904/ijee/stapleton.htm> (accessed 30 August 2006) and Roth et al., *Monograph on Terrorist Financing*, p. 27.
8 First Report of the Analytical Support and Sanctions Monitoring Team appointed pursuant to resolution 1526 (2004) concerning Al-Qaida and the Taliban and associated individual and entities, S/2004/679/, 25 August 2004. Online. Available HTTP: http://www.un.org./sc/committees/1267/monitoringteam.shtml (accessed 6 September 2006).
9 First Report of the Analytical Support and Sanctions Monitoring Team appointed pursuant to UN Security Council resolution 1526 (2004) concerning al Qaeda and the Taliban and associated individuals and entities, S/2004/679, 25 August 2004, p. 12.

10 R. Windrem, "FAQ: Osama Bin Laden," MSNBC, 12 January 2004. Online. Available HTTP: http://www.msnbc.msn.com/id/3907198/ (accessed 28 November 2006).

11 Boletin Oficial de las Cortes Generales, Congresso de los Disputades, VIII Legislatura, Serie D: General, 13 de Julio 2005, Numero 241, p. 18. The report estimates operational costs ranged between 41,000 and 54,000 Euros.

12 House of Commons, The Stationery Office, *Report of the Official Account on the Bombings in London on 7th July 2005*, HC 1087, 11 May 2006. Online. Available HTTP: http://www.official-documents.gov.uk/document/hc0506/hc10/1087/ 1087.pdf (accessed 6 September 2006).

13 M. J. White, "The Constitution, Terrorism, and Civil Liberties," 2004 Constitution Address at Dickinson College, 21 September 2004. Online. Available HTTP:<http://www.clarkecenter.org/content/occasionalpapers/Constitution-Civil%20Liberties-White.pdf#search=%22%22every%20dollar%20matters%22% 20Mary%20Jo%20White%22> (accessed 30 August 2006).

14 See M. Rudner, "Using Financial Intelligence Against the Funding of Terrorism," *International Journal of Intelligence and CounterIntelligence*, 19: 32–58, 2006, for a discussion of the cost structure of terrorist organizations, which includes planning, recruitment, training, procurement/preparation/delivery of materials, communications, persuasion/propaganda/incitement, infrastructure of safe houses/sleeper cells, reconnaissance of targets, and assault on targets.

15 D. Bugg, Speech to IAP Conference, 8 December 2003. Online. Available HTTP: <http://www.cdpp.gov.au/Media/Speeches/20030812db.aspx> (accessed 7 September 2006).

16 D. Rumsfeld, Memo to General Dick Myers, Paul Wolfowitz, etc., 16 October 2003 Online. Available HTTP: <http://www.globalsecurity.org/military/library/ policy/dod/rumsfeld-d20031016sdmemo.htm> (accessed 7 September 2006).

17 D. C. Rapoport, "The Four Waves of Modern Terrorism" in Audrey Kurth Cronin and James M. Ludes, eds., *Attacking Terrorism: Elements of a Grand Strategy* Washington, DC: Georgetown University Press, 2004.

18 M. Greenberg, W. Wechsler, and L. Wolosky, *Terrorist Financing: Report of an Independent Task Force Sponsored by the Council on Foreign Relations*, New York: Council on Foreign Relations, 2002.

19 R. Gunaratna, *Inside al Qaeda: Global Network of Terror*, New York: Columbia University Press, 2002. Stephen Coll, *Ghost Wars: The Secret History of the CIA, Afghanistan, bin Laden, From the Soviet Invasion to September 10, 2001*, New York: Penguin Press, 2004.

20 C. Smith, "North Africa Feared as Staging Ground for Terror, *New York Times*, 20 February 2007, p. 3. Online. Available HTTP: http://www.nytimes.com/2007/ 02/20/world/africa/20tunisia.html?_r=1&th=&emc=th&pag. . . (accessed 25 April 2007).

21 D. Byman, *Deadly Connections: States That Sponsor Terrorism*, Cambridge: Cambridge University Press, 2005.

22 L. Napoleoni, *Terror Incorporated: Tracing the Dollars Behind the Terror Networks*, New York: Seven Stories Press, 2005.

23 N. Fielding, "How al Qaeda Utilises Family Networks?," Presentation at Watson Institute, Workshop on the Financial and Transnational Dynamics of Terrorism, Providence, RI, 24–25 October 2003.

24 D. Farah, *Blood from Stones: The Secret Financial Network of Terror*, New York: Broadway Books, 2004.

25 This volume does not focus specifically on the use of the Internet to raise funds, but for more information, see B. Hoffman, "The Use of the Internet by Islamic Extremists," Testimony before the House Permanent Select Committee on Intelligence, 4 May 2006. Online. Available HTTP: http://www.globalsecurity.

org/intell/library/congress/2006_hr/060504-hoffman.pdf (accessed 24 April 2007) and Gabriel Weissman, Terror on the Internet: The New Arena, the New Challenges, Washington: United States Institute of Peace, 2006.
26 "UN Sanctions 'Hitting al-Qaeda'," BBC News, 11 January 2005. Online. Available HTTP: <http://news.bbc.co.uk/2/hi/americas/4164631.stm> (accessed 6 September 2006). See also US Department of State, *International Narcotics Control Strategy Report*, March 2005. Online. Available HTTP: <http://www.state.gov/p/inl/rls/nrcrpt/2005/vol2/html/42374.htm> (accessed 3 June 2007).
27 "Terrorist Assets Report, Calendar Year 2005," U.S. Department of the Treasury. Online. Available HTTP: <http://www.ustreas.gov/offices/enforcement/ofac/reports/tar2005.pdf> (accessed 7 September 2006).

Part I
The social organization of terrorism

2 Producing terror

Organizational dynamics of survival

Jessica Stern and Amit Modi[1]

In this chapter we use an organizational approach to explore terrorism as a definable and distinctive product rendered by groups or "firms." This approach allows us to analyze the production and "purchase" of terrorism, the evolution of groups, and the types of behaviors, shapes, and attributes that make groups more or less effective and resilient. Here we ask, what are the inputs of terrorism? How does resource scarcity or abundance affect organizational dynamics, such as competition and splintering? Why do terrorist organizations change their missions, and what factors affect their mission flexibility? What strategies do terrorist organizations choose in order to survive under changing environmental conditions? Under what set of conditions are the various organizational forms most efficient? By analyzing the organizational structures used for creating the "terrorist product," we can hypothesize how terrorist groups adapt in response to changes in their environment, in particular, to governmental counter-terrorism policies that limit a terrorist groups' access to funds.

The behavior of terrorist firms has always been responsive to and a reflection of the internal dynamics of the organization. Today, however, terrorist groups face extraordinary evolutionary pressures to adapt and evolve in the midst of the global war on terrorism. The argument presented here is that these internal and external dynamics encourage the development of terrorist organizations along a recognizable trajectory from creation to dissolution. Over time, groups that survive tend to evolve from the cause-maximizing end of the spectrum to the incentive-maximizing end. In this chapter we are primarily interested in groups that simultaneously pursue maintenance goals (providing incentives for labor) and collective goals. These groups, situated in the middle of the spectrum, are neither purely mission-driven (devoted to achieving the stated mission of the organization) nor incentive driven (devoted to securing the financial or emotional well-being of participants). By understanding this trajectory of development, we may create policies and strategies that are better poised to combat terrorism.

Analytical approach

Employing a slightly different method than that of the majority of scholars in the field, this chapter takes the internal dynamics of the terrorist organization as its starting point, and then proceeds to define the terms and outline the structure of the life cycle of a terrorist organization, with special emphasis on the professional or mature group. We have developed this organizational model attentive to the two dominant models that exist in the literature – the instrumental and expressive approaches – with the exclusion of all other models.

The instrumental model, which sees terrorism as a form of violent coercion and tacit bargaining, flows out of Thomas Schelling's *Strategy of Conflict* and subsequent works by Schelling and others.[2] The instrumental paradigm assumes that terrorists are rational actors who select strategies to maximize a clearly defined set of political objectives. Exhibiting a collective rationality, terrorists act in response to external stimuli, particularly actions by nation-states. Bruce Hoffman, a proponent of this view, argues that "the terrorist is fundamentally a violent intellectual" who uses force to attain goals that are "ineluctably political."[3] The instrumental model posits that the costs and benefits of a given attack can be calculated using measures based on the explicit mission of the organization rather than implicit group goals.[4] Therefore, an increase in the costs or a decrease in the benefits of violence will make terrorist attacks less likely.[5]

The expressive model, in contrast, assumes that terrorists are communicating with an audience – their supporters, the group itself, an enemy government, or a deity – but they are not primarily trying to alter the world outside the group. This focus on the internal dynamic of the group runs counter to the assumptions of the instrumental model. While the instrumental model assumes that terrorists may hope to attract attention and air grievances, in Schelling's words, these expressive acts serve only as an "an intermediate means toward political objectives."[6] The expressive model allows for the possibility that some individuals enjoy violence for its own sake or enjoy belonging to a group that employs violence. For instance, in her interviews of terrorists, Jessica Stern found that operatives are often more interested in the expression of a collective identity than they are in the group's stated goals.[7] According to psychiatrist Jerry Post, who is a proponent of this model, terrorists may feel "psychologically compelled" to commit violent acts and the political objectives they espouse are only a rationalization for their actions.[8]

In contrast, the organizational approach used here is most akin to that of Martha Crenshaw, who, in several articles published in the 1980s, emphasizes the internal politics of terrorist groups, concluding that "terrorist behavior represents the outcome of the internal dynamics of the organization rather than strategic action." She argues further that some terrorist groups can best be understood as self-sustaining organizations whose fundamental purpose is to survive.[9] The organizational approach assumes that making progress (or at least appearing to make progress) towards stated goals is an important consideration for terrorists, but rejects the assumption that the terrorists' principal aim is necessarily to achieve those goals.

Unlike the instrumental model, this organizational approach takes the terrorist group's mission as endogenous and assumes that it is not necessarily static. We reject the assumption that terrorist groups can most profitably be categorized according to their ideology or mission. On the contrary, our approach assumes that the group's ideology is just one of many variables that a group can control in order to enhance its survivability. Indeed, one of the requirements for long-term survival is a flexible mission. In keeping with the expressive model, the organizational approach assumes that terrorist organizations are made up of individuals with psychological and physical needs. However, even as we incorporate individuals into this organizational approach and relax the assumptions of the instrumental model, we nonetheless aim to give primacy to a model that considers the terrorist group's behavior in its entirety. In addition to drawing upon individual psychology, we also posit that terrorist groups depend on their sociopolitical contexts: the efficacy of behaviors, missions, and organizational forms depends on the terrorist group's interaction with its environment. Environmental changes act as stressors that may require an adaptive shift in the organization's strategy or structure.

This argument depends heavily on the definition of terms. In light of the fact that this volume concerns terrorist financing, it is fitting that we define the structure of terrorist organizations in terms commonly associated with business firms. We assess the missions, strategies, consumers, and products of the terrorist group. We also evaluate the conditions that favor networks versus hierarchies, vertical integration versus disaggregation, and pure competition versus network governance. And we consider how different organizational structures influence the long-term effectiveness of terrorist groups in an increasingly complex and polarized global environment.

The terrorist product: expressive and instrumental goals

Terrorists claim to be producing a great variety of things, depending with whom they are speaking and in what context. But the one thing they inevitably produce is violence, or the credible threat of violence. For the purpose of this discussion, we will call the terrorist product violence in the service of a collective goal. This simplification assumes that even those terrorists whose main goal is expressing rage or earning money are trying to affect the world in some way. The amount of terrorist product can be measured by the number of attacks a group produces, the symbolic importance of the targets, or the number of deaths or dollars in property damage per attack. We will use the term "quantity" to refer to the number of attacks an organization carries out in a given time period and "quality" to refer to a variable that combines the symbolic importance of the target, the type of weapons or tactics used, and the average number of deaths or dollars in property damage per attack.

The inputs of the terrorist product are not unlike the inputs of products manufactured by corporate firms in that both include capital, labor, and a branding or "mission." For terrorist groups, capital includes such things as weapons, camps, equipment, factories, and the physical plants for any businesses run by the terrorist firm. Labor includes the terrorist leaders plus all the personnel employed by the organization, including managers, killers, marketers, financiers, public-relations officers, etc.

Unlike goods produced by corporate firms, the product of terrorism – violence in service of a collective goal – is a public good. Terrorist activity is measured not only by the costs incurred by those who contribute but also by the benefits shared by a broader collective or group.[10] For example, when Jewish extremists attempt to lay a cornerstone for the Third Temple they hope to build, all like-minded messianic Jews (and messianic Christians) benefit. Only the participants pay: when they ascend the Temple Mount, they incur risks to their person, livelihood, freedom, and families. Given this, extremists should be asking themselves, why bother participating? Why not let others do the work and take the risks? The theory of collective action suggests that people tend to "free ride" on the contributions of others to collective goods.[11]

To address this free-rider problem, terrorist leaders encourage participation by offering two broad types of incentives to individual members: material incentives in the form of housing, food, and cash, and non-material incentives in the form of spiritual and emotional rewards. Financial rewards include cash payments for successful operations and money or housing for the families of "martyrs." In the spiritual realm, leaders hold out the promise of heavenly rewards and the threat of heavenly retribution. They provide adventure, camaraderie, and, most importantly, a collective identity with honor for their followers, who often describe themselves as humiliated. Some operatives participate because they fear being punished in the afterlife or because they desire to be virtuous (in their conception of the term) for virtue's own sake. Alternatively, those who refuse to obey orders in jihadi groups can be subject to corporal punishment, including, in extreme cases, death.[12]

In addition to these individual motivations for joining a terrorist group, terrorists also commit violence to advance a diversity of exogenous goals. Osama bin Laden, for example, has said at various times that his goals are (1) forcing US troops out of Saudi Arabia; (2) initiating an economic crisis in America; (3) impressing potential recruits with the aim of persuading them to join the al Qaeda movement; (4) changing US policies in Iraq, Israel, and elsewhere around the world; and (5) establishing a caliphate. In addition to these various instrumental goals, bin Laden has stated the expressive goals of (6) drawing attention to the plight of Muslims in various conflict zones around the world and (7) exacting revenge.

In a video produced shortly after the 11 September attacks, a senior al Qaeda manager listed the "benefits" of the 11 September strikes. He boasted:

The operations have brought about the largest economic crisis that America has ever known. Material losses amount to one trillion dollars. America has lost about two thousand economic brains as a result of the operations. The stock exchange dropped drastically, and American consumer spending deteriorated. The dollar has dropped, the airlines have been crippled.[13]

An additional goal was revenge. It was permissible to attack civilians, the al Qaeda manager said, because it was a "reciprocal" response to American sanctions and bombing of Iraq, which killed "millions of Iraqi Muslims."[14] Another objective was the inevitable psychological damage that many Americans received from the attacks. Shortly after 11 September, bin Laden boasted that seven out of ten Americans suffered psychological trauma as a result of the attacks, according to articles that he read in the press.[15]

Bin Laden also intended a "rift between the American people and their government" to result from the attacks by making Americans aware that the US Government was sacrificing people to serve the interests of the rich, especially the Jews.[16] Forcing the targeted government to overreact in a way that ultimately turns the people against their government, in what James Der Derian calls an "autoimmune response" to terrorism, may be the terrorists' main goal.[17]

In summary, the goals of terrorism fall on two continua: from the purely instrumental (aiming to achieve something) to the purely expressive (aiming to communicate something) and from promoting a mission to promoting the wealth or personal power, identity, or enjoyment of the participants. Organizational theorists distinguish between a rational system paradigm, which asserts that organizations seek specific, stated collective goals, and a natural system paradigm (now dominant in the literature), which asserts that participants in organizations pursue multiple interests, both disparate and common, instrumental and expressive, with the perpetuation of the organization as the single most important objective. Natural system theorists emphasize that even when the organization is pursuing its stated goals, it will also promote the needs of the individuals who belong to the group. These maintenance goals, required to secure the capital and labor needed to keep the organization in business, often "absorb much energy, and in the extreme (but perhaps not rare) case, become ends in themselves."[18] In this chapter we are primarily interested in groups that simultaneously pursue maintenance goals (providing incentives for labor) and collective goals. These groups, situated in the middle of the spectrum, are neither purely mission-driven (devoted to achieving the stated mission of the organization) nor incentive driven (devoted to securing the financial or emotional well-being of participants).

Organizational shapes: hierarchies versus networks

At this stage it is important to differentiate between two ideal types of terrorist group structures: commander–cadre and network. A commander–cadre organization is essentially a terrorist army. The leader of a commander–cadre organization provides both material and non-material incentives.[19] A network is generically defined in the literature as a set of actors connected by a set of ties. These actors are referred to as nodes. The nodes can be persons, networks, or hierarchical organizations. The term *network* refers to an organizational form characterized by a flat hierarchy, and we will use the term here in the same way. The pattern of ties among nodes may make some nodes more important by virtue of their access to information, but there are no leaders issuing instructions to followers in a network. The term *key player* describes the most important node in a network. A key player is defined as the node that, if removed, would maximally disrupt communication among the remaining nodes.[20] Nonetheless, the key player's importance does not stem from his or her position in a hierarchy. While a node within the network may be organized hierarchically, there will be no hierarchy at the superstructure level where the network exists. A network is different from a team, in that teams have identifiable leaders (e.g. coaches, captains), a hierarchical structure, and teams are usually governed by rules. Networks, in contrast, can be self-organized and self-enrolling.

We further differentiate between virtual and non-virtual networks. Non-virtual networks imply "long-term recurrent exchanges" that create inter-dependences, resulting in an "entangling of obligations, expectations, reputations, and mutual interests." Exchanges are protected – not by contracts as in a market, but by shared norms of trustworthy behavior.[21] Like participants in markets, nodes in networks have a shared social purpose. But unlike markets, networks depend on the assumption that participants are not solely self-interested.[22]

Non-virtual networks exist both within terrorist organizations (nodes within al Qaeda) and between them (for example, the consortium of terrorist groups with which bin Laden established ties while al Qaeda was based in Sudan). According to the *9/11 Commission Report*, bin Laden formalized relationships with terrorist groups from Saudi Arabia, Egypt, Jordan, Lebanon, Iraq, Oman, Algeria, Libya, Tunisia, Morocco, Somalia, and Eritrea. Each of the groups had its own leaders and operatives, but the groups met together in a coordinating body, the Islamic Army Shura. Bin Laden also established cooperative but less formal relationships with other extremist groups in these same countries as well as groups in Africa and Southeast Asia. For some groups he provided training and financial assistance, sometimes for particular operations.[23]

By contrast, within a virtual network, individuals take action on their own initiatives – raising their own funds, purchasing their own equipment, and creating and sustaining their own cells. The leader of a virtual network is *inspirational*. Rather than providing housing, cash, or training, as in a non-virtual network, the leader of a virtual network provides for the higher-order needs of operatives, such as a collective identity. A virtual network contracts almost all of its functions to the level of the individual node.[24] The network is a group of nodes (organizations or individuals) that come together to produce a particular product, but there are no formal or long-term ties among the nodes and no exchange of material things. Instead, shared world views link the nodes. In a virtual network, the leader's role is to articulate this shared world view and mission, suggesting strategies and targets and perhaps providing instructions, but never to any particular individual or node. The leader provides instructions and inspiration abstractly to a large, open audience.

In America, where virtual terrorist networks have become relatively common, terrorist leaders are likely to disseminate information in a way that is protected by the First Amendment. For example, Neal Horsley, a leader of the Army of God, a violent anti-abortion network, put up a website called The Nuremberg Files in 1995.[25] The site provides information about personnel at abortion clinics all over the country, and about judges and politicians "who pass or uphold laws authorizing child-killing." Visitors are urged to send names and birth dates of abortion providers' family members and friends; social-security numbers; license plate numbers; photographs and videos; affidavits of former employees, former patients, or former spouses; or "anything else you believe will help identify the abortionist in a future court of law."[26] When Dr. Barnett Slepian's name was crossed out within hours of his death, Planned Parenthood and a group of doctors filed suit, and Horsley's internet service provider took the site down.[27] But Horsley relaunched the site on his own server and has expanded it since he won the court case.[28] Horsley manages to keep the website up because he does not provide instructions to kill anyone. He is simply providing information on targets of opportunity.

In a virtual network, followers can become leaders at a moment's notice – either of their own cells, or of entire movements. Conversely, leaders may one day articulate the mission to followers and the next day become follower themselves by carrying out attacks on their own. A good example is Paul Hill, a former Presbyterian minister who was executed in 2004 for murdering two abortion-clinic personnel a decade earlier. Hill was both an operative and a leader in the doctor-killer movement. He advocated murdering Supreme Court justices and sending chemical and biological agents through the mail to abortion clinics.[29] He wrote a book while sitting on death row and regularly communicated his views to virtual followers through material published on the internet. From his prison cell, he admonished his followers not to remain at home, leaving others to respond to the "call from the womb." "Death opens her cavernous mouth before you," he said.

As evidenced by Paul Hill, the internet facilitates the spread of virtual subcultures, including those based on dissatisfaction and rage. It has greatly increased the capacity of loosely networked terrorist organizations. It enables inspirational leaders to communicate the mission to vast numbers of people they may never meet. It also allows people with "unusual interests" to find one another. An anti-government inspirational leader, James Dalton Bell, told Stern, "I'm as big a fan as it is possible to be of the internet," arguing that it "dramatically increased" the strength of anti-government movements. The internet has dealt a decimating blow to the government's strength, he said, a blow they have not even noticed. "Historically people couldn't talk to others around the world. To get your story out – maybe you'd write a letter to the editor. Today, anybody can get his or her word out." The internet means that "the story can't be killed," he told Stern.[30]

The internet is particularly useful for "gateway" organizations that spread a violent ideology without actually promoting violence, whose adherents are then susceptible to recruitment by violent groups. One example is the Islamist group Hizb-ut Tahrir (HT, "Liberation Party"). HT was established as a Palestinian Islamic movement in 1953, but is now active in approximately 25 countries with an estimated 15–20,000 members in Central Asia alone.[31] HT advocates conversion of the entire world to Islam and the urgent re-establishment of the caliphate. Perhaps in imitation of white supremacists' use of music as a means to indoctrinate and create a community of sympathizers, HT promotes technopop bands.[32] Influenced by HT, a group of American Muslims formed a rock group known as *Soldiers of Allah*, which spread HT's ideology to a broader audience. Song lyrics encourage "the masses [to] be joined under the banner of Allah and rise up in jihad against their 'oppressors' and 'occupiers' " in the United States and elsewhere around the world.[33] Ahmed Omar Saeed Sheikh, who was convicted in Pakistan of the 2002 murder of Wall Street Journal reporter Daniel Pearl, had been a member of HT, but it is not known whether HT facilitated his subsequent involvement in terrorist organizations linked to al Qaeda. Intelligence officials worry that al Qaeda and other Islamist groups could target HT cadres for recruitment.

The leader of a virtual network is not required to recruit or train personnel, raise money, or acquire weapons. The leader's job is to inspire rather than to command. Capital and labor are inputs to the terrorist product of virtual networks, but they are gathered by individual nodes rather than by central nodes. In a virtual network, the entire process is carried out by fluid cells that are independent of one another.

There are several advantages to the virtual-network organization from terrorists' perspective. First, redundancy of functions makes the network maximally resilient to disruption. Second, the internet facilitates the creation of virtual communities among people who have trouble finding others interested in fighting their chosen "enemy," whoever that enemy may be. Third, the internet allows people who have trouble cooperating with others to form cells without necessarily having to meet in person. Fourth, because communication among nodes in planning actual operations is minimal or nonexistent, it is harder for law enforcement personnel to disrupt attacks or penetrate the group. Indeed, "leaderless resistance" – the term American neo-Nazis use for virtual terrorist networks – was developed with precisely this goal in mind: to avoid detection and penetration by law enforcement personnel.

Louis Beam, who calls himself Ambassador-at-large, staff propagandist, and "Computer Terrorist to the Chosen," of the neo-Nazi group Aryan Nations, is one of the original promoters of the concept of leaderless resistance.[34] Beam writes that hierarchical organizations are dangerous for insurgents. This is especially so in "technologically advanced societies where electronic surveillance can often penetrate the structure revealing its chain of command," such as the United States. He writes: "Organs of information distribution such as newspapers, leaflets, computers, etc., which are widely available to all, keep each person informed of events, allowing for a planned response that will take many variations. No one need issue an order to anyone."[35] Beam's essay on the virtues of leaderless resistance has been picked up by radical Muslim sites, according to researcher Michael Reynolds.[36]

The disadvantage to virtual networks from the terrorists' perspective is that they are not well suited for carrying out complex tasks that require coordination among cells.[37] Unless terrorists acquire impenetrable means of communication, virtual networks will be incapable of carrying out large-scale, complex attacks such as the 11 September strikes.[38] However, technological developments will make virtual networks more dangerous over time as improved encryption and the dissemination of more and more powerful weapons to smaller and smaller groups continue to become available.

At the opposite end of the organizational spectrum is a commander–cadre organization, which enables terrorists to carry out big, complex strikes that require coordination. These terrorist bureaucracies are characterized by clear lines of authority, functional specialization, and centralized decision-making. There are separate departments responsible for particular tasks, and training takes place for operatives and managers at all levels. A commander–cadre organization, at least in its ideal form, is likely to possess many characteristics of Weber's "rational bureaucracy."[39] Hierarchies provide for lines of authority and responsibility and a clear division of labor. They facilitate the breaking down of complex tasks into specific jobs that can be handled more efficiently by the various sub-units or functional groups in the organization. They also facilitate complex, customized exchanges.[40]

Because terrorists violate laws and require secrecy to commit their crimes, a commander–cadre organization can exist only under particular circumstances – in weak or failed states, where governments are not able to impose a monopoly on the use of force; in regions within states that are outside of governmental control; or in countries where the government or parts of the government allow or facilitate terrorist groups to function. The CIA believes there are "stateless zones" in approximately 50 countries, and that terrorists are operating in half of them. These zones tend to appear in remote, rugged areas plagued by socioeconomic problems, where the central governments have inconsistent reach, the CIA finds.[41] As the war on terrorism progresses, terrorists are likely to move from their traditional hideouts to these stateless zones, where they can train personnel and plan and stage operations without interference from government authorities.[42] For instance, the most well-known stateless zone is the tribal area of Pakistan, where al Qaeda and other jihadi organizations are believed to be hiding. Others, likely to be important in the future, are in Bangladesh and in various parts of Africa, including the Horn and the Sahel.

Leaders who want to control the flow of information, resources, and status – possibly for personal gain, and possibly to keep information secure – will favor hierarchies over flatter structures. Moreover, the need for secrecy makes centralization of recruitment attractive because it facilitates protecting the identity of existing members. But, as Bonnie Erickson explained in regard to secret societies more broadly, "in risky situations members and hence the links they are part of may be frequently deleted: they may be informed on, etc." Unless there is link redundancy, she explains, "the secret society would be in continual danger of being cut to pieces"[43] because recruiters for secret societies operating under risk will tend to recruit individuals they trust based on a prior, reasonably strong relationship. This tendency introduces an inherent vulnerability. For instance, once law enforcement officials discovered the importance of family relationships in the structure of al Qaeda, parts of the organization became easier to map and unravel. A member of Lashkar-e-Jhangvi told Stern's interviewer that he joined that particular organization "due to my friends" and later shifted to a new group, also "due to my friends." He also admitted that the hierarchical tribal organizations known as biradri play a significant role in recruitment to jihadi organizations.[44]

Another disadvantage to pyramidal structures is that they can lull workers into focusing on the narrow task they are assigned rather than seeing how their work fits into the bigger picture. For this reason, hierarchies can reduce innovation and discourage initiative; this is as true for producers of terrorism as it is for producers of cars. As a result of a "do-as-I-am-told" mentality, new or cross-cutting issues may fall through organizational stovepipes.

In summary, hierarchies provide for lines of authority and responsibility and a clear division of labor. They facilitate the breaking down of complex tasks into specific jobs that can be handled more efficiently by the various sub-units or functional groups in the organization. They facilitate complex, customized exchanges.[45] As a commander–cadre or hierarchical terrorist organization grows and matures, it will develop certain operating routines and procedures for workers at different levels. This is fine in a static environment. But in a situation of rapid change and uncertainty, workers cannot rely on pre-specified routines or wait for clearance from those at higher levels of the bureaucracy before taking action.

Networks, which encourage innovation and initiative, are better suited to dealing with rapidly changing environments. It is noteworthy that the idea for the 11 September strikes came from a man who was not a member of al Qaeda at the time. He proposed a complex plot involving simultaneous attacks in several cities and using airplanes as weapons. Khalid Sheikh Mohammed, the mastermind of the 11 September plot, initially declined bin Laden's invitation to join al Qaeda, preferring to retain the option of working with a variety of terrorist groups as an independent entrepreneur. The plot he had in mind, however, required personnel, logistics, and money available only to a group like al Qaeda. Mohammed eventually joined al Qaeda when bin Laden approved his pet project to use planes as weapons, albeit in much simplified form.[46]

Increased law enforcement and intelligence cooperation internationally and a rapidly changing law-enforcement environment, including financial controls, reduce the reliability of inputs to the terrorist product – especially the supply of finance and skilled labor. In the current environment, skilled laborers working for al Qaeda are under increased threat of being captured or killed. Money to pay laborers, buy explosives, and provide training is also in shorter supply. Rather than destroying al Qaeda, law enforcement and intelligence efforts are forcing al Qaeda to evolve into an increasingly loose network. If each cell raises its own funds, less money is needed at the center. If each cell recruits its own labor, the organization, taken as a whole, is less vulnerable. If there is redundancy with respect to organizational requirements and tasks, the loss of a single node is less damaging. The looser the links between the cells – the more the network becomes a virtual one – the more resilient it will be with respect to law enforcement detection and penetration.

Having operationalized the terms *network* and *commander–cadre* relative to the structure of terrorist groups, we may now begin to understand these organizations in relation to the "product outputs" – attacks, as described previously. Attack quality, defined above, refers to the average number of deaths or dollars in property damage per attack. It also depends on the symbolic importance of the target and the shock value of employing sophisticated tactics or weapons, but these aspects of quality are difficult to measure. We will define capacity as the upper bound on the aggregate potential production of the organization – it is the summation of quality and quantity. In the context of terrorist networks, network capacity is the maximum death and destruction the nodes in the network are capable of generating in aggregate. Capacity is thus a function of the resources available to the network.[47]

A terrorist organization's effectiveness is then a measure of its actual production of outputs over time, or the sum of quantity and quality for a given time period. Efficiency is a measure of how well an organization transforms inputs into outputs, and resilience refers to the organization's ability to project capacity into the future, which in turn depends on its ability to withstand attack.

To be effective over time, an organization must not only have a high capacity to inflict damage, but must use its resources efficiently and be capable of surviving its adversaries' attempts to destroy it. In other words, it must be resilient. Virtual networks are designed to optimize resilience. Resilience requires both redundancy of nodes to reduce the effects of extraction (the removal of a node by enemy military or law enforcement personnel) and separation of nodes to reduce the effects of contagion (the process by which the discovery of one node leads to the discovery of additional nodes).

There is often an inherent tradeoff between efficiency and resilience in that maximizing efficiency requires coordination and communication (connectedness), which makes an organization vulnerable to penetration. The more connected the nodes, the easier it is to unravel the network in that identifying one node is likely to lead to the identification of others. In general, maximizing efficiency requires a more connected network, and resilience requires a less connected configuration.

It is important to point out that effectiveness does not necessarily imply success. An effective terrorist organization is one that produces civilian deaths or destroys property. A successful terrorist organization achieves its instrumental objectives.[48] An optimal network organizes a set of given resources, or nodes, in a configuration that most efficiently produces outputs, but is also maximally resistant to attack.

The terrorist mission: a goal or marketing strategy?

While labor, capital, and organization are all essential features, the most important requirement for a terrorist organization is its mission or ideology. Even the most diffuse organizations, in which small cells or lone wolves raise their own operating budgets and select targets on their own, need to articulate their grievances in a way that attracts recruits and capital. The mission serves many functions: it helps the group raise funds, it provides a *raison d'être* for action, and it provides a narrative about collective identity.

There are several things to note about terrorist missions. First, making progress toward achieving the mission does not guarantee organizational survival. Indeed, the two objectives – mission achievement and organizational

Table 2.1 Virtual network versus commander–cadre organizations

	Virtual network organization	*Commander–cadre organization*
Characterization	Flat hierarchy of largely independent nodes with inspirational leader(s)	Terrorist army
Incentive structure	Non-material	Non-material and material
Level of production	The unit node	The conglomerate organization
Organizational flow	Information and ideas from leader to non-specific nodes	Materials, information, and command flow within hierarchical structure
Command structure	Indirect Dynamic	Direct Rigid
Proficiencies	Resilience Resistance to extraction and infiltration	Quality Ability to perform complex and coordinated attacks

survival – are quite distinct. This is different from the for-profit world, where mission achievement (or value maximization), financial performance, and organizational survival are aligned. Maximizing profits is the firm's long-term goal, and the production of goods and services is a means to that end.

Second, terrorist organizations must make two calculations instead of one. They must attend to the financial performance of the enterprise and its long-term survival, and they must ensure that the enterprise is promoting, or at least appears to promote, its social objectives. For non-profit firms, including terrorist ones, revenues are not the objective but the means to the desired end of achieving social objectives.[49] (It is important to point out that some terrorist organizations evolve into organized criminal groups with no apparent mission other than generating profits. For example, the IRA appears to be moving in this direction.)

Third, terrorist groups, like other NGOs, have to raise money by "selling" their mission to donors and patrons, the terrorist groups' "customers." Some of these customers or donors, such as intelligence agencies, may buy more than the mission: they may buy particular attacks against particular targets. As is the case for more traditional NGOs, however, charitable donations – a contribution to the public good terrorism is supposed to provide, rather than the purchase of a particular attack – are often an important source of funding. Selecting and advertising a mission that will attract such donations is often important to the group's financial well-being.

This way of looking at terrorism suggests that the increase in religious terrorism after the breakup of the Soviet Union occurred in large measure because terrorist organizations realized that there was no longer money for purportedly promoting workers' rights or attacking enemies of the Soviet Union, but there was new money coming in to support religious causes. For instance, the Popular Front for the Liberation of Palestine (PFLP), a leftist terrorist group, lost influence, and Hamas, a nationalist Islamist group, became prominent. Why, then, did the PFLP not choose a new "brand" as a religious organization to capitalize on the popularity of this religious wave? Our analogy between legal NGOs and terrorist organizations continues, as both groups, seeking to assure their own survival, become hampered by an organization phenomenon called "mission stickiness."

The terrorist mission: Sticky or spry? Narrow or broad?

Terrorist missions can be sticky or spry. Most studies of terrorism assume that the mission is exogenously defined – the terrorists respond to an unmet societal need – and that the mission is static. Typologies of terrorist organizations are almost always based on their ideologies: left wing, right wing, irredentist, or secessionist. The assumption is that the group would not exist without its ideology and that its mission stays the same over time. But this assumption is not always correct. We will argue that groups that survive over the long term are likely to change their mission to attract more funding, support, or recruits, even at the risk of losing some of their original personnel or backers. They may form alliances of convenience with groups they once described as infidels or enemies. They may form temporary or even permanent alliances with groups with missions that are quite different from their own, or even with organized crime.[50] A flexible mission is an additional component that will affect the organization's resilience and, in turn, its effectiveness over time.

Why are some organizations "sticky" in regard to their mission and others "spry"? Three factors seem paramount for terrorist organizations: a reliable source of revenue, a flexible organizational structure that allows the organization to sell different products (violence in the service of different missions) at different times to different consumers, and a reliable source of recruits. In essence, these factors amount to a reliable source of inputs and a reliable demand for the products the group aims to sell.

Like other NGOs, terrorist organizations need to sell their mission to donors as well as recruits. As the environment changes, NGOs and terrorist organizations may find that their missions need to change to keep up with the desires of new or more generous donors. This need for flexibility can cause a variety of problems. Employees may be wedded to the original mission and resent the need to kowtow to donors, rather than focusing on the needs of the beneficiaries. Managers are vulnerable to charges of mission creep. From the viewpoint of the original stakeholders in the organization, there is a principal–agent problem if the group's mission shifts. An important example of this is when a state funds insurgent groups in the belief that it will have total control over the groups' activities. But if the groups find ways to diversify their revenue streams, they may eventually engage in activities that are counter to the state's interests.

The Islamic Movement of Uzbekistan (IMU) is an example of a group that shifted its mission to attract new donors and, like the Egyptian Islamic Jihad, the IMU eventually joined forces with al Qaeda. Its original mission was to fight the post-Soviet ruler of Uzbekistan, Islom Karimov, whose authoritarian rule continues to be characterized by corruption and repression. The IMU formed an alliance with Mullah Omar and began to pursue the Taliban's mission, reviling America and the West but also music, cigarettes, sex, and alcohol. This new agenda reduced the organization's appeal to its original supporters in Uzbekistan as many felt that the IMU no longer represented their interests.[51]

Terrorist groups need to maintain popular support. Perhaps ironically, overproduction of the terrorist product can undermine a group's appeal with the population it claims to represent. In Algeria, terrorists initially received support in their fight against the government. Algeria's autocratic regime responded with a brutal crackdown, but the terrorists who remained on the street continued to carry out even more vicious attacks. The terrorists fighting the government became so violent that al Qaeda backed away from them. The conflict between the government and the Islamic Army of Salvation resulted in an estimated 200,000 deaths between 1992 and 1997. "Instead of being seen by the general population as heroic warriors defending their interests, the militants became baby-killers whose campaigns were morally repugnant (and very bad for the economy)," Jason Burke explains. "Their legitimacy – and thus the crucial support from the community that is the key for any insurgent fighter – was gone."[52] Interestingly, Burke believes that the al Qaeda movement may be undermining its popular support in Saudi Arabia by carrying out vicious attacks against innocent civilians in that country.

State-sponsored groups that rely exclusively on funds supplied by the state presumably have little autonomy in selecting their missions. But groups that are partly funded by states, partly by charitable donations, and partly by licit or illicit businesses or other revenue-generating activities can change their missions more easily. In general, the more diverse the sources of revenue, the greater control the group will have to alter its mission at will. A large pool of donors means that no single donor can claim the right to control the core mission. This principle applies to any kind of NGO, including terrorist groups.[53]

Another factor affecting a mission's stickiness is its level of specificity. The mission statement describes the social justice problem the NGO was formed to alleviate. The broader the mission statement, the easier it is for managers of non-profits, including terrorist groups, to alter their organizations' stated goals to attract different consumers at different times.[54] Supporters of and volunteers involved in single-issue groups with narrowly defined missions might defect if the group abruptly changes its mission. For example, supporters and terrorist-volunteers for the Animal Liberation Front (a group that uses violence to protect animal rights) might object if the leader suddenly decided that the group would violently oppose abortion rather than singly focus on promoting animal rights. Mission statements vary on a continuum from narrow to broad and from abstract to specific and concrete.

Leaders need to balance the appeal of a narrow, specific mission that might be attractive to a particular set of donors and recruits in a particular region at a particular time with the flexibility and more general appeal of a broader mission. Al Qaeda, for example, has shifted its stated mission a number of times. Beginning in 1998, its main mission was to force US troops to leave Saudi Arabia. US troops, with the exception of some training personnel, have now left. The group's new mission – to fight the new world order – is sufficiently broad that it appeals to an extraordinary variety of individuals and groups from across the political spectrum – from anti-globalization groups on the far left to neo-Nazi and Identity Christian groups on the far right.[55] We believe that part of the reason al Qaeda has been able to make this shift is that the group itself has become a kind of brand as the only sub-national group able to frighten a superpower.

Sometimes large groups hive off sub-groups with narrower missions, enabling them to cater to the needs of a variety of donors and political supporters.

For example, several groups have broken off from the Pakistani religious party Jamiat Ulema-e-Islam (JUI). JUI offshoots attracted Pakistani and Saudi support when they aided the Taliban regime – for example, by providing "religious" training at madrassas preaching jihad to Afghani and Pakistani youth. And when JUI offshoots like Jamiat-ul-Mujahideen and Harkat-ul-Mujahideen focus their attention on Kashmir, the groups can bring in support from the Pakistani government and the Pakistani and Kashmiri diasporas. The splintering of the larger group can thus help the organization better cater to diverse market niches, but we will see shortly that splintering is not always adaptive.

A fourth factor in determining whether an organization's mission will be sticky or spry is the attitude of the employees and volunteers. Managers may be highly paid professionals willing to sell their expertise with little thought to the purported mission of the organization, but NGOs and terrorist groups often rely on staff or foot soldiers who are willing to work for below-market wages because of their commitment to the cause. These volunteers may be attached to the original mission. A management team that realizes there is a greater prospect of financial or political gain in a slightly different issue-area may find itself battling the staff. Managers may be forced to accept a diminished (but possibly more committed) staff, or they may have to attract new recruits if they change the mission. When bin Laden shifted al Qaeda's mission with his February 1998 fatwah, which instructed sympathizers to target American civilians, a number of operatives quit in protest, rejecting the new doctrine as counter to Islamic law.[56] An organization is more able to shift to a new mission when it is confident that there is a large pool of potential laborers from which to recruit and a reliable source of funding.

The bottom line remains that changing missions, and even keeping the mission constant in a changing environment, involves a risk of splintering. A subset of the management team of a non-profit group can break off from the main body of the organization for three reasons: (1) the splinter group may find a new source of funding for a new mission; (2) an "old-guard" faction, strongly attached to the organization's original mission, may oppose changing the agenda over time; and (3) a faction of "true believers" can break off because the main group has purportedly become ideologically flabby or is allegedly selling out to its enemies.[57] For example, a member of the Pakistani sectarian group Lashkar-e-Jhangvi (LJ), which split off from the group Sipah-e-Sahaba Pakistan (SSP), told Stern's interviewer:

> SSP leaders got addicted to their political success, and started compromising on the ideology. They were just sitting in the parliament, enjoying all the benefits, and doing nothing for the Shi'a. In fact they were sitting with Shi'a [considered by the group to be infidels]. The youth decided to stick to the ideology and formed LJ.[58]

Splinter groups commonly break off when peace processes move forward. The belief that the IRA was selling out seems to have inspired a group of IRA

operatives to create a splinter group called the Real IRA in 1997. Five operatives, taking some weapons with them, created the new group shortly after the
mainstream IRA had restored its ceasefire so Sinn Fein could be part of the
negotiations on power-sharing in government. All five members of the break-
off group were reportedly veterans of the IRA's managing executive body. In
1998, the splinter group set off a bomb in Omagh, a small town in Northern
Ireland, killing 29 people, the most violent single attack ever perpetrated by
IRA operatives.[59]

More generally, there are various ways that substitution of a terrorist
organization's objectives may come about. The organization may broaden or
change its mission as a result of an inability to meet its original objective. It
may be adapting to the needs of an evolving environment. A leader might
shift to a more diffuse mission in order to make it more difficult to assess
the group's success or the leader's competence. The tendency toward self-
preservation is one of several possible distortions of objectives. Those who
work for the organization inevitably seek to preserve its organizational structure above all.[60] As sociologist Alberto Melucci explains, "This analytical
perspective points up some of the central phenomena of the organizational
process and demystifies the image which movement organizations tend to
project of themselves through their ideology."[61]

Max Weber first observed the tendency for organizations to shift their
mission from achieving their objectives to promoting their own survival.
When spontaneous movements create bureaucratic structures, he argued, the
organization's ends are inevitably distorted, with the substitution of self-
preservation for the objectives it was formed to promote. James Q. Wilson
argued a quarter century ago that "Organizations tend to persist. This is the
most important thing to know about them."[62] Thus, terrorist organizations,
like other non-profits, can shift their missions in two principal ways – from
one stated objective to another stated objective or from their stated objectives
to no objective other than organizational survival or personal enrichment.

Who chooses the mission? Demand-driven versus entrepreneurial terrorist organizations

Non-profit organizations can be seen as responding to two different forces –
one on the demand side and the other on the supply side.[63] Problems such as
religious discrimination, poverty, and violence create demand for solutions.
Demand-driven organizations respond to the pull of these unmet needs.
Indeed, the existence of non-profit organizations is justified largely on the
basis of the assumption that they are catering to public needs that remain
unmet by governments and businesses. Most of the literature on non-profit
firms accepts the assumption that non-profits are demand-driven. But an
alternative supply-driven perspective sees social entrepreneurs, donors, and
volunteers advancing their own agendas, pushing forward their own ideas
and resources rather than responding to the pull of social needs.

Peter Frumkin argues that non-profit firms are often actually driven by "the people with resources and commitments who fire the engine of nonprofit and voluntary action. Drawn to the sector by visions and commitments, social entrepreneurs bring forward agendas that often operate independently of immediately obvious and enduring community needs."[64] Confusion over who is in control of the mission at any given level of the organization is in fact part of Frumkin's definition of the non-profit organization. The argument presented here assumes that donors and managers select the terrorist organization's mission, often at the expense of terrorists on the front lines or even the putative beneficiaries of terrorist activity. The balance of power between manager and donor therefore plays a key role in the direction and behavior of the terrorist organization.

Whose needs are being served? The terrorism consumer

Another key variable in the organization and behavior of terrorist groups is the definition of the customer. Non-profit organizations, including terrorist ones, typically describe their customers as the recipients of their largesse. Refugee International describes its customers as the refugees whose interests it promotes.[65] Save the Children describes its customers as the mothers and children it houses and feeds.[66] In its fund-raising literature, Lashkar-e-Taiba focuses on the Kashmiri Muslims it is assisting. NGOs have an interest in seeing and especially in describing their customers as the beneficiaries of their assistance.

Donors want to feel that they are making the world a better place, and often they are, but not necessarily in the most efficient way possible. In truth, donors' needs often eclipse beneficiaries' needs, according to some observers.[67] Pakistan's Interservices Intelligence (ISI) Agency provides one example. ISI actively promoted the Islamist groups who joined Kashmiri militants fighting India's rule in Kashmir. But over time, the ISI-funded groups shifted their sights to other agendas more consistent with the Pakistani regime's interests than the Kashmiri people's, such as carrying out strikes in India proper or serving as a counterweight to secular parties in Pakistani elections.[68]

Employees and volunteers working at NGOs are often partly donating their time. They do this because they benefit from the act of contributing to the objectives of the NGO. In some ways, they, too, are consumers – arguably of increased self-esteem. Referring to donors of labor or money as consumers is an admittedly unusual way to look at terrorism. "Drug dealers have customers; terrorists have supporters and victims," according to a study comparing the "war" on terrorism with the "war" on drugs.[69] However, ignoring the demand for terrorism may be equally as damaging as ignoring the demand for drugs.[70] Interestingly, according to Peter Reuter, suppliers of drugs are often simultaneously consumers.[71] The same is true for terrorism, although the suppliers/consumers of drugs consume a thing, whereas suppliers/consumers of terrorism consume the process of production.

Once we begin thinking of donors as consumers of the product, it becomes easier to understand why NGOs, including terrorist groups, act on behalf of individuals who do not really desire or need the kind of assistance they provide. For instance, the Kashmiri people are increasingly unhappy with the "assistance" of Pakistani jihadi groups. The local jihadi groups complain that they are being used as porters and guides, rather than as legitimate fighters in their own conflict.

Changes over time

As terrorist organizations become more concerned with self-preservation and securing benefits for laborers and less concerned about their ostensible *raison d'être*, the mission becomes a marketing tool for securing organizational survival or a source of social identity.

Although militant groups often start out with the interests of the public in mind, volunteers become attached to the organization and the benefits it provides at least as much as to the organizational mission. They become addicted to the sense of purpose they receive from "serving" the public and promoting "good," even when the public resents their assistance and disagrees with the group's conception of good. This is what James Wilson refers to as the purposive incentive: it is the satisfaction of pursuing a goal (which is different from the satisfaction one might get from achieving it). In Stern's interviews, terrorists reported becoming "addicted to jihad." This is partly a psychological attachment to living a certain way of life and promoting a purported public good and partly due to the fact that the longer a militant remains active, the harder it is to find alternative employment, especially for operatives who join in their youths. Sometimes operatives – or even whole organizations – lose all attachment to the purported mission and begin selling their expertise to the highest bidder.

In the for-profit sector, where organizations must provide profitable investment opportunities to shareholders to secure inputs, organizations adapt to trends of changing consumer demands. For example, when McDonald's redefines its core mission from provider of short-order hamburgers and sandwiches to provider of fast food, including "healthy food," it is adapting to changes in consumer preferences to maintain profitability and hence satisfy shareholders. Successful non-profit social-sector organizations also change their missions over time. The March of Dimes raised a large sum of money to find a cure for polio. After an effective vaccine was discovered, the March of Dimes shifted its mission to fighting birth defects.[72] The YMCA was founded during Prohibition as an organization committed to temperance. When the public mood shifted, the YMCA was able to transform its core mission from promoting temperance to promoting other kinds of healthy habits such as exercise.[73] Persisting organizations change their missions with changing environments.

Reducing environmental uncertainty

Like more traditional NGOs, terrorist organizations also find ways to commercialize their activities to supplement the revenues earned though "charitable donations." Some finance their operations in part through smuggling or weapons sales. Hezbollah, for example, is involved in smuggling cigarettes in the United States. Both sides in the conflict in Northern Ireland are heavily involved in drug smuggling.[74] The IRA is also linked with organized criminal groups in Croatia and Bosnia, trading in guns, bombs, and cigarettes.[75]

Many groups rely on robberies as a source of revenue. The leader of the Khalistan Commando Force admitted in an interview that his organization raised money by robbing banks and kidnapping for ransom.[76] The IRA raises money through a variety of illegal activities, in addition to drug smuggling. For example, a suspected IRA member was arrested in August 2001 as the alleged mastermind of a £150 million share-dealing fraud in Thailand. Authorities described the scam as the largest stock-dealing fraud ever perpetrated.[77] Operatives or groups sometimes sell or barter their expertise to other groups. Three suspected IRA operatives were arrested in August 2001 on charges of having provided training in explosives manufacture to Colombia's most violent leftist terrorist group, the Revolutionary Armed Forces of Colombia (FARC), as part of a multimillion-dollar deal between the two groups.[78] Ali Mohamed, a witness for the US Government in the Africa embassies bombing trial held in 2001, testified that bin Laden's al Qaeda maintained close ties to Hezbollah and to Iranian security forces through the 1990s. Hezbollah provided al Qaeda and its allies training in explosives at camps in Lebanon, Mohamed claimed, and received bombs "disguised to look like rocks" from Iranian security forces.[79]

While diversifying revenue streams gives terrorist organizations more flexibility in defining their missions, if the group ceases to attract "charitable" donors, it becomes more difficult to claim that it is fulfilling a humanitarian function. Terrorists claim to act on behalf of the people, and the people's support of the cause is important to them in maintaining their legitimacy. The defining source of revenue for non-profit organizations is charitable donations. This is an important part of what distinguishes NGOs – including terrorist organizations – from for-profit firms.[80]

As groups become more professionalized, this distinction may begin to wear thin. Operatives, or the group itself, may become more like mercenaries. Governments or sub-national actors may hire terrorists to carry out paramilitary operations. Charitable donations from ordinary people begin to pale in importance. Stern found in her interviews that leaders tended to emphasize small-scale charitable donations by ordinary people as the most important source of revenue for their groups while operatives, presumably less attuned to the public-relations implications of their words, admitted that smuggling, government funding, or large-scale donations by wealthy industrialists are the main sources of funding.[81]

When terrorist organizations rely on criminal activities to raise revenue, what distinguishes them from organized or petty crime? Ideology cannot be the whole answer, since organized criminal groups and drug smugglers often have codes of honor and promote various ideological perspectives, and since in professionalized terrorist organizations ideology is less important over time. But organized criminals and drug smugglers rarely solicit charitable donations. Revenue that can be described as charitable donations appears to be part of what makes NGOs and terrorist groups distinctive.

The competition for resources

When multiple groups purportedly promote similar goals, competition for scarce resources such as donors, government assistance, and personnel can make them fierce competitors. This leads to a dynamic in which marketing becomes increasingly important.[82] The group's competitors can become their actual enemies, rather than those enemies that they identify publicly. Interestingly, a public-affairs officer for the Pakistani group Lashkar-e-Taiba told Stern in an interview that he felt "happy" about the growth of Bajrang Dal, the purported arch-nemesis of the Pakistani militant groups. They provide a *raison d'être* for Islamic fundamentalism in Pakistan. He stated: "What is the logic for stopping the jihadi groups' activities, if the Indian government supports groups like Bajrang Dal?"[83] Bajrang Dal's activities can serve Lashkar-e-Taiba as a propaganda tool to enlarge the pool of available funds and recruits for which the leaders of Lashkar-e-Taiba and other jihadi groups know they must compete.

When groups are competing with one another, violence can become a critical marketing tool, directed at political and financial backers rather than at the "target audience" described in the literature. The day-to-day task of political combat becomes one of competition for supporters and financial backers. Neutralization of the competition can become the group's most important goal.[84]

Selznick's study of communist organizations shows that the communists' enemies were not the bankers, bosses, and imperialists they identified as their archenemies in public. Their real enemies were the socialists. Imperialists, unlike other socialist groups, did not challenge the communists at the source of power. They did not compete for the leadership of unions. And they did not appeal to the goodwill of liberal intellectuals. Most importantly, they were not equipped "to expose the communists as corrupters of the very ideas they claim[ed] to represent."[85] Thus, the communists could compromise with the class enemy, but they "dare[d] not tolerate the political existence of those who [offered] the target groups an alternative ideological leadership or [those who could] effectively expose the totalitarian practices of bolshevism in power."[86] Neutralization of the competition – especially groups potentially capable of winning over party cadres – became the most important objective. Tactics employed to accomplish this end included destruction of rival organizations by infiltrating them and disrupting their activities. This need to destroy the competition helps to explain the virulence of the attack against Titoism and Trotskyism, Selznick explains. The competition among various terrorist groups for funding and recruits is an important vulnerability that governments can exploit.

In other instances, competition benefits extremist terrorist organizations. The presence of more moderate groups seeking the same goals can strengthen the hand of the more extreme groups, according to Peter Merkl. When the government does not concede to the moderates, the terrorists have greater claims – "the perfect excuse for extreme action."[87] Moreover, the claims of the illegal groups make the moderates seem reasonable. Selznick explains, "The relation between the two, therefore, is apt to be one of conflict and collusion, and both types of interaction potentially serve the interests and objectives of each group."[88]

Conclusion

This chapter has shown that terrorists produce a definable product and that consumers "purchase" this product with their donations to a terrorist organization; these donations are made to support a perceived public good that the recipient terrorist group purports to promote. A terrorist group's resilience is enhanced when it diversifies its consumer base and its sources of labor and when it maximizes the flexibility of its marketing strategy and mission. But there is a tradeoff between the group's capacity for carrying out high-quality attacks and its resilience. The same factors that make terrorist bureaucracies capable of high-quality attacks – clear lines of authority and communication, ease of coordination, and centralization of tasks – reduce the resilience of commander–cadre organizations.

This finding suggests that a mature terrorist group will be both resilient at the network level and effective at the level of the node. In a rapidly changing environment, networks (rather than market-based transactions among separate terrorists or terrorist groups) become a more attractive organizational form, just as they are for legal organizations. When enhanced cooperation among intelligence agencies makes the supply of skilled labor uncertain, terrorist groups are likely to form networks with gateway organizations that can assist in indoctrinating potential recruits. And they are likely to network with other terrorist organizations, which may themselves be organized as networks or commander–cadre organizations. Terrorist organizations that are flexible – in terms of their structure, their funding sources, and their mission – are more resilient to counterterrorism measures. In such a network, effective terrorist nodes become, at least in theory, replaceable.

For all these reasons, a war on terrorism that is predominantly focused on killing terrorists – "hunting down the killers, one by one," in Vice President Cheney's words – is unlikely to be successful in the long run. It presumes a finite number of targets within a finite set of organizations. Given the characteristics of a mature terrorist network described above, this assumption is flawed.

Similarly, attempting to freeze terrorist bank accounts and shut down terrorist-supporting charities assumes that terrorist organizations are static and inflexible. This chapter argues the opposite. Successful terrorist organizations, such as al Qaeda, respond to changes in their environments by changing their missions and changing their shapes. If there is a threat to survival, they will form virtual networks. If there is a shortage of cash, they will network with other groups that are expected to raise their own funds. If the old mission is no longer attractive, they will find a new one that is more attractive to donors and potential recruits.

Defense Secretary Donald Rumsfeld asked in a memo in October 2003, "Are we capturing, killing, deterring or dissuading more terrorists every day than those [radical] clerics are deploying against us?" The answer appears to be no. Data compiled by the RAND Corporation show that nearly twice as many acts of terrorism were carried out in the two years after 11 September 2001 (4,422) than in the two preceding years (2,303). An increased number of attacks is joined by increasing efficacy: the number of people killed per attack has also risen, from an average of 0.65 deaths per incident to an average of 1. During this same period, al Qaeda evolved from an organization to a movement comprised of many autonomous, locally organized cells spread around the world. But it is not clear that this shift in organizational style is what led to the greater lethality of terrorism. While the number of incidents and their lethality might have risen still higher in the absence of the war on terrorism, our approach will be far more successful if we focus more of our efforts on the *demand* for terrorism. Terrorist organizations cater to the needs of their workers and supporters by supplying spiritual, emotional, and financial benefits to the alienated, disenfranchised, and humiliated. Until we understand that we need to compete with the producers of those benefits, our "war on terrorism" will continue to fail.

Notes

1 We would like to thank Thomas J. Biersteker, David Leheny, and Peter Reuter for their excellent comments and Steve Smith for research assistance.
2 T. Schelling, *The Strategy of Conflict*, Cambridge, MA: Harvard University Press, 1960; T. Schelling, *Arms and Influence*, Westport, CT: The Greenwood Press, 1967. When Thomas Schelling wryly observes that "despite the high ratio of damage and grief to the resources required for a terrorist act, terrorism has proved to be a remarkably ineffectual means to accomplishing anything," he is assuming that terrorists have substantively rational objectives and that their main purpose is to achieve those objectives. T. Schelling, "What Purposes can 'International Terrorism' Serve?" in R.G. Frey and Christopher W. Morris (eds.) *Violence, Terrorism, and Justice*, Cambridge: Cambridge University Press, 1991, pp. 20–21. See also Sun-Ki Chai, "An Organizational Economics Theory of Antigovernment Violence," *Comparative Politics*, October 1993, pp. 99–110.
3 B. Hoffman, *Inside Terrorism*, New York: Columbia University Press, 1998, p. 43.

4 A. Merari, "The Readiness to Kill and Die: Suicidal Terrorism in the Middle East," in W. Reich (ed.) *Origins of Terrorism: Psychologies, Ideologies, Theologies, States of Mind*, Washington: Wilson Center Press, 1998.

5 M. Crenshaw, "The Logic of Terrorism: Terrorist Behavior as a Product of Strategic Choice," in W. Reich (ed.) *Origins of Terrorism*, p. 8; M. Crenshaw, "Theories of Terrorism: Instrumental and Organizational Approaches," in D.C. Rapoport, *Inside Terrorist Organizations*, 2nd edn., Portland, OR: Frank Cass, 2001, p. 13.

6 Schelling explicitly excludes religious cults from his discussion. Schelling, "What Purposes," p. 20.

7 J. Stern, *Terror in the Name of God: Why Religious Militants Kill*, New York: Ecco/HarperCollins, 2003.

8 J. Post, "Terrorist Psycho-Logic," in Reich (ed.) *Origins of Terrorism*, p. 25.

9 Crenshaw, "The Logic of Terrorism"; M. Crenshaw, "An Organizational Approach to the Analysis of Political Terrorism," *Orbis*, Autumn 1985 vol. 29, no. 3, pp. 473–487; Crenshaw, "Theories of Terrorism," p. 13. In the first cited work, Crenshaw outlines an instrumental approach in response to works by a group of psychologists. In the second, she distinguishes an instrumental approach from an organizational one, but does not specify what the organization would entail.

10 The theory of collective action was developed in M. Olson, *The Logic of Collective Action*, Cambridge, MA: Harvard University Press, 1971. Many people find the application of this theory to terrorism surprising or even shocking. I do not subscribe to the notion that terrorists promote social justice, but it is critical to understand that terrorists and their sympathizers believe this. Given that, the same questions Olson raised with regard to voting or pollution abatement ought to apply when individuals are deciding whether or not to contribute to terrorist organizations. This section builds on the arguments in Stern, *Terror in the Name of God*.

11 Olson, *The Logic of Collective Action*.

12 For more extensive discussion of the findings from the author's interviews with terrorists, carried out between 1997 and the present, see Stern, *Terror in the Name of God*.

13 Alan Cullison, "Inside al-Qaeda's Hard Drive," *Atlantic Monthly*, September 2004, p. 68.

14 Ibid., p. 68.

15 Ibid., p. 70.

16 Ibid., p. 70.

17 J. Der Derian, "911: Before, After and In Between," in C. J. Calhoun, P. Price, and A. Timmer (eds.) *Understanding September 11*, New York: W. W. Norton & Company, 2002.

18 W. R. Scott, *Organizations: Rational, Natural, and Open Systems* 2nd edn, Englewood Cliffs, NJ: Prentice-Hall Inc., 1981, p. 52.

19 For much more on what we mean by inspirational leadership and virtual networks, please see Stern, *Terror in the Name of God*.

20 S. P. Borgatti, "The Key Player Problem," *Dynamic Social Network Modeling and Analysis: Workshop Summary and Papers*, National Academy of Sciences Press, 2003, p. 241.

21 S. P. Borgatti and P. C. Foster, "The Network Paradigm in Organizational Research: A Review and Typology," *Journal of Management*, 2003, vol. 29, no. 6, p. 995; See, for example, J.L. Bradach and R.G. Eccles, "Price Authority and Trust: From Ideal Types to Plural Forms," *American Review of Sociology*, 1989, vol. 15, pp. 97–118; and W. W. Powell, "Neither Market nor Hierarchy: Network Forms of Organization," *Research on Organizational Behavior*, 1990, vol. 12, pp. 295–336.

22 A. R. Elangovan and D. L. Shapiro, "Betrayal of Trust in Organizations," *Academy of Management Review*, 1998, vol. 23, no. 3, pp. 547–566.

23 National Commission on Terrorist Attacks, *The 9/11 Commission Report: Final Report of the National Commission on Terrorist Attacks Upon the United States*, New York: W. W. Norton & Company, 2004, pp. 58–59.

24 See S. Borgatti, "Virtual or Network Organizations." Online. Available HTTP: <http://www.analytictech.com/mb021/virtual.htm> (accessed 16 September 2005).

25 N. Horsley, "The Nuremberg Files." Online. Available HTTP: <http://www.christiangallery.com/atrocity/> (accessed 25 August 2002). As of 5 October 2004, only limited parts of this website are available online.

26 Ibid.

27 J. Gonnerman, "The Terrorist Campaign Against Abortion," *Village Voice*, 9 November 1998, p. 36; and S. Lerner, "The Nuremberg Menace," *Village Voice*, 10 April 2001. Online. Available HTTP: <http://www.villagevoice.com/issues/0114/lerner.php> (accessed 16 September 2005).

28 See US Court of Appeals for the 9th Circuit, *Planned Parenthood of the Columbia/ Willamette Inc.; Portland Feminist Women's Health Center; Robert Crist, M.D.; Warren M. Hern, M.D.; Elizabeth Newhall, M.D.; James Newhall, M.D., Plain-tiffs-Appellees, and Karen Sweigert, M.D., Plaintiff, v. American Coalition of Life Activists; Advocates For Life Ministries; Michael Bray; Andrew Burnett; David A. Crane; Timothy Paul Dreste; Michael B. Dodds; Joseph L. Foreman; Charles Roy Mcmillan; Stephen P. Mears; Bruce Evan Murch; Catherine Ramey; Dawn Marie Stover; Charles Wysong, Defendants, and Monica Migliorino Miller; Donald Tresh-man, Defendants-Appellants*, case no. 99–35320; See also F. Clarkson, "Journalists or Terrorists?" *Salon*, 31 May 2001.

29 Stern, *Terror in the Name of God*, pp. 167–188.

30 Stern, *Terror in the Name of God*, pp. 147–171.

31 M. Gruen, "Hizb ut-Tahrir," unpublished report, 30 January 2004. P. Baker, "Renewed Militancy Seen in Uzbekistan: Government Crackdown Threatens to Radicalize Previously Non-Violent Groups," *Washington Post*, 27 September 2003, A19.

32 Gruen, "Hizb ut-Tahrir."

33 Author interview with Rahmen, 15 May 2004.

34 Author interview with M. Reynolds, 11 October 1999.

35 L. Beam, "Leaderless Resistance," *Seditionist*, February 1992, no. 12. This system of organization, Beam claims, is almost identical to "the methods used by the committees of correspondence during the American Revolution." It is also similar in structure to communist revolutionaries' cells. The essay received significantly more attention after Beam republished it and presented it to the Aryan National Congress in 1992. The essay is published on different websites at different times. See, for example, <http://www.louisbeam.com/leaderless.htm> (accessed 16 September 2005), as well as <http://www2.mo-net.com/~mlindste/ledrless.html> (accessed 21 October 2002). The idea, at least as practiced in America, was origin-ally conceived by an American named Colonel Amoss in 1962, according to Beam, who refined the concept in his essay "On Revolutionary Majorities," published in the Inter-Klan newsletter and Survival Alert 4 (1984) and, again, in *The Seditionist* in 1992. Most published accounts have wrongly attributed the original idea to the 1992 essay.

36 Author interview with M. Reynolds, Summer 2003.

37 Hierarchical nodes within a virtual network would have the same strengths and weaknesses as commander–cadre organizations, discussed below – including their vulnerability to law enforcement detection and penetration.

38 But organizational theorists explain

> it would be incorrect to conclude that hierarchies are superior to more decentralized or equalitarian arrangements under all conditions ... [A]s

tasks become more complex or ambiguous, decentralized nets are usually superior to centralized structures . . . [F]ormal hierarchies aid the perform-ance of tasks requiring the efficient coordination of information and routine decision making, but they interfere with tasks presenting very complex or ambiguous problems.

There is a curvilinear relation between information processing requirements and the utility of hierarchy, Scott explains. We believe our conclusions differ from those of organizational theorists because of the added requirements of secrecy inherent in terrorist activity. See Scott, *Organizations*, pp. 158–161.

39 R. Stark, "The Organizational Age," *Sociology: Third Edition*; See also S. Borgatti, "Bureaucracy." Online. Available HTTP: <http://www.analytictech.com/mb021/bureau.htm> (accessed 16 September 2005).
40 C. Jones, W. Hesterly and S. Borgatti, "A General Theory of Network Govern-ance," *The Academy of Management Review*, October 1997, vol. 22, no. 4, p. 923.
41 G.J. Tenet, "The Worldwide Threat 2004: Challenges in a Changing Global Context," *Testimony of Director of Central Intelligence, George J. Tenet before the Senate Select Committee on Intelligence*, 24 February 2004. Online. Available HTTP: <http://www.cia.gov/cia/public_affairs/speeches/2004/dci_speech_02142004.html> (accessed 16 September 2005). See also J. Fearon and D. Laitin, "Ethnicity, Insurgency, and Civil War," *American Political Science Review*, February 2003, vol. 97, no. 1, pp. 75–90.
42 Tenet, "The Worldwide Threat."
43 B. Erickson, "Secret Societies and Social Structure," *Social Forces*, September 1981, vol. 60, no. 1, pp. 188–210.
44 Author interview with "Abu Bakar" (an assumed name), Jhang, Pakistan, 28 January 2004. Questionnaire administered by Muzamal Suherwardy.
45 Jones et al., "A General Theory," p. 923.
46 National Commission on Terrorist Attacks, *The 9/11 Commission Report*, p. 150.
47 Resources are represented by nodes, so capacity is a function of the number of nodes in the network. S. Toumpis and A. Goldsmith, "Ad Hoc Network Capacity," *Asilomar Conference on Signals, Systems, and Computers*, vol. 2, Pacific Grove, CA, October 2000, pp. 1265–1269.
48 Martha Crenshaw defines successful terrorism in this way in M. Crenshaw, P. Wilkinson, J. Alterman and T. Schaffer, "How Terrorism Ends," *Special Report 48*, Washington, DC: United States Institute of Peace, 25 May 1999, p. 3. Online. Available HTTP: <http://www.usip.org/pubs/specialreports/sr990525.pdf> (accessed 16 September 2005).
49 Stern conversations with Mark Moore, 2002–2003.
50 See J. Stern, "The Protean Enemy," *Foreign Affairs*, July/August 2003, vol. 82, no. 4, pp. 27–41.
51 A. Rashid, "The Taliban: Exporting Extremism," *Foreign Affairs*, November/December 1999, pp. 22–35; A. Rashid, *Jihad: The Rise of Militant Islam in Cent-ral Asia*, New Haven, CT: Yale University Press, 2002; R. Gunaratna, *Inside Al Qaeda: Global Network of Terror*, New York: Columbia University Press, 2002, pp. 168–172; C. J. Chivers, "Uzbek Militants Decline Provides Clues to U.S.," *New York Times*, 8 October 2002, A15.
52 J. Burke, "The Arab Backlash the Militants Didn't Expect," *The Observer*, 20 June 2004.
53 The Executive Director of one NGO expressed his frustration with the selection process of the Board of Directors. He wanted a board that was better equipped to attract a broad variety of private donors so that he would be less reliant on the foundations on which his organization had traditionally depended for support. But the board kept appointing members whom the foundations saw as experts,

arguably facilitating his ability to attract the usual sponsors, but not in any way enabling him to attract new money, in his view. Author interview with an executive director who asked not to be identified, 18 May 2001.

54 Stern conversations with Mark Moore, 2002–2003.

55 For more on this see Stern, *Terror in the Name of God.*

56 Cross-examination of Khertchou. *United States v. Usama Bin Laden, et al.,* Part 1, Book 3, 1409–92.

57 Examples of humanitarian relief organizations breaking up for such reasons include the group of doctors who broke off from the International Committee of the Red Cross (ICRC) to form *Médecins sans Frontières* (MSF). The splinter group was unhappy that the ICRC refused to speak out about the abuses it witnessed in the aftermath of the Biafra war. A few years later, another splinter group broke off from MSF to form *Médicins du Monde* (MDF). J. Fawcett. Email (4 August 2001).

58 Author interview with "Abu Bakar."

59 "Real Trouble," *The Economist,* 10 March 2001.

60 John Fawcett argues that a reliable funding stream is an important component in an NGO's evolution to an organization with no important mandate other than survival. "The process goes something like this," he explains. "The more donors or grants that an NGO has, the more labor intensive becomes the proposal and reporting process, which is called grant management. This means more people. More people means more overhead, which means the growth of a bureaucracy, a key component of an organization that is shifting towards bureaucratic survival. In my experience NGOs and UN agencies will always find justification for stretching or violating their mission, as long as money is available. The mission statement becomes a cover and something few of them take seriously. And donors, particularly the US Government, are complicit in this charade. They have to spend money to keep up budgetary allocations, and are content to justify spending on 'do-gooders.' " J. Fawcett. Email (4 August 2001).

61 A. Melucci, *Challenging Codes: Collective Action in the Information Age,* London: Cambridge University Press, 1996, p. 314.

62 J. Q. Wilson, *Political Organizations,* Princeton, NJ: Princeton University Press, 1995, p. 30.

63 This paragraph summarizes Frumkin's theory of non-profit activity. P. Frumkin, *On Being Nonprofit: A Conceptual and Policy Primer,* Cambridge, MA: Harvard University Press, 2002, pp. 20–22.

64 Frumkin, *On Being Nonprofit,* p. 21.

65 Author interview with board member of Refugee International, 19 May 2000.

66 Author interview with board member of Save the Children, 19 May 2000.

67 But fund-raising would be far more difficult if donors were told that they were the most important customers and that the product they are buying is improved self-esteem

68 See, for example, H. Abbas, *Pakistan's Drift into Extremism,* Armonk, NY: M.E. Sharpe, 2004.

69 J. P. Caulkins, M. A. R. Kleiman, and P. Reuter, "Lessons from the 'War' on Drugs for the 'War' on Terrorism," in A. Howitt and R. Pangi, eds., *Countering Terrorism: Dimensions of Preparedness,* Cambridge, MA: The MIT Press, 2003, pp. 96–97.

70 Any demand-side strategy for containing terrorism depends on the ability of the practitioner to implement tactics beyond the scope of violence and spying; simultaneously, such a strategy offers a status quo power (e.g. a government) opportunities both to consolidate its own power base and to undermine the social bases of support for terrorist groups.

71 Although Peter Reuter appears to reject the notion that there are consumers of terrorism, his arguments about the limits of supply-side controls seem to me to

apply to terrorism as well. See P. Reuter, "The Limits of Supply-Side Drug Control," *Milken Institute Review*, First Quarter 2001, pp. 14–23.

72 The March of Dimes reports on its website, "In 1938, President Franklin D. Roosevelt founded the National Foundation for Infantile Paralysis to search for a cure for Polio. In 1954, through March of Dimes funding, Dr. Jonas Salk discovered a vaccine to eliminate polio, making the March of Dimes the only national health organization to defeat the disease it was created to conquer." After achieving its original mission, the March of Dimes shifted its mission to reducing the incidence of premature birth. See March of Dimes, "History of Success." Online. Available HTTP: <http://www.marchofdimes.com/aboutus/789.asp> (accessed 16 September 2005).

73 E. L. Johnson, *The History of YMCA Physical Education*, Chicago, IL: Association Press, 1979.

74 J. Horgan and M. Taylor, "Playing the 'Green Card' – Financing the Provisional IRA," *Terrorism and Political Violence*, Summer 1999, pp. 1–38; A. Silke, "Drinks, Drugs, and Rock'n'Roll: Financing Loyalist Terrorism in Northern Ireland – Part 2," *Studies in Conflict and Terrorism*, 1 April 2000, vol. 23, no. 2, pp. 107–127.

75 See, for example, G. Tremlett, "Karadzic Family 'Arming Real IRA,' " *The Guardian*, 5 April 2001; "Real IRA Arms Purchasing in Croatia Indicates a Change of Tactics," *Jane's Terrorism & Security Monitor*, 23 August 2000.

76 Author interview in Lahore, Pakistan, 2 August 2001.

77 M. Bright and A. Barnett, "IRA Linked to Thai Share 'Scam,' " *Observer*, 19 August 2001, p. 1.

78 J. Forego, "Columbia Arrests 3 as IRA Bomb Experts," *New York Times*, 15 August 2001; Bright and Barnett, "IRA Linked," p. 1.

79 K. R. Roane, D. E. Kaplan, and C. Ragavan, "Putting Terror Inc. on Trial in New York," *U.S. News & World Report*, 8 January 2001, vol. 130, no. 1, p. 25.

80 This is Mark Moore's term.

81 Author interviews with Laskar Jihad, Jakarta, 9 August 2001, and Yogyakarta, 11 August 2001. Questionnaires administered in Pakistan.

82 Author telephone and email interview with J. Fawcett, 15 July 2001. Among humanitarian relief organizations, the drive to beat out other organizations in the competition for funds can replace the drive to provide humanitarian relief where it matters most. John Fawcett argues that donor agencies wanted the NGOs active in the former Yugoslavia to carve up the problem and coordinate their activities. But the aid agencies are actually competing for funding, he says. They did not want to coordinate; they wanted to out-bid each other. Each aid agency feared the others would steal its ideas.

83 Author interview with Lashkar-e-Taiba public affairs officer, 3 August 2001.

84 P. Selznick, *The Organizational Weapon: A Study of Bolshevik Strategy and Tactics*, Santa Monica, CA: RAND Corp., 1952, p. 229.

85 Ibid., p. 227.

86 Ibid., p. 227.

87 Ibid., p. 454.

88 Ibid., p. 468.

3   The evolution of al Qaeda

Rohan Gunaratna[1]

The evolution of al Qaeda from an operational group of several thousand members into an ideological vanguard of the Islamic terrorist movement consisting of tens of thousands of members may be the most profound development in the international security landscape since 11 September 2001. Although al Qaeda's operational capabilities have severely diminished since 2001, the ideology of global jihad articulated by Osama bin Laden and his group has catalyzed the proliferation of jihad groups across the globe, including numerous cells in the West. Reflecting this trend, al Qaeda itself has *not* been directly responsible for most of the terrorist attacks in the past four years; rather, attacks have been *inspired* by al Qaeda but carried out by its associated groups with origins in the Middle East, East Africa, Asia, and the Caucuses.[2]

After addressing the origins of this trend, this chapter discusses the consequences of these structural changes in how al Qaeda finances terrorism. What do recent events – especially the rise of Islamic terrorism in Europe and the ongoing insurgency in Iraq – suggest about the funding and operations of the global jihadi movement into the future? What approaches are best suited to countering the financing of al Qaeda in its present form? This chapter answers these questions in four parts.

First, I describe the current structure of al Qaeda and its central place in the global jihadi movement. Today, al Qaeda has supplemented the remaining elements of the original, core organization with geographically diverse affiliated groups and ideological cells. Together with other (primarily Sunni) extremist groups, these elements constitute the global jihadi movement, which represents an even greater threat to the US and its allies and friends than earlier iterations of al Qaeda alone.

Second, I trace the evolution of al Qaeda through four phases in its life-cycle. These relate to periods during which al Qaeda based its operations in Pakistan, Sudan, and Afghanistan, and its subsequent transformation to the global jihadi movement. Throughout its evolution, al Qaeda has served not only as a source of inspiration and training, but has also provided associated groups and cells with funding and the know-how to raise and manage finances to carry out their terrorist activities. Thus, it is not surprising that during each period of transformation, al Qaeda and its affiliated cells have similarly changed methods of raising funds – most recently shifting towards self-financed criminal activities and away from donations by wealthy Arabs or business investments.

Third, I focus on the US intervention in Iraq, showing how it has galvanized jihadi groups worldwide to the point that the threat posed by the global jihadi movement has surpassed the terrorist threat posed by al Qaeda. The effect of the intervention has been to infuse the global jihadi movement with new human and financial resources. Through this support, and by adapting strategies to reflect the organizational learning of Islamic terrorist networks over the years since 11 September 2001, the new jihadi is even stronger and more resilient.

In conclusion, I offer some thoughts on the kinds of counter-measures – financial and otherwise – that are needed to respond to the rise of the global jihadi movement. As terrorists of global reach have shown the ability to adapt their strategy and tactics in the post-11 September period, it is critical that the international community develop responses to the changing nature of terrorist threats.

Al Qaeda today: group, network, cells, and movement

The al Qaeda movement currently consists of three parts: (1) the al Qaeda group, founded by bin Laden and Abdullah Azzam in the late 1980s and severely weakened in the aftermath of the US invasion of Afghanistan; (2) the al Qaeda network, which is composed of the al Qaeda group and 30 to 40 associated groups located primarily in Africa, Asia, and the Middle East; and (3) ideologically affiliated cells worldwide acting in the name of or inspired by al Qaeda in pursuit of global jihad. Although the global jihadi movement embodies the ambitions of al Qaeda, global jihad is broader than the al Qaeda movement and has surpassed al Qaeda as the most significant threat to international security.

In 1988, bin Laden, the unofficial representative of the Saudi Kingdom to the anti-Soviet multinational Afghan jihad, and Azzam, bin Laden's Palestinian-Jordanian mentor, established the al Qaeda group. The al Qaeda group's global jihad ideology continues to hold great appeal for both associated groups waging local jihad in conflict zones and radicalized Muslim cells in the migrant and diaspora communities of the West. Also known as al Qaeda core, al Qaeda central, or al Qaeda classic, the al Qaeda group has been operationally weakened and largely depleted since the inception of Operation Enduring Freedom, but remains ideologically potent.

Operationally associated groups – the second major source of al Qaeda's support – form an umbrella of thirty to forty groups in Asia, Africa, and the Middle East known as the al Qaeda network. In Pakistan, Sudan, and Afghanistan, as well as in conflict zones such as Bosnia, Chechnya, and Mindanao, and through the internet, al Qaeda provides these groups with training, weapons, financing, and ideology. These groups hold declared or undeclared membership of the World Islamic Front for Jihad Against the Jews and the Crusaders, formed in February 1998. They include the Salafi Group for Call and Combat (GSPC), Moroccan Islamic Combatant Group (GICM), Takfir wal Hijra (TWH), Tawhid wal Jihad (al Qaeda of the Two Rivers), Lashkar-e-Taiba (LeT), Jemaah Islamiyah (JI), and Abu Sayyaff Group (ASG).

Al Qaeda's ideologically affiliated cells – the third component of al Qaeda – are operationally unconnected to al Qaeda but adhere to an ideology of a global jihad as articulated by al Qaeda. "The Supporters of al Qaeda,"[3] the cell responsible for the bombing of the trains in Madrid on 11 March 2004, and the disrupted British cell led by Omar Khayam[4] were self-financed and independent of al Qaeda's operational control. These local jihad groups are inspired by and seek to emulate al Qaeda. The robust, post-Iraq Islamist milieu in North America, Europe, and Australasia encourages the transformation of these support cells into execution cells.

Beyond al Qaeda are primarily Sunni groups that operationally are unconnected with al Qaeda but steadfastly advocate global jihad. This category contains violent and non-violent groups. For instance, extremist groups such as Hizb-ut-Tahrir and al Mahajaroon in the UK fit into this category, as well as violent groups like Laskar Jihad and Front Pembela Islam in Indonesia. Some of these groups have even criticized bin Laden and al Qaeda, but nonetheless share the belief in global jihad and are part of the global jihad movement.

The invasion and occupation of Iraq, as well as reports of abuse at Abu Ghraib and Guantanamo, have strengthened support for like-minded associated groups and affiliated cells, as well as for Islamist groups unconnected to al Qaeda. Exploiting the suffering, resentment, and anger of Muslims, terrorist and extremist groups are now able to replenish their human losses and material costs to continue and intensify the fight. Al Qaeda thus has morphed from a group of several thousand members to a movement of several tens of thousands of members. Add to this other elements of the global jihad and the result is a robust global jihadi movement that represents an even greater threat to the US and its allies and friends than does the classic and more limited al Qaeda behind the 11 September attacks.

Phases in the lifecycle of al Qaeda

In order to understand better how a terrorist group became a global movement, it is necessary to review the history of the various phases of al Qaeda. In doing so, I emphasize changes in the sources and methods used to finance al Qaeda operations.

Phase one: Pakistan

Al Qaeda Al Sulbha (solid base) was conceptualized by Abdullah Azzam in early 1988[5] and formally established by Osama bin Laden as an organization in Peshawar, Pakistan on 10 September 1988. Prior to its formation, however, al Qaeda existed as Maktab-il Khidamat (MAK – Afghan Service Bureau) for four years. As the premier Arab group supporting Afghan groups in their struggle against the Soviet Union, MAK received substantial financial support from the Saudi government and from Muslims living worldwide. MAK trained foreign supporters to fight against the Soviet occupation, which served to operationalize jihad as an ideology against communism.

In 1984, the Palestinian-Jordanian scholar Abdullah Azzam and his student and protégé, Osama bin Laden, established MAK with the purpose of facilitating recruitment, training, and fundraising for foreign mujahideen and chronicling the anti-Soviet multinational Afghan jihad. Both Azzam and bin Laden managed MAK, while Azzam also oversaw *Al Jihad*, a weekly magazine. As bin Laden controlled the funds, he served as the primary leader of operations while Azzam focused on ideology and popularizing the concept of jihad. Abdur Rasool Sayyaf and Gulbuddin Hekmatiyar (and his military commander Jalaludin Haqqani) – organizers of the anti-Soviet jihad with military and financial support of a multilateral coalition organized by the CIA and comprising the US, UK, Saudi Arabia, and Pakistan – were close to bin Laden, and a significant percentage of Arabs served in their groups. MAK built an infrastructure of guesthouses and training camps to support the flow of Arabs to fight against the Soviets.

MAK provided each visiting mujahideen with funds and accommodations. Mujahids would receive a Kalashnikov rifle, two hand grenades, a canteen, web gear, and ammunition. Guest houses included Beit al Ansar, Abdara Road, Peshawar; Beit al Salam, Peshawar; Beit al Quraba, Hyatabad, Peshawar; Beit al Shehada (House of Martyrs), Hyatabad, Peshawar; Miram Shah, Afghanistan–Pakistan border en route to Khost; another guesthouse in Torkhan en route from Pakistan to Afghanistan; and another guesthouse solely to house women – the wives of Arab mujahideen. Camps established beginning in 1987 included al Masada (Lions) Camp, Jaj – established by bin Laden; Areen Camp, also in Jaji; and the more specialized camps Khaled Ibn Waled and al Farooq, both in Khost.

In addition to the trainers, most of MAK's camps had a leader and a fundraiser. Sheikh Tameem Adnani, a Palestinian Jordanian who lived in the United States and raised funds internationally, oversaw finances at al Masada Camp. Although MAK did not receive support from the CIA or Western governments, MAK received support from the Saudi regime and the Muslim territorial and diaspora/migrant community, especially from the United States and the Gulf. From the MAK office in Peshawar, Abu Tariq – a Palestinian Jordanian – transported money to various camps.[6] In addition to providing false identities to the mujahideen as charity and school workers,

Abdel Quddous – a US citizen – bribed Pakistani officials and provided them with Pakistani residency visas.[7]

Having played such a vital role in supporting the Afghan factions against the Soviets, Azzam and bin Laden began to focus on Israel and its steadfast supporters, especially after the first Palestinian uprising in 1987.[8] Azzam, in 1987–1988, formulated the broad outlines of what would become al Qaeda; he envisaged an organization that would channel the energies of the mujahideen into fighting on behalf of oppressed Muslims worldwide and would play the role of a pioneering vanguard of the Islamic movement. Azzam and bin Laden wanted the success against the Soviets replicated in other regions where Muslims were suffering. Upon its creation, al Qaeda inherited from MAK a fully fledged infrastructure of trainers, camps, weapons, and sources of finance. In addition to the Afghan training and operational infrastructure, al Qaeda benefited from the worldwide network created by its predecessor, with 30 offices overseas.

In 1989, bin Laden and Azzam split over disagreements regarding al Qaeda's priorities – bin Laden wanted to fund the Egyptians and Algerians, while Azzam wanted to focus on Islamizing the Afghan government. Most followers joined bin Laden, despite Azzam's assurances that following Afghanistan's Islamization he would wage jihad starting with Tajikistan, Uzbekistan, and Chechnya.[9] Azzam took control of MAK and a building that housed the Sabalil (strong lion at night) Mosque and established Camp Khalden at Parachinar on the Afghanistan–Pakistan border. Azzam was assassinated by the members of the Egyptian Islamic Jihad in November 1989 with bin Laden's acquiescence. Following Azzam's death, MAK failed to generate "as much money,"[10] with some workers skimming money that was to be directed to support the Arab mujahideen.[11] After Abdullah Azzam's murder, MAK withered and bin Laden became the backbone and principal driving force of al Qaeda.

In this first phase of development, al Qaeda was primarily a commander–cadre organization as described by Jessica Stern in Chapter 2. Its operations were managed via a vertical leadership structure that provided strategic direction and tactical support to its horizontal network of compartmentalized cells or associated organizations. Separate operational committees – military, finance and business, fatwa and Islamic study, and media and publicity – were responsible for day-to-day operations.

Contributions from wealthy Arab benefactors served as al Qaeda's primary source of financing during its formative years. Initially supported by bin Laden's personal resources, al Qaeda fund-raisers increasingly approached wealthy financiers, charities, and businesses;[12] in fact, one of the key reasons al Qaeda re-established a presence in Saudi Arabia was the vast potential for recruitment and fundraising. A chart recovered from a computer in the Bosnia office of the Benevolence International Foundation on 19 March 2002 identified some of the respected individuals in Saudi Arabia, UAE, Kuwait, and Qatar who provided support. Wael Julaidan, alias Abu al Hassan al

Madani, a Saudi who managed the Pakistan office of the International Islamic Relief Organization (IIRO),[13] provided funds to Asadallah al Sindi, the treasurer. Abu Ibrahim al Iraqi, a relative of an al Qaeda leader, managed the Peshawar office of the Kuwaiti Red Crescent Society, lectured about jihad, and provided funds for the mujahideen. Another Iraqi, Mamdouh Salim, alias Abu Hajir al Iraqi, managed guest-houses in Pakistan and was appointed the first head of al Qaeda's finance and investment committee. To facilitate such transactions, businesses and banks in the Gulf were used as fronts. Al Qaeda also siphoned funds from legitimate Islamic charities and infiltrated NGOs.[14]

Evidencing the keen desire of al Qaeda's leadership to monopolize the financing from Saudi Arabia, bin Laden authorized the killing of Jamil Ur Rahman, an Afghan leader. Jamil Ur Rahman reportedly had close ties to representatives of the Saudi Arabian government and "had attempted to influence wealthy Saudis not to provide money to bin Laden and his al Qaeda network."[15] Abdullah al Roomi, an al Qaeda member, killed Rahman at the behest of Muhammad Atta, alias Abu Hafs, a military leader of al Qaeda.[16]

Phase two: Sudan

Following the Soviet withdrawal from Afghanistan, bin Laden returned to Saudi Arabia. The presence of "infidel" American troops on Saudi soil as part of Operation Desert Shield in 1990, and their continuing presence after the first Gulf War, led bin Laden to campaign against the Saudi regime. He joined the ranks of dissidents claiming those in the al Saud regime were false Muslims and that the regime needed to be replaced by a true Islamic state. Complaints that he was "financing subversive activities" in Algeria, Egypt, and Yemen, as well as his criticism of Saudi policies, caused bin Laden to fall out of favour with the Saudi government. After being warned of his impending arrest, bin Laden fled to Sudan, the headquarters of al Qaeda from April 1991 to May 1996.

Even before al Qaeda shifted its operations from Peshawar to Sudan, al Qaeda had established a small presence in Khartoum. In 1989, Azzam and bin Laden had dispatched Battan al Sudani, a trainer at Khaled Ibn Waled Camp in Afghanistan, and Abdul Halim Muhammad Dosman to Khartoum.[17] Having established an office to recruit mujahideen and begun training of the Eritrean Islamic Jihad, al Qaeda established a small organizational presence in Khartoum beginning in 1989. When the National Islamic Front (NIF) led by Hasan al Turabi came into office, al Turabi invited bin Laden to relocate to Sudan. In response, bin Laden dispatched his representatives to study the political, financial, and security environment. Bin Laden, satisfied with their findings, moved with Abu Ibrahim and Abu Hajir (also known as Mahmud Salim) to Sudan to establish a series of companies owned by al Qaeda.

Bin Laden's inherited wealth, which has been grossly exaggerated, nonetheless provided a basis to help establish businesses and diversify al Qaeda's finances while in Sudan. Al Qaeda's investments and economic ventures increased significantly and reportedly encompassed some 30 companies. These firms employed as many as 3,000 workers in Sudan in diverse fields, ranging from high-tech labs engaged in genetic research to civil engineering businesses. Al Qaeda trainer Battan al Sudani managed Taba Investments, one of bin Laden's key companies.[18] In particular, economic infrastructure and ambitious construction projects became key areas of investment. An al Qaeda camp builder, Abu Muath al Urduni, built both the Tahadi (challenge) road linking Khartoum and Port Sudan and another road linking Damazine and Koromuk.[19] Al Qaeda also cooperated directly with the government of Sudan, including co-investing to create al Hijra Construction, a firm managed by Abu Ibrahim for building roads and bridges. Bin Laden's extensive business ties with the Sudanese political and military leadership increased his stature and al Qaeda's influence. This was principally a period of consolidation for al Qaeda.

Although al Qaeda appears to have focused on its business investments from 1992 to 1996, its terrorist and militant activities continued unabated, with the economic ventures providing opportunities to further its agenda. Agricultural facilities owned by al Qaeda – the Soba and Damazaine farms – by night served as training facilities for jihadi groups. Likewise, al Qaeda transported camels from Sudan to Egypt for sale but also used the opportunity to smuggle weapons for the jihadists in Egypt. In addition to heading al Qaeda's finance and investment committee, Abu Hajir al Iraqi attempted to procure radioactive material for al Qaeda. While on a visit to Germany for such purchases in 1998, he was arrested for his alleged involvement in the African embassy bombings and extradited to the United States.[20] But, as he refused to cooperate with German and US authorities, Western nations remain in the dark about al Qaeda's financial and economic empire. There is no reliable estimate of the total value of Osama bin Laden's operations in Sudan to this point. During this period, al Qaeda also furthered its links with Islamic groups engaged in guerrilla warfare and terrorism, providing them with funds, training, and weapons.

After the 1995 failed attempt to assassinate Egyptian President Mubarak in Ethiopia attracted the attention of the intentional community, the United States used sanctions to intensify pressure on Sudan to expel bin Laden. Although bin Laden had some success in investing his personal wealth in Sudan, his enterprises ultimately lost money due to international sanctions. As his wealth evaporated, bin Laden's anger grew both against the West and against the Arab regimes that were close to the United States, notably Saudi Arabia and Egypt. By 1994–1995, Western and Israeli security and intelligence agencies identified bin Laden as a key financier of terrorism. Sudan finally bowed to international pressure in 1996 and asked the "Saudi businessman" and al Qaeda to leave.

Phase three: Afghanistan

The relocation of al Qaeda from Sudan to Afghanistan in May 1996 hastened the transformation of bin Laden into a true international terrorist. In Sudan, bin Laden invested in huge construction projects and certainly supported terrorism although he was not directly involved. Relocating to Afghanistan, a landlocked country where Western intelligence agencies had virtually no presence, enabled al Qaeda to revive and reorganize its training and operational infrastructure. With bin Laden's expulsion from Sudan, the Western intelligence community that had previously monitored bin Laden's activities entirely lost track of his operations.

Within months after bin Laden moved to Afghanistan, the Taliban seized control of most of Afghanistan, including Kabul. Supported by Pakistan's Inter-Services Intelligence (ISI), the Taliban drew support largely from Afghan youths who had grown up in Pakistan and mujahideen leaders in Pakistan. Bin Laden quickly consolidated his ties to the Taliban leadership by financing and materially assisting the regime. Specifically, al Qaeda formed a guerrilla unit to assist the Taliban, which, while functioning as a separate organization, integrated with Taliban troops for the purpose of fighting the Northern Alliance. The Taliban regime reciprocated al Qaeda's assistance by providing sanctuary, weapons, equipment, and training facilities.[21]

Bin Laden was warmly welcomed in Afghanistan. As the most prominent Arab who fought against the Soviets, both the Afghan and the Pakistani mujahideen groups considered him a hero. Among the several thousand Arabs who had remained in Afghanistan and Pakistan, unwelcome in their home countries after the Soviet withdrawal, he found a natural following. Especially after the first World Trade Center attack in February 1993, when the United States warned Pakistan to get rid of the mujahideen or be declared a "terrorist state," most of the Arab mujahideen located in Pakistan moved to Afghanistan where al Qaeda had established a presence.

Al Qaeda's relocation to Afghanistan in 1996 created the opportunity for bin Laden to build a truly global jihad network, consolidating old relationships and building new ones. Many of the North African and East African jihad groups that al Qaeda trained in Sudan established a presence in Afghanistan. Further, bin Laden deepened the traditional links to Middle Eastern terrorist groups, particularly those from the Persian Gulf, and through partnerships with regional leaders developed closer ties with Asian groups. As an organization with a global membership, al Qaeda used Afghanistan to train, finance, and indoctrinate Islamist groups from Asia, Africa, the Middle East, and the Caucasus. Almost all the recruited Muslims came from the conflict zones of Nagorno-Karabakh, Chechnya, Tajikistan, Dagestan, Bosnia, Kosovo, Kashmir, Rohingiya Myanmar, the Philippines (Mindanao), Indonesia (Maluku and Poso), China (Xingjiang), Somalia (Ogadan), Algeria, Egypt, Jordan, and Yemen. Al Qaeda described its goal as the capacitation of a core group of fighters to alleviate the suffering of Muslims at the hands of the repressive regimes and rulers supported by the US Government and its allies.

In addition to its own training camps in Afghanistan, al Qaeda dispatched trainers to establish or serve in the training camps of affiliated groups in Asia, Africa, the Middle East, and the Caucasus. For example, beginning in 1988 and increasing after 1994, al Qaeda made efforts to embed its influence in Southeast Asia. Al Qaeda began by dispatching Muhammad Jamal Khalifa, the brother-in-law of Osama bin Laden, to establish the Manila branch of the International Islamic Relief Organization, a respectable Saudi charity, and to provide assistance to Islamist groups in the region. In 1994, Khalid Sheikh Muhammad – the mastermind of 11 September – traveled to Southeast Asia with 1993 World Trade Center bomber Ramzi Ahmed Yousef carrying plans to destroy US airliners over the Pacific. Similarly, within the Moro Islamic Liberation Front (MILF) Camp Abu Bakar complex, al Qaeda's Kuwaiti trainer Omar Al Farooq established Camp Vietnam to train Southeast Asian groups in guerrilla warfare and terrorism. Al Qaeda replicated this model worldwide from the Caucasus to North Africa.

Financing three or four thousand al Qaeda members in Afghanistan and clandestine agents overseas is estimated to have cost at least $36 million a year, on top of which the group's set-up costs – weapons, technology, infrastructure, camps, offices, vehicles – are thought to have been under $50 million, an estimate computed by examining the budgets of terrorist groups in relation to their sources of finance, geographic distribution, organizational sophistication, size, and other factors.[22] The funds came primarily from charities, businesses, and individual contributions.

Immediately following the Soviet withdrawal from Afghanistan, and for the remainder of the century, the international community ignored Afghanistan and, to some extent, Pakistan. As a result, Afghanistan and Pakistan developed throughout the 1990s as the centers for ideological and physical training of Islamist guerrilla and terrorist groups. After the Oslo Accords in the early 1990s, Afghanistan replaced the Syrian-controlled Bekkaa Valley as the principal hub of international terrorism. As the West looked the other way, Afghanistan evolved into a "Terrorist Disneyland." Together, al Qaeda and the Islamic Movement of the Taliban – the ruling party of the Islamic Emirate of Afghanistan – trained upwards of 20,000 foreign mujahideen until the US-led coalition intervened in Afghanistan in October 2001.

Phase four: the global jihadi movement

Since the 11 September attacks, al Qaeda's core strength has shrunk from about three or four thousand to a few hundred members. With the loss of Afghanistan as an operational base following the US-led intervention, and nearly 80 percent of its operational leadership and membership killed or captured, al Qaeda entered a new phase of its development. Even though al Qaeda maintains a presence in Afghanistan and Pakistan, its capacity is significantly degraded, and exercising direct control over its wide-ranging affiliated groups is increasingly difficult. Now, instead of planning and executing attacks itself, al Qaeda's greatest success has been the transfer of its operational knowledge to other groups. The most hunted terrorist group in history has evolved into an ideological vanguard, working with and through associated groups, networks, and cells, which collectively are known as the global jihad movement.

Notwithstanding the loss of its territorial sanctuary, al Qaeda successfully disseminates its ideological agenda of global jihad to its followers. Through communications from bin Laden, al Zawahiri, al Zarqawi (until recently), and others, primarily delivered via the Internet, al Qaeda provides indirect but critical ideological and strategic direction. Al Qaeda's overarching ideological goals – to expel foreign forces from the Islamic world and ultimately to create an Islamic state – facilitate the organization of regional and local groups. The World Islamic Front for Jihad Against the Jews and the Crusaders, al Qaeda's umbrella organization created in February 1998, attempts to unite its Middle Eastern, African, Caucasian, and Asian groups and provide a common agenda. Several regional groups have developed alliances similar to al Qaeda's World Islamic Front. For instance, Hambali – both an al Qaeda and a Jemaah Islamiyah leader – convened a meeting of Southeast Asian groups in Malaysia in 1999 to form the Rabitat-ul-Mujahideen (Legion of God's Warriors). After 11 September, and especially after the US-led intervention in Iraq, the international security and intelligence community has reported unprecedented unity between these groups.

The attacks in Madrid (2004) and London (2005) point towards Europe as a primary target for al Qaeda. As in Spain and Britain, the phenomenon of near-autonomous "home grown" terrorist cells carrying out attacks conforms to a well-recognized model for al Qaeda's current operations. The invasion of Iraq spurred the radicalization of alienated diaspora communities in Europe, which received ideological incitements and material support from radical preachers and networks associated with al Qaeda. In particular, some of the most significant al Qaeda-affiliated cells planning attacks in Europe have origins and links to North Africa. For example, the north London cell, discovered by authorities in January 2003 to have manufactured ricin, was originally a cell organized to support the creation of an Islamist Algerian state. Throughout Europe, Algerian terrorist support cells had generated propaganda, funds, and supplies for their campaign. Likewise, many of the terrorists involved in the Madrid train bombings in March 2004 were from Morocco or from the Moroccan diaspora. While European governments initially responded slowly to this threat, the 2004 Madrid bombings and the 2005 London bombings jarred Europeans into recognizing the necessity for action against the wider al Qaeda network, not just individual cells.

Developments in Europe call into question some of the counter-measures pursued after 11 September, especially those in the financial sector. A key component of the "global war on terror" has been the effort to cut off financial support for terrorism. Since 11 September 2001, initiatives combating the financing of terrorism have gained greater prominence as part of the international counter-terrorism effort, which is described in Chapter 11 of this volume. But European Islamists who currently subscribe to al Qaeda's ideology have learned rapidly from the past mistakes of al Qaeda and its associated cells and have adapted to law enforcement initiatives targeting terrorist financing. Current dedicated operational cells of al Qaeda and its associated groups are now familiar with and can easily circumvent governmental measures, making the cells difficult to detect.

Largely as a result of national governments' efforts to cut off financial support, al Qaeda and its networks have been forced to further decentralize their financing methods. Although the core al Qaeda organization and its associated groups still raise funds and recruit members through front, cover, and sympathetic organizations – organizations used to established charities, human rights groups, humanitarian organizations, community centers, and religious associations – cells increasingly generate their own funds. Cells have adapted to the increasing pressure by becoming self-financing, primarily through criminal activities, as was demonstrated in the Madrid train bombings and as discussed by Phil Williams in Chapter 6.

With most of the operations now at the local or regional level, disrupting the financing of individual cells is increasingly important. Even though the CIA interrogation of Khalid Sheik Muhammad, the 11 September mastermind, revealed that al Qaeda had no shortage of funds immediately after the US attacks, most of the subsequent terrorist attacks are believed to have been financed locally through individual terrorists or self-financed cells.

Iraq

My discussion thus far is summarized in Table 3.1. To understand the post-11 September phase in the evolution of al Qaeda, however, it is necessary to focus on the Islamist response to the US-led invasion of Iraq in 2003. The Iraq war has provided a substantial impetus to al Qaeda and other jihadi groups, breathing new life into the movement and providing it with a base to recruit, train, and fight. As the major focal point for terrorist activity, Iraq has attracted "foreign fighters" from Islamic communities across the globe, serving as an experiential "training ground" of jihad, much as Afghanistan, Bosnia, and Chechnya inculcated generations of mujahideen into the terrorist lifestyle throughout the 1980s and 1990s.

Muslim public support for jihad depends on the ability of al Qaeda and like-minded groups to inculcate the belief that Islam is under threat by the United States and its allies. The Iraq war, the Abu Ghraib photographs, reports of prisoner abuse at Guantanamo, and Muslim loss of life in Iraq serve to encourage even moderate Muslims to support jihadi groups. Today, extremist and terrorist groups ably exploit Muslim suffering, resentment, and anger. In that process, several new "al Qaedas" have been created. Just as the

Table 3.1 The phases of al Qaeda and its financing

Phase	Financial source(s)	Organizational structure
Phase 1: Pakistan *(1984–1991)*	Solicitations of wealthy Middle Eastern benefactors, charities	MAK infrastructure under bin Laden and Azzam
Phase 2: Sudan *(1991–1996)*	Business fronts, Osama bin Laden's personal wealth	Hierarchical structure in consultation with Sudanese government, plus extended network
Phase 3: *Afghanistan* *(1996–2001)*	Taliban sanctuary, charity diversion, smuggling, solicitations	Hierarchical structure with extensive training camps, networks, and partnerships, including with the Taliban
Phase 4: Post–11 *September*	Self-financing of cells through petty crime	Weakened hierarchy providing inspiration and ideological justification to regional associates

Madrid bombers called their group "The Supporters of al Qaeda," jihadists now independently conduct al Qaeda-style coordinated simultaneous suicide and non-suicide attacks.

Underscoring the centrality of the war in Iraq to al Qaeda's current objectives and the global jihadi movement, Osama bin Laden endorsed Jordanian-born terrorist leader Abu Musab al Zarqawi as an al Qaeda affiliate and leader of operations in Iraq. Bin Laden characterized Iraq as a "golden and unique opportunity" to defeat the United States, and as the central battleground in a "Third World War, which the Crusader Zionist coalition began against the Islamic nation."[23] Zarqawi was responsible for coordinating the largest number of suicide and non-suicide attacks in Iraq, working with a dozen groups to amplify the threat. Although he trained with al Qaeda in the Heart Camp and even lost a leg in combat, he worked not only with al Qaeda but also with al Ansar al Islami in Iraq and al Tawhid in Europe. Bin Laden has encouraged Islamic elements in Iraq to work with other insurgent groups such as the Baathists.

Within Iraq, this network supports itself through many of the finance mechanisms used by al Qaeda, including:

> [F]unds provided by charities, Iraqi expatriates, and other donors, primarily in the Gulf, but also in Syria, Lebanon, Jordan, Iran, and Europe, and criminal activities such as kidnapping for ransom . . . narcotics trafficking, robbery, theft, extortion, smuggling, and counterfeiting (goods and currency).[24]

Many of the funds that come from external sources are smuggled into Iraq using cash couriers. This is the most convenient and preferred method of moving funds by virtue of the availability of smuggling routes across porous borders and the difficulty of tracing cash payments of US dollars in the primarily cash economy of today's Iraq. In addition to Syria's serving as such a conduit, the US Government maintains that Iranian-backed proxy groups transfer into southern Iraq funds and materiel provided directly by Iran.[25]

Al Qaeda has ideologically incited local and regional Islamist groups to fight what they perceive to be not only corrupt Muslim regimes and false Muslim rulers such as those in Algeria, Egypt, Jordan, Saudi Arabia, Morocco, Kuwait, Indonesia, and Pakistan but also those governments' patrons, the United States and its allies. This strategy has achieved a number of significant objectives. First, despite enhanced counter-terrorism law enforcement and detection initiatives in the worldwide hunt for members and supporters of al Qaeda, incidents of terrorism have increased. Second, although the ability of al Qaeda and other terrorist groups to mount attacks, especially against well-defended facilities or hard targets such as diplomatic missions, military bases, and other government targets, has diminished, terrorists remain intent to attack. One of the unforeseen consequences of the West's counter-terrorism policies has been a shift from hard targets to soft ones, such as commercial infrastructure, tourist resorts, and population centers. Such vulnerable targets are too numerous to protect, making mass fatalities and casualties inevitable. Considering the sustained terrorist drive to attack, the West is not likely to stop suffering periodic terrorist attacks any time soon.

In short, the Iraq conflict has provided al Qaeda with an infusion of new human and tactical resources. For the foreseeable future, Iraq and to a lesser extent Afghanistan (and possibly Chechnya) will remain the primary fronts of the global jihadi movement.

Conclusion: countering al Qaeda and the global jihadi movement

Since its emergence in the 1980s, al Qaeda has evolved from a core group of radicals determined to execute and facilitate acts of terrorism to an ideological vanguard inspiring a global jihadi movement. Al Qaeda as an organization has demonstrated its proficiency at adapting its structure and strategy in response to counter-terrorism measures taken by the international community since the 11 September attacks. To evade technical methods of monitoring, al Qaeda has developed greater discipline and operational security. Having lost its training and operational infrastructure in Afghanistan, al Qaeda has increasingly relied on and operated through associated groups.

As al Qaeda has evolved, its methods for raising and moving funds have varied. In response, Western governments have adopted a wide range of measures to suppress al Qaeda's operational and financial capability. However, while the threat of al Qaeda has evolved, to a large extent, the conception of al Qaeda utilized by security and intelligence services in the West has not. The unfortunate consequence is that our responses to the threat of al Qaeda today are designed to counter the al Qaeda of 2001, not the fragmented global jihadi movement of 2005. This is an important deficiency.

Therefore, we must ensure that our policies change to accurately reflect our understanding of the current threat, just as al Qaeda has changed in response to our efforts to suppress terrorism. If al Qaeda is truly atomized into self-financing cells, then our efforts must match this new understanding. Unfortunately, the US focus on Iraq and on eliminating the al Qaeda leadership has limited the ability of US officials to understand and respond to the changing threat. Equally pressing are the many gaps in our knowledge about the structure of today's al Qaeda. In these cases, recognizing our blind spots and holes in our understanding will serve to spur caution and further inquiry that may make a substantial difference in future attempts to disrupt al Qaeda and its affiliates.

In light of al Qaeda's evolution, counter-measures against the global jihadi movement should go beyond the tactical targeting of terrorist cells. Critically, we must act strategically to prevent the creation of terrorists. Strategies for fighting terrorism must include countering the appeal of abstract and hate-based ideology of jihad against the West, especially the United States, its allies, and friends. It is also necessary to send the message that al Qaeda and its associated groups are not Koranic organizations and that they are presenting a corrupt version of Islam by misinterpreting and misrepresenting the Koran and other texts. The jihadi movement uses Islam as a tool of mass mobilization through the manipulation of prophetic truths from the Koran. The West should work with the Muslim elite to confront and stop these jihadists from preaching and conducting violence and to create space and a platform for the moderate Muslims. Muslim leaders must get the *ulemas* (Muslim scholars) and *ustaz* (religious teachers) to preach that Islam is a religion of peace, not terror. Islam must be portrayed as tolerant of other faiths, as Muslim scholars in history have proudly asserted. It is also incumbent upon the international community to work together to roll back the threat of radical Islamism by helping the Muslim community recover from the current ideological crisis. Furthermore, conditions must be created under which Muslims can achieve a balance between personal piety, peace, freedom, and prosperity.

Overall, the key to defeating al Qaeda and reducing the terrorist threat is to develop a multi-agency, multi-juristic, and multinational strategy to combat the organization's ideology. Such a strategy will necessarily concentrate on combating regeneration – terrorist ability to replenish human losses and material costs. As strategies target the recruitment ability of such an organization and the impetus for any individual to attach his or herself to such an agenda, the group will start to decay over a period of time. Counter-strategies should seek to address grievances and aspirations. Such a perspective will discredit the ideology of al Qaeda, limit their activities, and undermine their ability to incite and enact violence. Therefore a both preventative and proactive strategy, in concert with continued law enforcement and financial measures, should be employed through all new policy initiatives.

Notes

1 I wish to express my gratitude to Peter Romaniuk, Sue E. Eckert, Arabinda Acharya, and Jaime Sarah Burnell for their assistance in writing this chapter.
2 Al Qaeda itself has conducted an average of only one terrorist attack per year since the 11 September attacks. Four times that number, or an average of one attack every three months, has been mounted by al Qaeda-associated groups.
3 Briefing by CNI, the Spanish Intelligence Service, December 2004.
4 Briefing on Operation Crevice, SO 13, New Scotland Yard, December 2004.
5 R. Paz, Personal Communication, December 2001. Dr. Paz, a former head of research of the Internal Security Agency (Shin bet) of Israel, was the first to bring to the attention of the operational and the academic community the founding charter of al Qaeda. The charter authored by Azzam was published in *Al Jihad*, the principal journal of the Arab Mujahideen in Peshawar, 1988.
6 Al Qaeda detainee commenting on Tareekh Osama, Folder 56, Document 136, recovered from Benevolence International Foundation's Bosnia Office, 19 March 2002, p. 9.
7 Ibid.
8 A. al Zawahiri, "The Knights under the Prophet's Banner," unpublished manuscript, December 2001.
9 Al Qaeda detainee commenting on Tareekh, Al Musadat, 86, 87, 88, Folder 8, Documents 301–347, recovered from Benevolence International Foundation's Bosnia Office, 19 March 2002, p. 5.
10 Ibid.
11 Ibid.
12 Considerable speculation has taken place as to Osama bin Laden's personal wealth. Bin Laden was alleged to have inherited upwards of $300 million when his father died, funds thought to have formed the basis for al Qaeda financing in Sudan and Afghanistan. Such exaggerations have been discredited, and his personal wealth has been estimated to be closer to $30–40 million – about a million dollars per year from about 1970–1994 according to the 9/11 Commission's *Monograph on Terrorist Financing*. In 1994, the Saudi government forced the bin Laden family to sell Osama's share of the family company and to freeze the proceeds, thereby depriving him of what could have been a $300 million fortune. J. Roth, D. Greenberg, and S. Wille, *Monograph on Terrorist Financing* (Staff Report to the Commission), National Commission on Terrorist Attacks Upon the United States, 2004. Online. Available HTTP: <http://www.9–11commission. gov/staff_statements/911_TerrFin_Monograph.pdf#search=%229%2F11%20 commission%20monograph%22>
13 IIRO functioned under Rabita al Islami, also known as MWLKA.
14 For a more detailed description of al Qaeda's financial network, see R. Gunaratna, *Inside al Qaeda: Global Network of Terror*, New York: Columbia University Press, 2002.
15 Al Qaeda detainee commenting on Tareekh, Al Musadat, 86, 87, 88, Folder 8, Documents 301–347, recovered from Benevolence International Foundation's Bosnia Office, 19 March 2002.
16 "Posing as a journalist Al Roomi visited with Jamil Ur Rahman and while interviewing him about his relationship with the Saudi government pulled out a small handgun and killed him. Al Roomi was killed by Jamil Ur Rahman's bodyguard.

Jamil Ur Rahman was killed after Abdullah Azzam, the ideological father of al Qaeda was killed, also by al Qaeda." Ibid.

17 Ibid.

18 Ibid.

19 Al Qaeda detainee commenting on Tareekh Osama, Folder 56, Document 136, recovered from Benevolence International Foundation's Bosnia Office, 19 March 2002, p. 7.

20 Al Iraqi attempted to procure a uranium canister for $1.5 million, but al Qaeda was duped. The canister had been irradiated from outside and sold. While in detention, al Iraqi used a sharpened comb to stab a US corrections officer in his eye.

21 Gunaratna, *Inside Al Qaeda*, p. 54.

22 Gunaratna, "The Lifeblood of Terrorist Organisations: Evolving Terrorist Financing Strategies," in Alex Schmid (ed.) *Countering Terrorism Through International Cooperation*, International Scientific and Professional Advisory Council of the UN Cooperation and the UN Terrorism Prevention Branch, 2001, pp. 180–205. R. Gunaratna, *Inside al Qaeda: Global Network of Terror*, New York, Columbia University Press, 2002, p. 61.

23 Bin Laden audio tape released 27 December 2004, Foreign Broadcast Information Service (FBIS) Report FEA20041227000762, 27 December 2004.

24 D. L. Glaser, "Who Pays the Iraqi Insurgents?" testimony of Daniel L. Glaser, Acting Assistant Secretary for the Office of Terrorist Financing and Financial Crimes, US Department of the Treasury before the House Financial Services Subcommittee on Oversight and Investigations and the House Armed Services Subcommittee on Terrorism, 28 July 2005. Online. Available HTTP:<http://financialservices.house.gov/media/pdf/072805dg.pdf> (accessed 21 October 2005).

25 Ibid.

4 The social organization of terror in Southeast Asia

The case of Jemaah Islamiyah

Zachary Abuza

Since the 11 September attacks on the United States, the Southeast Asian affiliate of al Qaeda, Jemaah Islamiyah (JI), has proven to be one of the most consistently lethal terrorist organizations in the world. Beginning with the simultaneous bombings that killed more than 200 people in Bali on 12 October 2002, JI has perpetrated major terrorist attacks at roughly one year intervals, including the JW Marriott hotel in August 2003 and the Australian Embassy in September 2004, both in Jakarta, and triple suicide bombings in Bali on 1 October 2005. Simultaneously, JI has continued to instigate and foment sectarian conflict in the outer islands of Indonesia. Despite counter-terror efforts across Southeast Asia that have led to the arrests of more than 300 members, including much of JI's leadership, the organization has proven remarkably resilient and lethal. This survivability is due to the organization's flexibility and its hybrid nature.

JI is neither a completely hierarchical commander–cadre system, nor a purely horizontal leaderless network. Overall, JI demonstrates many of the characteristics of both a commander–cadre organization and at other times, perhaps brought on by exogenous factors such as the "war on terror," JI displays characteristics of a "leaderless resistance." Jemaah Islamiyah, however, is first and foremost a socially-based organization. It is comprised of an intricate web of madrassas, foreign contacts, families, mosques, sub-organizations, and affiliates. On top of this network is superimposed a hierarchical authority structure that articulates the ultimate goals of the organization; but this authority structure is not highly institutionalized and it has often been a liability since the beginning of the war on terror. JI has demonstrated a capability to learn and adapt relying on the strengths of its informal social network structure. As Jessica Stern notes in Chapter 2, there is intense "evolutionary pressure to adapt." The organization's financing, too, demonstrates a shift from a more hierarchical organization with money coming in at the top from al Qaeda and filtering down, to a more socially based fund-raising system.

Jemaah Islamiyah is the Southeast Asian affiliate of al Qaeda. Many skeptics have questioned this assertion and argue that JI is an organization with a purely regional agenda. Indeed, some have contended that JI, which simply means "Islamic Community," does not really exist – though members and

internal documents consistently refer to it by that name. Arguments against
the affiliation of al Qaeda and JI do not take into account the close cooperation, financial flows, and personnel sharing between the two organizations.
It is clear that JI's immediate agenda is not at odds with al Qaeda's goals.
Moreover, the goal of JI – to establish a pan Islamic caliphate in Southeast
Asia – is not at all inconsistent with al Qaeda's vision of a pan-Islamic
caliphate across the Muslim world. JI is committed to the spread of Salafi
ideals into a region that in the past has been less than receptive, and al Qaeda
is at minimum a useful partner in that enterprise.

But al Qaeda provides more than simple inspiration for JI. Al Qaeda
encouraged the group's formation and helped it to develop; in the past they
have engaged in joint planning, assisted and coordinated with one another,
and jointly financed terrorist attacks. Indeed, intelligence officials were sur-
prised to learn how senior in the al Qaeda organization the JI operations
chief, Hambali, actually was at the time of his arrest in August 2003. There is
little understanding, however, of the current degree of cooperation between
the two groups after nearly five years of the "war on terror." Important for
our understanding of the organization is the fact that the image of JI as
purely independent of al Qaeda is based on a misunderstanding about al
Qaeda's organizational structure.

The al Qaeda network

Al Qaeda is not a top-down organization with a strong central leadership.
Even before the "war on terror" began, the central leadership of al Qaeda
was relatively small. What gave al Qaeda both its strength and depth was
its ability to form an international, "all channel" network that spanned the
Islamic world. Osama bin Laden himself views the organization – whose
official name is World Islamic Front for Jihad Against Jews and Crusaders
– as an international network of organizations that hitherto had more
parochial national agendas. John Arquilla writes that, "Terrorist networks
develop along the lines of 'diverse, dispersed nodes' who share a set of ideas
and interests and who are arrayed to act in a fully internetted 'all-channel'
manner."[1] He continues:

> Ideally there is no central leadership, command, or headquarters – no
> precise heart or head that can be targeted. The network as a whole (but
> not necessarily each node) has little to no hierarchy, and there may be
> multiple leaders. Decision-making and operations are decentralized,
> allowing for local initiative and autonomy. Thus the design may appear
> acephalous (headless), and at other times polycephalous (hydra-headed).[2]

All-channel networks are characterized by "relatively flat hierarchies, decentralization and delegation of decision-making authority and loose lateral ties
among dispersed groups and individuals."[3]

Because of the high degree of decentralization, these networks are not easy to maintain and "effective performance over time may depend on the presence of shared principles, interests, and goals – at best, an over-arching doctrine or ideology that spans all nodes and to which the members whole-heartedly subscribe."[4] An overarching philosophy facilitates the formation of an all-channel, "leaderless resistance" – a movement with "a central ideational, strategic and operational coherence that allows for tactical decentralization."[5] The organization's ideology sets "boundaries and provide[s] guidelines for decisions and actions so that the members do not have to resort to a hierarchy – 'they know what they have to do.' " However, when communication is necessary, "the network's members must be able to disseminate information promptly and as broadly as desired within the network and to outside audiences."[6]

Although Osama bin Laden serves as an inspiration to groups around the world, al Qaeda is not quite yet a "leaderless resistance." Though the organization has clearly been set back by arrests of key members around the world, it has still maintained a command and control system and demonstrated some of the characteristics of a commander–cadre organization.

JI and al Qaeda

In a network organization, nodes – and the relationships between and among the nodes – change over time, as does the organization's center of gravity. Ties between groups shift: strong and close working relationships can break down over time and vice-versa, or a seemingly marginal group can forge new ties and become an important actor in a new theater of operations. This is clearly what happened within Jemaah Islamiyah, which went from a nascent organization at al Qaeda's disposal from 1993 to 2000 to a bona fide terrorist organization in its own right starting in 2000.

Southeast Asia was an ad hoc theater of operations for Ramzi Yousef's 1994–1995 plot to down 11 jetliners, but after his operation was disrupted, the cell dispersed and Southeast Asia ceased to be a central front in al Qaeda's operations. Al Qaeda's links to the area remained, but oriented solely towards support activities. Southeast Asia was appealing to the al Qaeda leadership at the time because of the network of Islamic charities, the profusion of poorly regulated Islamic banks, available business-friendly environments, and economies that boasted scrutiny-free money transfers and money laundering. The region was treated, first and foremost, as a back office for al Qaeda's activities (especially to set up front companies, fundraise, recruit, forge documents, and purchase weapons). Only later did it become a theater of operations in its own right as its affiliate organization in Southeast Asia, the Jemaah Islamiyah, developed its own capabilities, having dispatched members to Afghanistan for training. At this time, al Qaeda and JI also began establishing training facilities in the territory of the Moro Islamic Liberation Front (MILF) in the southern Philippines.[7] Yet the relationship with al Qaeda remained very compartmentalized, known to only the most senior members and operatives. Rank and file JI members had little knowledge of al Qaeda, and only a handful of senior JI members pledged *bayat* (an oath of allegiance) to Osama bin Laden.

JI's organizational structure

JI exhibits characteristics of both formal and networked organizations. Although in relation to other militant Islamist organizations JI has a clear authority structure with defined rights, duties, responsibilities and geographic commands, JI also fits into a network model. JI has formed an integral part of the "leaderless" or "all-channel" al Qaeda network, while at the same time basing its inner workings on a commander–cadre cellular organization. JI founders wanted to codify their authority structures, rules, and regulations, and in a sense, this hierarchy and self-regulation foreshadows the group's ultimate goal of establishing an Islamic state. The attempt to formalize relationships, leadership selection, and decision-making procedures is also important for another reason: it demonstrates the importance the organization placed on maintaining its integrity, particularly the command and control structures. One must recall that JI, which was founded in 1992–1993, did not engage in terrorism until 2000. They spent seven to eight years patiently training, recruiting, indoctrinating, and building up a region-wide network of cells with specific functions such as procuring explosives and participating in sectarian conflicts.

JI places considerable importance on the religious piety and faith of its members. For example, in the fall of 2003, Pakistani officials arrested a 13-member JI cell, known as al Ghuraba, in a Lashkar-e-Taiba (LeT) madrassa.[8] The group, which was led by Abdul Rahim, Abu Bakar Ba'asyir's son, and Hambali's brother Rusman Gunawan, all had close familial ties to JI.[9] They were to be the core of the next generation of JI's leadership, and they were to be sent to Pakistan for advanced religious training. It is telling that JI did not send their future leaders to combat zones to gain jihad experience fighting America and infidels. Although there is evidence that Hambali called on them to provide operational assistance to JI and al Qaeda, it was primarily a religious study group.[10] Abdul Rahim, in a recent interview, said "al Ghuraba was formed purely for religious study and discussion. Saifudin said senior Jemaah Islamiyah members 'saw the urgency of regeneration in the movement' and sent their sons and their students to Pakistan to study to become ulamas."[11] They focused on *religion* to rebuild their depleted ranks. The most respected people within JI, as in al Qaeda, are not the Afghan Mujahidin or operatives with "street credibility," but highly esteemed religious leaders. This is not surprising as members of organizations tend to subordinate their own judgment and turn to an omnipotent leader who is lionized as a hero within a group (and pilloried by "out groups") for direction.[12]

Accordingly, as an organization JI utilizes a religious model centered on the *shura* (consultative leadership body) and subordinate regional *mantiqi* command structure. The *Pedoman Umum Perjuangan al-Jama'ah al-Islamiyah* (PUPJI), or *The General Guidebook for the Struggle of Jemaah Islamiya*, outlines the roles of these councils. In addition, an associated body, the Mujahidin Council of Indonesia (MMI) functions as a distinct political and fundraising organ. The next four sections outline the contents of two written documents, the PUPJI and the *General Manual of Operations* respectively, and discuss key organizational elements, including the shura, mantiqi councils and the Mujahidin Council of Indonesia.

The PUPJI

As JI recruited a cadre of members and developed its own capabilities, it set out to apply a more formal structure to its informal network of familial, kinship, and mosque–madrassa ties. Jemaah Islamiyah codified its formal structure in the PUPJI in 1996. The document may be a projection of how JI envisioned itself in the future. While the codified structure does not necessarily match reality or account for subsequent evolution, it provides important details concerning the goals and modus vivendi of the group.

The PUPJI outlines the authority structure, organization, goals, and rights and duties of its members. There are 15 chapters in addition to preambles, definitions, conclusions, and explanations. The fact that they took the time to develop and write such a thorough and complex document illustrates their patient and deliberative attempt to develop the network. The authors expected to be around for a long time. Much of the document is written in Arabic. The following is a summary of important chapters.

Chapter III states that the organization is led by an elected amir [(III (6.1–2)] and assisted by a *majlis* (council) that he can appoint and dismiss [IV (8.2)]. The most important function of the amir is as the spiritual educator of the members. Chapter V outlines the selection and responsibilities of the Qiyadah Councils that advise the amir. Though the Councils are elected by their *Qoid*, the election is done with the approval of the amir. One interesting aspect is the pre-eminence of the amir in decision-making. The PUPJI clearly states, "Should there be a difference of opinion between the amir and the majority of votes, the decision of the amir prevails" [IX (28.7)].

Chapter X identifies the criteria for membership [X (30)] and then the responsibilities [X (31)] and rights [X (32)] of those who are eligible. Membership criteria include piousness, understanding of Islam, comprehension of the teachings of Allah, and *bayat*, a pledge of loyalty to the amir. Responsibilities include living a life solely according to Islamic principles, obeying the PUPJI, obeying the amir and shura, defending and protecting the amir and brothers, and not performing any act that endangers the *jemaah* or community. Rights include social welfare, participation in discussion and debate, eligibility for election and appointment to new positions, and protection from the jemaah.

General Manual for Operations

The PUPJI contains the *General Manual for Operations*, which is a vague and somewhat philosophical document – a far cry from the al Qaeda training manual that was found in a Manchester terrorist safehouse. The *General Manual* does, however, discuss how operations should be conducted. It emphasizes planning: "the operation should be planned and carried out according to plan." It also outlines a schema for guerilla war: "View, analyze and explore all aspects of life in the enemy's body and in the environment," "View carefully and honestly all our potential strengths and effective powers we possess," "Determine points of target at the enemy and the environment to be handled in relation with our goals." The document calls for four stages of operations: (1) Planning, (2) Execution, (3) Reporting, (4) Evaluation. Emphasis is placed on education, meticulous planning, and learning from past acts (including mistakes).

Additionally, the document discusses how members should focus on Intelligence Operations, Strength Building Operations, Strength Utilization Operations, and Fighting Operations. Almost all emphasis is placed on Strength Building Operations, which are defined as a lengthy process that includes spiritual and physical strengthening. The goals of this educational period include enlightenment, discipline, instilling a sense of loyalty, physical readiness, and weapons skills, tactical and strategic thinking, and leadership development. The document also recognizes the dangers that members face. One of the goals of education is to "provide reserve powers as preparation to replace loss or destruction of forces."

The shuras and mantiqi

JI is organized into two sets of councils: the *shura* (a regional advisory council) and *mantiqi* (regional commands). Riduan Isamuddin, better known as Hambali, was the chairman of the five-member shura – "Regional Advisory Council." Other members included Mohammed Iqbal Rahman (Abu Jibril), Agus Dwikarna, Abu Hanafiah, and Faiz bin Abu Bakar Bafana. Beneath the shura were the secretaries and five functional sub-shura:

- Operations: This sub-shura was responsible for training members, dispatching members to Afghanistan or Mindanao for training, planning, conducting operations, and liaising with the MILF in the Philippines.
- Communications: This sub-shura was responsible for establishing primarily electronic communications. It was also in charge of maintaining web pages that were affiliated with JI such as fatidah.com.

- Security: This small sub-shura was responsible for internal control, discipline, and counter-intelligence.
- Finance: This sub-shura was in charge of fundraising, liaising with charities, establishing bank accounts, transferring money, and establishing front companies.
- Missionary (*dakwah*): This sub-shura was responsible for recruitment, training, and running JI's network of madrassas. It also engaged in Mosque outreach and fundraising for jihadi operations, particularly in support of the sectarian conflicts in eastern Indonesia in 1998–2001, and terrorist operations after 2000.

Also beneath the shura were the heads of the four regional commands, or *mantiqis*, below which were *wakalah* followed by *fiah*, or individual cells. JI has between 500 and 1,000 members spread throughout the region, though 500 is a more likely estimate.

- Mantiqi One covered peninsula Malaysia, Singapore and southern Thailand
- Mantiqi Two covered Indonesia
- Mantiqi Three covered the Philippines, Brunei, eastern Malaysia, Kalimantan and Sulawesi Indonesia
- Mantiqi Four was being developed to establish cells in Australia and Papua (Irian Jaya)

Mantiqi One, with an estimated 200 members, is perhaps the largest JI cell. It was led by Abu Hanafiah and Faiz bin Abu Bakar Bafana and it recruited actively among both Indonesian exiles and educated Malays – especially technical students. At least five senior JI members and recruiters were lecturers in the University of Technology Malaysia (UTM), and a significant number of JI members came from technical backgrounds, rather than simply madrassa education. Mantiqi One had four discernable functions. First, it worked very closely with the Kumpulan Mujahidin Malaysia (KMM) in Malaysia, with whom there is considerable overlap in membership. Second, it was the primary conduit between the JI and Osama bin Laden and al Qaeda in Afghanistan. The Malaysian cell was the logistical hub for up to 100 JI operatives who were sent to Afghanistan for training in al Qaeda camps, in addition to running its own camp in southern Malaysia. Third, Mantiqi One was responsible for recruiting and education. Much of the recruiting was done through two madrassas. Finally, Mantiqi One was responsible for establishing more than one dozen front companies that could be used to channel al Qaeda funds, and to procure weapons and bomb-making material.

Mantiqi Two provided the bulk of the JI membership. In the mid-1990s, there appears to have been very little JI activity in authoritarian Indonesia. Yet, following the fall of Suharto in May 1998, there was a surge in JI activity as hundreds of radical Indonesians returned to the archipelago. In addition to providing a large number of JI's members, it was in Indonesia that the JI developed its two paramilitary arms: the Laskar Mujahidin and the Laskar Jundullah, in 1998 to 2000. This Indonesian cell is thoroughly connected to Abu Bakar Ba'asyir's overt political organization, the Mujahidin Council of Indonesia (MMI), a large umbrella group covering approximately 100 small radical and militant groups from across the archipelago. In addition to recruitment and running a network of radical madrassas, the Indonesian cell was responsible for running a network of training camps, including some seven in Sulawesi and one in Kalimantan. The Indonesian cell was also very important, liaising with al Qaeda-linked Islamic charities, especially al Haramain, and became a very important conduit for foreign funding to JI and its paramilitary arms in the outer islands.

Mantiqi Three was important as a major logistics cell for the network – responsible for acquiring explosives, guns and other equipment, as well as liaising with the MILF and supporting al Qaeda operatives and trainers in the region. They included senior al Qaeda trainers Omar al-Faruq, al-Mughira al-Gaza'iri, and Omar al-Hadrani. These trainers also played an important role in establishing the MILF's own terrorist arm, the Special Operations Group in 1999. The cell leader was an Indonesian, Fathur Rohman al-Ghozi, who had studied at al Mukmin from 1984 to 1990 before going on to study in a Pakistani madrassa where he was recruited into Jemaah Islamiyah. In addition to explosives, al-Ghozi was responsible for the purchase of light arms and assault rifles that were used by the JI's two paramilitary arms engaged in sectarian conflicts in Indonesia, starting in 1999. These were shipped to Poso for Agus Dwikarna's Laskar Jundullah, and Ambon for Abu Jibril's Laskar Mujahidin.

Mantiqi Four was the smallest and least developed of the JI cells. It included Northern Australia, which the JI leaders frequented to recruit and fundraise from among the large population of Indonesian exiles.

The Mujahidin Council of Indonesia

The Mujahidin Council of Indonesia (Majlis Mujahidin Indonesia or MMI), has often been described as the overt wing of JI, akin to the Irish Republican Army's political wing, Sinn Fein. Although there is some overlap among the members of JI and MMI, they are separate entities. The organizations, however, share the same goal: the establishment of an Islamic state. Additionally, members of MMI have held key positions at Islamic charities suspected of funding Southeast Asian terrorist groups.

The MMI was established in mid-2000 by Abu Bakar Ba'asyir, ostensibly as a civil society organization that tries to implement *sharia* peacefully and through the democratic process.[13] However, many MMI leaders were also senior JI members. For example, the MMI's board included Mohammad Iqbal Rahman (Abu Jibril) and Agus Dwikarna. Both headed JI's two

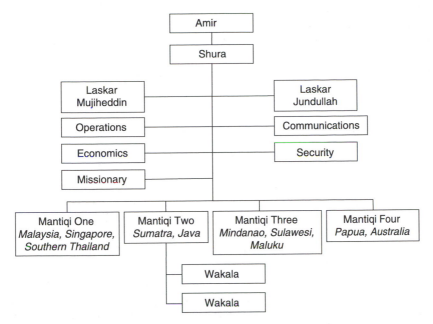

Figure 4.1 Organizational chart of Jemaah Islamiyah.

paramilitary arms and both were members of the JI shura. The head of the Fatwa council is Abdul Qadir Baraja. The MMI's director of daily operations is Irfan Suryahardy Awwas, the younger brother of Abu Jibril. Yet the MMI also includes many individuals who, while they may share a similar goal and worldview with JI, disagree about means and are not members of the organization. MMI remains a legal, though suspect organization.

The MMI also serves as an important financial conduit, especially for moving foreign money to the very small radical groups which would otherwise be unable to network abroad. Members of MMI have been involved with foreign charities thought to be used by al Qaeda to channel financial support to Southeast Asian terrorist organizations. Indonesian intelligence officials estimated that 15–20 percent of Islamic charity funds are diverted, either unwittingly or intentionally, to politically motivated groups and terrorists. JI and al Qaeda leaders assumed leadership positions[14] – often becoming regional branch chiefs – or formed alliances with several important Saudi charities, including the International Islamic Relief Organization (IIRO) and Al Haramain, as well as Indonesian charities that served as their counterpart or executing agencies such as KOMPAK or the Medical Emergency Relief Charity (MERC).[15]

In Indonesia, the leadership of these charities is overlapping. For example, Agus Dwikarna, the fourth in command of the MMI, was the local representative of the Saudi Charity al Haramain in Makassar in South Sulawesi –

which, one al Qaeda official admitted, was the largest single source of al Qaeda funds into Indonesia – and also a branch officer of KOMPAK.[16] Of the 13 regional officers of KOMPAK, four were senior JI commanders, which allowed them to siphon off funds for sectarian violence and other jihadi purposes. KOMPAK will be discussed in more depth in following sections.

Organizational flexibility and decision-making

JI's formal structure, explicitly delineated on paper, is not rigid, and the organization appears to be very adaptable and willing to adjust. While maintaining clear lines of command and control remains important today, the organization is not rigid and is able to adapt to new circumstances. This flexibility became more pronounced during the crackdown against JI following the Bali bombings in October 2002. The organization might have maintained more of its rigidity if the war on terror had not begun and the organization had not suffered so many arrests.

One of the lasting legacies of Hambali is the importance placed on maintaining the integrity of the organization. Press reports say that Hambali has confessed to being replaced by Zulkarnaen and Dr. Azahari, indicating that JI had contingency plans in place. Likewise, the organization quickly tapped new leaders when middle- to senior-level leaders were arrested. Nassir bin Abbas has confessed that the group was usually very quick to respond to arrests and secure new leaders, including the amir. In a mid-October 2002 meeting following Bali, Nassir commented: "We discussed reports from each Mantiqi head and the arrest of Abubakar Bashir and what position we should take. We decided to look for a new JI amir."[17] At that time Abbas was appointed the head of Mantiqi Three, following the arrest of his predecessor Mustapha.

JI made the conscious decision to ensure that the organizational command and control system remained intact. The changes followed a structured system of authority, and there were rituals, such as pledging *bayat*. There was always an attempt made to have a reasonable quorum of leaders when important decisions were made. Chapter IX of the *PUPJI* establishes parliamentary procedures for JI meetings including quorums and a rule stating that if more than one-third of cell members are not in attendance, the meeting is supposed to be delayed by a week. However, parliamentary details tend to be ignored in the heat of battle. Following the crackdown in Malaysia and Singapore in December 2001 and in Indonesia after October 2002, meetings became less frequent with fewer attendees.[18] It was simply too risky for them to meet often once all of the region's intelligence assets were focused on them.

JI is also a highly compartmentalized organization, judging by several examples from the Bali plot. For example, Nassir bin Abbas, the head of Mantiqi Three, had no idea who was responsible for the Bali bombing.[19]

Many of the individuals such as Wan Min Wan Mat, JI's treasurer who passed on the money to the Bali plotters, had no idea what the money would be used for. The organization clearly does not micro-manage its cells. For example, at the January 2002 meeting in Bangkok, in light of the rapid arrests in Malaysia and Singapore, Hambali gave the order to shift the focus of attacks onto small bombings in bars, cafés or nightclubs frequented by Westerners in Thailand, Malaysia, Singapore, the Philippines and Indonesia, rather than continuing to target larger, more symbolic, hardened targets. Yet Hambali never mentioned Bali or any other specific targets: it was left to the attendees to implement these new orders to the best of their ability.[20]

This meeting is also interesting for several other reasons. First, although this was a major strategy session, only five individuals attended the meeting in addition to Hambali: Noordin Mohammed Mop Top, Dr. Azahari, Wan Min Wan Mat, Ali Gufron (Mukhlas), and Mohammed Mansour Jabarah. Second, it demonstrates a high degree of coordination between JI and al Qaeda. Al Qaeda was under serious attack at the time. Mohammed Atef had been killed by US air strikes, and the December 2001 assault on Tora Bora convinced Hambali that he needed to conduct a major bombing to take the heat off al Qaeda. The Bali bombing was financed by al Qaeda and executed with their knowledge and support.

Since Bali, the meetings have grown smaller. Nassir bin Abbas indicated that major leadership meetings only included five or six individuals.[21] Apparently the organization is quite flexible in determining what constitutes a quorum and who can immediately fill in for others. Although the Mantiqi structure – the middle level of the organization based on geographical command zones – seems to be in disarray since the Bali bombings, there seems to be more direct interaction between the top leaders and the *wakalah* and *fiah* – the individual cells that have more operational autonomy. As Imam Samudra commented:

> In Islam, as we perform our alms, there is no terminology for superiors or subordinates. There isn't. Except for organizations that are really structured, or regular . . . no, there's no structure to it [JI]. No structure. I know there are attempts to describe our organization as a structured one. I understand that. The truth is, there is no structure. Of course it works, why wouldn't it? Allah wills it to work that way, so it works. In fact, such organizations are better, the ones like that, not rigid, very flexible. That's the truth. We have meetings, talked a bit, and there's a plan.[22]

So while the commander–cadre system is weaker than it was, JI has not yet completely morphed into a "leaderless resistance."[23] It remains a hybrid; perhaps the most resilient type of network. And it has had to be, owing to the concerted police and intelligence efforts out to undermine and infiltrate it. Since October 2001, there have been more than 300 arrests throughout the region.

Organizational challenges: factionalism

There is a debate whether JI is factionalized. Sidney Jones of the International Crisis Group (ICG) believes that JI is divided into distinct factions. Her thesis is based on the precept that the perpetrators of the Bali and Marriott attacks were in the Hambali faction that had internationalist ties and were close to the al Qaeda leadership.[24] Jones contends that the larger faction of JI sees those high profile attacks as symbolic but counter-productive. This faction, steeped in the Darul Islam tradition, advocates greater emphasis on sectarian conflict and a more domestic focus in their attempt to transform Indonesia into an Islamic state. Although the Hambali faction has been nearly decimated, the traditional faction remains quite strong. The ICG report is meticulous in its detail and analysis.

The one difference I have with Jones, is that she sees discernable *ideological* factions. While I do not discount them, I think she overstates the depth of the ideological differences. Instead, I contend that the factions are a natural result of compartmentalized cells across vast regions that are having more difficulty communicating with one another, especially as JI's command and control system has been badly damaged. The cells are more autonomous by default. It is also indicative of a multi-faceted strategy. The cells adopt different strategies according to different external environments and organizational needs.

We are in complete agreement, however, that JI seeks to foment sectarian violence, as it did in 1999–2000, as part of its strategy to regroup. While Jones sees a division between the advocates of international jihadism and proponents of sectarian violence, I do not. In JI's eyes, they are not mutually exclusive, but rather mutually reinforcing. For example, on 2 May 2005 Indonesian police arrested three suspects wanted in conjunction with the August 2003 bombing of the JW Marriott in Jakarta in a small village outside of Poso, Sulawesi. All three, as well as a fourth who escaped, were involved in not only the sectarian bloodletting in Ambon in 1999–2000, but also the 24 April 2005 sectarian attacks in Mamasa. We also have a clear connection between the same people engaged in both "international jihad" and sectarian conflict. A majority of JI members will want to focus on the "near enemy" and concentrate on sectarian violence, but a minority of the organization will continue to focus their efforts on engaging in terrorism. Individuals will shift. Membership in one camp does not preclude work in another.

There are clear differences between JI members over the timing of certain operations and strategies. For example, when Hambali was arrested in August 2003 he indicated that members were divided over the appropriate course of action. Some, including himself, were cognizant that the organization had suffered greatly in the past year and they needed to rebuild. Other members thought that the best course of action for the organization was to lash out with a wave of attacks in order to regain the initiative, boost their morale, and convince their constituency that they are still a viable force. Because JI is a small organization, serious ideological rifts would tear it apart. Operational disagreements are simply more likely than ideological factionalism at this time. If rifts do emerge in the organization, it would be more a manifestation of the difficulty of communication and coordination than the result of ideological or textual differences.

Informal ties and recruitment

There are contending views on what drives terrorist recruitment. Some studies focus on political factors; for instance some argue that individuals engage in violence because there are no legal means for them to redress their grievances. Other studies focus on economic factors, arguing that people experience relative depravity leading to frustration leading to aggression. Economic factors can be exacerbated by demographics, such as youth bulges in the population. Yet both of these explanations, which focus on the "push" towards joining militant groups are lacking. They may explain what makes these people angry and psychologically pre-disposed to violence, but they do not explain the actual process of joining a terrorist organization which is by its very nature elitist. The single most important determinant in terrorist recruitment is "pull," which is achieved through organizational and social networks.

JI is an elite organization and it is very selective in its membership. There is a potentially large pool of recruits for JI, and finding recruits is not a problem for the leadership. Their recruitment, however, is constrained by security considerations and the difficulties in providing training since, for the first time, regional security services are actively trying to penetrate JI cells.[25] Recruitment in such a commander–cadre based organization is based on personal ties; in this case through four central relationships: kinship, mosque, madrassa, and friendship. The commonality between them is that religious faith is the paramount trait that the JI leaders look for in their recruits.

The superb analysis of Jones and the ICG has concluded that these kinship ties, including marital ties, are the single most important determinant of membership in Jemaah Islamiyah.[26] Malaysian authorities have described JI as one hundred interconnected families. While an over-simplification, there is much truth to this statement. It is fascinating the degree to which JI has been based on familial Darul Islam relationships. In the example mentioned above of al Ghuraba, almost all of the 13 cell members have family ties to JI. The two Singaporeans are the sons of members of Jemaah Islamiyah and the Moro Islamic Liberation Front; in Malaysia, three of the five detained students' fathers are JI members.[27]

While there are no mosques that have been major epicenters of JI recruitment, the mosque remains a key recruitment conduit. JI "talent scouts" look for pious Muslims of a certain age who come not just to Friday prayers, but to prayers five times a day, every day. They are then invited to private "study sessions," in which they are slowly indoctrinated. This is a multi-stage process over the course of a year in which their commitment and religious understanding is tested and appraised. The mosque is important to understanding JI recruitment because religiosity is the paramount trait that JI leaders look for in their recruits.

The third network-based form of recruitment is through madrassa and other educational institutions, which are important for both the transmission of Salafi principles and recruitment.[28] Recruitment madrassas all have two commonalities: they were founded by Southeast Asian veterans of the anti-Soviet Mujahidin and/or founded by graduates of the al Mukmin madrassa in Ngruki, Solo, Indonesia.

Al Mukmin was founded in 1972 by Abu Bakar Ba'asyir and Abdullah Sungkar, the founders of Jemaah Islamiyah. The graduates of this school are a who's who of Southeast Asian terrorists.[29] Abu Bakar Ba'asyir and Abdullah Sungkar were arrested by the Suharto regime in 1972, and later fled to Malaysia while out on appeals, where they lived and preached openly for several decades and built up a large following of radical Indonesians, who had fled the Suharto regime, and radical Malays.[30] Even with Ba'asyir and Sungkar's flight to Malaysia in the 1980s, al Mukmin remained open, as it does to this day. The school has 1,900 students with plans to double in size with the construction of a girls' campus.

Indonesian intelligence and police officials are studying the entire network of graduates of Abu Bakar Ba'asyir's al Mukmin madrassa. In all, there is a network of some 60–100 madrassas that Indonesian security forces believe are centers of JI recruitment, most of which are run or staffed by Ngruki *alums* or veterans of the Afghan Mujahidin.[31] Established slowly and methodically, these madrassas include Mutaqin Jabarah in Central Java, Darul Syahadin, and the Madrassah Luqmanul Hakiem in Kelantan, Malaysia, and the Hidyatullah network throughout East Kalimantan and South Sulawesi, which is where many of the Bali bombers were hiding when they were arrested. Malaysian authorities have shut down the two JI-linked madrassas, Tarbiyah Luqmanul Hakiem in Johor, Malaysia, and Sekolah Menengah Arab Darul Anuar in Kota Baru. Madrassa-style recruitment also takes place further afield in schools in Pakistan, Yemen, Egypt, and in particular at one madrassa in Medina, Saudi Arabia. Characteristic of a command-cadre organization, Jemaah Islamiyah tries to provide livelihoods to its members, offering them employment in JI-controlled madrassas or companies.

Educational-based recruitment was not just centered on madrassas. Indeed, one aspect of JI that is so impressive is its ability to recruit across the board, irrespective of education or class. Recruits are not just students from the madrassas of the region, but young technical students and disenfranchised youth with few prospects. They are younger, angrier, and technically savvy. JI members pride themselves on being computer literate. JI members also include many technical faculty members, including architects, engineers, geo-physicists, chemists, and robotics engineers. JI has actively recruited in two leading technical institutes: University of Technology of Malaysia and Bandung Institute of Technology. JI's current leaders are divided among young radical firebrands from the madrassas (Zulkarnaen, Mustopha) and those with a technical-secular education (Dr. Azahari Husin, Noordin Mohammed Mop Top, Zulkifli Marzuki).

Finally, recruitment is often based on friendship with JI members and a desire to conform with the "in group." Friendship seems to be a very important variable in understanding the recruitment into JI's two paramilitary arms, the Laskar Jundullah and the Laskar Mujahidin. Membership in those organizations and participation in the jihad in the Malukus and Sulawesi was not the same as membership in JI, but it is clearly an important recruitment pool on which JI drew. "In-group conformity" is a very common phenomenon in terrorist organizations. The literature is rich with analysis based on small group dynamics, focusing on the pressure for conformity and consensus which tends to result in groupthink and a Manichean worldview; the socialization process that forges a sense of belonging to a community, and the way that the group becomes a surrogate family.[32]

Funding terrorism in Southeast Asia: what do social networks tell us?

While it is beyond the scope of this chapter to analyze the full extent of JI's funding and money laundering operations,[33] it is worth trying to explain how JI's social networks facilitate terrorist finance. To be sure, most of JI's operational funds come from external sources. Indonesian investigators of the Bali and Marriott bombings unequivocally stated that "Jemaah Islamiyah's jihad operations were funded by Al Qaeda."[34] The JI operations chief, Hambali, has revealed that JI depended on funds directly from Al Qaeda as many JI leaders were arrested and the organization fell into disarray. Of some $130,000 received through June 2003, Hambali allocated $45,000 to the Indonesian cell, including $15,000 to support the families of arrested JI members.[35] There are a number of other funding mechanisms in addition to money from al Qaeda, and the *zakat* and *infaq* that all members must pay. Chief among these is the use of social networks to facilitate skimming funds from Islamic charities and corporate entities.

Charities

Much of Jemaah Islamiyah's funding is thought to come from charities. As mentioned earlier, an estimated 15 to 20 percent of Islamic charity funds in Indonesia are diverted for Islamist purposes. In the Philippines during the 1990s it is estimated that as much as 50 to 60 percent of JI funds were siphoned off of charities.[36] The abuse of Saudi charities, especially the International Islamic Relief Organization (IIRO), which is part of the Muslim

World League – a fully Saudi state-funded organization whose assets were frozen by the US Treasury, the al Haramain Islamic Foundation, also based in Saudi Arabia, and the World Assembly of Muslim Youth[37] in Southeast Asia, has become a major point of diplomatic contention. Other Saudi-based charities have a lower profile in Southeast Asia, but they are still in operation.

Although most of the donations to Islamic charities go to legitimate social work (albeit work designed to win political support) such as mosque construction, NGOs, the construction of charities, cultural centers, and the production of translations of religious texts,[38] a significant amount of the money is diverted to terrorist and paramilitary activities. There is paltry oversight by the charities of how their funds are actually being used and allocated. In 2000 al Haramain signed a formal memorandum of understanding with the Indonesian Ministry of Religion that allowed it to finance educational institutions, including a Makassar *pesantren* called Darul Istiqamah al Haramain, al Irsyad, in the Central Java town of Salatiga, and the Gontor *pesantren* in East Java. But al Haramain's Makassar branch officer, a senior JI operative named Agus Dwikarna also used funds to finance his paramilitary group, the Laskar Jundullah – one of the JI's two paramilitary organizations.[39] Despite revelations by Omar al-Faruq that al Haramain was the primary conduit of al Qaeda funds into the region, it was not shut down until January 2004 when it was designated by the United States, Saudi Arabia, and the United Nations as a specially listed terrorist financier.[40] Though its offices were shut down, it soon re-opened under a new name and an al Haramain official continues to oversee the completion of the charity's new religious boarding school on the outskirts of Jakarta.[41]

Al Qaeda-linked charities were first established in Southeast Asia by Osama bin Laden's brother-in-law Mohammad Jammal Khalifa.[42] These included local NGOs, Islamic Wisdom Worldwide, and the Daw'l Immam al Shafee Center. The IIRO's activities have included establishing al Maktum University in Zamboanga, an orphanage and dispensary in Cotabato City, dispensaries and pharmacies in Zamboanga, including a floating dispensary that served remote coastal communities in Western Mindanao. It provided food and clothing to internally displaced people who fled war zones. In addition, IIRO funding went to schools and scholarships.[43] The IIRO asserted that it always did this, if not in cooperation with the government, at with least official approval.[44] All of these projects, though legitimate charitable works, were located in MILF zones or in urban population centers where the MILF was trying to make inroads as they began to focus on a political strategy and pursue an East Timor-like referendum process. "The IIRO which claims to be a relief institution, is being utilized by foreign extremists as a pipeline through which funding for the local extremists are being coursed through," a Philippine intelligence report noted.[45] An Abu Sayyaf defector acknowledged that "The IIRO was behind the construction of mosques, school buildings and other livelihood projects" but only "in areas penetrated, highly influenced and controlled by the Abu Sayyaf."[46] For example, in Tawi Tawi, the director of the IIRO branch office was Abdul Asmad, who was the Abu Sayyaf's intelligence chief before being killed on 10 June 1994. The report concludes: "Only 10 to 30 percent of the foreign funding goes to the legitimate relief and livelihood projects and the rest go to terrorist operations."[47]

Perhaps the most important charity established by Khalifa was the little-known International Relations and Information Center (IRIC) which was the primary funding mechanism for Khalid Sheik Mohammed, Ramzi Yousef, and Wali Khan Amin Shah's attempt to blow up 11 US jetliners in early 1995, in what was known as Oplan Bojinka. The charity was run by Abu Omar, Khalifa's brother-in-law, who was an Islamic student activist and supporter of the MILF at Mindanao State University when he first met Khalifa in the late 1980s. Unlike other charities, the IRIC had almost no humanitarian component; it was solely a front for terrorism.

In Malaysia, Hambali established a charity, Pertubuhan al Ehasan, in 1998 in order to fund jihad activities in the Malukus. The charity remained open until 2002 and raised a total of R500,000 (roughly $200,000).[48] The money went to purchasing weapons, training, clothing, and feeding recruits for the jihad in the Malukus and Poso, Indonesia in which some 9,000 people were killed. Much of the money came from donors within Malaysia, though foreign donors were solicited through the internet. It is not clear if the donors were aware that their money went to militant activities, as they were told that their money went to humanitarian causes in the Malukus.

KOMPAK and MERC

In Indonesia, JI and al Qaeda leaders assumed leadership positions at charities or formed alliances with important Saudi-backed charities, including Komite Penanggulangan Krisis (KOMPAK) and Medical Emergency Relief Charity (MERC). KOMPAK, an independent arm of the Dewan Dakwah Islam Indonesia (DDII), was founded on 1 August 1998 to address the humanitarian needs that arose from the sectarian conflict that erupted in the Maluku Islands in 1998.[49] KOMPAK officials, while acknowledging that they operate in regions torn by sectarian conflict (Aceh, Poso, Malukus, and Bangunan Beton Sumatra), assert they are there to alleviate the crises and provide necessary relief. By KOMPAK's own admission, between 1998 and 2001, they had some 8 billion Indonesia Rupiah (Rp) in disbursements.

While KOMPAK has denied links to "jihad activities,"[50] there is considerable evidence that KOMPAK played a very important role in supporting sectarian conflict in the Malukus and Poso while channeling money from al Qaeda to these causes. Even their humanitarian work – medicine and food distribution – supported the Muslim paramilitaries, freeing up their own resources for weapons and salaries. One KOMPAK official, Imam Hanafi, was in Mindanao buying weapons in March 2000 for the jihad in Ambon, while another JI member, Suryadi Mas'uf had made seven trips to the southern Philippines to purchase weapons with money from KOMPAK.[51]

Many KOMPAK officials have been tied to terrorism themselves. At least four of its 13 provincial representative officers were senior members of Jemaah Islamiya. Aris Munandar, one of Abu Bakar Ba'asyir's top lieutenants (suspected of purchasing much of the explosives for the bombings across the region on the anniversary of 11 September) was the head of KOMPAK's Central Java bureau. Munandar had been the head of Dewan Dakwah for Central Java and an original founder of KOMPAK. He was also a representative of the Jakarta branch of the Abu Dhabi-based charity Darul Birri. Munandar was labeled a terrorist financier by the US Department of the Treasury on 5 September 2003, one of 20 individuals designated terrorist financiers, and one of the few who had not yet been arrested; though he is currently being watched by Indonesian authorities.

The former chairman of KOMPAK's South Sulawesi office was Agus Dwikarna, and the head of the Jakarta office was Tamsil Linrung. Linrung, a member of the DDII and the former treasurer of the National Mandate Party (PAN) before quitting the post in January 2002, was identified by Omar al-Faruq as a JI operative and a participant in the three Rabitatul Mujahidin meetings in Malaysia from 1999 to 2000.[52] Dwikarna was the head of a group called the Committee to Implement Sharia in South Sulawesi and the number four official in Abu Bakar Ba'asyir's overt civil society organization, the Mujahidin Council of Indonesia (MMI). He established one of the JI's two paramilitary organizations, the Laskar Jundullah, and was arrested at Manila's international airport in March 2002 carrying C4 explosives in his suitcase.[53] When asked about the explosives, the Secretary of KOMPAK stated, "What he does outside of KOMPAK is not our responsibility."[54] Arguing that the provincial representatives were simply volunteers and not paid staff, he contended that KOMPAK itself had no link to militant activities. When asked how they can be sure that none of their money goes to the Laskar Mujahidin or the Laskar Jundullah, KOMPAK's secretary general curtly replied, "We have no link to them."[55]

Yet, KOMPAK also produced propaganda and recruitment videos for Dwikarna's paramilitary group the Laskar Jundullah and Abu Jibril's Laskar Mujahidin, emphasizing both their military strength and sense of Muslim persecution.[56] The videos are highly graphic and one sided, portraying the Muslim communities being victimized by Christian vigilantes, and small groups of poorly armed Muslim's fighting back. Although the KOMPAK videos do show the organization distributing food aid to beleaguered refugees, the context of the documentaries is highly biased. The highly graphic footage conveys a sense of brutality and utter victimization, justifying self defense. The narration justifies fighting in "self defense." Several of the videos are very professional in their footage, music, and with little narration. Moreover, a number of them viewed by the author were clearly produced by KOMPAK, with their logo on the screen throughout.

Aris Munandar's name appears in the credits of at least one of them as the video's producer.

The Medical Emergency Relief Charity (MERC) was established on 14 August 1999 also as a result of sectarian fighting.[57] They now have 12 offices in Indonesia, concentrated in the regions most directly affected by sectarian violence (Sulawesi, Malukus and Kalimintan). In 2000–2001, MERC produced two well-publicized jihadi videos for fund-raising purposes.[58] While MERC members were not implicated to the degree that KOMPAK was[59] in directly supporting Laskar Jundullah and Laskar Mujahidin paramilitary operations in the Malukus and Central Sulawesi, its one-sided approach to the Malukus conflict, as well as the actions of some individual members raised suspicions. A senior MERC official Haffiz, for example, was responsible for bailing a senior al Qaeda operative, Omar al-Faruq, out of jail when he was first arrested in Sulawesi for an immigration violation. MERC was very active in post-Tsunami relief, and has dispatched teams to work in Iraq.

Shell companies

The second way that JI funds itself through social networks is through front and shell companies. JI operatives established corporate entities, which with a minimum amount of capital investment, no substance or commercial purpose, and generating few if any profits, served the primary purpose of purchasing materials or cloaking other aspects of terrorist operations. Others were developed with the primary purpose of either revenue generation or commingling laundered money with revenue derived from legitimate business undertakings.[60] Examples of front companies include Konsojaya, a trading company established in 1994, that ostensibly exported Malaysian palm oil to Afghanistan and imported honey from Sudan and Yemen, but really played an important role financing and purchasing chemicals for Ramzi Yousef and Khalid Sheikh Mohammed's Oplan Bojinka. Another example would be Green Laboratory Medicine, a Malaysian-based company that was used to procure ammonium nitrate and other chemicals for planned bombings. We now know that Green Laboratory was the heart of the nascent attempt by al Qaeda to manufacture anthrax.[61]

Front companies were not the only businesses established by Jemaah Islamiyah. There are also cases in which JI members established businesses, received contracts and businesses from JI supporters, and then plowed the proceeds back into the organization. According to the Singapore Government's *White Paper*, "All JI-run businesses had to contribute 10% of their total earnings to the group. This money was to be channeled into the JI's special fund called *Infaq Fisbilillah* (Contributions for the Islamic cause or jihad fund)."[62] The *Infaq Fisbilillah* fund was controlled by the JI chief of operations, Hambali, and used to support the cost of travel and training of members to al Qaeda camps in Afghanistan and MILF camps, to purchase arms and explosives and subsidize JI-run madrassas. Examples of profit-oriented firms would include MNZ Associates, al Risalah Trading Company, Gulf Shores Sdn. Bhd., and Shafatex Niaga.

Social networks are important to understanding these firms in several different ways.

First, many of these companies had a close network of family members and friends on their board of directors. Many of the companies had overlapping board membership. A good example of this is Gulf Shores Sdn. Bhd., a general contractor and construction material supplier based in Johor Baru, Malaysia which was owned by JI members Abdul Nassir bin Anwarul and Amran bin Mansour, and run by Abdul's sister-in-law, Aliza Abas. Her sister is the wife of Mukhlas, the former head of Mantiqi One who was tried and convicted in Indonesia for masterminding the Bali plot. Aliza is also the sister of Hashim Abas, the former head of Mantiqi Three. Gulf Shores' former owner Abdul Nassir has been arrested under the Internal Security Act, along with his two brothers.

Second, JI began to invest in a network of nursery schools, kindergartens, orphanages, and primary/secondary schools across Southeast Asia. The brainchild of Zubair, a 28-year-old Malaysian who was recruited into al Qaeda while a student in Karachi, Pakistan, the schools were used to launder money for al Qaeda. Aliran Salam is one such example. It was established on 13 April 1996 as a private Selangor-based kindergarten and nursery. The most important example of this was the Om al Qura Foundation's school in Cambodia which addressed the dire needs of the country's aggrieved Muslim Cham population. These educational companies were also means to create a broader community.

Third, several companies are used to create propaganda and literature to promote their worldview, including Front Line Publishers and the Hidyatullah press based in Jogyakarta, which is run by Irfan S. Awwas, the brother of detained JI leader Abu Jibril, Abu Bakar Ba'asyir's aide, and the Director of the MMI.

Additional methods

There are several other ways that JI has funded itself by relying on social networks. Petty crime is one. According to the testimony of Mohammed Nassir bin Abbas, the former head of Mantiqi Three until his arrest during the trial of Ali Gufron [Mukhlas], Ba'asyir was frequently quizzed by his students whether computer hacking was Islamic. Justifying online fraud, Ba'asyir replied, "You can take their blood, then why not take their property?"[63] There is a long tradition of "*Fa'I*," in Southeast Asia, using money from crime to support religious causes. But, more importantly, ideological purists will often use criminals or find criminals who have discovered a religious calling and are trying to atone for sins. Sidney Jones writes of the close ties between jihadists and *preman*, thugs and common criminals.[64]

Mukhlas wrote in his treatise on the Bali bombing that becoming a muja-hideen and joining a jihad was always seen as a good way for sinners to repent, and thus criminals were actively courted. In the treatise he recounted a story in which he was criticized by a Muslim preacher for having a former *preman* as his commander of Laskar Mujahidin in the Malukus: "How can you call this a holy war when your commander is an ex-thug?" Mukhlas merely replied, "So where are your forces and why don't you become a com-mander instead of just sitting there counting your prayer beads."[65] Again, JI has relied on a close community for new members. Likewise, JI has relied on close networks of gem and gold traders with close familial ties to East Africa and South Asia to finance their operations. As these funding mechanisms are all based on close social networks and communities they will be very difficult to shut down and monitor, despite the regulatory efforts of states.

Conclusion

How has the post-Bali environment and war on terror affected the JI organi-zation? Jemaah Islamiyah has been severely degraded in more than five years of counter-terrorist operations. The Bali investigations, in particular, have led to a far greater understanding of how the network operates and a better com-prehension of their command and control structure, leading to subsequent arrests. Across Southeast Asia, more than 300 people have been arrested, including much of the organization's leadership and Hambali, who was arrested in Thailand in August 2003. Though estimates on the size of JI vary from around 500 to several thousand, it is not a large organization and, given the rate of arrests, JI's survival is in doubt. Although there are a number of leading operatives still at large, including those with operational experience and bomb-making know-how, many of their madrassas are being monitored and they are less able to send their recruits abroad for advanced training.

That said, despite being on the run, JI has been able to perpetrate three major terrorist attacks in Indonesia since the Bali bombing of October 2002: the JW Marriott in Jakarta (August 2003), the Australian Embassy (September 2004), and Bali (October 2005). These attacks have been carried out at roughly one-year intervals, suggesting that they do not have the resources, manpower or capabilities to perpetrate attacks at a faster rate. One JI member who was arrested following the September 2004 bombing of the Australian Embassy has stated that Dr. Azahari's goal is to be able to increase the rate of attacks to every six months. To date there is no indication that JI has the capability to do this. JI's leaders, however, are highly charis-matic and have been able to successfully recruit people for six separate suicide bombings. Other detained JI members have admitted that they were recruited to engage in suicide operations.

Following the October 2005 Bali attacks, Indonesian police suggested that the perpetrators were a "new group": "A new generation means that they are not known by the old group."[66] Yet, this is not a new group, a distinct organization, with its own command system, hierarchy, and goals. JI is just a very horizontal and exceptionally compartmentalized organization. It has a very rigid cell structure that places paramount importance on operational security. Of course leaders do not know who cell members are. That is the point of a cellular-based organization; so that an arrest can never lead police to more than a handful of other members. These cell members often form their own organizations (KOMPAK in Ambon, for example) that simply have a more local geographical range of operations and activities. But that does not mean that they are completely autonomous or that they are working at odds against JI's goals. Moreover, we have to understand that when Indonesian officials say that this is a new organization, we have to understand the political realities.

In September 2004, newly elected president Susilo Bambang Yudhoyono (SBY) announced that he would ban JI only after he had proof that the organization exists. Under the current law, membership within JI is technically not illegal, and Indonesian officials have hidden behind ludicrous claims that since JI is not registered, it cannot be banned, nor can they claim that it is pointless to ban something that "is not a formal organization with card-carrying members." There is intense international pressure on the Indonesian government to ban JI, but no politician in the world's largest Muslim community has the political courage to ban an organization that simply translates as "Islamic community," and many Muslims do not believe really exists. If SBY is going to ban any organization, it cannot be called "Jemaah Islamiyah," but must be a new "fringe group."

Looking to the future, how will JI try to regroup? The arrest of a JI cell in Karachi, Pakistan is telling. The cell was comprised of the siblings or children of senior JI members. They were not engaged in military training, nor had they joined up with Taliban remnants, nor were they fighting the Americans in the streets of Fallujah. They were there for advanced religious training. Though we often denigrate the terrorists for not knowing their religion, the senior leadership is deeply steeped in the Koran. The writings and analysis of Mukhlas and others, analyzed by US-based religious scholars, are surprisingly sophisticated. We should expect JI to focus on religious indoctrination and spiritual purification; all overt and legal.

The second direction for JI will be to provoke sectarian conflict. This is what JI and its leaders were consumed with in 1998–2000 when they established the two separate paramilitaries. This was an important tool for JI in indoctrinating its members, giving them a sense that they were defending their religion, and reinforcing their Manichean view of the world. In 2004 a number of bombings, attacks, and assassinations occurred which must be seen as an attempt to break the uneasy truce that has held since the negotiation of the Malino Accords in 2002. In March 2005, Indonesian police raided an Islamist militant safe house and seized a cache of 95 improvised explosive devices and ammunition; they are bracing for a new wave of sectarian conflicts. On 24 April 2005 another sectarian conflict flared in Mamasa, Sulawesi.

A gang of JI members and other Muslim "Kommandos" torched houses in a Christian community, killing six. The arrest of a suspect was followed by two bombings in April in Poso. Two bombs were detonated in Tentana, Sulawesi, on 28 May 2005, killing 22 and wounding 40. At the same time sectarian conflicts spread in the Malukus. There are also attempts to provoke sectarian strife in Mindanao and there is some alarm that the conflict in Southern Thailand is spiraling out of control and that JI will try to take advantage of it, as they did in the Malukus and Sulawesi in 1998.

When assessing JI's future direction, it is important to keep in mind that JI has a very long-term strategic view. As in the philosophical underpinnings of al Qaeda, there is no shame to strategic retreats. Indeed there is a Koranic precedent: the Prophet Mohammad, himself, had to retreat from Mecca to Medina where he regrouped, recruited, trained, and only then went on to fight the enemies of Islam. The *PUPJI* has a 30 year time-frame for jihad, and it outlines a schema for guerilla war: "View, analyze and explore all aspects of life in the enemy's body and in the environment," "View carefully and honestly all our potential strengths and effective powers we possess," and "Determine points of target at the enemy and the environment to be handled in relation with our goals." While JI may have weakened, the complex organization appears resilient, and it remains a threat to Southeast Asian security.

Notes

1 J. Arquilla, D. Ronfeldt, and M. Zanini, "Networks, Netwar and Information-Age Terrorism," *International Organization*, Ian O. Lesser, Bruce Hoffman, John Arquilla, David Ronfeldt, and Michael Zanini (eds.) *Countering the New Terrorism*, Washington: RAND Corporation, 1999, p. 49.
2 Ibid., p. 51.
3 Ibid., p. 61.
4 Ibid., p. 51.
5 Ibid., p. 51.
6 Ibid.
7 P. J. Smith, "Transnational Terrorism and the Al Qaeda Model: Confronting New Realities," *Parameters*, 2002, vol. 32, pp. 33–46.
8 This is a very important point. Contacts between JI and the LeT keep appearing in the course of research on JI. The LeT has evolved from an ethno-nationalist group to a group much more committed to the cause of international Islamic terrorism. In many ways, security experts warn that the LeT is poised to replace al Qaeda as a truly global organization. This truly needs more study. Not only were members of the al Ghuraba cell studying in LeT madrassas, but several fought with the Kashmiri militant group, and were trained in their camps, or in Al Qaeda camps in Afghanistan with other LeT cadres. E. Nakashima, "Indonesian Militants 'Keep Regenerating,' " *Washington Post*, 25 March 2004. Ministry of Home Affairs, "Singapore Government Press Statement on the Detention of 2 Singaporean Members of the Jemaah Islamiyah Karachi Cell," 18 December 2003.
9 Nakashima, "Indonesian Militants 'Keep Regenerating.' "
10 Ministry of Home Affairs, "Singapore Government Press Statement."
11 Nakashima, "Indonesian Militants 'Keep Regenerating.' "

12 R. Hudson, *The Psychology and Sociology of Terrorism*, Library of Congress Federal Research Division, 2000, pp. 20–55. Online. Available HTTP: <http://web.archive.org/web/20021209181134/http://www.loc.gov/rr/frd/Sociology-Psychology+of+Terrorism.htm> (accessed 9 December 2002)

13 "The MMI is an institution where a lot of people from a lot of Muslim groups including the NU [Nahdlatul Ulama] and Muhammadiyah gather at one table to discuss how to get our vision of *sharia* implemented into national laws. . . . The long-term strategy is to get Indonesia 100 percent based on *sharia*. As long as Muslims are the majority, the country should be ruled by *sharia*." Interview with Abu Bakar Ba'asyir, Ngruki, Solo, 11 June 2002.

14 Baden Intelijen Negara, "Interrogation Report of Omar al-Faruq," Jakarta, June 2002.

15 KOMPAK officials, while acknowledging that they operate in regions struck by sectarian conflict (Aceh, Poso, Malukus, and Bangunan Beton Sumatra), assert they are there to alleviate the crises and provide necessary relief. They denied any links to "jihad activities." Interview with Dr. H. Asep R. Jayanegara, Secretary, Komite Penanggulangan Krisis, Dewan Dakwah Islam Indonesia, Jakarta, 8 January 2003.

16 Badan Intelijen Nasional (BIN) Interrogation Report of Omar al-Faruq, June 2002. The office was in Makassar, Sulawesi. Also see R. Ratnesar, "Confessions of an Al Qaeda Terrorist," *Time*, 23 September 2003, pp. 34–41.

17 Indonesian National Police, "Interrogation of Mohammad Nasir bin Abbas," Jakarta, 18 April 2003.

18 Ibid.

19 Ibid.

20 Canadian High Commission, Malaysia, "RE: Mohammed Mansour Jabarah," 13 May 2002.

21 Indonesian National Police, "Interrogation of Mohammad Nasir bin Abbas," Jakarta, 18 April 2003.

22 BBC Transcript, Tape 2, p. 20.

23 For more on these organizational structures, see J. Stern, *Terror in the Name of God: Why Religious Militants Kill*, New York: HarperCollins, 2003, pp. 141–145.

24 International Crisis Group, *Indonesia Backgrounder: Jihad in Central Sulawesi*, 3 February 2004.

25 Interview with a senior Indonesian National Police intelligence official, Jakarta, 10 March 2003.

26 International Crisis Group, *Jemaah Islamiyah in Southeast Asia: Damaged But Still Dangerous*, 26 August 2003; ICG, *Indonesia Backgrounder: Jihad in Central Sulawesi*, 3 February 2004. For more on the history of JI see Z. Abuza, *Militant Islam in Southeast Asia: Crucible of Terror*, Boulder, CO: Lynne Rienner, 2003.

27 Nakashima, "Indonesian Militants 'Keep Regenerating.' "

28 The main centers included: Tarbiyah Luqmanul Hakiem school, Johor, Malaysia; Sekolah Menengah Arab Darul Anuar, Kota Baru, Malaysia; Pesentren Hidayatullah in Balikpapan, Kalimantan; al Islam, East Java, Indonesia; Pesentren Darul Aman, Gombara, Ujung Pandang; Laskar Jihad's schools around Yogyakarta; Burana Islamic School.

29 The two met when they were both leaders of the Geragan Pemuda Islam Indonesia, an Islamic youth movement. In 1972, Abu Bakar Ba'asyir and Abdullah Sungkar, a fellow cleric, established an Islamic boarding school in Solo, al Mukmin. The land was donated by Kiai Haji Abu Amman an *ulama* in Solo who was notable in the 1960s for his fervor to create an Islamic state. The school which opened with 30 students grew rapidly and in 1976 they moved to a four hectare compound outside of the city; it now has 1,900 students, with plans to

expand. For more on al Mukmin, see B. Bektiati, I. Rosyid, and L.N. Idayanie, "Exclusive and Secretive," *Tempo*, 29 January to 4 February 2002, no. 21.

30 Their escape and resettlement was arranged by Abdul Wahid Kadungga, a radical Muslim who had fled to Europe in 1971 and formed the Muslim Youth Association of Europe, which put him into close contact with Muslim leaders from around the world, and especially the Muslim Brotherhood. The preachers lived in a small town on the Malacca Straight that had a ferry service to Indonesia and heavy flows of traffic between the two states. The two served as a way station for Indonesians and Malaysians who were on their way to Afghanistan and Pakistan to study and fight the Soviets or train in one of the 40 al Qaeda camps that were established in the late 1990s. Sungkar traveled to Pakistan and the Afghan border region in the early 1990s where he met Bin Laden and other senior al Qaeda members, and where he pledged *bayat*, effectively absorbing his movement into al Qaeda.

31 Interview with a senior Indonesian National Police intelligence official, Jakarta, 10 March 2003.

32 For more on this phenomenon see, Hudson, *The Psychology and Sociology of Terrorism*, pp. 20–55. Also S. Atran, "Mishandling Suicide Terrorism," *The Washington Quarterly* vol. 27, no. 3, pp. 67–90.

33 For more see Z. Abuza, *Funding Terrorism in Southeast Asia: The Financial Network of Al Qaeda and Jemaah Islamiyah*, NBR Analysis, 2003, vol. 14, no. 5.

34 S. Elegant and J. Tedjaskmana, "The Jihadis' Tale," *Time Asian Edition*, 27 January 2002.

35 S. Elegant, "The Terrorist Talks," Time Asian Edition, 5 October 2003.

36 Interview with a Major of the Intelligence Service, Armed Forces of the Philippines (IS-AFP), Camp Aguinaldo, Quezon City, 24 January 2001; Interview with a Colonel in Philippine National Police (PNP) Intelligence, Manila, 27 June 2002.

37 The President of the World Assembly of Muslim Youth is Sheikh Saleh al-Sheikh, the Saudi Minister of Islamic Affairs. He is also the "superintendent of all foundation activities for Al Haramain. M. Levitt, 'Combating Terrorist Financing, Despite the Saudis,' Washington Institute for Near East Policy, Policy Watch no. 673, 1 November 2002.

38 The Saudi Arabian Religious Affairs Office attached to its embassy in Jakarta, for example, translates religious texts into Indonesian; distributing some one million texts annually.

39 Al Faruq organized training for the Laskar Jundullah at Wafa Humanitarian Organization facilities and then at the Hidyatullah Islamic school both in Balikpapen, Kalimantan.

40 For example, al Haramain moved its office from a large villa on the outskirts of Jakarta, to a smaller office nearby. See, J. Perlez, "Saudis Quietly Promote Strict Islam in Indonesia," *New York Times*, 4 July 2003.

41 Ibid.

42 Starting in 1985, Khalifa ran the Peshwar office of the Saudi Muslim World League, where he was active in sending recruits to join the Mujahidin. He had close ties to two of Bin Laden's top financiers, Wael Hamza Jalaidin and Yasin al Qadi, who was the head of the Muwafaq Foundation that was designated by both the Saudis and the Americans as a terrorist front. Muwafaq, which had a $20 million endowment, was found to have sent millions of dollars to al Qaeda in the 1990s before it was shut down. Wael Hamza Jalaidin, a 45-year-old Saudi businessman, was described by US intelligence officials as a founding member of al Qaeda, and a key financial backer of bin Laden. He was designated as a terrorist funder by the US Government in September 2002. He sits on the board of the Pakistani-based charity Rabita Trust, also accused by the US as a terrorist funder and supporter of al Qaeda. The Saudi Arabian government announced in 2001, that Jalaidin cut ties with Osama bin Laden in 1992. M. Levitt, "Saudi

Financial Counter-Terrorism Measures (Part II): Smokescreen or Substance," Washington Institute for Near East Policy, Policy Watch no. 687, 10 December 2002; D. Frantz, "Front Companies Said to Keep Financing Terrorists," *New York Times*, 19 September 2002; Levitt, "The Political Economy of Middle East Terrorism," p. 51; Gerth and Miller, "Threats and Responses: The Money Trail."

43 The IIRO was established in 1978 in Saudi Arabia as a non-governmental humanitarian organization. It has more than 30 offices, and its activities cover more than 75 countries in different parts of the world. It was used extensively by Saudi Arabian intelligence services to channel Saudi, American, and Gulf-state funding to the Afghan Mujahidin from 1979 to 1989.

44 Dr. A. K. Basha, "Largest Islamic Relief Organization Maligned," Letter to the Editor, *Philippine Daily Inquirer*, 22 August 2000.

45 C. Herrera, "Bin Laden Funds Abu Sayyaf Through Muslim Relief Group," *Philippine Daily Inquirer*, 9 August 2000.

46 Ibid.

47 Ibid.

48 Associated Press, "Terror Suspects Used Donations to Fund Bombings, Train Islamic Extremists," 1 January 2003.

49 The Dewan Dakwah is one of Indonesia's most important Islamic social organizations that was founded in February 1967 by Muhammad Nasir, the first Prime Minister of the Republic of Indonesia. The group, comprised of hard-core Islamists from the Muhammadiyah, is committed to the implementation of sharia, or Islamic law.

50 Interview with Dr. H. Asep R. Jayanegara, Secretary, Komite Penanggulangan Krisis, Dewan Dakwah Islam Indonesia, Jakarta, 8 January 2003.

51 International Crisis Group, *Jemaah Islamiyah in Southeast Asia: Damaged but Still Dangerous*, ICG Asia Report no. 63, August 2003, p. 20.

52 Ratnesar, "Confessions of an Al Qaeda Terrorist," Badan Intelijen Negara, Interrogation Report of Omar al-Faruq.

53 Dwikarna asserted that he was framed. "I Don't Have a History of Violence," interview with Agus Dwikarna, *Tempo*, 6 January 2003, pp. 38–41; "Suspected Terrorists Arrested at NAIA," *Philippine Daily Inquirer*, 15 March 2002; "Jakarta Asks Manila to Clarify Arrests," *Philippine Daily Inquirer*, 17 March 2002.

54 Interview with Dr. H. Asep R. Jayanegara.

55 Ibid.

56 Dwikarna was also the head of the Dewan Dakwa Islam Indonesia, South Sulawesi branch. Dewan Dakwah founded KOMPAK. KOMPAK had very close ties with the Saudi charity MERC. Omar al-Faruq admitted to sending large amounts of aid through KOMPAK to Ambon and Poso. The funding of such video production was seen also in Bosnia. The charity Benevolence International Foundation (whose office in Chicago was raided in December 2001 by US Government authorities), also funded the production of such propaganda videos. In March 2002, its Bosnian office was investigated for missing funds. M. Levitt, "The Political Economy of Middle East Terrorism," p. 58.

57 MERC website. Online. Available HTTP: <http://web.archive.org/web/20041027094523/http://www.mer-c.org/background.htm> (accessed 27 October 2004).

58 A communications division of the charity, Studio MERC, produced the two videos: "Pasir Hitum Teluk Galela" ("The Black Sand of Galela Bay") and "Dan Kesaksian Pun Menangis" ("And the Witnessing Despite the Crying"). Both are available from the MERC website. Online. Available HTTP : <http://web.archive.org/web/20040721081633/http://www.mer-c.org/vcd_01.htm> (accessed 21 July 2004).

59 For its part, KOMPAK, a charitable relief agency affiliated with the Dewan

Dakwah Islam Indonesia, has maintained a very low profile in the Achnese relief efforts. KOMPAK was also founded in 1999 as a result of the sectarian bloodletting. It was actively engaged in supporting JI's two paramilitaries; three of KOMPAK's 13 branch officers were senior JI officials who were able to skim funds earmarked for humanitarian purposes to paramilitary activities. KOMPAK also produced a number of jihadi videos for fundraising and recruitment purposes. KOMPAK was an executor agency for several Saudi charities including al Haramain and the IIRO, which Omar al-Faruq, a senior al Qaeda operative has acknowledged were the key conduits of al Qaeda funds into Southeast Asia. KOMPAK's relief efforts for Aceh have been conducted out of the Bandung field office.

60 Financial Action Task Force on Money Laundering, *Report on Money Laundering Typologies, 2002–2003*, 14 February 2003, 3.
61 C. Simpson, "US Seeks Access to Malaysian Al Qaeda Suspect," *Chicago Tribune*, 7 December 2003.
62 Ministry of Home Affairs, *White Paper: The Jemaah Islamiyah Arrests and the Treat of Terrorism*, Singapore, 2003, p. 6.
63 C. Munro, "Muklas Confessed to Bali, Court Told," *The Age*, 23 July 2003.
64 International Crisis Group, *Jemaah Islamiyah in Southeast Asia: Damaged but Still Dangerous*, pp. 24–25.
65 A. Gufron (Mukhlas), *Jihad Bom Bali*, Unpublished Manuscript, April 2003.
66 I Made Mangku Pastika cited in "Bali Bomb Intelligence Bungled: report," *The Age*, 7 October 2005.

Part II

The financial organization of terrorism

The raising and movement of funds

5 Terrorism, charities, and diasporas

Contrasting the fundraising practices of Hamas and al Qaeda among Muslims in Europe[1]

Jeroen Gunning

Since 11 September, links between "Islamic charities" in the West and organizations categorized as "terrorist" in the Middle East have come under intense scrutiny. Dozens of charities with alleged ties to al Qaeda have had their assets frozen in an unprecedented international clampdown. Most prominently, family members of the 11 September victims have sued six charities and their subsidiaries in a $116 trillion lawsuit for their alleged role in financing the 11 September attacks.[2]

The allegation that those involved in political violence use charities, or more broadly non-profit organizations, to raise or channel money is not new. The Provisional Irish Republican Army, the Palestine Liberation Organization, Hamas, Hezbollah, the Tamil Tigers, and others have been similarly accused.[3] The notion of fighting "terrorism" by targeting charities believed to be channeling funds to those perpetrating terroristic acts is similarly well established. What distinguishes the current situation from previous ones is the increased commitment of the international community, as embodied in United Nations Security Council 1373, which demands that Member States "prevent and suppress the financing of terrorist acts," and the increased use of legally binding lists to blacklist accused organizations and charities.[4]

What further distinguishes the current situation is the apparently exclusive focus of the international community on "Islamic charities," defined as charities involving a predominance of Muslims in staff and recipients,[5] and specifically on Islamic charities affiliated with two groups: al Qaeda and the Palestinian resistance movement Hamas. Both the Bank of England's "Consolidated List of Financial Sanctions Targets in the UK" and the European Union's "List of Persons and Entities Subject to Financial Sanctions" included, at the time of writing, some 20 charities thought to be affiliated with al Qaeda and affiliates (the number fluctuates somewhat depending on how one delineates a "charity"), and two with alleged links to Hamas.[6] No other charities were listed in relation to non-state "terrorist-designated" organizations – even though both lists included both non-Muslim and other Muslim entities.[7]

Al Qaeda's inclusion on the list of those using charitable "fronts" is not surprising given claims by terrorism experts and intelligence services that "the most important source of al-Qaeda's money is its continuous fundraising efforts" through a worldwide charitable network.[8] The inclusion of Hamas is similarly predictable given the widespread belief among intelligence services that the organization raises much of its funding through charitable "fronts" in the West.[9] Even the fact that only Islamic charities with a predominantly Islamist disposition – where "Islamist" refers to the political ideology that advocates Islam as the blueprint for political society – are listed is predictable, given that an Islamist organization attacked the United States and thereby triggered the "war on terror."

Closer observation, however, raises the serious question of why, if the abuse of charities is so widespread, so few charities have been found guilty of funding terrorism. When considering Islamic charities registered in Europe (as opposed to those operating internationally from non-European countries, such as Saudi Arabia, Somalia, or Pakistan), the divergence between the view that al Qaeda and Hamas raise much of their "resistance" funds through European-based Islamic charities and the actual number of charities identified by European governments raises questions about the true extent of the use of charities by targeted organizations. Narrowing our focus to the United Kingdom (or, more precisely, England and Wales)[10] and the Netherlands – two key European states that have been regularly linked with al Qaeda and Hamas fundraising activities[11] – we find that only two charities have been found guilty of funding al Qaeda, only four of having trustees with links to al Qaeda, and only one of funding Hamas. Of these, all charities found guilty of funding terrorism are registered in the Netherlands.[12] This disjuncture is particularly striking when evaluating the claim that al Qaeda has infiltrated one-fifth of all Islamic charities[13] – which, even if we limit ourselves to the jurisdictions of England and Wales and the Netherlands, would amount to some 2,000 charities (if the rough estimate that there are in the order of 10,000 Islamic charities in these two jurisdictions is correct).[14]

Contrary to this expectation, only one Europe-based charity, admittedly with various national branches, has been found guilty of funding Hamas's resistance wing.[15] This low figure, coupled with the fact that the accusations against this charity appear to revolve around providing money to the relatives of suicide operations rather than funding the armed struggle directly,[16] calls into question the validity of the claim that Hamas raises substantial amounts of capital for its resistance activities (as opposed to its charitable network) through charitable fronts.

Though the number of successful court cases and, in the case of the UK, Charity Commission investigations is of course not necessarily the same as the number of charities actually involved in such fundraising, it serves as a proxy on the basis of which one can arguably predict at least the order of magnitude of the number of charities involved. In addition, despite intense international scrutiny, the number of collapsed court cases or "unsuccessful" Charity Commission investigations is of the same order of magnitude and the number of these cases has not been dramatically affected by the relaxation of rules governing the use of evidence gathered by intelligence services in court.

If this proxy is acceptable, two key discrepancies need to be addressed. First, the number of charities accused of funding either al Qaeda or the resistance wing of Hamas and the number of charities expected to do so by intelligence analysts diverge. Second, there is a discrepancy between the significantly larger number of charities accused of funding al Qaeda and the smaller number of charities accused of funding the resistance activities of Hamas. In addition, there is a discrepancy between the nature of the claims against the al Qaeda and Hamas affiliates. In order to account for these discrepancies, we must take into account the ideological, sociological, organizational, and historical contexts of al Qaeda and Hamas and consider them in relationship to the development of Muslim political activism in Europe.

On the basis of publicly available evidence, al Qaeda and Hamas appear to rely less on Western-based charities to fund their violent activities than is typically believed. Furthermore, the relationship between a violent organization and sympathetic charities is not uniform but dependent on the organization's ideology, self-image, historical development, and the nature of its relationship with the larger community or society it claims to represent. In the case of Hamas, these factors discourage the redirection of funds to anything other than officially stated, usually humanitarian, ends – although this is not to say it does not occur. Because funding for political resistance is readily available from other sources, Hamas furthermore has no pressing need to pursue this path.

In the case of al Qaeda, its ideology, self-image, and historical development all fail to discourage abuse of charities for the redirection of funds. As such, one would expect al Qaeda to use charitable fronts extensively. However, the relative scarcity of charities with proven links to al Qaeda in Europe can be explained by the, until now, relative incompatibility between al Qaeda's ideology and methods and the life experience, practices, and beliefs currently found among the majority of Europe's Muslims – thus rendering the option of fundraising through charities too uneconomical to compete successfully with other available sources of finance.

Regarding terminology and the definition of terrorism

The absence of an internationally agreed upon definition of "terrorism" poses serious problems for delineating what constitutes "financing terrorism." According to Article 2.1 of the International Convention for the Suppression of the Financing of Terrorism, a person commits a punishable offence "if that person by any means, directly or indirectly, unlawfully and wilfully, provides or collects funds with the intention that they should be used or in the knowledge that they are to be used, in full or in part, in order to carry out [terrorist activities]."[17]

Problems arise not only from the fact that terrorism is a contested concept but also from the political use of the term. Because current international practice is to designate an entire organization as "terrorist" and to make all dealings with that organization illegal, it becomes impossible to distinguish between terrorist activities on the one hand and resistance activities carried out according to the Geneva Convention or humanitarian activities in support of a suffering population on the other. The consequences of this unresolved problem will become more evident in the course of the following discussion. To avoid this problem, I will reserve the term "terrorist" to denote solely acts of political violence (and not organizations perpetrating them) aimed at terrorizing civilians for the purpose of influencing a third party.

Organizational differences between al Qaeda and Hamas

Though al Qaeda and Hamas are sometimes treated as if they were the same type of organization on the grounds that both organizations are Islamist,[18] the two are significantly different and represent different ends of the Islamist spectrum. Historically, Hamas grew out of the Muslim Brotherhood movement. Established in Egypt in 1928, the Brotherhood was both an Islamic revival movement and a grassroots organization concerned with welfare, social justice, and ending (British) imperialism. Though increasingly engaged in the political violence that characterized Egyptian politics in the 1930s, at its core it was a movement of middle- and lower-middle-class professionals and entrepreneurs whose main interests lay in reform, not revolution.

In 1945–1946, the Muslim Brotherhood established branches in Palestine. Following Israel's establishment and the subsequent Arab–Israeli war of 1948, the Palestinian Brotherhood increasingly focused on providing humanitarian services for the estimated 700–800,000 refugees who had flooded Gaza and the West Bank. During the 1970s, when the Brotherhood re-emerged following a decade-long repression in Gaza and disruption in the West Bank,[19] it returned to these humanitarian roots and focused on welfare. Until the outbreak of the first Intifada in 1987, the Brothers largely refused to engage in resistance activities.

At the start of the 1987 Intifada, the Palestinian Muslim Brotherhood established Hamas as its resistance wing; as such, it reflected the thinking of the mainstream Muslim Brotherhood. Though increasingly radical in its attitude towards Israel, Hamas's focus on gradualism and welfare, typical of the larger Brotherhood, continued to characterize its domestic outlook. Although begun as the resistance wing of the Brotherhood, Hamas soon eclipsed the mother organization by taking on its socio-political mantle and welfare network and delegating the task of fighting to its newly established resistance wing, the Izz al Din al Qassam Brigades.

Al Qaeda – or, more precisely, what is usually described as al Qaeda[20] – traces its origins to the Muslim Brotherhood and the *takfiri*[21] movements of the 1970s. Inspired by Sayyid Qutb, an Egyptian Muslim Brother ideologue who became radicalized in prison and was hanged in 1966, the *takfiri* movements capitalized on disillusionment with the Brotherhood's political effectiveness and with the leadership's decision to compromise with the political status quo under President Sadat. According to the ideologues following in Qutb's footsteps, including Shukri Mustafa of al Takfir wa al Hijra and Abdessalam Faraj of the Egyptian Jihad, the very principles of gradualism and compromise had caused the Brotherhood's ineffectiveness.[22] They advocated a radical break with the status quo in anticipation of a comprehensive revolution. Society as a whole was depicted as having been corrupted and a radical withdrawal from society was considered necessary to safeguard the newfound ideological purity. Because all of society was to blame, deception and even violence against its members were deemed acceptable.

Al Qaeda appears to have emerged as a loose network out of the confluence of *takfiri*-inclined volunteers who had participated in the Afghan guerrilla war against the Soviet invasion. Those who joined the struggle in Afghanistan were increasingly either hardened radicals from Islamist movements across the Middle East, North Africa, and Asia, many of whom were university graduates or professionals, or members of the lower classes with little grounding in Islam or experience of local, embedded Islamist politics.[23] If they had originally been part of a socially embedded movement in their home states, they became uprooted and radicalized by the Afghan war. Upon return to their home states, they usually did not fit in with the more moderate, embedded Islamist movements and congregated instead around other Afghan "alumni" and radical fringe groups.[24] Unlike those involved with the accommodationist offshoots of the Muslim Brotherhood movement, theirs was a strategy of violent revolution, inspired by their belief that they had forced the Soviet superpower to withdraw from Afghanistan and made feasible by their relative isolation from local communities.[25]

The differences in the historical trajectories of Hamas and al Qaeda are reflected in fundamental variances in ideological, sociological, and organizational make-up (see Table 5.1). Ideologically, Hamas has adopted a gradualist approach to building an Islamic state, with a heavy emphasis on institution-building and social welfare. Al Qaeda favors a revolutionary approach, emphasizing violence and terrorism over institution building. Hamas's Islamic state includes most of the features one would expect a modern state to have and is heavily influenced by nationalist discourse. Al Qaeda's end goal is less well defined and appears to reject many of the features of a modern state. Hamas has shown an increased willingness to compromise domestically – and even, though to a far lesser extent, in its attitude towards Israel[26] – and to accommodate other-thinkers, resulting in partnerships with both Western and local non-Islamist institutions. Al Qaeda nurtures an absolutist attitude, typically limiting its partnerships to fellow Islamist organizations of a radical

Table 5.1 Ideological, sociological, and organizational differences between Hamas and al Qaeda

Hamas	al Qaeda
• Gradualist	• Revolutionary
• Accommodationist	• Absolutist
• Non-*takfiri*	• *Takfiri*
• "Jihadist" only vis-à-vis Israel	• "Jihadist" vis-à-vis world, including "corrupted" Muslims
• Socially embedded (national)	• Minimal welfare structure
• Welfare structure	• No political representation
• Political representation	• Little social emphasis besides military emphasis
• Social emphasis besides military activities	• Little local accountability
• High level of local accountability	

bent. Hamas usually limits its use of the word *jihad* to the struggle against Israeli occupation, and largely refrains from calling dissenting Muslims "apostates." Al Qaeda and affiliates use the term *jihad* to describe their struggle against not only the West but against all Muslims they consider "lapsed" (or dissenting).[27]

Sociologically, Hamas is an embedded organization of grassroots activists. Because Hamas's "military" strength does not match that of the (pro-Fatah) Palestinian Authority's security services, its power stems largely from the level of popular support it galvanizes in the annual professional and student union elections (which functioned as a barometer of popular support in the absence of national elections) and, most recently, in the municipal and legislative elections of 2005–2006. As a result, Hamas depends for its very survival largely on championing the interests of its various constituencies. The middle and lower-middle classes, particularly professionals and the petty bourgeoisie, form the backbone of Hamas's constituency.[28] Among these classes, gradualism, accommodation, and institution-building tend to be the tactics of choice.[29]

Even the many students who support Hamas tend to be gradualist rather than revolutionary in domestic terms – although they simultaneously provide much of the impetus for a sustained radical attitude towards Israel.[30] Because the bulk of Hamas's leadership comes from the same constituency as its supporters, its policies naturally reflect the social preferences of this constituency. Institution-building, gradualism and ensuring integrity, moreover, are precisely the type of practices that have catapulted Hamas to its 2006 electoral victory, as illustrated by the fact that a national survey found that only 7 percent of respondents believed that voters had elected Hamas to be "a fighting authority that resists occupation," as against 36 and 37 percent respectively believing people wanted "a clean authority that fights corruption" or "an Islamic authority that rules according to Shari'a and religion."[31] Consequently, Hamas's emphasis is as much on social welfare, social transformation, and local politics as it is on fighting Israel.

Al Qaeda, by contrast, is primarily a transnational network with limited local roots. Its various constituent and affiliated parts are largely un-embedded and typically have no welfare network of note.[32] They do not seek to participate in local politics, except in a parasitic manner (as illustrated by al Qaeda's behavior in Sudan and Afghanistan),[33] and this is precisely what appears to attract those who are disillusioned with the grinding gradualism of local politics. Their constituencies do not appear to be as well defined as those of Hamas. They include both well-educated members of the upper and middle classes and social dropouts or members from the lower classes.[34] The one thing that appears to unite these disparate groups is a feeling of uprootedness.

Al Qaeda and affiliates can "afford" to maintain an uncompromising approach to the status quo because they are less embedded and do not need to gain mass acceptance for their survival. Their immediate goal is not political power through mass support; instead they seek influence through daring and symbolic violent actions. For this, they need dedicated members, not mass membership. Al Qaeda and affiliates thus derive their power from their ability to elicit dedication from their followers, to escape detection by the authorities, and to raise the funds and the means to carry out the revolution – not from their participation in elections, institution-building, or charitable work.

Impact of organizational differences on use of charities

Taken together, the ideological, sociological, and historical differences between Hamas and al Qaeda can help explain the current divergence in their relationships with charities.

Hamas

Hamas's particular historical trajectory provides one of the chief explanations for the organization's structural make-up and the place of charities therein. The original activities of the Muslim Brotherhood in the area of welfare, education, and institution building have provided, and continue to provide, much of the *modus vivendi* of Hamas. To some extent, Hamas's resistance activities are secondary to this larger movement's social agenda – despite their centrality in Palestinian Islamist discourse. This reality is reflected not only in the fact that far fewer people are involved in resistance activities than in welfare[35] but also in the fact that the charities considered to be affiliated with Hamas are organizationally independent from the political and resistance wings.

Each of the charities has its own administration and is answerable to its own board of trustees. Since the boards of trustees typically consist of a cross-section of people considered upright by their communities, they tend to include both Hamas and non-Hamas members (although a majority are typically Hamas affiliates).[36] Those involved in the charities often become involved because of a concern for social justice or Islamic education. As a result, the charities' agendas do not necessarily coincide with the agendas of Hamas's political or resistance wings; however, many trustees do share these ideological commitments and some serve as political leaders. However if Hamas's political or resistance agenda is likely to jeopardize the charity's well-being, those involved in the charities may well put the charity's survival first – as many did during the 1970s and 1980s when they supported the Brotherhood's refusal to join the resistance.

Although the charitable "wing" is organizationally independent from Hamas's political structure, Hamas derives a considerable amount of political clout from its affiliated charities (just as the charities derive status from their affiliation with Hamas). Because Hamas is socially embedded, ideologically non-*takfiri*, and because its power is largely dependent on maintaining popular support,[37] it has a strong incentive to present itself as socially involved. To be seen to be involved in charitable work and in fundraising for charity helps Hamas to bolster its image as a socially active and "caring" organization. This in turn is likely to increase its fundraising potential. It is thus not surprising that, according to Israeli intelligence estimates, 80 to 90 percent of the money raised by "Hamas" (to be understood in the widest sense as those who are part of the larger social movement of which Hamas is the political expression, and thus not just the charities) is spent on charitable, educational, and medical institutions – leaving only 10 to 20 percent for "military" endeavours.[38]

Equally important for Hamas's political standing is the fact that the charities have a reputation for financial transparency. For both ideological and political reasons, Hamas has chosen to make incorruptibility its selling point. Helped by the fact that the general population views its rival, Fatah, as deeply corrupt,[39] incorruptibility has gained Hamas both political popularity (see election victory details above) and a steady flow of voluntary donations. This reputation has been supported by Hamas's affiliation with various highly regarded NGOs (many of those employed in financial positions by the United Nation's Relief and Works Agency (UNRWA), the agency running Palestinian refugee camps, are affiliated with Hamas). It has also ensured the continued support of financial contributors, both inside Palestine and abroad. Save the Children, USAID, Médecins sans Frontières, and Medical Aid for Palestine are among the international, non-Islamic charities that have contributed at one time or another to charities affiliated with Hamas, precisely because they have observed that contributions reach their intended destination.[40]

Locally, many Palestinians, including those who do not subscribe to Hamas's political program, prefer to contribute to Hamas-affiliated charities rather than to charities with a reputation for less transparency. Consequently, Hamas has a vested interest not only in ensuring that the charities thrive but also that they maintain a reputation for financial transparency. Given the close-knit nature of Palestinian society, the intense scrutiny charities are under from the Israeli government (as exemplified in various army raids on charity buildings), the permanent presence on the ground of international aid workers, and the requirement of providing annual accounts (scrutinized by an authority that, until the 2006 elections, was hostile to the charities concerned) this reputation would be difficult to maintain if irregularities occurred on a large scale.

If there were a hint of suspicion that money was spent on projects other than those advertised, charities would risk losing donor confidence. This holds for Western donor charities whose activities are scrutinized by both regulatory bodies and watchful pro-Israeli organizations.[41] It also holds for local Palestinians, a significant number of whom would not give money if it could be linked to terrorism – whether for ethical or ideological reasons or, until recently, for fear of being implicated in Hamas's resistance wing and imprisoned (under the previous Palestinian Authority). Just as the charities' boards consist of both Hamas and non-Hamas members, so do the donors to these charities. Thus it is in both the charities' and Hamas's interests to keep humanitarian and "military" fundraising apart. This does not mean that such a distinction is always upheld. Significantly, however, Matthew Levitt, who dedicated an entire book to making the claim that charities are integral to Hamas's terrorist activities, only mentions a few instances where charitable money is believed to have been used for armed activities, and where he does, he generally fails to provide the level of detail needed to make these claims stick. Instead, his argument rests on the overlap in personnel between the political, military and charitable wings and on the fact that the charities help Hamas spread its ideology, and provide an infrastructure and jobs (which he describes as "covers").[42]

The fact that financial resources are readily available to support the violent struggle facilitates Hamas's commitment to keep welfare and resistance fundraising apart. The Qassam Brigades' funding is shrouded in secrecy, as is the identity of its financial sources. The Israeli Ministry of Foreign Affairs has claimed variously that the Brigades' budget is $10 million, "at least $20 million," and "several tens of millions of dollars per year."[43] However large its actual budget, sufficient funds appear to be available from a wide variety of sources, including those intent on keeping the conflict with Israel alive, those wishing to sustain an effective opposition to Fatah, and those seeking to strengthen Islamism region-wide.

Even if the post-Saddam Middle East "order" may have diminished the sources of funding for the organization's resistance wing,[44] other non-charitable sources are potentially available to Hamas, such as money laundering[45] and smuggling. These, if conducted out of sight from ordinary Palestinians (for instance in the notorious tri-border area between Brazil, Paraguay, and Argentina where Hamas affiliates have allegedly been active),[46] and used solely for funding clandestine activities, are unlikely to damage Hamas's local image as a "clean operator."

Following the above analysis, it is hardly surprising that only one European-registered Islamic charity has been linked by courts to Hamas's resistance – even though, arguably, the disincentives to behave "impeccably" detailed above are less immediate for overseas charities than for charities inside Palestine. Equally unsurprising is the fact that the accusations against this charity are limited to spreading propaganda and funding the families of suicide bombers. In the eyes of Hamas and many Palestinians, neither of these activities constitutes direct military struggle nor do they compromise the charity's clean reputation. In this particular instance, Hamas's position is supported by the rulings of the Charity Commission for England and Wales[47] and the Geneva Convention. According to Article 33 of the latter, no person in a conflict situation "may be punished for an offence he or she has not personally committed."[48] Refusal of humanitarian assistance to a family on the grounds that the father (or mother) of the family has committed a terrorist act would thus arguably constitute a breach of the Geneva Convention.

The amount of money believed to be typically paid to a martyr's family ($5,000) is insufficient to provide a decisive incentive to volunteer for a suicide operation, at least compared to the sums Saddam Hussein allegedly provided ($25,000).[49] Research, moreover, suggests that those volunteering for suicide operations are typically not poor (in some cases even the sons of millionaires), generally relatively well-educated, and employed – thus drastically reducing the incentive of pecuniary "re-imbursements."[50] On the basis of this evidence one cannot conclusively state that providing money to the families of martyrs constitutes "intentionally financing terrorism," thus throwing some doubt on the Dutch government's decision to indict Stichting al Aqsa.

Al Qaeda

The logic that cautions Hamas against mixing humanitarian and "military" fundraising is hardly persuasive to a network like al Qaeda's. Al Qaeda has no extensive welfare structure to maintain nor does it see creating one as one of its core goals.[51] Its primary goal is to promote violent struggle. Because it is a *takfiri*, revolutionary-minded, and socially isolated organization, it has few incentives to invest heavily in welfare networks. It may raise money to cater to its fighters.[52] It may use charities to raise money surreptitiously and at the same time spread its ideology.[53] It may even use the benefits charities can offer to attract potential recruits.[54] But its ideology and structure do not necessitate the maintenance of charitable structures or local patronage networks. Its reputation rests on being a radical organization successful in unconventional warfare, not on being a social benefactor. Indeed, in contrast to the charities affiliated with Hamas, none of the charities accused of links with al Qaeda was publicly affiliated with it.

Unlike Hamas, al Qaeda does not occupy a recognized position in a struggle for national liberation that is considered legitimate by both a large local constituency and, internationally, by a number of state governments. Moreover, unlike Hamas, al Qaeda has denounced as apostate a number of the governments that might support it.[55] It is thus less likely to attract funds from friendly governments than is Hamas, and it has had more incentive to develop clandestine ways of raising money.

Since al Qaeda has no reputation to lose as a socially active or a financially transparent organization, it can abuse the charitable system without costs to its reputation and siphon off money donated for charitable purposes to fund its violent campaigns. This may explain why, in the case of charities linked to al Qaeda, a high percentage of the funding was found to have been exfiltrated surreptitiously or skimmed off of raised funds in small percentages without the knowledge of the donors.[56] It may also explain why, wealth and religious/cultural affinity apart, al Qaeda has targeted so many Saudi charities since, for both political and religious reasons, the Saudi state has traditionally lacked adequate mechanisms to monitor money flows.[57]

There are further historical explanations both for al Qaeda's close links with Saudi charities and for its readiness to mix humanitarian and "military" fundraising – reasons largely lacking in the case of Hamas. At the height of the guerrilla war against the Soviet invasion of Afghanistan, the states most involved in sponsoring the mujahideen – the United States, Saudi Arabia, and Pakistan – encouraged fundraising and recruitment for the struggle through the global network of Islamic charities. According to various analysts, the CIA was involved both in securing visas for radical "preachers" such as the Egyptian Shaykh Omar Abd al Rahman and in encouraging the establishment of charities such as the al Kifah Afghan Refugee Center in Brooklyn – in both instances to facilitate fundraising and recruitment for the Afghan mujahideen.[58] The Saudis similarly encouraged the establishment of charities in aid of the Afghan struggle, some of which were directly involved in funding the "Arab Afghans" (through, for instance, the Maktab il Khidamat of Abdullah Azzam and bin Laden).[59]

Such a policy was encouraged to spread the financial burden but, more importantly, to raise awareness of the struggle – and of the sponsoring states' roles in it. The Saudis, in particular, were determined to cement their position as the chief custodians of Islam, specifically following the creation of a rival "Islamic center" in the Islamic Republic of Iran, and to spread their particular brand of Islam, Wahhabism, to Central Asia.[60] At that time, and within the jurisdictions of these particular states, the mujahideen's struggle was considered legitimate. Thus, fundraising for "military" purposes through the offices of humanitarian networks was considered both acceptable and legitimate. It was only when the mujahideen's, and later al Qaeda's global jihadist struggle, became "illegitimate" that groups such as al Qaeda turned to subterfuge to raise funds – as exemplified by Ayman al Zawahiri's reputed attempts in the early 1990s to raise funds for al Qaeda's armed operations by claiming to collect money for Afghan widows and orphans.[61]

However, two factors limit al Qaeda's potential interest in charities, one relating to charities in general, and the other applying to charities registered in the West. The amount of money that one can surreptitiously siphon off from charitable funds is relatively small compared to the amounts of money to be made elsewhere – particularly if one has no ideological or socio-political aversion to using criminal sources. Information concerning al Qaeda's income streams is imprecise, and the following estimates must there-fore be taken as indications of orders of magnitude only. Intelligence reports estimate al Haramain and other Saudi charities with possible al Qaeda links raise $40 to 50 million annually[62] – of which, by general acknowledgement, the "vast majority [goes] to feed hungry Somali orphans, educate poor Indonesian students and help sick Kenyan children" rather than to al Qaeda.[63] A 2002 report speculated (not without contestation) that al Qaeda received $300–500 million in funding directly "from wealthy businessmen and bankers representing about 20% of the Saudi GNP."[64] Claims of a similar order of magnitude have been made for the income from counterfeiting, credit card scams, falcon smuggling, and the diamond trade.

Second, Western-based charities pose a particular set of problems for al Qaeda. Against the $40–50 million in estimated annual donations to al Haramain, estimates for charities believed to be linked to al Qaeda in the United States are a mere $6–9 million.[65] If Jean-Charles Brisard is right in his estimate that charities used by al Qaeda channel only 10 percent of their income to al Qaeda, the US charities would provide al Qaeda with $600,000–900,000 per year. Compared to the sums believed to be raised from the alter-native sources listed above, such contributions from the charities based in the United States and the West are small. The strict controls typically applied to charities in Western states are an important factor, and the absence of historical connections with oil-rich families is another. However, there appear to be additional reasons why al Qaeda has had difficulties in infiltrating Western-based charities.

European Muslims, political alienation, and al Qaeda

One of the reasons al Qaeda appears to have infiltrated only a relatively small number of European-registered Islamic charities may be the make-up and socialization of Europe's Muslims and the political environment they inhabit. My hypothesis is that, though the conditions exist for Muslims in Europe to become radicalized – as graphically illustrated by the fact that the perpet-rators of the London 7 July 2005 bombings were British-born European Muslims – al Qaeda's ideology and chosen methods are nevertheless, at least currently, too dissonant with the life experiences and ideological frameworks of the vast majority of European Muslims to become their focus of alle-giance.[66] Because the number of charities open to funding al Qaeda is con-sequently likely to be small, al Qaeda has to surreptitiously infiltrate charities if it is to raise funds this way. Because this is a laborious process – made more difficult by the new procedures (and increased vigilance) created since

11 September 2001 – al Qaeda is more likely to focus its efforts on activities with more immediate benefits such as credit card scams or smuggling, or on activities that are absolutely essential to its survival such as gaining recruits who can carry out operations from the inside (e.g. the London bombings).

When analyzing the level of support for al Qaeda among Europe's Muslims, one has to distinguish between sympathy for al Qaeda's anti-Americanism and the plight of Muslims in conflict zones such as Iraq, wholesale subscription to al Qaeda's ideology and methods, and readiness to carry out operations. That, for example, 8 percent of British Muslims questioned in a 2002 survey believed al Qaeda to be justified in attacking Britain is not a reliable proxy for measuring the latter two levels of support – particularly as this question was asked after Britain had initiated military action against Afghanistan with 56 percent of the respondents not believing al Qaeda to be responsible for the events of 11 September.[67]

In Britain only a few fringe Islamist groups have expressed qualified support for al Qaeda.[68] The majority of both mainstream Muslim and larger Islamist organizations, as well as most mosques, have unequivocally distanced themselves from al Qaeda and sought to marginalize those expressing views close to it.[69] In the Netherlands, mainstream Muslim organizations and mosques have similarly condemned 11 September – and more recently, the 2004 murder of Dutch filmmaker Theo van Gogh – and typically sought to cooperate with the government to marginalize al Qaeda's influence by banning al Qaeda sympathizers.[70] The 1,000-strong Islamist Arab European League called the 11 September attacks a "sweet revenge" but its leader has stated "we are against violence."[71] Only three charities, two of which linked to "radical" mosques, and an unidentified number of fringe mosques (situated in private homes) were, at the time of writing, under investigation for expressing views close to bin Laden's.[72]

A more direct, though by no means exact, indicator of al Qaeda's support level in Europe can be found in the number of European volunteers it has succeeded in recruiting. The typical al Qaeda recruit residing in Europe is an Arab, usually of North African descent, recently migrated, and relatively unembedded in the local Muslim community.[73] The profile of the European-based 11 September bombers matches this description. The same holds true for the perpetrators of the 2004 Madrid bombing, the alleged perpetrators of the Tunisian bombing of 2002, and most of the cells arrested on suspicion of working on behalf of al Qaeda. Indeed, according to one of the most extensive analyses of the known profiles of al Qaeda suspects apprehended in Europe and the United States, 87 percent of those studied were immigrants.[74]

The fact that the 7 July London bombers were British-born may point to a shift in al Qaeda's fortunes, although we should be wary of jumping to hasty conclusions (after all, the 21 July London bombers were not British-born). However, taken together with the 2004 arrest of eight British-born Muslims on suspicion of planning a terrorist attack in Britain (although the allegations have not yet been proven) and the fact that a number of those behind the ritual murder of Theo van Gogh in the Netherlands were Dutch citizens of Moroccan descent born in the Netherlands, these data seem to point to a growing constituency for al Qaeda – although the exact relationship between what is usually described as al Qaeda and these European militants is far from clear.[75] Equally portentous may be the fact that a number of those providing logistical support for al Qaeda cells, as well as a number of al Muhajiroun's recruits, have been "white" converts to Islam.[76]

Nevertheless, until now, the average profile of those arrested on suspicion of working for al Qaeda and those known to have died as al Qaeda operatives suggests that al Qaeda has largely failed to recruit among European-born Muslims – and certainly to the level necessary to infiltrate thousands of charities. Given al Qaeda's isolationist, absolutist ideology and practices, and in view of the profile of past al Qaeda recruits, support for al Qaeda can be expected to be highest among those who feel socially or politically isolated and are in search of an absolutist identity (in the case of the 7 July bombers, isolation appears to have occurred in the mind, rather than at the physical level). Those who are socially or politically embedded are unlikely to be attracted by an isolationist ideology as their identity and ideological preferences are bound up with their place in the community. There may be a tension between their identity and the (presumed) identity of the majority population. They may feel politically isolated outside of their community, yet remain sufficiently embedded within their own communities not to feel the need for a radical break. Moreover, their level of social integration (even if limited to their "own" sub-community) makes them more likely to be averse to absolutist notions because integration usually encourages compromise. Conversely, those who feel profoundly dissatisfied with both their own community and the larger political community are more likely to be attracted by an isolationist, absolutist ideology. Muslims who are un-embedded and alienated from both the local Muslim communities and their host societies are, according to this logic, most likely to be open to al Qaeda's ideology.

Terrorism and identity

A theoretical framework that captures these twin notions of isolation and identity, and may provide the beginnings of an insight into al Qaeda's failure to recruit widely among European Muslims, is the theory of political alienation developed by David Schwartz in his 1970s study of political activism in the United States. In this work, Schwartz postulates that an individual's level of political alienation influences his or her propensity towards political violence. Schwartz defined political alienation as a function of three variables: perceived threat from value conflict, perceived personal political inefficacy, and perceived systemic inefficacy.[77] The latter two variables describe the level of isolation a person feels. The first variable, and to some extent the second, are linked to a person's notion of identity.

According to Schwartz, political alienation is expected to occur when "individuals perceive a fundamental conflict between their basic politicized values and those exhibited in the polity, under the conditions that they perceive both themselves and the political system to be inefficacious to reduce this conflict." This sense of political alienation leads to a "behavioral orientation," the particular nature of which is influenced by socioeconomic status, personality, and the process by which alienation was reached. Behavioral orientations encompass a scale from conformity, ritualism, and retreat to reformism and, finally, rebelliousness. Only the latter type of orientation, typically associated with a high level of perceived threat to values and a predisposition to participatory activism, may lead to political violence (though not necessarily terrorism). For this to occur, the orientation needs to be stimulated by an intensification of the perceived threat to values or the sense of personal and systemic inefficacy, as well as by the emergence of a "reference group" (counter-elite, counter-group, counter-culture) which can convince the individual that "his value conflict and his perceptions of inefficacy will . . . be reduced or reversed" by his identification with the group. The individual's investment in the political system is withdrawn and reinvested in the identity of the dissident organization.[78]

The dissonance between European Islamists and al Qaeda can be made more intelligible with reference to Schwartz's theoretical framework – although it must be emphasized that in the absence of extensive, reliable data the following explanation is largely conjectural. The evolution of European Islamism is a function of both international and domestic changes. Internationally, these include the rise of Islamism as a popular ideological framework in the Middle East and elsewhere. Most prominent among domestic changes have been the shift from a migrant to a post-migrant perspective (with a concomitant rise in expectations towards the "host" society; often, a weakening of ties to the parental "homeland;"[79] and the shift from a cultural/racial identity to a self-consciously Islamic identity (as opposed to a particular "national" identity) among a significant sector of Europe's Muslims. Prior to the 1990s, both Muslims of migratory descent and officialdom conceived political and social exclusion in cultural or racial/ethnic terms. In Britain, there was no official category of "Muslim" in public surveys, only Pakistani, Bangladeshi, etc., until the census of 2001. In the Netherlands, the category of "religion," originally introduced to differentiate between Protestants and Catholics, was removed from the census in 1983 and has not been re-introduced although the category "Islamic" has come to play a central role in public discourse.[80] Though exclusion and cultural alienation were real, immigrants did not cast their alienation in the overtly existential terms of religious discourse until the mid- to late-1980s (the precise date varies according to location).[81]

The failure of al Qaeda to gain widespread support, not just among Muslims generally, but among European Islamists in particular, can be explained, in part and tentatively, with reference to Schwartz's theory of political alienation. On the one hand, there are sufficient structural inequalities for a significant section of European Muslims to experience both personal and system inefficacy. In the UK, 40 percent of Muslim households are allegedly classified below the poverty line, while unemployment among British Muslims is three to four times higher than the national average. Meanwhile, educational achievement, according to one report, is only 5 percent below the average, leading to an acute tension between expectation and achievement.[82] Finally, levels of political representation are far below the representation of Muslims in the general population, both in Britain and in the Netherlands. Even those who have escaped such economic and educational marginalization may not be fully accepted by non-Muslim society (see, for example, al Qaeda affiliate Zacarias Moussaoui),[83] or may continue to feel aggrieved on behalf of their community.

Whether or not this leads to political alienation hinges, at least within Schwartz's framework, on one's perception of value threat, which in turn is influenced by the make-up of one's identity. Those who, in response to globalization and the post-migrant turn, have adopted a self-consciously "Islamic" identity while remaining secular in outlook,[84] do not inevitably experience "a fundamental conflict between their basic politicized values and those exhibited in the polity" – as reflected in the fact that 67 percent of British Muslims interviewed in the aforementioned 2002 survey felt patriotic towards Britain (only 10 percent behind the national average). According to Schwartz's framework, this group of European Muslims is not likely to become involved in political violence.[85] For European Islamists, the sense of value conflict is potentially more acute – domestically in terms of a (perceived) conflict between Islamist and secular values, and globally in terms of the (perceived) clash between Western and Muslim countries. But even among this group, al Qaeda's appeal is limited.

Significantly, marginalization and value conflict notwithstanding, a number of well-established political and civil outlets exist for those seeking to reform the system or become personally active. An increasing, though still relatively small, number of Muslims has been successful in politics[86] while a plethora of charities exist aimed at improving the lot of European Muslims. Though slow in response, most governments have made some efforts at combating marginalization. As such, (limited) alternatives are available to al Qaeda's strategies for those who feel politically ineffective or believe the system to be unresponsive. In this, the presence of moderate Islamist organizations such as the Muslim Association of Britain (MAB), and their perceived success in affecting voting outcomes,[87] are vital in neutralizing the appeal of al Qaeda as these organizations cater to those disillusioned by the (apparent) inefficacy of non-Islamist options.[88]

The existence of well-established, embedded organizations catering to Muslims in Europe and abroad also means that al Qaeda faces fierce competition. Because the majority of these organizations are highly integrated into society, including European Islamist organizations, and run by Muslims with a post-migrant outlook and an acute awareness of both the possibilities and the shortcomings of the local political system, they are likely to be vigilant against those advocating a radical break with their host societies. However, these organizations may also be less vigilant against those advocating support for resistance struggles abroad (particularly if they have adopted a self-consciously "Islamic" identity, increasing affinity with the plight of Muslims worldwide). Available evidence suggests that affinity with the Muslim *umma*, or global community, is most typically translated into charitable activities (donations to relief organizations, fundraising) or political action (awareness-raising, lobbying, electioneering) – rather than raising funds for overtly terrorist acts abroad. This helps to explain why al Qaeda sympathizers have typically raised funds under false pretence[89] (and why the charities funding Hamas appear to limit their funding to the humanitarian realm, even if this term is stretched by involving funding for the families of suicide bombers).

Finally, even to those radical Islamists who feel acutely alienated, al Qaeda's program may not necessarily seem appealing. For al Qaeda to be attractive, they have to feel comfortable with a *takfiri* perspective, a response more suited to those residing in overwhelmingly Muslim societies in the process of secularization (which poses a more acute threat to their Muslim identity than the relatively disinterested non-Muslim secular societies in which European Islamists live). They must also feel comfortable with a radically violent strategy, both internationally and domestically, and with the repercussions such a strategy will provoke. Such a strategy is more attractive in a situation where a large Muslim constituency exists with a revolutionary potential. In Europe, such a constituency does not exist.

The ideology of the larger, more moderate Islamist organizations in Europe is typically too pragmatic and accommodating to engage in terrorism. Their preferred methods are education, awareness-raising, electioneering, and lobbying. They also tend not to divide the world starkly into good and evil. The ideology of the more radical organizations such as Hizb ut-Tahrir and al Muhajiroun, is better suited to employing terrorist means. They tend to divide the world starkly into good versus evil and seek to distance themselves from corrupt society. Like al Qaeda, they operate within a *takfiri* mindset. "Al muhajiroun," for example, means "the migrants" and the term is used in *takfiri* circles to denote withdrawal from society. But even among these *takfiri* groups, not all unequivocally support violent struggle, let alone the use of terrorist means. The British branch of Hizb ut-Tahrir, though vociferous in its condemnation of Western society, has thus far condemned violence and refrained from using it.[90] The Arab European League has similarly refrained from advocating violence. Al Qaeda thus appears to have largely failed to convince politically alienated European Muslims, including most Islamists, that its strategies will effectively "reduce or reverse" both their sense of being threatened in their core values and their sense of the system being unresponsive to their needs.

Al Qaeda's future in Europe

Whether al Qaeda's appeal among European Muslims will increase is a function of a complex relationship between poorly understood factors. On the one hand, after 11 September, President Bush's response and the prospect of a fifth column in Europe's midst has given rise to increased suspicions towards Muslims in general, and Muslim migrants in particular. On the other hand, Muslims, and particularly embedded European Muslims, have seen their political influence increase.

In Britain, an unprecedented number of Muslims have been politically galvanized by 11 September and the war against Iraq. Unlike the situation during the 1991 Gulf War, Muslim activists found themselves among a broad alliance of Christians, left-wingers, and liberals who opposed the war against Iraq and the war on terror for very similar reasons. The aforementioned Muslim Association of Britain is a product of this new climate and has, together with other Muslim and non-Muslim organizations, managed to make its mark on British politics, even affecting the outcome of municipal and national elections.[91] In these instances, Muslims have become visible and have come to see themselves as full-fledged, fully participant citizens.

It is far from certain which of the two trends will prevail. The gains made in British local and European elections in 2003 and 2004 were countered by only one Muslim winning a seat in the European Parliament (although four won seats in Britain's 2005 parliamentary elections).[92] The success of the 2003 anti-war demonstrations in which Muslims played an important part was nullified by the fact that the British government, supported by a two-third majority in Parliament, went to war nonetheless. The de-securitizing effect of the Charity Commission's refusal to close down Islamic charities on unsupported accusations from the US Treasury has been diluted by continued allegations, often conjectural, from certain media outlets about charities and institutions with an Islamist bent.[93] More recently, the July 2005 London bombings appear to have both encouraged dialogue and increased fear and suspicion. The situation in the Netherlands is much the same as the wildly contradictory responses of both the public and the government reveal, ranging from appeals for dialogue to fire bombs aimed at mosques and calls for the withdrawal of citizenship from Netherlands-born Muslims with radical Islamist views or a criminal conviction.[94]

It is similarly not certain that further marginalization will lead to the adoption of al Qaeda-like tactics by European activists. Further marginalization could lead equally to an increase in criminalization, riots, or the emergence of a broad, united Muslim social movement. A decrease in marginalization similarly does not inevitably lead to the eradication of radical groups. The inclusion of the more moderate and successful Muslim organizations into the political system may result in the emergence of violent fringe groups, just as the cooption of the mainstream Communist Party into the Italian political system of the 1970s led to an increase in the violence of radical left-wing groups such as the Red Brigades.[95]

Conclusion and policy implications

This chapter has shown that contrary to some popular narratives, the number of charities thought to have provided funding for either al Qaeda or Hamas is relatively small, and that there is a marked discrepancy between the number of charities linked to al Qaeda and the number of those funding Hamas's military wing. I have attempted to provide an explanation for this discrepancy by looking at each organization's ideology, self-image, historical development, and relationship with its constituency. In the case of Hamas, each of these factors was seen to inhibit the organization from using charitable fronts to finance acts of violence. Because Hamas is an embedded organization dependent on maintaining local popular support, and because it has chosen to gain this support through building a reputation for incorruptibility, it can ill afford to be seen to embezzle charitable funds. The ready availability of alternative financial sources enables it to maintain a strict separation between fundraising for charitable and resistance ends. In the case of al Qaeda, none of the listed factors particularly discourage it from using charitable fronts. As a transnational, un-embedded organization whose power is not primarily based on gaining a local support base, al Qaeda has little to lose by abusing charities for terrorist purposes. As an isolationist, *takfiri* organization, it can justify abusing charities by claiming that these charities are part of a corrupted society with which al Qaeda is at war.

One explanation for why the number of European-registered charities with links to al Qaeda has remained so small despite the lack of disincentives revolves around the apparent dissonance between the views of European Muslims and al Qaeda's ideology and methods. The presence of a relatively strict fiscal climate (particularly compared to the lack of regulation in countries such as Saudi Arabia and Somalia) and the absence of historical relations with rich benefactors and their charities (compared to the presence of such links elsewhere, such as in Saudi Arabia) also play a role. But the fact that the majority of Europe's Muslims and their charitable institutions are deeply embedded in local communities means that al Qaeda's isolationist, *takfiri* ideology has little to offer. Though European Muslims may feel politically marginalized, the vast majority, including most Islamists, do not appear to have experienced the level of threat to their basic values and identities or the level of alienation from their own faith communities needed to make al Qaeda's ideology attractive. Consequently, because recruitment in Europe is unlikely to provide al Qaeda with a large pool of activists, at least for now, and because infiltration into existing Islamic charities is likely to be difficult and time-consuming, the most cost-effective option for al Qaeda is to focus its European activities on gaining recruits who can carry out its terrorist projects relatively undetected, and to raise funds through different channels.[96]

Beyond these empirical observations, a number of lessons can be drawn from the above analysis. First, the fact that differences in organization, ideology, and history appear to shape the way charities are approached underlines the importance of adopting a more differentiated approach to Islamist organizations more generally, and to organizations labelled "terrorist" in particular. Of particular importance is the level of embeddedness of the organization in question and the impact of this embeddedness on the organization's ideology, structure, and practices. A related issue concerns the way terrorism is used to designate entire organizations engaged in terrorist acts – regardless of whether the bulk of their activities is terrorist. Not only does this practice obscure our understanding of the organization in question, but it also serves to delegitimize the otherwise legitimate social reform aspects of such organizations as well as all forms of resistance, even those conducted according to the rules of the Geneva Convention. If Schwartz's theory of political alienation has any validity, such a blanket delegitimization is likely to alienate the constituencies one is trying to win over and decrease system responsiveness, thus increasing the attractiveness of unconventional forms of warfare. The delegitimization of social welfare activities in particular, especially if accompanied by the freezing of charitable assets, is likely to contribute to human suffering as it has already done in Palestine[97] – which similarly may increase the attractiveness of unconventional forms of warfare.

Second, the grounds on which the Stichting al Aqsa has been indicted raises important questions about what exactly constitutes "financing terrorism." If al Aqsa's primary crime has been providing money to the families of those responsible for suicide operations, it is questionable whether such an act constitutes financing terrorism – although the act itself raises a number of ethical issues. More broadly, if a European-registered charity donates money to a charity that is loosely affiliated with an organization engaged in terrorism, does such an act constitute "financing terrorism"? Is it sufficient to be "associated" with an organization that carries out terrorist acts to be open to the charge of "financing terrorism"? What exactly constitutes "associated"? Given the potential for human suffering if a charity is closed down and the potential for radicalization if it is closed down on dubious grounds, stricter rules on what constitutes "financing terrorism" and what constitutes evidence for such claims are advisable.[98]

A related issue concerns the fact that the evidence against the Stichting al Aqsa was, for perfectly legitimate intelligence reasons, only shown to the judge presiding over the Stichting's appeal against closure. Because the Stichting was deprived of a chance to challenge the accusations, this practice arguably served to render its closure more contentious and thus potentially radicalizing. This highlights the importance of devising more transparent procedures, an issue taken up in more detail in Chapter 11 of this volume.

A third set of lessons can be drawn from differences in the way the British and Dutch governments monitor suspect charities, producing fundamentally different outcomes. In Britain, the body investigating an accused charity is the Charity Commission. This Commission is an independent branch of government responsible for both defending the interests of British charities and regulating them. It alone has the authority to instigate an inquiry and to decide on the type of sanction to impose, if any.[99] As such, the Charity Commission serves as a buffer between the political pressures surrounding the government and the charities, and typically attempts to find a solution that does not result in the closure of a charity but in its reform.[100] Because the charities recognize that the Commission's purpose is to both regulate and defend them, crises are more readily averted, and charities are more willing to voluntarily ensure transparency than would be the case if the only tools available were police investigation, covert surveillance, or legal proceedings.

In the Netherlands, the government carries out investigations, often with the help of intelligence services (AIVD), making it easier for the process to become politicized and antagonistic. Because authority rests with the government, the Ministers are regularly questioned in Parliament over their decisions concerning charities, providing both Ministers and opposition politicians a ready platform to score political points on the back of the charity debate. It also increases the likelihood that opposition politicians pressure relevant Ministers into making decisions on the basis of political expediency rather than simply security concerns or verifiable evidence. In both the case of Stichting al Haramain and of Stichting al Aqsa, there seems to have been considerable political pressure, both domestic and international, which may have forced the government into a hastier or a more politically motivated decision than might have been chosen if responsibility for the case could have been deferred to a charity commission.[101] Moreover, had the process been conducted by a commission simultaneously charged with defending the interests of charities, the outcome might have been reform, thereby preventing the humanitarian and political costs of closing the charity while reducing the likelihood that charitable money is channelled into terrorist activities.[102] The government might have made use of the notion of an "accreditation seal," which the Dutch Central Bureau on Fundraising has already developed to signal to the public which fundraising charities can be trusted to spend their money on the projects specified[103] – a policy that, if handled sensitively, is likely to be similarly welcomed by Hamas-affiliated charities overseas. To be fair, however, in both cases the AIVD did withstand the political pressure for a considerable length of time, and in the case of al Aqsa would, according to one insider, have been prepared to consider reform if the charity had been more forthcoming in considering reform (which, if the investigating party had been a charity commission rather than the intelligence services, might have been more readily the case).[104]

Finally, if al Qaeda's dissonance with European Muslims is to be maintained, Europe's governments must pay more attention to the needs and sensitivities of their Muslim citizens. These concern both the foreign policies governments pursue, bearing in mind that Muslim citizens may have different loyalties than their governments in conflicts involving Muslims, and the way governments allow Muslims to express their Islamic identity domestically. A government should seek not merely to decrease the sense of exclusion many Muslims feel by making the system more responsive (which includes a greater commitment to tackling structural problems of unemployment and exclusion from education), but also on decreasing the perception of value conflict. Some level of value conflict is inevitable in any democracy, let alone one consisting of multiple cultural communities. But the state could be more willing to accommodate religious claims and identities in the public arena, which would involve a rethinking of the concept of secularity.

Of particular importance is the state's attitude to Islamism. In the current climate, mainstream politicians too readily characterize Islamism as incompatible with democracy. Yet in its most accommodating forms, Islamism is compatible with democratic practice. It is vital to distinguish between different forms of Islamism and to recognize that some of them are not only "acceptable" within a secular context but vital to reducing the sense of value conflict felt by a significant number of Muslims. The Muslim Association of Britain (MAB) has empowered British Muslims by convincing them that the (perceived) value conflict between them, the state, and society is not insurmountable. Significantly, it has succeeded in channelling the energy of angry young Muslims into democratic avenues of protest, thereby lessening the sense of both personal and systemic inefficacy. By doing so, it has helped to delegitimize al Qaeda and its methods. Similarly, Islamist charities such as Interpal (Palestinian Relief and Development Fund) play a role in directing the concern of self-consciously Islamic European Muslims for the plight of Palestinians into humanitarian channels. If organizations such as MAB and Interpal are demonized, al Qaeda may become more attractive to disenfranchised Muslims. At the same time, organizations such as MAB and Interpal must be encouraged to pay greater heed to accusations that some of the things they advocate (e.g. regarding suicide operations in Israel), and the way they advocate them, are offensive to other members of the community (e.g. British Jews).

Such an approach is particularly imperative in the face of changes in the way the al Qaeda network appears to be recruiting. Having been hounded from the few charities and mosques it had infiltrated, its recruiters appear to have moved into small, private mosques, informal groups of disgruntled youths, and onto the internet – a shift away from structures that are observable by the authorities. This parallels patterns in the financing of terrorism. As a result, the authorities now have to rely more than before on information from those who frequent Islamist circles. For such cooperation to be possible, European Islamists must be persuaded that their governments have their best interests at heart. This means that European domestic systems must become more sensitive and inclusive, and foreign policies may have to take Muslim concerns more explicitly into account and, rather than focus primarily on suppressing terrorism, focus also on transforming the structures that help cause terrorism.

This approach will be more likely to succeed if one distinguishes meticulously between financing humanitarian networks affiliated with resistance groups, and financing terrorism. It militates against equating ideological support for a resistance struggle with financing terrorism. It cautions against providing undisclosed, and thus incontestable, evidence, and against using the logic of "crime by association." It similarly cautions against labelling an entire organization "terrorist," instead favouring an approach that encourages constructive engagement with the non-terrorist aspects of an organization, while clamping down hard on its terrorist aspects (this policy, however, does not currently seem to be applicable to al Qaeda). Finally, such an approach calls for legislation to be applied across the board, regardless of religious or political affiliation.

Notes

1 I am indebted to Tom J. Biersteker, Sue E. Eckert, Frazer Egerton, Toni Erskine, Alastair Finlan, and Doug Stokes for their insightful comments.
2 "$116 Trillion Lawsuit Filed by 9/11 Families," *CNN.com/LawCenter*, 16 August 2002. Online. Available HTTP: <http://archives.cnn.com/2002/LAW/08/15/attacks.suit/> (accessed 24 November 2004). The charities concerned are the Benevolence International Foundation, al Haramain Islamic Foundation, International Islamic Relief Organization, Rabita Trust, Saar Foundation, and World Assembly of Muslim Youth. See *Burnett, et al. v. al Baraka Investment and Development Corp., et al.* Online. Available HTTP: <http://news.findlaw.com/cnn/docs/terrorism/burnettba81502cmp.pdf> (accessed 22 May 2005).
3 See Adams on the PIRA's and the PLO's financing and Napoleoni on the PIRA's and the Kosovo Liberation Army's fundraising. J. Adams, *The Financing of Terror*, London: New English Library, 1986, pp. 86–89, 135–155; L. Napoleoni, *Modern Jihad: Tracing the Dollars Behind the Terror Networks*, London: Pluto, 2003, pp. 29–33, 166–167; M. Levitt, "Islamic Extremism in Europe: Beyond al-Qaeda: Hamas and Hezbollah in Europe," Testimony to the Joint Hearing of the Committee on International Relations, Subcommittee on Europe and Emerging Threats, United States House of Representatives, 27 April 2005; D. Ranetunge, "British Charities Fund Terrorists," *The Island*, 4 October 2000. Online. Available HTTP: <http://www.priu.gov.lk/news_update/features/20001004British_charities_fund_terrorists%20.htm> (accessed 17 October 2005).
4 UN Security Council Resolution 1373 (2001). Online. Available HTTP: <http://www.unodc.org/images/resolution%201373.pdf> (accessed 22 May 2005). UNSCR 1373 followed a number of earlier initiatives, such as the International Convention for the Suppression of the Financing of Terrorism (1999) and the Financial Action Task Force on Money Laundering (1989). Lists of prohibited entities include the United States' "Executive Order 13224 Blocking Terrorist Property," the Bank of England's "Consolidated List of Financial Sanctions Targets in the UK," and the European Union's "List of Persons and Entities Subject to Financial Sanctions."
5 The fact that such charities are operated by and for Muslims does not necessarily determine their behavior. As Sunier rightly observes, Islamic organizations do not necessarily "take on similar shapes, irrespective of social setting." Instead, "the interests of Muslims are . . . not self evidently based on Islamic principles, as is often assumed. They are contextual and dynamic and change according to altered circumstances . . . the mechanisms underlying interest struggle are general and

applicable to any interest group." T. Sunier, "Islam and Interest Struggle: Religious Collective Action among Turkish Muslims in the Netherlands," in S. Vertovece and A. Rogers (eds.) *Muslim European Youth–Reproducing Ethnicity, Religion, Culture*, Aldershot: Ashgate, 1998, pp. 40–41. In this chapter, I will analyze Islamic charities from a social movement perspective, assuming that such charities are collective actors following rational strategies within particular political and discursive opportunity structures.

6   The charities accused of links with al Qaeda were Afghan Support Committee, al Furqan, al Rashid Trust, al Haramain and al Masjed al Aqsa Charity Foundation, al Haramain (Islamic/Humanitarian) Foundation, Barakaat International Foundation (Sweden), Benevolence International (Foundation/Fund), Bosanska Idealna Futura, Global Relief Foundation, Jam'yah Ta'awun al Islamia, Lajnat al Daawa al Islamiya, Makhtab al Khidamat/al Kifah, Nada International Anstalt, Nasreddin Foundation, Rabita Trust, Revival of Islamic Heritage Society, Somali International Relief Organization, Taibah International Aid Agency (Bosnia), The Aid Organisation of the Ulema Pakistan, Ummah Tameer e-Nau, Wafa Humanitarian Organization. The charities linked with Hamas were Holy Land Foundation for Relief and Development (USA), al Aqsa Foundation. Only organizations that appeared to be explicitly registered as charitable foundations have been included. Banks, financial networks, trading companies, and business organizations have been excluded from this count – although the distinction is not always clear (some of the charities included appear to be financial networks rather than charities in the proper sense of the word, e.g. Barakaat International Foundation, Nada International Anstalt, and Nasreddin Foundation). Where a charity's national branches have been listed separately, I have counted the different branches as one charity. See lists online. Available HTTP: <http://www.bankofengland.co.uk/ publications/financialsanctions/current/index.htm> <http://europa.eu.int/comm/ external_relations/cfsp/sanctions/list/version4/global/e_ctlview.html#en845> (accessed 22 May 2005).

7   The only prohibited non-Muslim entity with aspects of a charity was the International Sikh Youth Foundation.

8   M. Greenberg, W. Wechsler, and L. Wolosky, *Terrorist Financing: Report of an Independent Task Force Sponsored by the Council on Foreign Relations*, New York: Council on Foreign Relations, 2002, p. 13; R. Gunaratna, *Inside al-Qaeda: Global Network of Terror*, London: Hurst, 2002, pp. 6, 68.

9   See Napoleoni, *Modern Jihad*, 70–73; Levitt, "Hamas and Hezbollah in Europe"; *Rapportage werkgroep/Terrorismefinanciering en terrorismebestrijding*, 8 July 2003, p. 45. Online. Available HTTP: <http://www.fecinfo.nl> (accessed 24 June 2004).

10   Because of differences in the legal systems between England and Wales, Scotland, and Northern Ireland, as reflected in the existence of different Charity Commissions, I will focus on England and Wales.

11   The UK has been identified as a hub for both Islamist activities generally and al Qaeda actions specifically. See G. Kepel, *Jihad: the Trail of Political Islam*, London: I.B. Tauris, 2000, pp. 303–305; R. Gunaratna, *Inside al Qaeda: Global Network of Terror*, New York: Columbia University Press, 2002, pp. 116–121. The Netherlands have been identified as a significant hub for financial and coordinational activities of al Qaeda-related cells. See Gunaratna, *Inside al Qaeda*, pp. 126–129; A. Anthony, "Amsterdamned, Part One," *The Observer*, 5 December 2004; H. de Vreij, "Dutch Link in Madrid Bomb Plot?" *Radio Netherlands*, 21 October 2004. Online. Available HTTP: <http://www2.rnw.nl/rnw/en/ currentaffairs/region/westerneurope/10610251> (accessed 17 October 2005); de Vreij, "Behind the Dutch Terror Threat," *Radio Netherlands*, 22 July 2004. Online. Available HTTP: <http://www2.rnw.nl/rnw/en/currentaffairs/region/netherlands/ ned040722.html> (accessed 17 October 2005); "Not Saying the 'AQ' Word,"

Geopolitical Review, 16 November 2004. Online. Available HTTP: <http://www.geopoliticalreview.com/archives/000500.php> (accessed 17 October 2005).

12 The Charity Commission for England and Wales had investigated 17 charities for possible wrongdoing at the time of writing; 10 were subsequently subjected to formal inquiries. Aalami Majlise Tahaffuze Khatme Nubuwwat and the Islamic Foundation were found to have trustees with possible links with bin Laden's network. The trustees were removed and the charities continued to operate. The North London Central Mosque Trust (the "Finsbury Park mosque") was investigated because its main preacher, Abu Hamza al Masri, was believed to have abused the mosque's charitable status by overtly promoting extreme political goals. Various al Qaeda suspects (e.g. Richard Reid, Zacarias Moussaoui) are said to have worshipped at the Finsbury Park mosque. See M. Sageman, *Understanding Terror Networks*, Philadelphia: University of Pennsylvania Press, 2004, p. 50; "U.S. Indicts British Cleric on 11 Charges," *MSNBC News*, 27 May 2004. Online. Available HTTP: <http://www.msnbc.msn.com/id/5071534> (accessed 17 October 2005). The charity's trustees (who had been ousted by al Masri) welcomed the Charity Commission's decision to remove al Masri. Interpal (Palestinians Relief and Development Fund) was investigated following allegations by the US Treasury that it funded Hamas. Benevolence International (UK) was similarly inspected because the US Treasury believed it to have links with the Saudi-based Benevolence International Foundation (blacklisted on both the EU and Bank of England lists). No evidence of wrongdoing was found in either case. See <http://www.charity-commission.gov.uk/investigations/inquiryreports/inqreps.asp> (accessed 17 October 2005).

In the Netherlands, Benevolence International Nederland and Stichting al Haramain Humanitarian Aid were found to have links with the bin Laden network. Stichting al Aqsa, a local branch of the German-based al Aqsa Foundation, was believed to have funded Palestinian organizations that were thought to fund Hamas. The al Muwaffaq charity was found to have two members designated by the US Government as persons implicated in bin Laden's network. Though the Dutch Intelligence and Security Services (AIVD) stated in 1998 that they believed al Muwaffaq to have "supported the armed Islamic struggle," no further action was taken. Stichting Tawheed, which runs the Tawheed mosque and As Siddiq school in Amsterdam, remains open although it is believed to have close links with the al Haramain Foundation. The Al-waqf Al-islaami Stichting in Eindhoven is thought to have been involved in training and recruiting volunteers for "the international jihad" through the affiliated al Furqaan mosque. See <http://www.aivd.nl> (accessed 1 July 2004): "Antwoorden op kamervragen over financieringen vanuit Saoedi-Arabië," 31 December 2002; "Antwoorden op kamervragen over de mogelijke financiering van de Al-Tawheed moskee in Amsterdam," 2 March 2004; "Brief aan de Tweede Kamer over de stichting Al Waqf al-Islami," 25 April 2003; "Antwoorden op kamervragen over de organisatie Al-waqf Al-islaami die in de Al Furqaan moskee in Eindhoven opleidingen verzorgt tot strijder in de heilige oorlog," 24 June 2003; "Antwoorden op kamervragen over onderzoek naar een mogelijke tijdelijke sluiting van de Al-Fourqaan moskee in Eindhoven," 24 June 2003. Gunaratna, *Inside al Qaeda*, p. 126.

13 Gunaratna, *Inside al Qaeda*, pp. 6, 68.

14 No precise figures are available on the number of "Islamic" charities in England, Wales, and the Netherlands. Considering that there were 187,000 charities registered in England and Wales in July 2004 and that 3 percent of the population in England and Wales declared itself "Muslim" in the 2001 census, a rough estimate would be that some 3 percent of the 187,000 charities, or 5,610, are "Islamic." In the Netherlands, 151,190 charities ("stichtingen") were registered with the Chamber of Commerce in July 2004. With Muslims making up 4.4 percent of the

total population (the Dutch census does not record religion; this figure comes from the *CIA World Factbook* and is presumably based on an approximation on the basis of the original nationality of immigrants and their descendants), a rough estimate of the number of Islamic charities would be 4 percent of the total number, or 6,000. However, if we base our calculations on the (estimated) number of Muslims in each country, 700,000 in the Netherlands versus 1.5 million in England and Wales, the number of Islamic charities in the Netherlands is likely to be half that of those in England and Wales, i.e., 2,800 (assuming levels of socio-political activity among Muslims are similar). Charity Commission Homepage <http://www.charity-commission.gov.uk/>; Census 2001: Ethnicity and Religion in England and Wales <http://www.statistics.gov.uk/census2001/profiles/commentaries/ethnicity.asp#religion>; Chamber of Commerce Homepage <http://www.kvk.nl>; CIA World Factbook <http://www.cia.gov/cia/publications/factbook/geos/nl.html#People> (all websites accessed July 2004).

15 Europe-wide, three other charities have been accused by the Israeli and American governments of funding Hamas's violent struggle (the Comité de bienfaisance et de secours aux Palistiniens in France, the Association de secours palestinien in Switzerland, and the Palestinian Association in Austria). The governments in question have so far refused to take action for lack of evidence.

16 Though the official accusation against Stichting al Aqsa states that the charities it has funded are believed to have either carried out or facilitated terrorist acts, the information available in the public domain only suggests that its money has been used to pay the families of martyrs, including the families of suicide bombers, rather than funding armed actions directly. "Tegoeden Al-Aqsa bevroren na onderzoek AIVD," AIVD Press Release, 9 April 2003, Online. Available HTTP: <http://www.aivd.nl/algemene_onderdelen/tegoeden_al-aqsa> (accessed 17 October 2005). This assumption was corroborated by an anonymous source close to the investigations into Stichting al Aqsa (consulted in 2005). Even Levitt, who accuses European-based charities of funding Hamas's armed struggle, does not produce any concrete evidence of a charity (as opposed to individuals) funding Hamas's armed struggle beyond providing money to the families of martyrs but makes his case on the basis of the argument that the charities are integral to the armed struggle. Levitt, "Hamas and Hezbollah in Europe"; Levitt, *Hamas: Politics, Charity, and Terrorism in the Service of Jihad*, New Haven, CT: Yale University Press, 2006, pp. 154–157. For Israeli intelligence reports, see, e.g. "Saudi Money Transfers to the Hamas and to Extremist Groups Identified with It," Report of the (Israeli) Intelligence and Terrorism Information Center at the Center for Special Studies, February 2003. Online. Available HTTP: <http://www.intelligence.org.il/eng/bu/saudi/saudi.htm> (accessed 17 October 2005); " 'Charity' and Palestinian Terrorism – Spotlight on the Hamas-run Islamic Al-Tadhamun 'Charitable Society' in Nablus," Intelligence and Terrorism Information Center at the Center for Special Studies, February 2005. Online. Available HTTP: <http://www.intelligence.org.il/eng/sib/3_05/charity_2.htm> (accessed 17 October 2005); M. Dudkevitch, "Army Seals Offices of Hamas Charity Organizations," *Jerusalem Post*, 8 July 2004.

17 United Nations, *International Convention for the Suppression of the Financing of Terrorism*, 1999. Online. Available HTTP: <http://untreaty.un.org/English/Terrorism/Conv12.pdf> (accessed 17 October 2005).

18 Y. Amidror and D. Keyes, "Will a Gaza 'Hamas-stan' Become a Future Al-Qaeda Sanctuary?" *Jerusalem Issue Brief*, vol. 4 no. 7, 8 November 2004. Online. Available HTTP: <http://www.jcpa.org/brief/brief004-7.htm> (accessed 17 October 2005); Levitt, "Hamas and Hezbollah in Europe."

19 In Gaza (under Egyptian administration between 1948 and 1967), the Brotherhood suffered from the clash between the Egyptian Brotherhood and President Nasser

and was decimated by Nasser's heavy-handed clampdown. In the West Bank (under Jordanian administration), the Palestinian Brothers were subsumed under the Jordanian Brotherhood, which meant that when the West Bank was occupied by Israel in 1967, the local branches were effectively leaderless. Palestinian Islamism, moreover, was initially eclipsed by the ascent of Palestinian nationalism as the Palestinian response to the defeat of 1967. See, for example, B. Milton-Edwards, *Islamic Politics in Palestine*, London: Tauris Academic Studies, 1996, pp. 36–80.

20 In the absence of extensive, reliable data regarding the exact nature of al Qaeda, and given the contested nature of available data, this caveat is essential. See, for instance, J. Burke, *Al-Qaeda: Casting a Shadow of Terror*, London: I.B. Tauris, 2003, pp. 7–22. See also Chapter Three by Rohan Gunaratna in this book describing the transformation of al Qaeda from an organization into a global jihad movement.

21 *Takfiri* denotes the practice of labelling Muslims considered to have "lapsed" apostate (*kafir*) and worthy of summary execution.

22 Kepel, *Jihad*, pp. 83–87.

23 Burke, *Al-Qaeda*, pp. 71–72.

24 Ibid., p. 78, 109, 139; Kepel, *Jihad*, pp. 254–258, 276, 286.

25 The 1997 targeting of tourists by Egyptian radical Islamists in Luxor illustrates the extent of their isolation from the larger community whose livelihood largely depended on tourism, and whose anger and subsequent alienation was one of the factors leading to the radicals' demise. Kepel, *Jihad*, pp. 277, 289, 297.

26 J. Gunning, "Peace with Hamas? The Transforming Potential of Political Participation," *International Affairs*, 2004, vol. 80, no. 2, pp. 241–255.

27 For details on Hamas's political ideals and practice, see Gunning, *Re-Thinking Western Constructs of Islamism: Pluralism, Democracy and the Theory and Praxis of the Islamic Movement in the Gaza Strip*, doctoral thesis, Durham: Centre for Middle Eastern and Islamic Studies, 2000, Chs 6–8. See also my forthcoming monograph on Hamas, Cambridge: Cambridge University Press. For details on al Qaeda's political ideals and practice, see, e.g. Gunaratna, *Inside al Qaeda*, pp. 84–94, 156–159; Burke, *Al-Qaeda*, pp. 23–39, 69–72, 85–89, 109, 141, 145–150; Sageman, *Understanding Terror Networks*, pp. 1–59.

28 G. Robinson, "Hamas as Social Movement," in Q. Wiktorowicz (ed.) *Islamic Activism: a Social Movement Theory Approach*, Bloomington: Indiana University Press, 2004, pp. 117–123; Gunning, "Hamas, Socialisation and the Logic of Compromise," in J. Tirman, M. Heiberg and B. O'Leary (eds.) *Terror, Insurgency, and the State*, Philadelphia: University of Pennsylvania Press, 2007.

29 See also Kepel's analysis of the divergent dispositions of the core constituencies of the radical and more moderate forms of Islamism. Kepel, *Jihad*, pp. 254, 292, 359, 375.

30 See, for example, survey findings of Palestine Center for Policy and Survey Research (PSR). Online. Available HTTP: <http://www.pcpsr.org> (accessed 5 November 2005).

31 PSR, Poll No. 19, 16–18 March 2006 (accessed 30 June 2006).

32 Al Qaeda "proper" does not have an embedded charitable network or consist of embedded members. Sageman notes similarly that the individuals joining the "global jihad" were typically "socially alienated, or temporarily disembedded" and makes the important observation that "this absence of connection is a necessary condition for a network of people to join the global jihad." Sageman, *Understanding Terror Networks*, pp. 146–147. The Egyptian Jihad, some of whose leaders dominate al Qaeda's upper echelons, distinguishes itself from other Egyptian Islamist groups by its lack of concern for society and what Kepel calls "the process of resocialization," which both the Muslim Brotherhood and its

radical offshoots, the Gamaat Islamiyya, emphasize. G. Kepel, *The Prophet & Pharaoh: Muslim Extremism in Egypt*, London: Al Saqi Books, 1985, p. 193; Kepel, *Jihad*, p. 282. The Algerian GIA, another (according to some) close associate of al Qaeda's, has similarly been primarily focused on violence (Kepel, *Jihad*, pp. 254–258). The Indonesian Jemaah Islamiya, another affiliate, is similarly primarily a jihadi organization with little interest in transforming society through charitable activities. The fact that many of its leaders were recruited while in exile and performed the role of "itinerant preachers" underscores this point. Z. Abuza, *Militant Islam in Southeast Asia: Crucible of Terror*, London: Lynne Rienner, 2003, pp. 125–140.

33 Gunaratna, *Inside al Qaeda*, pp. 156–159; Burke, *Al-Qaeda*, pp. 150–177.

34 Illustrations of both ends of this spectrum are Mohammed Atta and Richard Reid. For an analysis of the socioeconomic status of a sample of "global salafi mujahedin" (Sageman's term for the pool of people from which al Qaeda and affiliates draw), see Sageman, *Understanding Terror Networks*, pp. 73–77. Sageman's sample contains 18 percent members from the upper classes, 55 percent from the middle classes, 28 percent from the lower classes. In the sample, 83 percent had been educated in secular (as opposed to religious) schools, 71 percent had a university or college education, and 17 percent did not have a high school education.

35 According to one (arguably very conservative) estimate, Hamas's Qassam Brigades consisted of only 200–500 "hard-core members" in 2003. "Special Report: Terror Groups," *The St. Petersburg Times*. Online. Available HTTP: <http://www.sptimes.com/2003/webspecials03/alarian/terror.shtml> (accessed 17 October 2005). The US State Department merely describes the strength of the Brigades as "unknown." US Department of State, *Patterns of Global Terrorism*, 21 May 2002. Online. Available HTTP: <http://www.state.gov/s/ct/rls/pgtrpt/2001/html/10252.htm#hamas> (accessed 17 October 2005). The precise number of charitable workers is unknown but certain to be considerably higher.

36 Gunning, *Western Constructs*, Ch. 7.4.1.

37 Gunning, *Socialisation*.

38 According to Israeli intelligence sources, 90 percent of Hamas's funding before the al Aqsa Intifada was spent on social-service programs, 10 percent on its military wing. Since the start of the al Aqsa Intifada, the same sources believe 20 percent of total funding is now directed towards Hamas's military program. T. Roule, "Post–911 Financial Freeze Dries Up Hamas Funding," *Jane's Intelligence Review*, 17–19 May 2002, no. 14, p. 17.

39 According to a recent opinion poll, 82 percent of Palestinians believe that "corruption is most prevalent in the Governmental sector." The Coalition for Accountability and Integrity, "Opinion Poll on Corruption in the Palestinian Society," 30–31 December 2004. Online. Available HTTP: <http://www.transparency.org/surveys/dnld/palestine_poll.pdf> (accessed 17 October 2005).

40 Conversations with personnel from UNRWA, Pharmaciens sans Frontières, Save the Children, and Mennonite Central Committee, Gaza, 1998.

41 See, for example, the accusation levelled by the Board of Deputies of British Jews against Interpal. C. Dyer, "Charity Sues Jewish Board over Hamas Claim," *The Guardian*, London, 20 October 2003. In the Netherlands, the Centre for Information and Documentation on Israel (CIDI) plays a similar role, having prompted investigations into a number of charities, including. Stichting al Aqsa. See "CIDI vraagt onderzoek naar stichting Al Aqsa Rotterdam," *Rotterdams Dagblad*, 7 August 2002; or CIDI Homepage, <http://www.cidi.nl> (accessed 17 October 2005).

42 Levitt, *Hamas*, pp. 52–106.

43 D. van Natta and T. O'Brien, "Flow of Saudi Cash to Hamas Is under Scrutiny by U.S.," *The New York Times*, New York, 17 September 2003; L. Kaplow,

"Backgrounder: Israel's Adversaries: Hamas: Back-seat Driver to Arafat Group," *Atlanta Journal-Constitution*, 24 January 2002, quoted in J. Stork, *Erased In A Moment: Suicide Bombing Attacks Against Israeli Civilians*, New York: Human Rights Watch, 2002, p. 94; D. Eberhart, "Hamas Touts Untouchable 'Secret' Funding Sources," *NewsMax.com*, 5 December 2001. Online. Available HTTP: <http://www.newsmax.com/archives/articles/2001/12/4/175008.shtml> (accessed 17 October 2005).

44 The removal of Saddam Hussein has resulted in the suspension of the $25,000 payments to the families of suicide bombers that Saddam is said to have instigated (although it is unclear how regular such payments were; see, for example, Stork, *Suicide Bombing*, 100–101, 104). The presence of US troops in the region has made both the Syrian and Iranian regimes more cautious, although it remains to be seen whether this will result in a drop in financial and other aid.

45 See, for example, allegations and court case against Mohammed Salah, a Palestinian living in the United States. Boim v. Quranic Literacy Institute (291 F.3d 1000); D. Pipes, "A New Way to Fight Terrorism," *Jerusalem Post*, 24 May 2000.

46 Rex Hudson, "Terrorist and Organized Crime Groups in the Tri-Border Area (TBA) of South America," Report prepared by the Federal Research Division, Washington, DC: Library of Congress, July 2003.

47 See the Commission's ruling on Interpal. Online. Available HTTP: <http://www.charity-commission.gov.uk/investigations/inquiryreports/inqreps.asp> (accessed 17 October 2005).

48 Geneva Convention Relative to the Protection of Civilian Persons in Time of War, 12 August 1949. Online. Available HTTP: <http://www.unhchr.ch/html/menu3/b/92.htm> (accessed 17 October 2005).

49 An Israeli government report argued that Hamas-affiliated charities provided "one-time grants of between $500–5,000" for "the families of those who have been killed and wounded in perpetrating acts of terror." "Hamas's Use of Charitable Societies to Fund and Support Terror," Israeli Ministry of Foreign Affairs, 22 September 2003. Online. Available HTTP: <http://www.mfa.gov.il> (accessed 23 May 2005). Stork sets the amount of money given to martyrs' families by the Islamist as-Salah charity (which, though separate from the Hamas network, operates according to a similar logic) at $5,300 (106). Until the fall of Saddam, families of suicide bombers were said to receive $25,000 from the local Iraqi Bath party (see Stork, *Suicide Bombing*, p. 104; Goldberg, "The Men behind the Suicide Bombers," *The Guardian*, London, 12 June 2002, p. 13.).

50 Claude Berrebi, "Evidence About the Link Between Education, Poverty and Terrorism Among Palestinians," Mimeo, Princeton University, 2003, pp. 37–39; Alan Krueger and Jitka Maleçková, "Education, Poverty and Terrorism: Is There a Causal Connection?" *Journal of Economic Perspectives*, Fall 2003, vol. 17, no. 4, pp. 135–136.

51 See also M. Basile, "Going to the Source: Why Al Qaeda's Financial Network Is Likely to Withstand the Current War on Terrorist Financing," *Studies in Conflict and Terrorism*, 2004, vol. 27, no. 3, p. 173.

52 See, by way of comparison, the original Maktab al Khidamat which bin Laden oversaw during the Afghan conflict.

53 Many of the charities that have been linked to al Qaeda are humanitarian charities providing aid to the war-torn areas in which al Qaeda affiliates operate. Some of these charities have allegedly been founded by people close to bin Laden. See, for example, Gunaratna's claims regarding Benevolence International and Brisard's claims regarding the IIRO and the Muslim World League. Gunaratna, *Inside al Qaeda*, pp. 112–113; J. C. Brisard, *Terrorism Financing*, Report prepared for the President of the UN Security Council, New York, 2002, p. 27. Others appear to have been infiltrated subsequent to having been founded.

54 A Dutch government report notes that "a recruiter [for the international jihad] will welcome a prominent position in a mosque . . . [because] it gives him more possibilities to arrange matters for other brothers and recruits (logistics, material and financial)." AIVD, "Recruitment for the Jihad in the Netherlands." Online. Available HTTP: <http://www.aivd.nl/contents/pages/2285/recruitmentbw.pdf> (accessed 17 October 2005).

55 See, for example, bin Laden's denunciations of the Gulf State rulers in his 4 January 2004 speech on *al Jazeera*. Online. Available HTTP: <http://www.mideastweb.org/log/archives/00000155.htm> (accessed 17 October 2005).

56 See also Basile, "Going to the Source," p. 173.

57 Because the Saudi state has not traditionally levied tax (the so-called "rentier state" model, which funds itself through oil proceeds), there is no regular audit system. Similarly, until recently, no records have been required for the giving of *zakah* (a religious "tax" that both individuals and businesses voluntarily give to charity). Napoleoni, *Modern Jihad*, 123.

58 J. Cooley, *Unholy Wars: Afghanistan, America and International Terrorism*, 2nd edn, London: Pluto Press, 2000, pp. 83, 87; Kepel, *Jihad*, 300–301; Burke, *Al-Qaeda*, p. 57.

59 Burke, *Al-Qaeda*, pp. 57–58; Basile, "Going to the Source," 173.

60 Burke, *Al-Qaeda*, pp. 57–58; D. Kaplan, "The Saudi Connection," *U.S. News & World Report*, Washington, 15 December 2003.

61 D. McGrory and J. Doran, "Bin Laden Funded by Bogus Charities," *The Times*, London, 25 September 2001.

62 For estimates of the budgets of al Haramain, the Muslim World League, and the International Islamic Relief Organization, see Kaplan, "The Saudi Connection."

63 "Al-Qaeda Skimming Charity Money," *CBSNews.com*, 7 June 2004. Online. Available HTTP: <http://www.cbsnews.com/stories/2004/06/07/terror/main 621621.shtml> (accessed 18 October 2005).

64 Brisard, *Terrorism Financing*.

65 I. Key, "Bin Laden's Money Network," *The Express*, Manchester, 1 October 2001, pp. 8, 9.

66 See also J. Gunning, "Making Sense of al-Qaeda in Europe," Oxford-Princeton Conference on Muslims in Europe post 9/11, Oxford, 26 April 2003. Online. Available HTTP: <http://www.sant.ox.ac.uk/princeton/gunning-full.pdf> (accessed 23 May 2005).

67 ICM/BBC Radio 4 Today poll, December 2002. Online. Available HTTP: <http://www.icmresearch.co.uk/reviews/2002/bbc-today-muslims-dec-02.htm> (accessed 5 November 2005).

68 Most prominently, Abu Hamza al Masri's Supporters of Shari'ah and Omar Bakri's now disbanded al Muhajiroun. The number of supporters of Shari'ah has been in decline since al Masri's removal from Finsbury Park Mosque. Estimates for al Muhajiroun range between a few hundred and a few thousand. Omar Bakri himself set the total number at 800. Interview in A. Mesoy, *How Does Political Alienation Cause Muslims in London to Engage in Radical Political Behaviour?*, Masters dissertation, Aberystwyth, 2004, p. 15.

69 For mainstream rejection, see letter sent by the Muslim Council of Britain to all UK mosques. "Letter to Mosques and Muslim Leaders," *The Guardian*, London, 31 March 2004. For reaction of larger Islamist organizations, see telephone interview with Dr. Azzam Tamimi, Institute of Islamic Political Thought and Muslim Association of Britain, April 2003.

70 "Saoedische invloeden in Nederland. Verbanden tuseen salafistische missie, radicaliseringsprocessen en islamitisch terrorisme," AIVD report, 9 June 2004, 11. Online. Available HTTP: <http://www.aivd.nl/contents/pages/8931/rapportsaoedischeinvloeden.pdf> (accessed 18 October 2005).

71 A. Esman, "The Arabian Panther," Foundation for the Defense of Democracies, 14 June 2004. Online. Available HTTP: <http://www.defenddemocracy.org/research_topics/research_topics_show.htm?doc_id=228652> (accessed 18 October 2005).

72 See note 12.

73 See also Sageman's comment on the necessity of un-embeddedness, n. 33. A significant number of those who were European-born, such as Zacarias Moussaoui, Richard Reid, and David and Jérome Courtailler, appear to have become uprooted from their communities before "succumbing" to al Qaeda.

74 R. Leiken, "Immigration: Is Integration Failing?" panel discussion, International Summit on Democracy, Terrorism, and Security, Madrid, 9 March 2005. Online. Available HTTP: <http://english.safe-democracy.org/keynotes/immigration-is-integration-failing.html> (accessed 17 October 2005).

75 "Young Islam: Hardline Youths Fuel Bitter Divide," *The Observer*, London, 4 April 2004; Anthony, "Amsterdamned"; "Not Saying the 'AQ' Word," *Geopolitical Review*, 16 November 2004. Online. Available HTTP: <http://www.geopoliticalreview.com/archives/000500not_saying_the_aq_word.php> (accessed 17 October 2005).

76 Among Sageman's sample of "global Salafi mujahedin," 7 out of 172 are converts of Western origin (*Understanding Terror Networks*, 185–189). On white converts among al Muhajiroun members, see B. Wazir, "Essex Boys Sign up for 'Holy War,' " *The Observer*, London, 24 February 2002.

77 The strength of this definition lies in the fact that it straddles both individual psychological and systemic factors and therefore can incorporate a wide variety of findings, ranging from aspiration–achievement gap theories to systems-level analyses, as well as more contemporary notions of identity and culture.

78 D. Schwartz, *Political Alienation and Political Behavior*, Chicago: Aldine Publishing, 1973, pp. 14–16, 25–28, 235.

79 I borrow the term "post-migrant" from Sunier, "Islam and Interest Struggle," pp. 52–54.

80 See, for example, notions of "Islamic terrorism" and "Islamic education" used in AIVD publications. AIVD Homepage. Online. Available HTTP: <http://www.aivd.nl> (accessed 17 October 2005).

81 Sunier, Cesari, and Samad all date the emergence of self-consciously Islamic organizations and identities among Turkish immigrants in the Netherlands, Muslims in France, and Muslims in Britain to the 1980s. Sunier, "Islam and Interest Struggle," 46; J. Cesari, "Islam in France: Social Challenge or Challenge of Secularism?" in Vertovec and Rogers, *Muslim European Youth*, Aldershot, UK: Ashgate Publishing, 1998, 33–36; Y. Samad, "Imagining a British Muslim Identification," in Vertovec and Rogers, *Muslim European Youth*, 61–72. Kepel dates this shift in France to the late 1980s and early 1990s G. Kepel, *Allah in the West*, Stanford, CA: Stanford University Press, 1997, pp. 202–203. This shift from a more secular identity to a self-consciously religious one should, however, not be exaggerated. Religious identity played a role in secular self-understandings while secular notions such as national identity continue to play a role in the self-consciously religious construction of identity.

82 Home Office Report (*Briefing on British Muslims*, March 2004) quoted in David Leppard, "Soaring Jobless Total Feeds the Extremist Fires," *The Sunday Times*, London, 30 May 2004; observations by Lord Ahmed, quoted in Jason Burke et al., "Hardline Youths Divide Muslims," *The Observer*, London, 4 April 2004.

83 See, for example, Kim Willsher, "My Son Wouldn't Lie to Me," *The Sunday Telegraph*, London, 1 September 2002; Abd Samad Moussaoui, "My Brother Zac," *The Guardian*, London, 19 April 2003.

84 Cesari, "Islam in France," pp. 29–31.

85 Schwartz distinguishes between "socio-cultural" and "political" alienation, and argues that, in 1960s America, the two were not "significantly associated with each other" (*Political Alienation and Political Behavior*, pp. 42–44).

86 On most recent developments in Britain, see M. Abdel-Halim, "Four British Muslims Make It to Parliament," *IslamOnline.net*, Cairo, 6 May 2005. Online. Available HTTP: <http://islamonline.net/English/News/2005–05/06/article03.shtml> (accessed 18 October 2005).

87 George Galloway, MP, was one of those who benefited from MAB's endorsement. "Muslim Vote Pivotal to General Election Outcome," press release, *MABonline.net*, 6 May 2005. Online. Available HTTP: <http://www.mabonline.info/english/modules.php?name=News&file=article&sid=378> (accessed 18 October 2005).

88 An alternative reading is that increased openness in a political system either marginalizes the violently inclined or leads them to believe that violence "worked." In both cases, increased openness is likely to produce more violence, at least in the short term. See D. della Porta, "Left-Wing Terrorism in Italy," in M. Crenshaw (ed.) *Terrorism in Context*, University Park, PA: Pennsylvania State University Press, 1995, pp. 105–159.

89 Zawahiri's subterfuge has already been cited above. According to Special Branch in Britain, a number of unregistered fringe organizations have similarly "[preyed] on mosques, colleges and communities who believed that they were giving to orphans in Afghanistan or the homeless from an Indian earthquake." McGrory and Doran, "Bin Laden Funded by Bogus Charities."

90 Despite local government accusations to the contrary, experts appear to believe that the Central Asian branches of the party similarly refrain from advocating and perpetrating political violence. J. Page, "Muslims Seeking Paradise Turn to Extremism in the Face of Poverty," *The Times*, London, 21 May 2005; T. Makarenko, "The Changing Dynamics of Central Asian Terrorism," *Jane's Intelligence Review*, February 2002. Online. Available HTTP: <http://www.janes.com/security/international_security/news/jir/jir020129_1_n.shtml> (accessed 13 April 2007).

91 For national impact, see notes 86, 87. For an overview of local and European election strategies, see O. Saeed, "Labour Has Forfeited the Muslim Vote," *The Guardian*, London, 25 May 2004.

92 E. Asaad Buaras, "War Costs Labour the Muslim Vote," *Muslim News*, 30 May 2003, no. 169; H. Chapman, "Lib Dems Delighted at Gaining Britain's Only Muslim MEP," *Muslim News*, 25 June 2004, no. 182. See also n. 88, 89.

93 S. O'Neill, "British Islam Colleges 'Link to Terrorism.'" *The Times*, London, 29 July 2004.

94 A. Browne, "Hatred Engulfs a Liberal Land," *The Times*, London, 13 November 2004; I. Traynor, "Liberal Culture under Threat in Dutch Religious and Ethnic Crisis," *The Guardian*, London, 12 November 2004.

95 della Porta, "Left-Wing Terrorism in Italy," pp. 105–159.

96 Gunaratna has recently argued that al Qaeda's influence in Europe has grown since the Madrid bombings and that compromised Islamic charities need to be targeted by European intelligence agencies if al Qaeda's threat is to be countered effectively. However, Gunaratna does not provide a single example of a compromised charity, instead focusing on small-scale cells of suspected al Qaeda affiliates. R. Gunaratna, "The Post-Madrid Face of Al Qaeda," *The Washington Quarterly*, Summer 2004, vol. 27, no. 3, pp. 91–100.

97 T. Kafala, "Palestinians Suffer as Charities Close," *BBC News Online*, 30 January 2002. Online. Available HTTP: <http://news.bbc.co.uk/1/hi/world/middle_east/1789093.stm> (accessed 18 October 2005); S. Taylor Martin, "Frozen Accounts Jeopardize Learning, Healing in Gaza," *St Petersburg Times Online*, 15 September

2003. Online. Available HTTP: <http://www.sptimes.com/2003/09/15/Worldand-nation/Frozen_accounts_jeopa.shtml> (accessed 18 October 2005); "PCHR Calls upon the Palestinian Authority to Cancel Its Decision to Freeze Funds of Charitable Societies," press release, Palestinian Centre for Human Rights, Gaza, 28 August 2003.

 98 See the precise distinction made in Boim vs. Quranic Literacy Institute (291 F.3d 1000) between "giving money to a group which then sponsored a terrorist act" and "international terrorism."

 99 Any member of the public has the right to bring suspicions to the Commission's attention and the Commission is obliged to look into these suspicions (30–40 percent of cases originate from the Commission's own investigations; 30 percent from other regulators, for example, the police; 30 percent from members of the public). However, the decision whether to instigate an inquiry rests solely with the Commission. Telephone interview with Simon Gillespie, Director of Operations, Charity Commission, 21 July 2004.

100 Telephone interviews with Gillespie (2004) and Antony Robbins, Head of Communications, Charity Commission, 8 July 2004. For reform outcomes, see n. 12.

101 In conversations with an anonymous source close to the investigation, that source hinted at strong pressure from Israel on the AIVD (and the government) to revise its earlier stance that Hamas's political and social wings could be differentiated from its military wing.

102 A similar solution was suggested in a hypothetical situation by Gillespie, the Charity Commission's Director of Operations (Interview with Gillespie, 2004).

103 See R. Bekkers, "Trust, Accreditation, and Philanthropy in the Netherlands," *Nonprofit and Voluntary Sector Quarterly*, December 2003, vol. 32, no. 4, pp. 596–615.

104 Conversation with anonymous source close to the investigations.

6 Terrorist financing and organized crime

Nexus, appropriation, or transformation?[1]

Phil Williams

On 11 March 2004 a coordinated series of train bombings in Madrid killed 191 people and injured more than 1,500 others.[2] The death toll would have been even higher had not one of the bombs failed to explode. Significantly, the unexploded bomb provided forensic clues that facilitated the succeeding investigation. In the ensuing months, Spanish investigators not only succeeded in identifying and arresting most of the perpetrators, but also pieced together the activities that preceded the attacks, including the fundraising efforts. The investigators found that the financial activities of these terrorists were intimately connected to those of a drug trafficking group, thus lending credence to arguments that there is a growing cooperation – and perhaps a nexus – between organized crime and terrorism.

This notion of a nexus between organized crime and terrorism is far from new. In the 1980s the US Ambassador to Colombia coined the term "narco-terrorism" to describe the terrorist acts perpetrated by drug trafficking organizations, especially the Medellin Cartel. During the 1990s there was increasing concern that linkages between organized crime and terrorist organizations could make the latter a much more formidable threat. As one commentator notes:

> The growing global inter-connectivity of organized crime – with its vast resources and its ability to move money, share information, exploit and manipulate modern technology, and provide endless quantities of black market commodities – has forever changed the way terrorists do business. Terrorists have always sought leverage to penetrate international power and influence. A major change today is that otherwise small and insignificant terrorist groups can join with organized crime to exercise disproportionate leverage. We used to think that small groups could only execute small acts of violence. Because of the benefits accruing from these new criminal arrangements, however, this may no longer be the case.[3]

The implication of this argument is that alliances between criminal organizations and terrorist groups have provided major synergies – for both entities, but especially for terrorist organizations – and will become not only increasingly frequent, but also of great strategic significance. Even though there is no strong empirical evidence supporting this nexus, there are some grounds for anticipating that criminal organizations and terrorist groups will forge closer links with one another. Both terrorist and criminal organizations operate in the same underworld and often in the same geographic areas, such as weak states. In addition, they have similar needs in terms of false documentation, weapons, and money; and both types of organization could derive benefits from cooperation with the other, especially in their efforts to counter law enforcement and government agencies. It would hardly be surprising, therefore, to find examples of cooperation between criminal organizations and terrorist networks.

It is important, however, not to mistake particular incidents for a secular trend, not to endow specific linkages with a significance that is unwarranted, and not to highlight a few examples of cooperation without also looking at the barriers to more extensive cooperation. Analyses rarely specify the nature of the connections involved, resulting all too often in broad allegations about the organized crime–terrorism nexus that obscure more than they reveal. While terrorists and criminals are often co-located, usually in regions or countries where good governance is absent, proximity alone does not necessarily mean that they actively cooperate with each other. Lumping together disparate phenomena under a simple heading such as the crime–terror nexus, therefore, is unhelpful conceptually and dangerous for policy.

As Karl Weick and Kathleen Sutcliffe have noted, in order to maintain an effective understanding of the environment and its attendant challenges, it is essential to reappraise and re-evaluate concepts and categories – and to do so continually and not just sporadically.[4] Although Weick and Sutcliffe's comments are directed primarily at organizations seeking to develop a culture of watchfulness and to transform themselves into high reliability organizations, they are equally compelling for analysts of organized crime and terrorism. Therefore, we must reconsider the traditional distinctions and demarcations between organized crime and terrorism. This chapter seeks to develop a conceptual framework that offers a more refined understanding of the relationships between terrorism and organized crime, to identify specific examples of the various relationships in action, and to assess the relative importance of terrorist links with criminal entities compared with terrorist appropriation of organized crime methods and activities. It also identifies a trend likely to become increasingly important – that is, the radicalization of criminals and their transformation into terrorists. Transformation, of course, can also take place in the other direction and as pointed out below, striking examples exist of terrorists abandoning the cause and becoming profit-seeking criminal enterprises.

Framework for analysis

Although the nexus between organized crime and terrorism is often treated as a given rather than as something that needs to be assessed, there are a few notable exceptions. Tamara Makarenko, for example, has contended that the term " 'crime–terror nexus' refers to a security continuum with traditional organized crime on one end of the spectrum and terrorism at the other. In the middle of the spectrum is a 'gray area,' where organized crime and terrorism are indistinguishable from one another."[5] The gray area includes traditional criminal organizations using terrorist tactics as an operational tool to pursue political objectives. Also in the gray area are terrorist groups that initially use criminal activities as a source of financing, but subsequently change from political to financial motivations. In a further development of this analysis, Makarenko identifies four general crime–terror relationships: alliances, operational motivations, convergence, and the "black hole" syndrome, in which "convergence between criminal and political motivations within a single group allows it to subsequently gain economic and political control over a state."[6]

Refreshing as Makarenko's analysis is, difficulties remain. Part of the problem is that the term nexus has been stretched to a point where it has lost any clear meaning, and some of the categories need to be disaggregated much more fully. Makarenko seems to use the term alliance, for example, to cover any form of cooperation between criminal and terrorist organizations. Certainly, the term is appropriate for joint ventures in which criminal and terrorist organizations cooperate extensively with one another, but to use it to cover supplier relationships, which are simply a function of the market, endows these relationships with either a formality or a degree of closeness that they do not deserve. The notion of the black hole syndrome is also problematic: both terrorist and criminal organizations flourish in "lawless areas" where the state is weak, but there is a huge gap between this flourishing and obtaining joint control over the state. Makarenko's analysis, nonetheless, is significant because it acknowledges the dynamic nature of these relationships and organizations, recognizing that terrorist groups can morph into criminal organizations and vice versa.

A study of criminal and terrorist organizations in Western Europe, undertaken in 2002 by the Library of Congress, provides greater analytic clarity. The authors of this study conclude:

> The association of the two types of groups has occurred in three broad patterns. The first pattern is alliances for mutual benefit, in which terrorists enter agreements with transnational criminals solely to gain funding, without engaging directly in commercial activities or compromising their ideologically based mission. This arrangement normally has been the first form of contact between the two types of group [sic]. The second pattern is direct involvement of terror groups in organized

crime, removing the "middleman" but maintaining the ideological premise of their strategy. The third pattern is the replacement of ideology by profit as the main motive for operations.[7]

Significantly, the report found that the second pattern is the most prevalent while also suggesting that a "natural progression seems to occur from the first category toward the third."[8] This last assertion is disputable, as insufficient empirical evidence exists to conclude that there is a "natural progression." Nevertheless, the third pattern highlights another dimension that needs to be considered: transformation. Moreover, as noted above, transformation can occur in either direction – not only from terrorist to criminal, as the Library of Congress study suggests, but also from criminal to terrorist. The Library of Congress study also draws an important, but in some ways confining, distinction between objectives and activities.

This chapter builds upon the distinction between objectives and activities and develops an analytic framework that further differentiates between entities and activities, while accepting that some entities are defined in large part in terms of their activities. In effect, the approach distinguishes between the essence of organizations (which covers both the purpose or mission and the core activities that are central to their identity) and the instrumental use of peripheral activities. Some activities can be used by different kinds of entities but are usually part of the core mission and core identity of only one kind. In this connection, the essence of terrorism is the effort to bring about political change through what one definition refers to as "the use, or threat of use of anxiety-producing, extra-normal violence ... which is intended to influence the attitudes and behavior of a target group wider than the immediate."[9] Often the victims are innocent civilians. The violence is intended to shock, coerce, and have other political effects. But it is not the violence per se that defines a terrorist organization; rather it is the peculiar combination of ends (which might be religious or ideological in origin but translate into political objectives) and means (extra-normal violence) that is critical to the very identity of terrorist organizations. Similarly, the combination of profit-seeking with the systematic use of criminal activities is the essence of organized crime and differentiates criminal enterprises from licit business. With this notion of essences in mind it is now necessary to consider the distinction between organizations and activities.

Organized crime as entity

Organized crime as an entity can be understood as an organization, whether networked or hierarchical, that systematically adopts criminal activities in pursuit of profit as its ultimate objective. Organized crime groups are Clausewitzian: criminal activity is a continuation of business by criminal means. Perhaps the best way to understand these entities, therefore, is to treat them as criminal enterprises. Such entities are pragmatic rather than ideological. While they can have a political dimension, sometimes creating what Roy Godson terms a political–criminal nexus, their political activities are almost invariably intended to protect their illegal activities.[10] Similarly, they tend to use violence selectively to eliminate rivals (e.g. gang war), to remove threats (e.g. contract killings of law enforcement personnel or judges), or to remove obstacles (e.g. killing of intractable businesspeople who are fighting against organized crime infiltration of a firm, factory, or economic sector). It is rare that criminal enterprises use violence against innocent civilians in the way terrorist organizations do. Among criminal enterprises, the use of contract killings is usually a carefully chosen strategy linked to the desire for financial gain: it is designed to expand the opportunities for such gains or to remove threats to either profits or the enterprise itself. Criminal violence of this kind, brutal though it is, does not involve the indiscriminate use of violence against innocent civilians that is the hallmark of terrorism. Consequently, such killings should not be confused with terrorism.

Organized crime as method

Organized crime can also be understood as a method or a set of activities that many types of entities may employ to obtain funds. Ethnic factions, terrorist organizations, insurgent groups, and even some governments, which ultimately have political ends, may appropriate organized crime methodologies as a means for funding their political agendas. In other words, the defining characteristic of these groups is not the activity so much as the purpose: organized crime is an instrumental activity. Pariah regimes in particular tend to engage in organized crime activities to maintain a hold on power in the face of international isolation. Perhaps the best example of this is the North Korean regime, which has developed an extensive portfolio of criminal activities ranging from heroin trafficking and methamphetamine production and trafficking to smuggling in endangered species and various forms of financial fraud. Such activities can be described as do-it-yourself organized crime. This phrase is particularly apposite in the sense that not all those who engage in organized criminal activities are members of traditional criminal enterprises or part of the profession of organized crime. Indeed, in the North Korean case, extensive criminal activities, usually involving some form of trafficking, have been carried out by diplomats. Fundraising through illicit activities became necessary as Pyongyang demanded that North Korean embassies become self-sufficient. Do-it-yourself organized crime is equally useful for terrorist organizations and has become an increasingly important source of funding for Islamist terrorist organizations as actions by the United States and the international community have made funding from charities and from sympathetic financiers more problematic.

Terrorist entities

Terrorist organizations can be understood as entities – quintessentially political organizations with a commitment to large-scale political change and to the use of violence to enable that change. As suggested above, the pursuit of political change through violence is the very essence of terrorist organizations. For terrorist organizations, violence is not simply instrumental nor is it merely a tactic; rather, it is a defining characteristic that differentiates terrorists from other political activists. Any other activities in which terrorist organizations engage are generally designed to facilitate the campaign of violence the groups employ in pursuit of their political, religious, or ideological objectives.[11] In this way, terrorist organizations remain distinct from criminal enterprises, and conflating the two serves neither the cause of sound analysis nor that of effective policy-making.

Terrorist activities

Alternatively, terrorism may be understood as an activity that can be adopted by entities, such as criminal enterprises, that are not predominantly political in orientation. The best examples of this include the terror campaign initiated by Pablo Escobar and Carlos Lehder of the Medellin drug trafficking organizations. This campaign included the assassination of the Colombian Justice Minister, Lara Bonilla; the attack on the Palace of Justice by M–19, in which records of drug traffickers were among the many things destroyed; a bomb explosion on an Avianco airliner; and a variety of other incidents. The Mafia initiated a similar campaign in Italy in response to what it saw as a betrayal by the Christian Democrats. The campaign resulted in the killing of the two leading anti-Mafia magistrates, Falcone and Borsellino; damage to some of Italy's historic monuments; and a series of train bombings. The overall result, however, was a popular backlash. In both the Italian and the Colombian cases, terrorist tactics backfired, leading to a full-blown confrontation with the state in which the state won. The implication of these events is that for criminal enterprises, terror tactics are far from ideal – in most cases, criminal enterprises are better off using corruption and cooption rather than confrontation.[12] Indeed, the Cali drug trafficking organizations that for a short time succeeded the Medellin group used violence only as a last resort but devoted significant resources to corruption and efforts to co-opt state authorities.

The distinction between entities and activities has important implications. It makes clear that any entity can use organized crime as a mechanism to generate resources to assist in the pursuit of its political agenda, whether that agenda is to obtain control or to remain in control of a country, to inflict psychological and physical harm onto enemies, or to engage in ethnic cleansing. Similarly, a variety of entities can resort to terrorism as a strategy whether or not they are committed to bringing about large-scale political change.

Hybrid forms of organization

There is, however, an important wrinkle in all this. Helpful as the distinction between terrorist entities and profit-oriented criminal enterprises might be as a starting point, it captures only part of a more complex reality. In several regions, amalgamation has resulted in hybrid forms of organization that combine an explicit political agenda and a quest for power with a desire to make profits through illegal activities and a willingness to use significant levels of violence – both discriminate and indiscriminate. This hybrid dual dynamic is evident in many weak or collapsing states or states embroiled in military conflict. The Tajik civil war from 1992 to 1997, for example, was partly an extension of old clan rivalries and traditional power struggles, partly a religious and ideological conflict, and partly a struggle for control of opium and heroin trafficking routes and markets. In cases like this, the major players are hybrid organizations: part criminal enterprise, part terrorist group, part mercenary, and part political or religious faction.

The most fully amalgamated of these hybrid organizations are warlords or insurgents who typically engage in criminal activities (including drug trafficking or extortion of traders who transit the territories under their control) and in insurgent or military activities while also providing a modicum of governance in areas under their control. The FARC in Colombia, for example, has imposed law and order on some towns that were previously lawless while also committing acts of terrorism targeting civilians.[13] FARC is conducting a political insurgency (something the United States has lumped with terrorism) with ideological objectives relating in large part to notions of social justice. FARC has become what Steven Metz terms a "commercial insurgency": the group uses its involvement in the drug business to acquire considerable wealth, not all of which is directed towards the political cause.[14] In fact, it is arguable that serious divisions now exist within FARC as a result of these distinct agendas. These divisions have manifested themselves over arguments about the FARC's drug business. FARC has multiple fronts or units. Some of these – particularly the 16th Front – are heavily engaged in drug trafficking, while others are willing to tax the farmers and traffickers but are reluctant to become more directly involved, and yet others want nothing to do with the business. Despite the internal discord, FARC has clearly benefited from its involvement in the cocaine industry, if only in enhancing its ability to perpetuate the armed struggle against the Colombian state. FARC's extensive involvement with the drug business and use of terror against civilian targets has given the notion of "narco-terrorism" both a new twist and new life: a term that was initially coined to describe criminal enterprises' use of terror tactics is now applied to an insurgent organization's use of organized crime, and specifically the drug trade, to fund the politically motivated use of indiscriminate violence.[15]

Other groups exemplify both mixed motives and mixed strategies. In South Asia, for example, Dawood Ibrahim's organization, known as D-Company, constitutes a hybrid entity that pursues crime for profit and for a political agenda, including direct involvement in terrorism and support for terrorist activities. D-Company has a broad portfolio of criminal activities for profit. The group has also been responsible for some terrorist attacks, including most notably the 1993 Mumbai bombings, which killed at least 257 people. As a criminal organization, D-Company has become involved in geopolitical rivalry in South Asia. Pakistan, and more particularly its intelligence agency, the ISI, support and protect D-Company and employ the group as a channel for funding anti-Indian terrorist organizations. D-Company, with ISI approval and support, has reportedly provided arms, ammunitions, and explosives to Lashkar-e-Taiba, which is playing an increasingly important role in the global jihad movement.[16] Dawood Ibrahim has also provided financial support to al Hikma, an anti-Indian group in Bangladesh which claims West Bengal is part of Bangladesh.[17] Consequently, D-Company does not fit comfortably into traditional notions of either criminal or terrorist organizations.

Dynamism and transformation

The evolution of both FARC and D-Company underlines Makarenko's observation that social phenomena are not static. Indeed, recognition of changes in either objectives or methods needs to be incorporated into effective analyses of organized crime and terrorism. It is not inconceivable that a terrorist or a criminal group can transform itself from one kind of entity into another. This is perhaps more likely in the case of terrorist groups and occurs when the political cause begins to recede in importance – either because the group has achieved some political success or because the goals have proved futile – and the rewards of profitable criminal activities take on increasing importance. A good example of this transformation is the Pentagon Gang, which formed out of a splinter group from the Moro Islamic Liberation Front and became heavily involved in kidnappings and other criminal exploits designed strictly for profit for its own sake.[18] As well as engaging in kidnapping, the group obtained funding from the extortion of Chinese-owned businesses. Initially these criminal activities were intended to fund a terrorist agenda, but the Pentagon Gang became so embroiled in its fundraising activities that, in effect, it ceased to be a terrorist organization, abandoned its political agenda, and became a criminal enterprise focused entirely on profits.[19]

The converse is also possible: a criminal organization could become highly politicized and radically alter the focus of its activity from accruing profit through illicit business to bringing about political change through the use of violence against civilians. A close examination of those involved in the Madrid train bombings of 11 March 2004 reveals that a critical role was played by a drug trafficking organization that, under the leadership of Jamal Ahmidan, morphed into a terrorist organization. Such transformations can be described respectively as the commercialization of terrorist (or insurgent) organizations and the radicalization of criminal organizations. In some cases, the transition can be quick and relatively direct; in others, the change leads through the rise and decline of a hybrid organization. Hybrid organizations can be end states in and of themselves or transitional phases in either the transformation of a criminal enterprise into a terrorist organization or the transformation of a terrorist organization into a criminal enterprise.

This discussion, in effect, suggests a range of possible relationships between entities of different kinds and between entities and activities as well as the possibility of transformation from one kind of entity into another. This range of possible relationships and transformations is encapsulated in Figure 6.1.

The next section examines evidence of cooperation between criminal and terrorist entities while the subsequent section explores terrorist use of organized crime methods for funding. The final section explores the phenomenon of transformation and shows how it was critical to the Madrid bombings.

Cooperation between criminal and terrorist entities

The evidence for linkages between organized crime entities and terrorist groups is often circumstantial and has rarely been buttressed by solid empirical evidence. The assertion that Russian organized crime groups cooperated with al Qaeda may only reflect the observation that the Islamic Movement of Uzbekistan, an al Qaeda-affiliate organization, was involved in

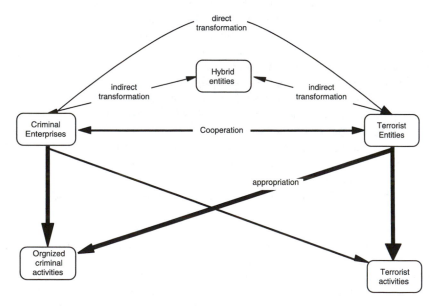

Figure 6.1 Possible relationships and transformations between terrorist organizations and criminal enterprises.

drug trafficking from Afghanistan, where it seems almost inevitable that some cooperation would have occurred. In cases where terrorist organizations engage in do-it-yourself organized crime, especially drug trafficking, it is highly likely that they cooperate with criminal enterprises by supplying drugs. Conversely, criminal enterprises involved in weapons trafficking may well supply arms to terrorist organizations.

Cooperation between criminal enterprises and terrorist organizations, when it does arise, is usually based on expediency and mutual convenience: one type of organization wants something the other type has and is willing to pay for it. More often than not, the reasons for cooperation are rooted purely in commercial considerations on the part of the criminal enterprise and in need or expediency on the part of the terrorist organization. In other cases, cooperation develops for less instrumental and more substantive reasons, such as when crucial members of a criminal enterprise sympathize with a terrorist organization. This type of cooperation has been evident in Italy, for example, where it was reported that "a member of the Camorra, the Neapolitan Mafia, converted to Islam and recently set up an exchange of arms for drugs between the Camorra and Islamic terrorists."[20] According to Pierluigi Vigna, Italy's national anti-Mafia prosecutor, these cooperative links were formed in prison.[21]

The tri-border region of South America, where Brazil, Argentina, and Paraguay come together, is characterized by opportunistic relations between criminal enterprises and terrorist organizations and by allegiances or affiliations between the two types of groups. The region has become a haven for criminal enterprises and terrorist organizations (or, perhaps more accurately, for terrorist support structures linked to Hamas, al Gama'a al Islamiyya, and Hezbollah). According to one report, the Sung-I and Ming organized crime groups in the region have worked very closely with the Egyptian al Gama'a al Islamiyya in carrying out criminal activities, including intellectual property theft, with counterfeit software and other counterfeit goods coming into the tri-border region.[22] The profits from these criminal activities are sent to the Middle East. On some occasions, these organized crime groups trade other illicit commodities. In December 2000, Sung-I reportedly sold the Islamic Group munitions, which were subsequently sent by ship to Egypt under the disguise of "medical equipment," but which were intercepted in Cyprus.[23] In an even more intriguing relationship, another Chinese group, the Ming family, actually managed Islamic Group funds, moving them through Guyana and the Cayman Islands in what was probably an elaborate deception or laundering operation.[24] Unfortunately, details of this operation are sparse and it is not clear whether it represented an enduring and close relationship or was simply a one-time venture in which the Ming family was paid for its expertise. Whatever the case, it is clear that the cooperation was direct and that it benefited all those involved.

Direct cooperation has also been evident in India, where ties have been formed between Islamic militants and "traditional organized crime groups," especially that group led by Aftab Ansari. Cooperation here appears to involve training and exploitation of each other's resources. One of Ansari's lieutenants, who received military training at a camp in Afghanistan run by Lashkar-e-Taiba, claimed that Pakistani militant groups were trying to utilize Ansari's criminal network "for the purpose of jihad," while Ansari was trying to use the militants' networks "for underworld operations."[25] Although exploitation of this kind can enhance the effectiveness of both the criminal and the terrorist networks, it may amount to little more than a mutually convenient but temporary relationship. To describe such a relationship as a nexus could be premature, endowing it with a significance that it might, but does not necessarily, warrant.

While claims about an organized crime–terrorism nexus tend to exaggerate the degree of cooperation and to endow these relationships with a strategic importance they usually lack, cooperation between criminal enterprises and terrorist organizations has taken place – and in a few cases at significant levels. Moreover, in the future it is very likely that connections between terrorist and criminal organizations will become increasingly frequent and important. The involvement of terrorist organizations in do-it-yourself organized crime brings them into contact with traditional criminal organizations as part of the natural workings of the criminal market. As al Qaeda has become more of a network, in which other groups carry out terrorist strikes that are inspired rather than directed by bin Laden and his core group, independent funding becomes crucial. For these organizations, "institutional funding" from al Qaeda is likely to be modest at best.[26] As Stephen Brooke notes:

> Even if they were able to tap into al-Qaeda coffers and apply for a grant, so to speak, they would still have to contend with a worldwide financial crackdown on terrorist financing. These impediments to utilizing established funding networks will force bands to increasingly turn towards small-scale criminal enterprises to finance their operations. . . . Crime is self-starting and requires no particular training or expertise. . . . Strands of the Algerian GIA in Europe provided the bulk of the organization's funds through petty theft and credit card fraud. The network headed by Abu Musab al-Zarqawi, al Tawhid, got its start trafficking in forged documents and immigrant smuggling between the Middle East and Europe.[27]

In France, for example, most of the terrorist cells dismantled by the authorities financed themselves though criminal activities. Terrorist groups justify criminal activities and drug trafficking both in terms of the benefits they bring for the cause and the fact that they are directed against "the infidel."[28] Accordingly, the next section provides a more thorough examination of the way in which terrorist organizations appropriate organized crime methods for funding.

Terrorist organizations using crime

As suggested above, cooperation between criminal enterprises and terrorist networks is increasing. Nevertheless, this cooperation remains far less significant than the appropriation of organized crime methods by terrorists. One of the pioneers of the use of racketeering and other organized crime activities to finance terrorist activities was the Provisional Irish Republican Army (PIRA) which developed a broad portfolio of criminal activities to fund its political–military campaign. According to British law enforcement estimates in the early 1990s, the large-scale copying and distribution of illicit videos made up more than 2 million pounds (approximately $3.5 million) of the estimated 10.5 million pounds (nearly $16 million) the PIRA raised each year to fund its activities. In the early 1990s the Royal Ulster Constabulary seized over 100,000 pirated videos worth an estimated 4.5 million pounds (nearly $7 million) as well as electronic equipment such as color enhancers, anti-copy signal decoders, shrink wrappers, and VCRs. Another 100,000 tapes were seized in the Republic of Ireland.[29] The PIRA extended these activities into the manufacturing of forged compact discs and tapes. Another source of funds was Eurofraud. As one report observed:

> The borders of Eire and Northern Ireland . . . provide a lucrative source of income for the IRA. Cattle moved across the border attract an EU subsidy per head. It is a simple matter to smuggle the animals back again under cover of darkness and repeat the whole process. Effective surveillance of about 244 roads on a 270-mile stretch is nearly impossible at night, when para-military organizations claim much of the territory as their own. A "levy" is said to be paid by the farmers on each animal that is smuggled.[30]

A third source was the theft and sale of construction equipment taken from Britain and smuggled to Ireland. This was an extensive phenomenon and authorities only believed part of it to be connected with the IRA.[31] The development of protection rackets, or what James Adams called the Provisional IRA's "Capone discovery," offered a fourth source of criminal funding.[32] Protection money from shopkeepers and small businesses became a major source of revenue:

> The payment had two results for a typical shopkeeper. First, it guaranteed Provisional IRA protection for the business in case of trouble (but this was not the prime motivation for the payment). The second and major purpose was to keep the Provisional IRA from attacking the owner's property or family.[33]

John Horgan, who has carefully examined the PIRA's funding of its campaign of violence, has highlighted the extensive range of criminal activities employed by the organization. He notes too that the PIRA's portfolio of criminal activities included not only pirating videos and computer games but also "income tax frauds involving the use of false tax exemption certificates (on Northern Ireland building sites), the smuggling of livestock grain, cattle and pigs . . . trading in livestock growth promoters and the theft of cars . . . the sale of contraband cigarette lighters in Belfast."[34] The PIRA has also used kidnapping for ransom and armed robbery.[35] In addition, the PIRA has used its criminal proceeds to purchase licit businesses. Although the exact amount of money obtained through these activities is uncertain, it has clearly been substantial.

The PIRA offers a striking example of the effectiveness with which a terrorist group can appropriate organized crime as fundraising method. It has to be acknowledged, however, that there is considerable variety in the skill and effectiveness with which terrorist organizations use criminal methods. Some terrorist groups engage in do-it-yourself organized crime very effectively and with a high degree of professionalism. Other terrorist groups employ organized crime in a way that is not only amateurish, but also increases the danger of exposure.

Such caveats notwithstanding, it is possible to discern at least three different channels through which organizations direct or carry out criminal activities for the purpose of fundraising. First, high-level involvement in organized crime reflects a strategic decision about the importance of criminal enterprises in providing financial support; a particularly important example is drug trafficking. Second, on a lower level, members of particular cells sustain themselves through organized crime. Finally, members of transnational ethnic networks may support either nationalist or religious violence through organized crime. This last type can be subcategorized to distinguish between those already involved in organized crime who sympathize with the terrorist cause and therefore funnel some of their profits to the support of militancy, and those who would otherwise not be involved in organized crime, yet who engage in criminal activities to help the terrorist cause.

Examples of all three channels are plentiful. In some instances, a terrorist network will be involved in organized crime at both the strategic and the operational levels and will also obtain funds from organized criminal activities in the diaspora. In other instances, criminal activities are simply channeled through one level rather than all three.

The Liberation Tigers of Tamil Eelam (LTTE) group has made more extensive use of criminal activities and has raised funds at all three levels – the strategic level, the cell level, and throughout the diaspora. The LTTE group itself has reportedly established cells in as many as 38 countries in Europe, the Middle East, and North America.[36] Generally the LTTE cells obtain financial support from the Tamil communities, either through voluntary contributions or intimidation and extortion. They also engage in a wide variety of criminal activities that extend well beyond the Tamil community. The Tamil drug connection, facilitated by Sri Lanka's proximity to both the Golden Triangle and the Golden Crescent, became evident during the 1980s. The presence of LTTE representatives or supporters in Thailand – where they have reportedly procured arms and possibly heroin – provided an excellent opportunity for entry into the business.[37] At the other end of the drug supply chain, the presence of Tamil refugees in Western Europe provided ready outlets for drug sales. Evidence of Tamil involvement in the drug business emerged in the mid-1980s, with several members of the LTTE arrested for heroin trafficking in Italy in 1984.[38] This did little to stop the trend, and during the 1980s, Tamil traffickers were responsible for one fifth of all heroin seized in Switzerland, leading Swiss authorities to focus on the "Tamil connection."[39] Subsequent reports point to Colombo as a major transshipment point for heroin destined for the United States and Europe.[40]

If the LTTE has used Pakistan, particularly Karachi, as a base for its drug-trafficking activities, Dawood Ibrahim's D-Company has supplied the Tamil Tigers with heroin and insured their shipments. In the late 1990s, however, the LTTE diversified into alien smuggling or human trafficking. According to the Sri Lankan government, R. Visendrarajan (who heads the Tamil Tigers' finance division and owns two shipping companies used for gun-running and drug trafficking) began an alien smuggling business that in 1999 alone moved 17,000 people to 11 countries.[41] Reportedly this business earned $340 million. The government's assessment concluded that the operation was "one of the LTTE's major fund raising devices for its ongoing war with Sri Lankan government troops."[42]

Tamil networks within the diaspora also became involved in a wider range of criminal activities including credit card fraud in Britain and Canada, extortion in Germany, social security fraud in France,[43] and currency counterfeiting in several European countries and Australia. In a report completed in 1999, the Royal Canadian Mounted Police claimed to have "clear evidence" that Tamil street gangs in Toronto and other Canadian cities were sending the proceeds from bank and casino fraud, immigration fraud, drug smuggling, and trafficking in weapons to the LTTE to support terrorist activities.[44] These Tamil street gangs also extort money from the Tamil communities and funnel the profits back to the LTTE.[45]

An example of the strategic use of crime is provided by the Islamic Movement of Uzbekistan (IMU), which relies mostly on drug trafficking and kidnappings for ransom to fund its operations. In one instance of kidnapping, the IMU received somewhere between $2 and $6 million when it agreed to release a group of Japanese geologists it had taken hostage.[46] It is also clear that IMU involvement in the drug trade has been extensive. Ralf Mutschke, assistant director of Interpol's Criminal Intelligence Directorate, reported that IMU "may be responsible for up to seventy percent of the heroin and opium that is transmitted though" Central Asia.[47] Although this figure was widely repeated, it was almost certainly an inflated estimate based largely on allegations by governments in the region rather than any serious analysis of drug flows.[48] Prior to the US intervention in Afghanistan there were even claims that the IMU was not really a terrorist organization and that its annual military campaign was little more than an attempt to divert attention from its real preoccupation – making money through drug trafficking. The assertion that IMU was no more than a criminal enterprise, however, was undermined by the way in which the organization fought alongside of al Qaeda in Afghanistan. For the IMU, participation was costly; the group lost Namangani, its military leader. All this is not to deny that the IMU profited from drug trafficking; it is merely to argue that drug trafficking was simply a means of funding the cause. This was an example of do-it-yourself organized crime, but the extent of the profits from drug trafficking should not be exaggerated.

Even where a terrorist organization does not use organized crime activities for funding at the strategic level, criminal activities in the diaspora can provide considerable support. Members of the Lebanese diaspora, for example, have systematically undertaken professional criminal activities on behalf of Hezbollah.[49] Such support is crucial, as Hezbollah has established its legitimacy in Lebanon by providing public and social services in Muslim areas and is unique in "the scope and range of the social and public services that it provides compared to other parties in Lebanon and fundamentalist organizations in the region."[50] These public service activities, however, do not come cheap. Fortunately for Hezbollah, Lebanese criminal networks in the tri-border region of South America are involved in "smuggling, money laundering, and product piracy" and contribute at least some of the proceeds to the organization.[51] Perhaps the most significant figure in the region in terms of financial support for Hezbollah was Assad Ahmad Barakat, who reportedly also provided funds to al Qaeda.[52] Barakat used a variety of methods to raise money, including sales of pirated software and video games. Other Lebanese linked either to Barakat or his businesses were involved in drug trafficking throughout the region. Although Barakat was arrested in July 2002, Argentine officials contend that Lebanese communities remain involved in money laundering, counterfeiting of US dollars, and other illicit financial activities, citing "thousands of U.S. dollars bearing stamps from Lebanese currency exchange banks, tens of thousands of dollars in phony bills, and receipts from wire transfers made between the tri-border area and the Middle East."[53] Nevertheless, the arrest of Barakat and some of his associates has probably reduced the flow of money to Hezbollah from the tri-border region.

Other diaspora support has come from Lebanese diamond merchants in Africa, some of whom have been involved in the trafficking of conflict or blood diamonds. According to reports by Douglas Farah in the *Washington Post* and by the London-based NGO Global Witness, Lebanese diamond merchants in Liberia, Sierra Leone, and the Democratic Republic of Congo (DRC) purchased and traded illicit diamonds mined by Revolutionary United Front (RUF) forces, reintegrating the diamonds into the licit trade in Antwerp. Some of these merchants were, at the very least, sympathetic to Hezbollah, and some of the proceeds from cut diamonds found their way into Hezbollah's coffers.[54] Reportedly, al Qaeda also became involved in the diamond business – although it is uncertain whether this involvement was for profit or simply to exploit the security of possessing highly portable, high-value commodities.[55]

Even in the United States, Hezbollah supporters have engaged in criminal activities – most notably cigarette smuggling from North Carolina, where cigarette taxes were low, to Michigan, where taxes were high. Led by Mohammad Hammoud and his brother Chawki, members of the group engaged in smuggling activities for over four years until their arrests in July 2000. At least some of the profits were channeled directly to Hezbollah or used to buy weapons and equipment such as night-vision goggles, laser range finders, and GPS systems for the organization.[56] In 2002 the Hammoud brothers were found guilty on a variety of charges and given heavy sentences (see Box 7.2 for more information). Reportedly they had sold at least $7.2 million dollars worth of cigarettes in Michigan.[57]

One group that has not had the advantage of a diaspora but has used criminal activities quite extensively is Abu Sayyaf, based in the southern Philippines.[58] At an early stage, the group clearly made a strategic decision to use crime as a fundraising mechanism. The most important of its activities has been kidnapping, which has served the dual purpose of sowing fear and providing what at times has been a highly significant source of income. In July 2000, for example, an Abu Sayyaf kidnapping reportedly resulted in the transfer of as much as $25 million in return for freeing hostages from Malaysia and Europe.[59] The organization has succeeded in generating a fairly steady revenue stream through the kidnapping of Christian missionaries, businesspeople, and tourists. The group has supplemented this activity with extortion, or the imposition of revolutionary taxes on vulnerable communities,[60] and trafficking of marijuana on and from the island of Basilan which is sometimes known as "Little Colombia."[61]

Other organizations also resort to kidnapping as a fundraising device. The Salafist Group for Prayer and Combat (GSPC), based in Algeria and highly active in Western Europe, has used kidnapping as a source of funding.[62] Although much less successful than its Filipino counterpart, the GSPC in 2003 received an estimated 5 million euros for the release of 14 European tourists.[63] Perhaps a more important and more regular source of funding has come from the extortion of Algerian farmers, who pay a "jihad tax," and from sand and gravel smugglers in the Sebaou Oued valley, who pay for access to and exit from the area.[64] Financial support from expatriates in Europe, especially France, also appears to be common, although the extent to which the payments are coerced as opposed to voluntary is uncertain. GSPC members or affiliates in France have also been involved in "petty crimes such as car-theft, credit-card fraud and document forgery."[65] Several Salafist members were arrested in Paris in October 2002 for the production and sale of counterfeit clothing and watches, as well as for car theft and export.[66] Similarly, in Spain, Mohammed Belaziz, a Salafist, was arrested on 25 September 2001 as part of the crackdown after the 11 September attacks. It turned out that Belaziz and other members of his cell had been financing their operations through credit card fraud.[67] Police discovered equipment for forging documents – an activity that not only facilitates relatively free movement of terrorists, but also generates criminal proceeds.

There have also been reports that GSPC deliberately recruits members who have some experience in committing petty crimes and that these new recruits are encouraged to use their experience to help raise funds for the organization.[68] Although most GSPC terrorist plots seem to have been thwarted or aborted, the group remains a close affiliate of al Qaeda and is still dangerous. Nevertheless, there are some signs that GSPC's focus on fundraising is eclipsing its political–religious agenda. As the Algerian government has become more successful in its efforts to combat both the Armed Islamic Group (GIA) and the GSPC, at least some of the terrorist cells appear to be abandoning the cause in favor of using crime for profit. Increases have been reported in drug trafficking, human trafficking, car theft and counterfeiting,[69] and it appears that some of the terrorist cells have morphed or are morphing into criminal enterprises intent on profit for its own sake.

A similar pattern of criminal activities (although without the morphing) is evident in the case of Lashkar-e-Taiba (LeT) in Pakistan, which reportedly has been involved in heroin trafficking and opium production and the kidnapping of Indian businesspeople.[70] LeT has also used insurance fraud – falsely reporting cars as stolen and collecting the insurance money – to strengthen its financial base.[71] In the case of Jemaah Islamiyah (JI), support for attacks has come from al Qaeda (see Chapter 4 by Zachary Abuza for a detailed description of the relationship between JI and al Qaeda). Nevertheless, JI has also been involved in criminal activities such as gold and gem smuggling as well as in other low-level crimes.[72] In August 2002, for example, JI members robbed a gold and jewelry store in West Java, subsequently using the funds for the Bali bombing.[73] Interestingly, JI has a religious justification for such activities in the doctrine of fa'i, which justifies crimes against infidels if the profits are used for jihad.[74] Nevertheless, it has not used crime as extensively as some other groups, partly because the funds raised have been rather modest while the costs incurred have proved to be rather high in terms of arrests. JI has been more successful in its use of terror than in its use of crime.

In some cases, of course, the crime is so basic and low-level that it is better described as petty crime than organized crime. This pattern of low-level, almost amateurish criminal activity was evident in the case of Ahmed Ressam, the Algerian who was caught trying to enter the United States with explosives to be used at Los Angeles International Airport on the eve of the millennium. Although Ressam had been given $12,000 in seed money by al Qaeda on completion of his training in Afghanistan, while in Montreal he was forced to become self sufficient and resorted to petty theft, stealing luggage from hotel rooms, and stealing money, passports, credit cards, and travelers' checks from tourists.[75]

Transformation from terrorists to criminals and from criminals to terrorists

Terrorist organizations morph into criminal enterprises for various reasons. One reason is that members become disillusioned with the progress of the political struggle. Another is that groups become so enamored of their moneymaking activities that the political struggle becomes secondary. A third possibility is that a peace settlement or political agreement gives the terrorists much of what they want. While some of the members of the group might return to a normal life, others – hooked on the excitement and recognizing the potential profits – might well be tempted to continue their criminal activities for pecuniary rather than political reasons. This appears to be the case with the PIRA in Northern Ireland. In spite of the peace process, PIRA criminal activities have not ceased. On the contrary, the expertise developed in organized crime methods initially used for funding the cause is now being used for personal and group enrichment. It is not surprising, therefore, that Horgan has concluded that the "IRA has become an increasingly obvious criminal conspiracy, engaged in significant money raising and money laundering operations, in the absence of an 'armed struggle.' "[76]

In a reverse scenario, a criminal enterprise could become highly politicized and radically alter the focus of its activity from accruing profit through illicit business to bringing about political change through terrorist activities. At this point, the cause supersedes profit considerations. Even though the group still engages in organized crime activities, these activities are now used to fund the political cause. Perhaps the best example of this transformation is the hashish trafficking group that became involved in the Madrid bombings. At first glance, this appeared to be an example of close cooperation between terrorists and a criminal enterprise. On closer inspection, however, it was more accurately an example of transformation, where the transformed criminal organization became a key part of the Madrid terrorist network that carried out the train bombings. Indeed, as one commentator has observed, the Madrid bombers were a strange mix of "longtime extremists and radicalized gangsters."[77] The immediate leadership of the network was reportedly provided by Jamal Ahmidan, a well-known Moroccan drug trafficker, and Sarhane Ben Abdelmajid Fakhet, a 35-year-old Tunisian student of economics – both of whom (along with five others) blew themselves up in a confrontation with police on 3 April 2004. Although the network was also linked to Imad Yarkas (also known as Abu Dahda, who had been arrested for collaborating with the 11 September hijackers) and to the perpetrators of the Casablanca bombings, it was the drug traffickers who provided both the money and much of the expertise that ensured the successful implementation of the attacks.

Spanish authorities, after an exhaustive and detailed analysis of 185 bank accounts linked to 55 defendants, concluded that the attacks cost between 41,000 and 54,000 euros.[78] Significantly, they also concluded – contradicting many earlier reports – that "it was not possible to determine the existence of transnational transfers or financial transactions that might have contributed to the funding of the attacks."[79] Rather than the money coming from an outside source, the train bombings were both perpetrated and financed by Jamal Ahmidan and his drug-trafficking-turned-terrorist organization. Ahmidan acquired the explosives and detonators from a miner, Suarez Trashorras, and paid for them with a stolen Toyota Corolla and hashish worth between 32,000 and 45,000 euros.[80] In addition, Ahmidan helped to provide a "contingency fund" of over 52,000 euros and had a stash of drugs in reserve worth between 1.35 and 1.53 million euros.[81] He also brought logistical expertise to the terrorist group. According to one analysis:

> [The drug traffickers] took charge of obtaining money, weapons, phones, cars, safe houses and other infrastructure. Ahmidan rented a rickety rural cottage . . . turning it into a headquarters and bomb factory. . . . Days before he and a dozen others allegedly planted the backpack bombs on four commuter trains, Ahmidan flew to the island of Majorca, apparently to arrange a sale of hashish and Ecstasy, police say. The cash went into a war chest for follow-up plots, among them a foiled attempt to blow a high-speed Madrid–Seville train off its tracks.[82]

The contribution of Ahmidan and his group to the success of the Madrid bombings is difficult to overestimate. Indeed, without the drug traffickers, it is not clear that the other planners, such as Fakhet, would have been able to transform their terrorist aspirations into reality.

What makes this all the more disturbing is the possibility that more members of organized crime will be transformed into terrorists. Radicalization seems especially likely to occur in prison. According to one Belgian law enforcement official:

> The intermingling of terrorist networks with the criminal milieu is becoming more and more important. . . . It's in prisons where political operatives recruit specialists whom they need to run their networks – specialists in fraudulent documents, arms trafficking, etc. They use concepts that justify crime, that transform it into redemption. The prisons of today are producing the terrorists of tomorrow.[83]

The radicalization of criminals can also occur outside prisons. This is particularly the case in Morocco, where a traditional emphasis on the cultivation and trafficking of hashish coexists with the growth of Islamic militancy in many of the shantytowns. In Algeria, too, organized crime has had to operate in such a radicalized and fraught political environment that some radicalization of criminal groups – along with the transfer of expertise from criminal entities to terrorist entities – has been inevitable.

Concluding observations

The foregoing analysis suggests very clearly that there are three distinct trends in the relationship between terrorist networks and organized crime: growing but still limited cooperation between the two types of entities, the use of criminal methods by terrorist groups, and the radicalization of criminal enterprises resulting in their transformation into terrorists (with some transformation in the opposite direction).

The cooperation between terrorist groups and organized criminal organizations is not insignificant, but remains the least important of the three trends and hardly merits the term nexus. Most of the relationships between terrorists and criminals are predominantly matters of commercial convenience and there is little evidence of any congruence of objectives and interests between criminal enterprises and terrorist networks. Much more important is the appropriation of organized crime methods by terrorist organizations. This is far from new as the discussion of the Provisional IRA demonstrated. Although the use of organized crime activities for fundraising is sometimes implemented in a very amateurish manner, appropriation of methods is the most pervasive of the three trends. It is also something that could contribute in the longer term to a closer criminal–terrorist relationship. When terrorist organizations start to adopt organized crime methods, they inevitably come into contact with traditional criminal enterprises. Mutual convenience, common opportunities, and the simple search for customers or suppliers push them towards more cooperative relationships. Yet the differences of purpose and objective, along with very different approaches to the use of violence, inhibit the development of anything more than temporary and tactical cooperation. Perhaps the most serious long-term threat, therefore, is the transformation of criminals into terrorists.

As suggested above, without the radicalization of Jamal Ahmidan and his drug-trafficking organization, it is unlikely that the Madrid attacks would have been nearly as devastating – and they might not have taken place. Such a transformation, therefore, is particularly disturbing, and is unlikely to be offset by transformations of terrorists into criminal enterprises concerned only about profits and not about politics. If the politicization and radicalization of organized crime groups becomes more frequent, then the capacity of terrorists to carry out large-scale attacks will be significantly augmented. There is an up side to this, however. If terrorist networks integrate transformed criminal enterprises or even individual radicalized criminals, then the opportunities for infiltration by law enforcement – with all the benefits of good human intelligence – might be increased. The more immediate danger, however, is that the terrorist use of organized crime activities will render the attack on terrorist finances by governments ineffective and ensure that the funding for further attacks, which after all are relatively modest in their costs, remains readily available.

Notes

1 The author would like to express his appreciation to Patrick Dutton, Paul N. Woessner, and Robert Volkert, former students and researchers at the Graduate School of Public and International Affairs, University of Pittsburgh. Their impeccable and massively detailed work on terrorist financing was a source of inspiration. In addition, he would like to thank all those students in the Graduate School of Public and International Affairs, University of Pittsburgh who were in his Capstone seminars on "Organized Crime and Terrorism" and "The Financing of Terrorism." Not only did these students provide excellent overviews for some of the themes developed in this chapter, but they also provided many pertinent examples. Where the author has drawn on these examples, both the original source and the specific authors of those sections of the Capstone reports are cited.
2 Associated Press, 3 March 2005.
3 R. H. Kupperman, "A Dangerous Future," *Harvard International Review*, Summer 1995, vol. 17, no. 3, p. 46.
4 K. E. Weick and K. M. Sutcliffe, *Managing the Unexpected: Assuring High Performance in the Age of Complexity*, San Francisco: Jossey Bass, 2001.
5 T. Makarenko, "Crime, Terror and the Central Asian Drug Trade," *Harvard Asia Quarterly*, Summer 2002, vol. 6, no. 3. Online. Available HTTP: <http://www.fas.harvard.edu/~asiactr/haq/200203/0203a004.htm> (accessed 19 September 2005).
6 Makarenko, "A Model of Terrorist–Criminal Relationships," *Jane's Intelligence Review*, 1 September 2003.
7 Federal Research Division, Library of Congress, *The Nexus Among Terrorists, Narcotics Traffickers, Weapons Proliferators, and Organized Crime Networks in Western Europe*, December 2002. Online. Available HTTP: <http://www.loc.gov/rr/frd/pdf-files/WestEurope_NEXUS.pdf> (accessed 19 September 2005).
8 Ibid., p. 23.
9 This quote is taken from an abridged version of the ITERATE database and is used in an excellent paper by Dr. Tore Bjørgo of the Norwegian Institute of International Affairs (NUPI) entitled "How Violent Groups Transform: a Comparison of Terrorism, Organized Crime and Violent Subcultures" Presented at the XIII World Congress of Criminology, Rio de Janeiro, 10–15 August 2003.
10 R. Godson, "Special Focus: The International Fight against Money Laundering," *Trends in Organized Crime*, Spring 1999, vol. 4, no. 3, pp. 1–7.
11 For an excellent discussion of similarities and differences between organized crime and terrorism, see A. P. Schmid, "The Links between Transnational Organized Crime and Terrorist Crimes," *Transnational Organized Crime*, Winter 1996, vol. 2, no. 45, pp. 40–81.
12 Makarenko, "A Model of Terrorist–Criminal Relationships."
13 C. Villalon, "Cocaine Country," *National Geographic Magazine*, July 2004, pp. 34–55.
14 S. Metz, *The Future of Insurgency*, 10 December 1993. Online. Available HTTP: <www.au.af.mil/au/awc/awcgate/ssi/metz.pdf> (accessed 19 September 2005).
15 The author would like to thank Erin Wick for her work on FARC and Amy Weber for her work on the tri-border region. Heather Bragg, Laura Feltz, and Tami Schrader also provided insights on organized crime and terrorism in Latin America.

16 For work done on Lashkar-e-Taiba, I am grateful to Patrick Dutton as well as Mardann Olsen and Bryan McDowell. For the specific reference, see R. Sharma, "LeT Turning Global: Dawood's Links Come to the Fore," *The Tribune*, 19 January 2003. Online. Available HTTP: <http://www.tribuneindia.com/2003/20030119/main1.htm> (accessed 19 September 2005).

17 "Bangladesh Bans Dawood-Funded Terrorist Group," *The Hindustan Times*, 17 February 2003. Online. Available HTTP: <http://www.hvk.org/articles/0203/207.html> (accessed 19 September 2005).

18 "Philippine Gang Leader Shot Dead," *BBC*. Online. Available HTTP: <http://news.bbc.co.uk/2/hi/asia-pacific/2215382.stm> (accessed 19 September 2005).

19 "Pentagon Gang Leader, 15 Others Yield," *ABC-CBN News*, 11 October 2004.

20 "Islamic Militants Linked to Italian Mafia Group," *The New Zealand Herald*, 20 April 2004. Online. Available HTTP: <http://www.nzherald.co.nz/category/story.cfm?c_id=340&objectid=3561599> (accessed 19 September 2005).

21 Ibid.

22 Federal Research Division, Library of Congress, *Terrorist And Organized Crime Groups In The Tri-Border Area (TBA) Of South America*, July 2003, p. 3.

23 Ibid., p. 43.

24 Ibid.

25 J. Stern, "The Protean Enemy," *Foreign Affairs*, July–August 2003, pp. 27–40.

26 S. Brooke, "Outside View: Financing Al-Qaeda 2.0," *United Press International*, 29 June 2004. Online. Available HTTP: <http://washingtontimes.com/upi-breaking/20040629–112719–2610r.htm> (accessed 19 September 2005).

27 Ibid.

28 Ibid.

29 P. Dean, "Pirate Videos Fund IRA Terrorism, U.K. Government Says," *Billboard*, 6 August 1994, pp. 67–9.

30 T. Glover, "A Continent of Crooks: Fraud in the European Community," *EuroBusiness*, February 1995, vol. 2 no. 9, p. 23.

31 J. Steele, "Building Site Thefts Funding Terrorism," *Daily Telegraph*, 9 December 1996.

32 J. Adams, *The Financing of Terror*, New York: Simon and Schuster, 1986.

33 J. R. White, *Terrorism: an Introduction*, 2nd ed., Belmont, CA: Wadsworth/West, 1998, p. 42; P. K. Clare, *Racketeering in Northern Ireland: A New Version of the Patriot Game*, Chicago, IL: Office of International Criminal Justice at the University of Illinois at Chicago, 1989, p. 16.

34 J. Horgan and M. Taylor, "Playing the 'Green Card' – Financing the Provisional IRA: Part 1," *Terrorism and Political Violence*, Summer 1999, vol. 11, no.2, pp. 1–38.

35 Ibid.

36 Mackenzie Institute, "Funding Terror: The Liberation Tigers of Tamil Eelam and their Criminal Activities in Canada and the Western World," *Mackenzie Briefing Notes*, Toronto: Mackenzie Institute, 1996.

37 D. Pathan, "Tamil Tiger Foothold Shows Security Flaws," *The Nation*, 31 March 2000.

38 *Funding Terror*.

39 *Funding Terror*.

40 "Sri Lanka Seen as Important Drug Conduit," *United Press International*, 10 March 2000.

41 "Sri Lanka: Sri Lanka's Rebels Involved In Trafficking Human Cargo," *Xinhua News Agency*, 7 April 2000.

42 Ibid.

43 *Funding Terror*.

44 A. Abocar, "Canada Police Say Tamil Gangs Funding Rebels," *Reuters*, 28 March 2000.

45 J. Kingstone, "Clear Evidence of Links between Tamil Gangs and LTTE," *CanTYD Media*, 2003.

46 Ibid., p. 163.

47 See A. Rashid, *Jihad: The Rise of Militant Islam in Central Asia*, New Haven, CT: Yale University Press, 2002, p. 165.

48 Although the IMU was decimated by the US intervention in Afghanistan, the flow of opium and heroin through Central Asia was not disrupted. On the contrary, drug trafficking through Central Asia actually increased, which suggests that many other actors were also involved.

49 The author would like to thank Dan Flynn, Steve Ligday, and Walter E. Trynock III for their work on Hezbollah.

50 J. P. Harik, *Hezbollah: The Changing Face of Terrorism*, London: I.B. Tauris, 2004, p. 81.

51 R. Hudson, *Terrorist and Organized Crime Groups in the Tri-Border Area (TBA) of South America*, Washington, DC: Library of Congress, 2003, p. 3.

52 Barakat's company, Mondial Engineering and Construction Company, with offices in Ciudad del Este and Beirut, was suspected of contributing funds to al Qaeda using proceeds from real estate fraud. Other Barakat businesses reportedly also sent funds to al Qaeda, using "charitable contributions to orphanages" as the cover. There was even speculation that Barakat was in touch with Ramzi bin al-Shibh, who was one of the main planners for the 11 September attacks in New York and Washington. See ibid., p. 22.

53 Quoted in Ibid., p. 27.

54 See, for example, "Hezbollah and the West African Diamond Trade," *Middle East Intelligence Bulletin*, June/July 2004, vol. 6 nos. 6–7. Online. Available HTTP: <http://www.meib.org/articles/0407_l2.htm> (accessed 19 September 2005) and Mungo Soggot, "Conflict Diamonds are Forever," Center for Public Integrity, 8 November 2002. Online. Available HTTP: <http://www.publicintegrity.org/bow/report.aspx?aid=152> (accessed 19 September 2005).

55 See Chapter 9 of this volume, and D. Farah, *Blood from Stones: The Secret Financial Network of Terror*, New York: Broadway Books, 2004.

56 J. A. Damask, "Cigarette Smuggling: Financing Terrorism?" Mackinac Center for Public Policy, 1 July 2002. Online. Available HTTP: <http://www.mackinac.org/article.asp?ID=4461> (accessed 19 September 2005).

57 M. Roig-Franzia, "Man Convicted of Using Smuggling to Fund Hezbollah," *The Washington Post*, 23 June 2002.

58 The author would like to thank Joseph Gulino, Scott Jablonski, and Martin Lawther for their work on Abu Sayyaf, from which this section draws.

59 Estimates vary between $10 and $25 million. See L. Niksch, "Abu Sayyaf: Target of Philippine–U.S. Anti-Terrorism Cooperation," *Congressional Research Service*, 25 January 2002. Online. Available HTTP: <http://fpc.state.gov/documents/organization/8046.pdf> (accessed 19 September 2005).

60 "Extremist Rebels Demand 'Revolutionary Taxes' in the Philippines," *Deutsche Presse-Agentur*, 26 September 1998.

61 "An Embarrassing Dominance in Marijuana Supply," *Xinhua News Agency*, 10 April 2002.

62 The author would like to thank Christopher Hawn, Plesah Mayo, and David Rocchi as well as Jayna Keller for their work on the Algerian groups. The section on GSPC draws on many of the sources they found.

63 "An Unforgotten Ransom," *Expatica*, 5 September 2003. Online. Available HTTP: <http://www.expatica.com/source/site_article.asp?subchannel_id=19&story_id=1974> (accessed 19 September 2005).

64 El Kadi Ihsane, "In the Heartland of the GSPC," *Algeria Interface*, 16 December 2002. Online. Available HTTP: <http://www.algeria-interface.com/new/article.php?article_id=657&lng=e> (accessed 15 May 2004).

65 A. Keats, "In the Spotlight: the Salafist Group for Call and Combat (GSPC)," *Center for Defense Information*, 14 January 2003. Online. Available HTTP: <http://www.cdi.org/terrorism/gspc-pr.cfm> (accessed 19 September 2005).

66 "French Police Arrest Three Linked to Algerian Islamist Group," *Global News Wire – Asia Africa Intelligence Wire*, 19 October 2002.

67 E. Vermaat, "Bin Laden's Terror Networks in Europe," *Mackenzie Institute*, 2002. Online. Available HTTP: <http://www.mackenzieinstitute.com/2002/2002_Bin_Ladens_Networks.html> (accessed 19 September 2005).

68 Keats, "In the Spotlight."

69 Overseas Security Advisory Council, *Algiers, Algeria 2005: Crime and Safety Report*, 28 April 2005. Online. Available HTTP: <http://www.ds-osac.org/Reports/report.cfm?contentID=28081> (accessed 24 October 2005).

70 "UNI Report: Security Experts for Steps to Destroy Terrorist Network in Eastern States," *Jammu Daily Excelsior*, 10 December 2001.

71 J. Dey, "Sources Say Mumbai Remains Key Conduit of Lashkar-I-Taiyibah Funds," *The Indian Express*, New Delhi, 13 June 2002.

72 The author is grateful to Maria Mallo and Shawn McClearn for their work on JI, on which he has drawn.

73 "Jemaah Islamiyah in South East Asia: Damaged But Still Dangerous," *International Crisis Group* ICG Asia Report no. 63, 26 August 2003, p. 24.

74 Ibid.

75 "A Terrorist's Testimony," *PBS Frontline*. Online. Available HTTP: <http://www.pbs.org/wgbh/pages/frontline/shows/trail/inside/testimony.html> (accessed 19 September 2005).

76 J. Horgan, "The Provisional IRA in 2005: the Final Moments of an Increasingly Irrelevant Movement?" prepared for International Workshop on Global Terror and the Imagination, University of Pittsburgh, 24–27 March 2005.

77 S. Rotella, "Jihad's Unlikely Alliance," *Los Angeles Times*, 23 May 2004.

78 "Spanish Police Identify Financial Mastermind of Madrid Bombings," Madrid, *El Pais*, 17 May 2005, Foreign Broadcast Information Service (FBIS) Document EUP20050517950058.

79 Ibid.

80 Ibid.

81 Ibid.

82 Rotella, "Jihad's Unlikely Alliance."

83 A. Grignard quoted in Rotella, "Jihad's Unlikely Alliance."

7 Trade diversion as a fund raising and money laundering technique of terrorist organizations

Donald E. deKieffer

International trade diversion is one of the most sophisticated methods of laundering large amounts of money. Unlike other techniques, trade diversion relies upon "hiding in plain sight" – large transactions are disguised as legitimate, using well-known and respected firms to accomplish the transfer. While international diversion is more commonly used by transnational organized crime, it is also well suited to fund terrorist activities. Not only is trade diversion difficult to detect, it is also versatile in that it can allow funds to remain in numerous countries (including the United States) without prompting serious inquiry by the authorities. Trade diversion, therefore, has important implications for terrorist financing in that it potentially enables terrorist groups to raise and hide funds while evading government scrutiny. As will be discussed, groups engaged in acts of terrorism have already used trade diversion for money laundering.

The threat for terrorist financing is not only theoretical, but has been extensively discussed in the US State Department's annual *International Narcotics Control Strategy Report* (INCSR). According to the 2003 INCSR, "Trade-based value transfer is prevalent in many parts of the world that are vulnerable to terrorist financing. At present, it is impossible for law enforcement and customs to interdict all suspect transactions in this underworld of trade."[1] The INCSR goes on to observe:

> Terrorist financiers are increasingly likely to use fraudulent trade-based practices in international commerce to launder, earn, move and integrate funds and assets. US Customs officials define trade-based money laundering as the use of trade to legitimize, conceal, transfer and convert large quantities of illicit cash into less conspicuous assets or commodities. In turn, the tangible assets or value are transferred worldwide without being subject to financial transparency laws and regulations.

The 2005 INCSR reiterated this warning by noting, "Trade-based money laundering is used by organized crime groups and, increasingly, by terrorist financiers as well. This method involves the use of commodities, false invoicing, and other trade manipulation to move funds."[2] While transfer pricing mechanisms such as import overpricing and export underpricing were widely utilized by multinational corporations when national capital controls were common, trade diversion is a different and sophisticated practice, and the number of people who are actually masters of the technique is fairly limited. These individuals, however, move millions of dollars every day in international commerce, largely undetected.

How trade diversion works

Diversion schemes are extremely varied, but most tend to rely on a system of arbitrage. Since most consumer goods vary in price from market to market, large amounts of cash can be generated by diverting these products from low-price to high-price countries. To accomplish this, diverters often create shell companies to affect the transfer, but are usually careful to give these entities the trappings of legitimacy.

For a diversion scheme to work, the perpetrators must first acquire easily sold merchandise at prices far below that for which they can be purchased in other markets. This can involve ordinary commercial fraud, but has numerous variants. For example, the "U-Boat" diversion involves a foreign "buyer" (the diverter) approaching a US manufacturer with a large order. When asked where the goods are destined, the buyer indicates a market that is underserved by the manufacturer. When the deal goes through, several things may happen. First, the goods may wind up in a prohibited destination or sold to a prohibited party.[3] Second, the goods may be diverted and sold in the country of origin. Third, the products may be transferred to a third-country market in competition with legitimate products the manufacturer is already selling in that country.

The reason this particular scheme is called a "U-Boat" scam is that the goods are frequently transshipped via an intermediary location (e.g. Rotterdam) before they reach their intended destination. They are "stripped and stuffed" – loaded from one shipping container to another – and re-shipped back to the country of origin, oftentimes a developed country like the United States. Upon entering the US, for instance, the goods do not require tariffs to be paid since US law provides "duty free" treatment for "US goods returned."[4] The goods are then distributed in the market indicated by the buyer.

This technique succeeds because consumer products have become important commodities in international markets. Famous brands such as Kraft, Coca Cola, Gillette, and even pet food such as Alpo are sought in markets throughout the world. This reality has engendered a thriving arbitrage trade in which branded goods flow from low-priced to high-priced markets. Thus, when a large US company offers goods in foreign markets at lower prices than those same goods would be offered in the "home market," "reverse trade" flourishes.

Differing prices are caused by a variety of factors, including exchange rates and tax policies. Just as often, however, the manufacturer is responsible for the discrepancy, as it may lower prices to achieve market share in a foreign country. In other cases, the offshore buyer will demand discounts from usual US wholesale because it does not receive the advantage of the imbedded costs of advertising, inventory control, etc. Whatever the reason, ultimately international trade in branded goods is highly vulnerable to manipulation by sophisticated money launderers and illicit financiers.

In the third variant of a U-Boat transaction described above – in which products enter a third-country market in competition with legitimate products the manufacturer is already selling in that country – the putative foreign buyer almost always has a confederate located in the United States. This confederate, whether a co-conspirator or an arms-length dealer, accepts the goods when they re-enter the United States and arranges for their ultimate sale. When the goods are sold, the US confederate retains a percentage of the proceeds and sends the balance of the funds back to the offshore buyer.

This technique has the dual advantage of laundering money by creating a legitimate pedigree for the funds and of actually making a profit on the transaction. The transfer of funds need not be to an offshore account, but may be retained in the US for financing other activities, including the funding of terrorist groups already there.

There are dozens of trading companies in Canada, the UK, Switzerland, Singapore, Dubai, and elsewhere, that specialize in U-Boat transactions. This type of fraud generally involves large amounts of a product, rarely less than $100,000, and more often in the millions. Fraud can go undetected for months and can ruin marketing plans and profits for the US exporter.

Diversion in the US market

Some manufacturers intend to distribute their products in limited domestic markets. Examples include manufacturers of professional hair-care and beauty products, who intend their products only for salon use and sale, or other manufacturers who intend their products to be sold only by select full-service retailers. Product diversion severely disrupts the channels of distribution established by manufacturers and authorized distributors. Because the products usually cannot be obtained outside of the authorized distribution channels through any legitimate means, diverted products are often acquired by deception and fraud. Discount and warehouse retailers, supermarket chains, and drug store outlets have handled diverted merchandise, so they can profit from the efforts of the manufacturers and authorized distributors to develop and support the market for their products.

It is often difficult to differentiate goods acquired in the gray market from those sold through legitimate transactions. This is especially true in the case of pharmaceuticals, where major wholesalers purchase a vast majority of their inventory from manufacturers but supplement their bottom lines by buying heavily discounted identical goods on the gray market.

This is a fairly common activity among supermarkets and variety stores and is not illegal. Frequently, supermarkets overstock goods that they then sell to competitors at a slight discount from wholesale. This saves inventory costs and allows the goods to be sold prior to the expiration date. A supermarket may in fact consciously order more goods than it can foreseeably sell at retail to take advantage of regional or seasonal discounts offered by manufacturers. This practice, of course, horrifies manufacturers, but is very difficult to detect. Furthermore, the legal remedies are slim. It is highly unlikely that the manufacturer will retaliate by refusing to sell to its best customers.

Usually, diversion of this type is done on a business-to-business (B2B) basis, where the seller is transferring the goods directly to another retailer. In some cases, however, even large chains will purchase goods at below manufacturer's wholesale from the huge gray market "facilitators" such as Quality King (QK). This company is one of dozens that acquire and resell goods almost wholly on the gray market. QK has over $2 billion in annual sales, almost all of which goes to legitimate retailers. One of the problems in frequenting the gray market, however, is that QK and its peers are sometimes less than punctilious about the sources of their acquisition. Counterfeit and even stolen goods often find their way into this supply chain. One large retailer found that it was actually buying back goods stolen from its own stores when dealing with a major diversion "facilitator." These goods were stolen by a group of "boosters" who were suspected by Cincinnati police investigators to have facilitated terrorist operations.[5]

"Boosting" as a component of diversion

Organized theft rings in the United States cause more monetary damage than any other type of crime affecting retailers. So-called "booster rings" prey upon retailers across the nation. These groups of coordinated shoplifters steal millions of dollars of consumer products every day. Most often targeted are high-value, low-bulk items such as over-the-counter pharmaceuticals, spices, infant formula, condoms, film, and computer hardware.

Unlike many other thieves, "boosters" offer their stolen property through many of the same channels used by diverters who use fraud rather than theft to acquire their inventory. Organized "booster rings" with potential links to Middle East terrorist groups operate in several states, including Michigan, Texas, New York, and Florida. In Detroit, for example, some of the rings are fully integrated. That is, both the ringleaders of the theft crews and the fences are members of the Chaldean community, which has been implicated in several money laundering cases where the funds allegedly found their way to groups identified as "terrorist" by the US Government.

In 2002, for example, federal authorities investigated more than 500 Muslim and Arab small businesses across the United States to determine whether they were dispatching money raised through criminal activity in the United States to terrorist groups overseas. The investigation into Arab businesses, many of

Box 7.1 Case study – Possibility of terrorist financing via stolen goods

In April 2004, Mohammed Khalil Ghali was convicted on 15 counts of a superseding indictment that charged him with various federal felony violations relating to organized retail theft in north Texas. Six of Ghali's co-defendants pled guilty to conspiracy to commit offenses. Ghali was convicted on one count of conspiracy to commit offenses against the United States, one count of theft from an interstate shipment, three counts of interstate transportation of stolen property, nine counts of money laundering, and one count of conspiracy to commit money laundering (violations of 18 USC §371, 18 USC §659, 18 USC §2314, 18 USC §1956(a)(3)(A), and 18 USC §1956(h), respectively). Ghali faces a maximum sentence of 245 years imprisonment and a $3.75 million fine.

At trial, the government presented evidence that Ghali was the organizer and leader of the "Ghali" organization and controlled every aspect of its activities, and that the other seven defendants charged were members of his organization. From September 2001 through May 2003, Ghali directed members of his organization to purchase stolen property, which was held at various Fort Worth convenience stores by store owners/operators who served as "fences" for the Ghali organization. Ghali was the de facto owner or secret partner in several businesses, all of which were in the name of members of the Ghali organization or associates. The government presented evidence that Ghali orchestrated the shipment and distribution of the stolen property throughout the United States, and although he avoided directly dealing with thieves, he closely supervised and directed other members of his organization to conduct the activity, using them as a buffer to avoid detection by law enforcement authorities.

Ghali, his co-defendants, and their co-conspirators, including other owners and operators of convenience stores in and around Fort Worth, advertised by word of mouth that the Ghali organization would pay cash for certain property, including infant formula, pharmaceuticals, cigarettes, health and beauty aids, medicinal products, glucose test strips, nicotine gum and transdermal patches, and razors and razor blades. Encouraged by this, thieves would shoplift or steal up to $2,000 worth of property per day from retail stores and supermarkets. The defendants assisted some of the thieves by providing vehicles and, in the event thieves were arrested, the defendants even provided bail money.

The defendants paid the thieves 30–50 percent of the average retail sales price of the stolen goods. The stolen property was then collected and delivered to their warehouses where price tags and anti-theft devices were removed. The property was repackaged and placed on pallets for delivery to a common carrier for shipment throughout the United States. The operation also sold stolen infant formula to stores operating in Texas and Arizona under the Women, Infants, and Children (WIC) program, which provides free supplemental foods to meet specific nutritional needs of pregnant, postpartum, and breast-feeding women, and infants and children of low-income families determined to be "at nutritional risk." Ghali also sold 1600 Viagra® sildenafil citrate tablets, which were taken in an $800,000 burglary of a warehouse in Grand Prairie, Texas, to a government confidential informant. The Viagra® tablets had been preordered by the Department of Veterans Affairs. The government also presented evidence that Ghali used the monetary proceeds of these activities to purchase residences using straw buyers.

The investigation began after 11 September 2001, when federal authorities received information from Muslim Americans and Arab sources that proceeds from a money laundering operation were being sent overseas, possibly to support terrorism. Law enforcement officials believe some of the proceeds were sent to the Middle East. According to investigators, "We have identified where some money has gone over to the Middle East, but [we] can't tell you how much money, and once it hits the West Bank, [we] can't tell you what happens to it. At this time, the Palestinian Authority has not been able to assist."

Millions of dollars were laundered by the Ghali organization over a two-year period. Since the public documents in this case do not cite terrorist groups as having received funds from this operation, the legally provable "money trail" was unavailable at the trial.

Source: USDOJ Press Release 6 April 2004. Online. Available HTTP: <http://www.usdoj.gov/usao/txn/PressRel04/ghali_convict_pr.html> (accessed 5 November 2005)

them convenience stores, was launched after 11 September, when law enforcement agents stepped up scrutiny of small-scale scams that they believed were generating tens of millions of dollars a year for militant groups. The criminal activity included skimming the profits of drug sales, stealing and reselling baby formula, illegally redeeming huge quantities of grocery coupons, collecting fraudulent welfare payments, swiping credit card numbers, and hawking unlicensed T-shirts. These investigations were undertaken on speculation that some of the money had gone to Palestinian groups engaged in suicide bombings, including the Islamic Resistance Movement and the Popular Front for the Liberation of Palestine.

Booster rings with ties to suspected terrorist organizations were especially active in targeting branded infant formula between 1997 and 2000. At least three independent groups were active throughout the US South and Southwest in repackaging boosted product. The fruits of this scheme disappeared into accounts located in Egypt and have never been fully accounted for. Repackaging infant formula was a very poor idea. The federal government did not spare the horses in tracking down the perpetrators. Infant formula is an iconic product in the United States, and those who tamper with these goods are not appreciated.[6]

Smuggling and diversion

Smuggling, by definition, involves the transport of contraband goods. "Contraband" includes legitimate products that are restricted or taxed differently in the target market than in the home market. This is especially true for goods such as tobacco and liquor. Tobacco, for example, is taxed at substantially higher rates in some states than in others. In the high-tax jurisdictions, this situation has bred a substantial gray market in cigarettes that is filled by both diverted goods and products physically smuggled by politically motivated individuals as well as by organized criminal enterprises.

Cigarette diversion often involves the purchase of tax-free products ostensibly destined for offshore distribution, but re-introduced into the US under the regulatory radar. Until four years ago, such re-importation was actually legal, as far as the federal government was concerned.[7] Of course, the federal government did not condone the tax evasion component that such diversion generally involved.

Smuggling follows the same pattern, using many of the same outlets and personnel as diversion fraud schemes. For example, a group of residents of North Carolina (where cigarette taxes are low) conspired with a diversion ring in Michigan to transport truckloads of tobacco products to the Detroit area. The goods supplemented other gray market sources for cheap cigarettes. Portions of the proceeds from these operations were then transferred to Hezbollah. In an earlier case in 2002, two brothers, Mohamad and Chawki Hammoud, made large purchases of cigarettes in North Carolina and then shipped them to Michigan, where they were resold at a profit of 70 cents a pack. Mohamad Hammoud had a close relationship with Ayatollah Mohammed Hussein Fadlallah, spiritual leader of Hezbollah. Trial evidence included a receipt from Fadlallah to Mohamad Hammoud for $1,300 he wired to Hezbollah and a photo of Mohamad at age 15 holding an assault rifle at a Hezbollah site in Lebanon. In June 2002, the Hammouds were convicted in federal court of running a cigarette smuggling operation, and Mohamad Hammoud was convicted of funneling money to Hezbollah. The ring, which sold $7.5 million in cigarettes, also arranged for the delivery of military equipment such as mine detection gear, blasting equipment, and night-vision goggles to Hezbollah.

Because tobacco and liquor distribution is strictly regulated, disposition of diverted and smuggled goods in these categories often follows slightly different routes than other types of consumer products. It is sometimes difficult for diverters and smugglers to sell their goods to "legitimate" diversion

Box 7.2 Case study – Terrorist finance via cigarette diversion

Recent cases in Illinois and Michigan demonstrate the ease with which illicit cigarette transfers can be made. In March 2004, police raided a seemingly small retail store in Detroit. Prosecutors alleged that the Chapel Market was in fact a major wholesaler and fence for stolen property that resold its goods into the wholesale gray market. Bernard Zeki Butris, Zeki Abdul Butris, and Karim Seiba were arrested on 31 counts of racketeering. They had laundered millions of dollars in merchandise through their operation in only three years. Similarly, the Central Grocery in Chicago was raided in December 2004. Its proprietor, Mahmoud Okab, and three others were arrested for massive money laundering through a "Mom & Pop" convenience store that was fencing over $50,000 each business day.

On 23 January 2003, a federal grand jury in Detroit indicted 11 people on charges of conspiracy to commit a pattern of racketeering activity. The indictment charged that the defendants agreed to participate in a criminal enterprise through a pattern of racketeering activity that included contraband cigarette trafficking, possession of counterfeit cigarette tax stamps, credit card fraud, money laundering, arson, and witness tampering. The indictment also charged Elias Mohamad Akhdar with an additional count of traveling between the states of Michigan and New York in aid of committing arson.

The indictment charged that the enterprise would obtain low-taxed or untaxed cigarettes in North Carolina and the Cattaraugus Indian Reservation in New York and bring them into Michigan for the purpose of evading Michigan cigarette taxes. In Michigan, cigarette taxes are $12.50 per carton. In North Carolina, cigarette taxes are 50 cents per carton. Cigarettes on the Cattaraugus Indian Reservation are untaxed. The enterprise sometimes used counterfeit tax stamps to make it appear that the Michigan taxes had been paid. The enterprise also used fraudulent credit cards to purchase contraband cigarettes. The indictment also charges that, as part of the enterprise's pattern of racketeering activity, some members of the enterprise traveled from Michigan to New York in 2001 where they set fire to the Indian Express tobacco shop located on the Cattaraugus Indian Reservation after removing untaxed cigarettes from the store and sending them to Michigan to be resold.

See also Superseding Bill of Indictment Docket No 3:00CR 147-MU 03/28/01 *US v. Mohamad Youssef Hammoud et al.*, which includes the state's case against the defendants in a scheme to smuggle cigarettes from North Carolina to Michigan in order to fund activities and make purchases for the terrorist group, Hezbollah.

Mohamad Youssef Hammoud is the sole defendant found guilty of providing material support to a terrorist organization. His case is also the only one to predate 11 September 2001. Indicted in 2000 on a litany of money laundering, racketeering, and immigration fraud charges in addition to several counts of providing material support to terrorists, Hammoud was convicted two years later. The jury found him guilty of funneling profits from a cigarette smuggling operation to Lebanon's Hezbollah. In February 2003, Judge Graham Mullen of the Western District of North Carolina sentenced him to 155 years imprisonment. Hammoud appealed to the 4th Circuit which affirmed his sentence.

Most of the other defendants pleaded guilty to other charges and were sentenced to various periods in federal custody and ordered to pay millions of dollars in fines and penalties.

Source: Siobhan Roth, "Material Support Law: Weapon in War on Terror," *Legal Times*, 9 May 2003. Online. Available HTTP: <http://www.law.com/jsp/article.jsp?id=1051121856896> (accessed 11 April 2007)

fences, so "dark gray" wholesalers (who also handle stolen goods) and even retailers are often enlisted as outlets.[8] In the case of the above-noted cigarettes, for example, the conspirators enlisted numerous convenience stores in the Detroit area as outlets for their goods.

Product counterfeiting and diversion

Product counterfeiting is a common component of diversion schemes. For example, every single one of the 65 cases investigated by the Food and Drug Administration (FDA) Office of Criminal Investigation in the past four years involved counterfeit drugs that have found their way to legitimate US pharmacy shelves via the diversion pipeline. The FDA is so concerned about terrorists using diversion as a method by which to introduce dangerous drugs into the US market that it formed special task forces in 2003 to investigate this threat.[9]

There is no question that the US drug distribution chain is vulnerable to infiltration by counterfeit medications. It is also understood that diversion is the favored means of doing so. Finally, it is clear that terrorist groups have used diversion as a means to raise (and launder) money. What has *not* been conclusively demonstrated to date, however, is that terrorists have actually used their diversion skills to insert bogus medications into the United States.[10] All of the counterfeit pharmaceutical cases that have been prosecuted to date have involved diversion, but none have been definitively linked with terrorists. It has been tempting to conclude that terrorists would find drug diversion an attractive target, and the FDA takes this threat seriously. In 2003, the FDA formed task forces on both pharmaceutical and food surety, which filed reports late that year. The reports concluded that although there had been no confirmed terrorist participation in the dozens of instances to date, the US drug distribution network was indeed vulnerable to this sort of scheme. The fact that terrorists have not yet been found to enter this criminal enterprise does not mean that they have not done so – only that they have not been detected.[11]

Counterfeiting per se has long been a favored activity of terrorist groups and their supporters. These counterfeited goods are almost always smuggled merchandise.

Sampling diversion

Many companies provide products for promotional purposes at low or no cost. Often, these goods are acquired under false pretenses and sold to diversion "facilitators" or directly to retail outlets. Although sampling scams are a well-known "niche crime" in the United States, they have not yet been definitively linked with persons involved with terrorist funding operations.

Charity fraud

One of the major sources of diverted goods is an array of "charity fraud" schemes that operate internationally. One of the most common of these scams is for a seemingly legitimate charity to solicit goods from well-known manu-facturers. This is particularly common in the health-care field. The alleged charities claim that they plan to distribute donated (or below-wholesale priced) products to deserving victims overseas. In many cases, a portion of the donated products will indeed be provided to sufferers, but a major portion of the goods are re-introduced into high-price markets via the standard "diversion facilitators" mentioned previously.

This scheme is particularly prevalent in Africa and in regions suffering either from pandemic diseases or from natural disasters. Pharmaceutical companies have been defrauded of hundreds of millions of dollars from these schemes, especially with the provision of HIV/AIDS medications. In a single case in 2002, government officials in a West African country who were com-plicit with the diversion scheme cheated one pharmaceutical manufacturer of almost $18 million in less than a year.[12] Only a portion of the proceeds of that scam has been recovered.

Even charities that do not resell items are alleged to have had duplicitous dealings with donors. In some cases, "charities" have been said to have approached donors for humanitarian goods allegedly destined for such clearly benign causes as schools, hospitals, and refugee camps, only to convert donations into materiel for armed terrorist groups. The issue of diversion from charities is considered more fully in Chapter 5.

Although the United States and several foreign governments have identi-fied numerous suspect "charities," both political and practical problems have largely thwarted these efforts. It is often difficult to isolate the "charitable" functions of a group from other activities. Hamas (among others) is a political movement that has a well-deserved reputation for providing succor for victims of the occupation, but also conducts armed resistance against Israel. Further, charities often (rightly) claim that the products donated by well-meaning Western companies and individuals do not serve the immediate needs of the victims, who sell these goods to raise money for purchasing more sorely needed products. The most obvious way to do this is by dumping the unneeded goods on the gray market, which is always willing to accept below-wholesale products. Even the best-run charities (such as the Red Cross/Red Crescent) have engaged in this practice. In fact, the Red Cross actively discourages donations of products by either individuals or companies and routinely disposes of unnecessary goods as quickly as possible to raise funds for more efficient distribution of relief to affected victims.[13]

Laundering the proceeds of a diversion transaction

As noted above, the first critical step in any diversion scheme is to acquire products cheaply and sell them dearly. This is standard arbitrage, but with the added element of fraud at the inception of the transaction. Nevertheless, this fraud is not immediately apparent to the seller, who often acts as a facilitator for the more elegant part of the transaction – laundering the cash.

In a standard "U-Boat" scam described previously, the manufacturer in the developed world – for instance, the US – is actually paid for the goods at the outset. If the manufacturer is sophisticated in international trade (as most are), he or she will insist that payment be made by irrevocable Letter of Credit (L/C) or its equivalent. This means that the perpetrators of the scheme must have relations with well-known overseas banks that can issue a L/C acceptable to the seller. This is an essential element in the more complex schemes.

Establishing credit is fairly easy with many of the most respectable banks if a substantial deposit accompanies it. These deposits can often be arranged with a satisfactory explanation that the seller will not accept a L/C from another bank (e.g. a Cypriot account). The account in the reputable bank is generally established in the name of a trading company or other such nominee domiciled in the country of the bank itself. In most European countries, establishing a local trading company is straightforward. All that is needed is a pliant collaborator like an attorney specialized in such matters. These are often called "brass plaque" or shell companies and are almost always properly registered. The shell trading company can receive cash from a suspect bank, but uses these funds to establish the account with a Blue Chip bank in a Western country.

Sometimes, there is a "cut-out" trading company – one to receive the funds from abroad and another to establish a trading account with the legitimate bank. These companies can have cross-signatures so that the shift from one company to another can be difficult to detect. The transfer is carried on the books of the two companies as an internal transfer, and the bank itself may be unaware of the shift if the diversion broker has set up the scheme with the sleight of hand for which many are famous. Once the deposit is made, an L/C can be arranged for almost any sum that is less than the amount in the account.

When the original order for goods is placed (i.e. in the "U-boat example"), the buyer will request a "pro-forma invoice" listing the quantity and quality of the goods, as well as the total price. The buyer then instructs its bank to open a Letter of Credit in favor of the seller in that amount. The buyer's bank then notifies the seller's bank (i.e. a reputable bank located in the United States) of the open L/C in the seller's favor. The seller's bank confirms the L/C with its customer. The seller then ships the goods in conformity with the terms of the Letter of Credit and presents its bank with supporting documentation (e.g. Bills of Lading, Manifests, etc.). The seller's bank then notifies the buyer's bank, requesting payment of the L/C. This payment is made and is credited to the seller's account.

Note that the above transaction is the most common method by which legitimate international sales are commonly made. The transactions are, of course, reported to the monetary authorities of the respective banks'. countries and are undoubtedly detected by other governmental agencies (e.g. FinCEN). Such detection, however, is not of concern to the conspirators. After all, if questioned, *all* of the parties can confirm that the payment was made for the purpose of paying for the shipment of perfectly legitimate merchandise in a standard wholesale transaction. Further, the paperwork for this transaction is in full conformity with both international agreements and national law.

Once the foreign "shell" has diverted the goods, the ultimate buyer of the goods must pay them. In this event, the US confederate of the foreign diverter merely wires the funds to the offshore bank account of the diverter (i.e. the same one which set up the original Letter of Credit). Generally, the funds thus transmitted will be in excess of what was originally paid from that company. This final transaction is also "in the clear." That is, it is likely to be detected by monetary authorities, and will be reported as required by law. If questions arise, the transaction is again correctly described as payment for legitimate product.

Although these procedures may appear cumbersome, they are routine in international commerce. All that needs to be done to transform a legitimate commercial transaction into a money laundering mechanism is "hidden in plain sight."

There are numerous variations of this scenario, including the falsification of shipping documentation (especially Bills of Lading) to save shipping costs, but the most careful diverters do not deign to engage in this sort of thing. The beauty of a well-executed diversion transaction is that very few laws are actually broken. Those that are, for example, wire fraud, are extremely difficult to detect and the likelihood of prosecution is low.

Ostensible "Trading Companies" in the Middle East (especially in Dubai and Lebanon) have raised diversion to a subtle art. The sources of their initial funds are often unknown, and the return funds disappear without a trace once repatriated. It is certain that Saddam Hussein's regime used diversion via trading firms in Jebel Ali, but rarely with the intent of profiting directly thereby. It was merely a simple tool to evade sanctions imposed by the United Nations, and it worked wonderfully.[14]

In other cases, however, the mechanisms described above have been used by much more shadowy organizations. In the Middle East these primarily consist of groups that do not wish to be identified, including several on the OFAC list of prohibited parties. For example, the Saddam Hussein regime used Al-Bashair Trading Company, which was the largest of Iraq's arms procurement front companies, to engage in a range of sanctions busting and corruption schemes. Al-Bashair reported directly to the Organization of Military Industrialization, which was responsible for Iraq's military procurement programs and was headed by former Deputy Prime Minister Abd-al-Tawab Mullah Huwaysh. Huwaysh was named by the UN as a senior official of the former Iraq regime on the list established pursuant to UNSCR 1483.

Documents removed from Al-Bashair's headquarters describe a variety of deals involving sham contracts, kickbacks, falsified export documentation, and money laundering designed to deceive UN inspectors and deliver, among other things, missile components, surveillance equipment, and tank barrels to the former Iraqi regime. The company also allegedly helped senior officials of the former regime launder and hide Iraqi government funds.

Operations

As can be seen from the above description, international diversion schemes can be extremely complicated. These are not techniques commonly used by amateurs. Most commercial diversion operations are actually set up and managed by specialists who act as brokers on behalf of such groups. These brokers are experts in commercial logistics as well as the intricacies of international financial transactions.

There are only a few truly great diversion brokers in the world. They infrequently handle goods themselves, and their names rarely appear on any financial documents. Like black market peso exchange brokers, diversion brokers do not often finance their own transactions, but "place" funds for others. A good broker can set up shell companies in "safe" countries (e.g. Switzerland); establish bank accounts; arrange shipping logistics; find US confederates in "U-boat" transactions; locate pliant freight forwarders who will ask few questions about the nature of a transaction; identify "diversion facilitators" who will accept the diverted goods; "paper" a transaction with legitimate documentation; take out Letters of Credit and confirmations; and monitor the entire transaction from initial order through repatriation of the funds.

Diversion brokers work on a commission basis – generally in the 5 to 7 percent range, but sometimes lower, depending upon the size of the transaction. The commission is generally paid upon the successful completion of the transaction, but they are often "fronted" expenses (e.g. for shipping costs or establishment of shells) from the inception. Although most brokers reside overseas, especially in the United Kingdom, France, Switzerland, and the United Arab Emirates, several are located in the United States (they favor Miami, New York, and Southern California). By and large, diversion brokers are well educated, worldly, and have clean criminal records.

Although most expert brokers are extremely inventive and change the details of their schemes frequently, many have adopted *modus operandi* that are recognizable "signatures." Some diversion brokers have been so successful that they actually trade on their own behalf. That is, they do not need a patron, but finance million-dollar deals themselves. The most skilled brokers can accomplish this by "pre-cooking" deals whereby they persuade a buyer to guarantee payment even before the goods are acquired. Using this guarantee, they can often get friendly bankers to lend sufficient cash to cover a Letter of Credit. This, however, is an exception that demonstrates the rule. Most diversion brokers would rather have someone else's money in play rather than their own.

In less sophisticated operations, diverters may rely upon the simple skills of a commodities broker. These individuals, while necessary to a diversion transaction, do not actually manage the deals. They merely place goods that have been acquired by offshore companies. There are thousands of commodities brokers around the world – a few hundred of which have sales exceeding $100 million. They are located in many countries, and can "deal" goods wherever located. Although commodities brokers (as the name implies) generally handle such goods as wheat, cement, urea, and petroleum, many will place internationally famous brands in wholesale quantities that have acquired "commodity" status of their own (e.g. branded apparel, packaged food, cigarettes, etc.).

When dealing through a commodities broker, diverters are merely trying to dump product that they have fraudulently acquired. Commodities brokers' commissions are generally less than that of full-service diversion brokers because inventory costs and the speed with which goods are placed can reduce overall profits to the diversion plotters. Dealing through commodities brokers, however, has the advantage of disguising the conspiracy itself, since the broker is rarely part of any underhanded transaction, but is merely arranging for the goods to be sold. The mere identification of a commodities broker in a transaction does not do much to unravel the entire scheme. Thus, brokers (especially in Singapore, the UAE, India, and Malta) can operate with relative impunity, secure in their lack of knowledge about exactly how the goods they are placing have been acquired.

Commodities brokers even advertise on specialized websites known as Trade Bulletin Boards (TBBs). There are around 30 major TBBs and 400 to

500 more specialized sites. Unlike auction sites such as eBay, TBBs offer wholesale quantities of "commodity" consumer goods to all comers. Prices are negotiable. The sales terms are generally standard (i.e. Confirmed L/C, fob port). Commodities brokers are not usually involved in any "after-market" exchange of funds. They take payment, deduct their commission, and pass along the balance to the seller. The final arrangements for the shipment are made between the buyer and seller; the broker rarely has anything to do with this part of the transaction. The relative anonymity of deals arranged by commodities brokers offers obvious benefits to a seller interested only in laundering cash, but does not provide much opportunity for profit unless the spread between the initial cost of the goods and the ultimate selling price is substantial (20 percent or more).

These deals have the downside, however, of being relatively easy to detect. Although it is possible for commodities brokers to short-circuit TBBs by maintaining "favored customer" lists to whom offers are emailed rather than being publicly posted, once a commodities broker is identified as dealing in diverted goods, they are (or should be) "on the radar" for anti-diversion specialists. Diverters themselves know the identity of major commodities brokers who will place large quantities of goods and offer favored brokers large quantities of product if the broker has a proven track record. These brokers act as wholesale pawnshops where few questions are asked. Classic "diversion brokers," on the other hand, are more akin to private bankers who know their customers well, have personal contacts with buyers, and are extremely discreet.

Terrorist groups have used both types of brokers in the past decade, but tend to favor commodities brokers over the more sophisticated diversion brokers.[15] There are several explanations for this. One reason may be that many specialist diversion brokers are Jewish. While there are numerous examples of Jewish diversion brokers handling deals for world-class crooks (including suspected narcotics dealers), there may be some reticence (either on the part of the broker or the "placer") to use a Jewish "fixer" to launder cash for groups like Hamas. Rather, the reason might be the relative secrecy of a transaction placed through a commodities broker. This method is much more "survivable" in the event that the broker is compromised. The arrest of a single component does not necessarily result in the dismantling of the entire enterprise.

Unlike organized criminal groups, terrorist groups appear less concerned about maximizing profits than they are about risking compromising the supply of funds associated with diversion operations. This, of course, is speculation in that the alternative (i.e. using a specialized "diversion broker") is extremely safe, but finding a suitable broker is somewhat difficult.

Dealing with diversion

There are a variety of currently available means to deal with diversion through legal processes. To begin, counterfeiting and diversion in the United

Box 7.3 Case study – Hezbollah and the tri-border region of South America

"Khalil Saleh, a Paraguayan of Arab origin, registered a business, Saleh Trading Limited, in the Free Zone of Iquique (Chile), contributing the larger part of the initial $50,000 in capital. Assad Ahmad Barakat contributed $1,000, and a Paraguayan attorney from Iquique, Juan Eduardo Lecaros, contributed an additional $500. The next day, Barakat Limited was registered with a capital of $20,000, of which Barakat contributed $19,800 and Lecaros the remaining $200. Barakat Limited has not yet initiated operations, but Saleh Trading Limited is an import mercantile business, dealing in various goods from clothes to electronic devices. It is managed by another Lebanese citizen, Arafat Ismail."

A Brazilian resident of Lebanese origin, Bakarat remains a fugitive and is reported to be living in the Brazilian Triple Border city with his Brazilian wife and children. Barakat was considered the top fund-raiser for Hezbollah in the Paraguay, Brazil, and Argentina tri-border area. He is well regarded by the Hezbollah leadership. In fact, Paraguayan police discovered a letter in which Hassan Nasrallah, the Hezbollah leader, thanked Barakat for his efforts on behalf of children orphaned when their fathers were killed.

"Barakat arrived as a teenager in Paraguay in 1985, along with his father. Other family members followed, and, according to a news source, 'today the Barakat family numbers about 90' in the country, all of them 'devout Shi'ite Muslims.' Bakarat claims that the accusations against him are due to a rival Lebanese merchant who aims at grabbing Barakat's exclusive rights to distribute a video game made in Hong Kong, and that Paraguayan police are pursuing him for purposes of extortion, with the excuse of seeking terrorists. But according to officials, Bakarat, who operated a farm in the outskirts of Foz de Iguazu, created a 'business-screen' in Ciudad del Este. Barakat left his former residence in Paraguay shortly after the Paraguayan authorities commenced operations in Ciudad del Este in December 1999, working with its neighbor cities in a search for suspected anti-Israeli terrorists. Nevertheless, the Paraguayan branch of Interpol said that they suspected Barakat was still in the zone."

Source: Blanca Madani, "Hizbollah in South America." Online.
Available HTTP: <http://www.jdo.org/hezbollah.htm>
(accessed 11 April 2007)

States are both subject to federal and state law. Counterfeiting usually constitutes a violation of the manufacturer's Intellectual Property Rights. Diversion often involves a fraud scheme that may give a manufacturer the right to collect damages for breach of contract and lead to criminal prosecution of the diverter.

Of the charges brought against trade diverters, the most common civil remedy is action based on trademark infringement. Infringement actions, however, tend to work much better in counterfeit cases than in diversion. It is almost always preferable to bring lawsuits alleging civil fraud if the facts so warrant. The most common criminal charges are mail and wire fraud. In a great number of cases the diverter makes false statements about the destination of the goods. In some cases, the RICO Act has also been used.[16] Pharmaceutical diversion has become subject to recent legislation, notably 18 USC §1365, which makes tampering with and mislabeling of consumer products unlawful.

Although there are laws that affect specific types of goods (e.g. prescription pharmaceuticals), there is no general prohibition of diversion in either federal or state statutes. In many cases of diversion, however, the perpetrators rely upon deception to accomplish their objectives or commit other offenses that constitute a criminal enterprise. There have been several attempts at the federal level in the US to criminalize activities such as "decoding" products (i.e. removing manufacturers' product codes so as to make product tracing impossible), but these attempts have not been successful to date. There are, however, several state laws that in some cases can address the decoding problem. Notwithstanding the lack of federal legislation on the decoding issue, there have been numerous cases in which diverters have been found guilty of criminal activity or civil fraud.

The federal government, of course, can prosecute diversion cases using an entire quiver of charges if they are so inclined. False statements to a federal official, wire fraud, mail fraud, and money laundering are often the "hooks" that are used.[17] Underlying these charges, of course, are the even more serious allegations of supporting terrorist organizations, the Trading with the Enemy Act, and a host of others.[18]

Penetrating a diversion scheme

Law enforcement has traditionally been reluctant even to investigate diversion schemes. This is understandable. These schemes almost always involve commercial fraud, and the "victims" are generally well-heeled multinational companies with vast resources of their own. Further, the victims have often been paid at least a nominal amount for their goods, so the controversy often appears to be a mere contract dispute. Finally, many multinational companies are at least partially at fault for failing to protect themselves from scoundrels in the marketplace. In some cases, it could be argued that the companies have even been complicit in their own victimization by actually seeking out questionable characters to open new markets. This is compounded by the perverse incentives many companies have adopted which encourage sales representatives to move product. Those within the company regard any questions about the integrity of an account as a threat to sales commissions.

Another reason for the dearth of criminal proceedings is the relative complexity of the cases and the difficulty of obtaining evidence. Many of the activities in diversion schemes take place overseas where US law enforcement is at a significant disadvantage. Further, although criminal conduct of some kind is almost always present (at least wire fraud), the underlying nature of additional crimes is usually obscure. As can be seen from the explanations above, diversion can be used both to raise money and to launder it. It is very difficult to tell exactly who is behind the plots when they are first discovered. Diversion is often used by organized crime (especially Russian), narcotics dealers (Central Asian, Southeast Asian, and South American), and terrorist organizations. There are also large freelance operations with no known relationship with any of these groups. Law enforcement prefers to know their target, even when criminal activity is evident.

Law enforcement also has difficulty in sorting data in diversion cases. The financial transactions are cleverly camouflaged as legitimate. Discerning transactions motivated by fraud or "cleaning" operations is tedious and often unproductive.

Prosecutors do not favor diversion matters since they rarely have much "jury appeal" and consume substantial investigative resources. These are not "low hanging fruit" cases, and they are routinely ignored by even the most zealous prosecutors (such as those in Miami) who have hundreds of "emergency" cases involving violent crime or massive narcotics trafficking, that are much easier to prove. Juries often have trouble differentiating a diversion case involving money laundering from a commercial contract gone bad. In fact, most prosecutors will only take these cases where there is substantial evidence of other, "sexier" crimes.

Notwithstanding the reluctance of law enforcement to investigate these cases, there have been notable prosecutions. The most numerous of these have involved other threats represented by the diversion activity, especially threats to public health. As noted above, targeting infant formula and pharmaceuticals were especially poor choices by diverters. However, the most vigorous enforcement has taken place where the diverters have gotten greedy and "salted" diverted shipments with counterfeit goods.[19]

There have only been a few "pure" federal cases brought against diverters where no public safety issues were involved.[20] Even these, however, have been justified on the basis that either the government itself had been defrauded or that public health *could* have been endangered. There have been no cases brought in the past decade where the principal charge was money laundering. This latter count has, of course, been added to several criminal indictments, but generally as an "enhancement" to the primary charges.

The chances of apprehension and prosecution are so low and the penalties so light that diverters have every incentive to continue their operations.

For law enforcement to penetrate a diversion web, they would not only have to devote substantial resources, but more importantly, understand how the systems work and cooperate with different agencies with disparate knowledge bases.

Conclusion

There are indications of recent and, more importantly, increased potential use of trade diversion as a method of raising funds for terrorist groups. Given the noted vulnerabilities, the existence of the know-how for trade diversion in conflict-ridden regions, and the large transaction volume of international trade, this is a *modus operandi* that policy-makers need to be familiar with and pay close attention to. The current regulatory and enforcement environment, however, neglects this type of misconduct, thereby posing significant risks to US security and economic interests.

The policy implications outlined below are consistent with the arguments set out in other chapters of this book. As collaboration between criminal and terrorist groups raises concerns (see Williams, Chapter 6), so must trade diversion be included in the list of offenses more thoroughly scrutinized. Trade in specific commodities (see Farah, Chapter 9) is indeed non-transparent and enables the commission of serious crimes supportive of terrorist groups. The financial controls against terrorism should not focus exclusively on some areas, such as informal value transfers and money service businesses (see Passas and Maimbo, Chapter 8), but also on trade in an effort to anticipate, detect, and stop attempts by terrorist groups or their supporters to take advantage of this mechanism. Some practical recommendations and steps can be taken in the short and medium term.

US goods returned

The Customs Service verifies many goods declared as "US Goods Returned" to assure that no dutiable goods are disguised as domestic products. Customs already has electronic records of these entries, so it can determine which US importers are handling goods that they clearly did not manufacture. With some exceptions (e.g. pharmaceuticals), this is not illegal, but having a database of known importers of consumer goods that are made in the United States would at least narrow the suspects for subsequent investigation. Many US importers of these goods are known diverters. To the extent that they are complicit with foreign conspirators, investigators already have immediate access to these records. The Customs records will also reveal the identity of the foreign shipper of the products. This can be particularly valuable if investigators then present this information to victims, asking for any information on the subject.

Tracking payments to offshore trading companies

While FinCEN and other government agencies track trillions of financial transactions every day, their biggest challenge is to identify suspect transactions. In diversion cases, the incoming transfer to a reputable US manufacturer is unlikely to be particularly revealing – at least at the outset of an investigation. More interesting would be the outgoing payment for goods later sold in the United States. This payment is often made by a co-conspirator of the offshore diverter. Sometimes, the same person or entity that acted as the importer of record for the "US Goods Returned" makes the payment. In other cases, it can be a company located in the United States. In addition, the destination of these funds can often be revealing. Even when it is made to a reputable international bank (as is usually the case), the underlying transaction is rarely revealed. Small companies that send millions of dollars to shell companies abroad are particularly suspicious. Often, the offshore firm then transmits the funds to other entities located in third countries. It is at this point where the link can sometimes be made with terrorist funding operations.

Establish working relationships with victims of diversion

Large US manufacturers are victimized daily by diversion schemes. Many of these companies have staff that monitor suspicious sales and are knowledgeable about currently operating diverters nationally and internationally. Unfortunately, the "Not Invented Here Syndrome" seems to pervade many federal law enforcement agencies. Suspicious activity is well known to victims of diversion – it merely requires someone to ask for it. Most victims are unaware of precisely who is profiting from a diversion scheme. They generally only know that a particular account is involved in the plot. They have neither the means nor the inclination to find out who is directly profiting. Their goal is to stop the losses to their company. It is only when they can actually seize goods or identify an entity that is not "judgment proof" in the US that they are interested in pursuing the matter further. Law enforcement, however, can take these cases for their own purposes. Using the information provided by the victim, they can follow the money trail to the real perpetrators and their sources of funding. This is where terrorism links may emerge.

Law enforcement has been reluctant to use this resource. Since companies generally do not know the full cast of conspirators in any given scheme, many of the suspects appear involved in nothing more than commercial fraud with no connection to terrorism or organized crime. When, however, law enforcement can identify companies that have aroused suspicion, US manufacturers can often provide a wealth of data, including original documentation. In these cases, the companies are usually anxious to cooperate with law enforcement, so none of the problems sometimes associated with getting companies to produce documents are present.

Note that data gleaned from victims of diversion may not always be accurate. Diversion plots almost always involve subterfuge, including falsified shipping documents, phony letterheads, aliases, "accommodation addresses," and similar ploys. Nevertheless, having access to this material can lead to more questions about these transactions. The most skilled diversion brokers will use as many genuine documents and names as possible to avoid raising suspicions, but even they often resort to setting up new fronts using the same address once one of their shells has been detected.

Track trade bulletin boards

As explained above, commodities brokers actually advertise on the internet through Trade Bulletin Boards. Although there are hundreds of these, US law enforcement can monitor their offerings. In fact, such monitoring is already being done in the private sector. There are several private databases with historical records of all major commodities brokers. Although it is difficult to match brokers with names gleaned from the US goods returned data (since they usually do not act as the exporter), matches can sometimes be made by comparison of volumes or weight. This technique has been successful in identifying numerous shipments of diverted goods over the years. Once a shipment is identified, reliance on the US Food and Drug Administration's OASIS system (Operational and Administrative System for Import Support) or the Hong Kong Trade Development Council's PIERS system (Port Import Export Reporting Service) to cross-index the data is fairly straightforward.

Coordinate with other agencies

One of the major weaknesses in the US ability to recognize diversion transactions and who is behind them is a lack of coordination among agencies. Customs has a wealth of information on cross-border trade and can isolate suspicious accounts with relative ease. However, customs officials lack the ability to determine what happens in the financial chain. Working with FinCEN, OFAC, and the Justice Department, the combined resources of the US federal government could make life extremely difficult for terrorist groups and other criminal groups that use this as a method of money laundering. Anti-diversion efforts will net all sorts of other scoundrels unrelated to terrorism, but this is a bonus.

However skilled investigators may be, it is critical that the Justice Department make prosecution of these crimes a priority. US attorneys will simply refuse to prosecute these cases unless instructed to do so. Failure to follow up has already led to a relatively open door for terrorists and other antisocial elements to use diversion as the most sophisticated – and profitable – money laundering tool available.

Notes

1 US Department of State, *International Narcotics Control Strategy Report 2003*, Bureau for International Narcotics and Law Enforcement Affairs, March 2004. Online. Available HTTP: <http://www.state.gov/p/inl/rls/nrcrpt/2003/vol2/html/29910.htm> (accessed 16 April 2007)

2 US Department of State, *International Narcotics Control Strategy Report 2005*, Bureau for International Narcotics and Law Enforcement Affairs, March 2005. Online. Available HTTP: <http://www.state.gov/p/inl/rls/nrcrpt/2005/vol2/html/42380.htm> (accessed 16 April 2007)

3 The US Government has outright prohibitions on trade with several countries (e.g. Cuba and North Korea) and severely restricts trade with several others (e.g. Burma, Sudan). Further, the US Government lists numerous companies and individuals as "prohibited parties" or "specially designated nationals" because of their involvement in a wide variety of illegal activity, including terrorism and narcotics trafficking. See especially the discussion in Chapter 10 of this volume. These lists rarely identify money laundering operations, per se, as "prohibited."

4 Harmonized Tariff System of the United States 19 CFR 1–199; HTSUS 9801.00.

5 In October 2003, Cincinnati police shut down a massive theft ring that fenced stolen goods through retailers, oppressed poor neighborhoods by gouging customers, and possibly sent at least $37 million to bank accounts in the Middle East. Nineteen people were arrested, five of the stores were padlocked, and a total of 23 people indicted on 105 charges, from receiving stolen property to money laundering and engaging in corrupt activity. Omran Saleh, a Palestinean immigrant, and other market owners made huge profits by paying people 5 to 10 cents on the dollar for stolen goods like Crest Whitestrips, over-the-counter painkillers, and cigarettes. Professional thieves also worked for the store owners, hijacking trucks filled with merchandise. Saleh was indicted on charges of tampering with records, money laundering, conspiracy, and engaging in a pattern of corrupt activity. Investigators found dozens of bank transactions for $9,995 – just below the $10,000 that would trigger an automatic report to the government. S. Coolidge and J. Prendergast, "Markets Gouged the Poor, Laundered Money," *The Cincinnati Enquirer*, 3 October 2003.

6 In 1998, for example, a federal grand jury indicted four persons and three companies in an alleged multi-state conspiracy to sell baby formula packaged in cases bearing bogus expiration dates and designed to resemble original packaging. According to the indictment, Lexington Wholesale had "runners" across the country pay cash at grocery stores for baby formula on sale for below-cost prices. The companies named in the indictment would then repackage the several brands of formula to look new. They would then resell at a profit to grocery stores without disclosing that the formula had been repackaged or that they were not affiliated with the registered manufacturers. In 2000, four individuals were convicted of selling infant formula to wholesalers that had been stolen from retailer's shelves by shoplifters or that had been fraudulently obtained under government food assistance programs. The defendants repackaged the baby formula into counterfeit cardboard cases and trays that were made to look identical to the manufacturers' cartons. The defendants also counterfeited the trademarks of well-known brands such as Similac, Isomil, Enfamil, Nutramigen, Prosobee, Pregestimil, and Lactofree. Originally, 14 defendants were charged in a 154-count indictment that was returned in February 1999. Ten of the defendants pleaded guilty to various charges prior to trial. The four remaining defendants were Ibrahim Elsayed Hanafy, Adel Hisham Saadat, Mohamed M. Mokbel, and Samer Samad Quassas. See *US v. Hanafy et al.* 302 F 3rd 485. The defendants were found guilty of money

laundering, mislabeling, and trademark infringement. The US District Court, however, overturned the jury verdict.

7 Until 2000 the Federal Trade Commission issued licenses for companies desiring to re-import previously exported cigarettes. This practice was halted as a result of anti-tobacco activists and a spate of lawsuits filed by tobacco companies.

8 The distinctions among "gray market," "parallel market," "diversion market," and "black market" in many products (such as pharmaceuticals, for example) are ambiguous because of differing legal terminology and usage in various countries. In the United States, for example, "counterfeit" drugs include those which bear an infringing trademark, and are thus "black market." In other countries, falsification of a trademark may not render the goods "counterfeit" if they are generically identical to the trademarked product. The "parallel market" is generally composed of legitimate, branded goods which are acquired in one market and sold in another via arbitrage. "Gray market" products are similar, but are usually produced under license for sale in one country, and later sold in unauthorized locales. In general, "black market" products are illegal in the country where they are sold, but not necessarily in the country where they are manufactured.

9 In 2003, the FDA issued a contract to New Mexico State University Physical Sciences Laboratory (PSL) to develop recommendations for the food and pharmaceutical industries for assuring the safety of these products from terrorist attacks. PSL convened a series of meetings around the country to solicit views on this topic from various experts. The groups were composed of representatives from government, the respective industries, and technology providers. Among other things, the final report recounted a number of ways, including diversion, that terrorist groups could penetrate food and pharmaceutical supply chains.

10 For a somewhat contrary view, see GlobalOptions, Inc., *An Analysis of Terrorist Threats to America's Medicine Supply*, Gaithersburg, MD: Signature Book Printing, Inc., 2003. This book outlines the threat of terrorists infiltrating the pharmaceutical distribution system, their means of doing so, and includes a discussion of how terrorist groups have already engaged in counterfeiting and diversion. It implies (but does not state explicitly) that terrorists have already targeted this country with bogus drugs as part of diversion schemes and terrorist plots. This has not been conclusively demonstrated to date.

11 In the past few years, counterfeit drugs have become a significant issue in the US market. The number of counterfeit drug cases opened by the FDA each year has grown steadily since 1997. The following figures illustrate the growth of counterfeit drug cases. Counterfeit drug cases opened by FDA per year: 1997: 9; 1998: 5; 1999: 11; 2000: 6; 2001: 21; 2002: 27; 2003: 30, and 2004: 58. Food and Drug Administration, "Combating Counterfeit Drugs: a Report of the Food and Drug Administration, Annual Update," Rockville, MD: US Department of Health and Human Services, 18 May 2005. Online. Available HTTP: <http://www.fda.gov/oc/initiatives/counterfeit/update2005.html> (accessed 12 October 2005).

12 European wholesalers diverted 28 shipments of Combivir, Epivir, and Trizivir from Africa to markets in Germany, the Netherlands, Switzerland, and the United Kingdom between July 2001 and July 2002. The 28 shipments comprised three million doses of the drugs and had an estimated retail value of $18 million; they were intended for distribution in five central African nations. Although only two individuals were arrested in conjunction with the smuggling, officials suspect that a whole chain of businesses and individuals is involved in the fraud. See, for example, *The Wall Street Journal*, 4 October 2002.

13 Red Cross, "Donate Goods." Online. Available HTTP: <http://www.redcross.org/donate/goods/> (accessed 12 October 2005).

14 See the report of the Independent Inquiry Committee into The United Nations

Oil-for-Food Programme (The Volcker Commission Report) for further details. Available at: <http://www.iic-offp.org/story27oct05.htm> (accessed 16 April 2007).

15 It is, of course, impossible to quantify the actual practices of terrorists and brokers given publicly available information. Nevertheless, a survey of relevant cases seems to indicate this is true. By contrast, the example contained in Box 7.3 illustrates one case of a more sophisticated operation.

16 The Racketeer Influenced and Corrupt Organizations Act of 1970 (also referred to as the RICO Act or, simply, RICO) is an American federal law which allows prosecutors to press for greater penalties if a suspect has engaged in more than one criminal act during a 10 year period as part of a larger pattern of offences. The Act is commonly employed in the prosecution of organized crime groups in the US.

17 18 USC 1001, 18 USC 1343, 18 USC 1342, 18 USC 1956.

18 For example, the USA PATRIOT Act of 2001 and ancillary laws, 8 USC 1182, 22 USC 2656, 18 USC 2339.

19 In July 2003 a Florida grand jury indicted 19 individuals in a drug diversion and counterfeiting scheme. The first indictment charged Michael Carlow and 17 co-conspirators with various crimes associated with selling to the wholesale market adulterated, relabeled, stolen, illegally imported, and improperly stored prescription drugs. The charges varied by individual and included Racketeering, Conspiracy to Commit Racketeering, Organized Scheme to Defraud, Grand Theft, Sale or Delivery of a Controlled Substance, Possession with Intent to Sell Prescription Drugs, and Purchase or Receipt of a Prescription Drug from Unauthorized Person. Online. Available HTTP: <http://www.fdle.state.fl.us/press_releases/expired/2003/20030721_Adulterated_Drugs.html> (accessed 12 October 2005).

20 For example, in March of 1998, the US Government indicted Duty Free Selva and its principal, Orna Vainstein, for diverting Nestlé products. Nestlé had falsely claimed about 681,000 lbs (299,824 kg) of sugar credits. The scam was phony orders allegedly for US Military Post Exchanges in South America. Other persons and entities indicted were Fernando Nissenbaum and his company, Compania Argentina de Productos de Beliza, and William J. Coleman, Jr. and his company Coleary Transport. *United States v. William J. Coleman and Orna Vainstein*, Criminal No. 98–71 (SMO), filed 1998.

8 The design, development, and implementation of regulatory and supervisory frameworks for informal funds transfer systems

Nikos Passas and
Samuel Munzele Maimbo

Following the events of 11 September 2001, authorities around the world came under pressure to regulate and supervise certain informal funds transfer systems (IFTS). *Hawala*, in particular, a traditional IFTS, was identified as especially vulnerable to abuse by criminal organizations and terrorist groups.[1]

On 10 October 2001 the Financial Action Task Force (FATF) issued eight special recommendations – and a subsequent ninth recommendation on cash couriers (2004) – aimed at combating terrorist financing. Special Recommendation VI (FATF SP.VI) called on countries to either license or register informal remittance businesses and to subject them to all FATF recommendations that apply to banks and non-banks:

> Each country should take measures to ensure that persons or legal entities, including agents, that provide a service for the transmission of money or value, including transmission through an informal money or value transfer system or network, should be licensed or registered and subject to all the FATF Recommendations that apply to banks and non-bank financial institutions. Each country should ensure that persons or legal entities that carry out this service illegally are subject to administrative, civil or criminal sanctions.[2]

Arguing that money or value transfer systems appear vulnerable to misuse for money laundering and terrorist financing purposes, the FATF sought to increase the transparency of payment flows by recommending that jurisdictions impose consistent anti-money laundering (AML) and countering the financing of terrorism (CFT) measures on all forms of money and value transfer systems. Financial regulators began the process of re-examining existing regulations, and in some cases, designing, developing and implementing new financial regulations.

In the rush to create a regulatory and supervisory framework for informal remittances, practice has preceded a comprehensive debate as to the costs and benefits of regulation, as well as the empirical research to determine the possible effects. Consequently, fundamental concerns remain over the appropriateness and cost of current regulatory arrangements. Although well-intentioned, this "express top-down route" to regulation has had serious, adverse effects not only on the effectiveness of these regulations and the capacity of supervisors to implement them, but also on the flow of significant migrant labor remittances to developing countries, which are estimated to be about $250 billion annually.

There is, therefore, a need for a concerted and systematic evaluation of the regulatory objectives, strategies, tools and mechanisms that are being advanced in the international and domestic design, development and implementation of regulatory and supervisory frameworks for informal funds transfer systems. Our chapter begins by defining the terms used to describe informal remitters and discussing regulatory concerns and objectives, then identifies the challenges faced by regulators and controllers, continues with an overview of some developments in regulatory practice, and concludes with policy implications and recommendations.

Defining the regulatory objectives

Although the FATF has adopted the term Alternative Remittance Systems (ARS) to describe "financial services, traditionally operating outside the regulated financial sector, where value or funds are moved from one geographic location to another," the term remains subject to definitional debate. The specific words used have significant implications for regulatory policy. The terms define the entities and instruments of transfer targeted by regulators, and in turn, define the response of market service providers, participants and clients. Ill-defined terms and concepts may lead to unintended regulatory and supervisory effects.

The term Alternative Remittance System has been criticized for being inaccurate and misleading along the same lines that the prevalent term "underground banking" has been disputed. Banking is rarely, if ever, involved in these transactions, which take place quite openly in many parts of the globe. The word "alternative" is also not well chosen, because it implies the existence of other, mainstream or conventional, remittance systems. This is clearly not the case in scores of regions in the global South, where the operations of informal remitters and financiers (with a variety of names but quite similar mechanics) often predate contemporary banking facilities. For millions of people in many countries, formal banking facilities remain inaccessible. "Alternative," thus, is too ethnocentric a designation to apply in this context. In many instances, it emerged that value rather than money is transferred from place to place. Passas therefore introduced the term informal value transfer systems (IVTS) in 1999, in order to demystify and describe more accurately and inclusively the phenomenon under study.

Starting from the premise that IVTS refers to "mechanisms or networks of people facilitating the transfer of funds or value without leaving a trail of entire transactions or taking place outside the traditionally regulated financial channels,"[3] we distinguish between two types of IVTS. At one end of the spectrum there are informal funds transfer systems (IFTS)[4] and at the other extreme are "pure" transfers of value in the form of goods for their monetary value. In between, there is a continuum of combinations, generally referred to as informal value transfer methods (IVTM) but for which a clear categorization would be impossible.[5]

First, IFTS, which refer to financial transfers, have the following features: they constitute traditional ethnic fund and value transfer operations and businesses; they are generally thought to have originated in the Indian sub-continent and in China, but have spread throughout the globe following waves of immigration and economic globalization; they are currently subject to regulations designed for so-called "money services businesses" (MSBs); and their clients and services are for the most part well established, known to their respective local community. Examples of IFTS are *hawala* (India), *hundi* (Bangladesh), *fei chien* (China), *phoe kuan* (Thailand), *padala* (Philippines) and other similar services (including couriers). The underlying characteristic is that the transfer is originated, transferred and delivered as a financial asset.

On the other end of the spectrum, there is the physical transfer of goods. In this case, goods are purchased by the sender/remitter with the sole under-standing that once the goods reach the recipient's jurisdiction they will be sold by the remitter in order to acquire the monetary value those goods represent. Except for the profit that might arise from the sale, the monetary value of the goods is what might otherwise have been transferred through the financial system. In its purest form, this is a very inefficient method of transferring value.

In between, individuals, networks and organizations employ a variety of methods of transferring both money and value informally (IVTM). It is this gray area that causes regulators the most concern, because for the most part, there appears to be a direct correlation between the degree to which funds and goods co-mingle and the likelihood of a criminal intent to conceal or deceive. These methods demonstrate the following characteristics: they do not require the existence of widespread networks of people; most of them can be accomplished by a few individuals on an ad hoc or regular basis (hence the term "method" as opposed to "system" or "network"); and they can involve the use of the formal financial system, but they leave no trail for anyone wishing to monitor or reconstruct the route of a transaction. They are very often part of legitimate or legitimate-looking trade transactions, which effectively obfuscate substantial value transfers. Where there is intent to conceal, the transactions are usually combined with other offenses (e.g. tax evasion, subsidy fraud, embargo busting, capital flight, terrorist funding or smuggling).

Examples of IVTM include the following: in-kind payments and transfers; use of gifts services; invoice manipulation; trade diversion; stored value; use of credit and debit cards; use of correspondent accounts; use of brokerage accounts; options and futures trading; and e-payments. This list is not exhaustive, but does include the main methods identified and focused on so far.

The distinction between IFTS and IVTM is analytical but also offers a prima facie indicator of legitimate as opposed to suspicious operations. However, in both IFTS and IVTM individuals use a wide variety of channels for the transfer of funds or value without leaving traces and serious misconduct may be perpetrated or facilitated by these channels, many of which involve regulated and formal sectors or institutions. The (frequent) combination of a number of transfer methods should raise regulatory concern that illicit value transfers may be hidden behind apparently legitimate and ordinary transactions. As will be stressed below, the distinction between IFTS and IVTM also draws attention to possible unintended effects of authorities seeking to regulate IFTS (e.g. displacement effect from IFTS to IVTM).

Identifying the regulatory challenges[6]

Despite media mythology and instant expertise on the internet linking *hawala* with the 11 September operations, al Qaeda relied upon formal sector US and Western financial institutions for funding the attacks. Notwithstanding aggressive efforts to clamp down on all unregulated money remitters, law enforcement officers still have not found a single case in the US in which al Qaeda used *hawala* and have found only one very recent case in Europe. Nevertheless, just like any other financial vehicle, *hawala* can and has been used for the support of terrorist actions in many parts of the world, especially in South Asia and Africa. Informal financial networks furnish essential services to expatriates, traders, NGOs and even government agencies in several countries. However, they are also vulnerable to abuse for all sorts of financial misconduct, hence the challenge of finding an appropriate and effective way of allowing the positive services to continue without jeopardizing crime control and security objectives.

As we have explained in detail elsewhere, there are many varieties of IFTS (including *hawala*) transactions and ways in which the books are balanced. Certain characteristics that appear to be rather common include: (a) a general absence of long-term record keeping and know your customer (KYC) practices, (b) the mixing of IFTS with other activities, (c) unintended and collateral damages and (d) the difficulty of knowing for sure whether a policy relative to IFTS is actually producing the intended effects. In particular, (a) and (b) effectively create obstacles to law enforcement efforts and block investigative trails.

Absence of transparent transaction audit trail

Due to the very informality of transactions and typically low-overhead operations, record keeping by IFTS operators is mostly a short-term exercise that lasts until the accounts with counterparts are balanced. Transparency is essentially lacking, as most transactions are conducted by telephone and fax machines. In some cases, internet or telephone banking may be used for the payment of money to ultimate recipients, which is a double-edged sword. It may create some trail for investigators, but at the same time, IFTS transactions can be lost in the massive numbers of daily transactions going through internet or telephone banking.

Informality and lack of regulation bring about a lack of standardization in the kind of records each operator keeps. IFTS ledgers are often insubstantial and in idiosyncratic shorthand. Initials or numbers that are meaningful to the operators are useless if they reveal nothing about transactions, amounts, time, and names of people or organizations. Personal ledgers are often destroyed within a short period of time. In some cases, especially when operators know that their clients are breaking the law, no notes or records are kept at all. In other cases, *hawaladars* or IFTS operators may serve customers without asking many questions about their true identity, the origin of their money or the reason for the transfer. In such cases, even if operators decided to cooperate with authorities, they would have no knowledge or useful information to share. Without records, paper trail or some documentary basis, there is very little that investigators can pursue and may thus face a dead end in their efforts to build a case against an IFTS operator or his criminal customers.

Difficulty in interpreting IFTS records

The opposite challenge is also possible. Contrary to conventional wisdom, some IFTS operators do keep records even after the accounts have been balanced with counterparts overseas; some records go back many years. In many cases in the US and Europe, as well as South Asia, investigators end up finding masses of records, ledgers or notes kept by the operators. The details include the sender, recipient, amount, exchange rate, commission charged, date, cash-flow and balances. However, records are generally kept in ways hard to decipher without the cooperation of those who created the records. Sometimes they are kept in different languages or use initials and codes. In other instances, there are third party accounts of individuals or companies involved within the same country or abroad.

In the end, a paper trail often does surface, but it becomes difficult to interpret and reconstruct accurately. The task of putting everything together for investigators, and ultimately for judicial proceedings, gets more complicated as the production and interpretation of documents may require the cooperation of operators or controllers in multiple jurisdictions.

Business combinations

IFTS is not always an independent or separate business. Some people run such operations on the side or as a free or extra service to clients (e.g. of a travel agency or grocery store). The transfer of clients' money may be combined with gold, diamond or other commodity deals. *Hawala* and criminal activities can be concealed in the mass of other ordinary and non-suspicious transactions. For example, mis-invoicing of exports or imports can assist operators in balancing their books; under-invoicing by $20,000, for instance, "pays" this amount to the importer of computer equipment, who will make profits higher by this amount upon resale of the goods. If the remittance amounts are not excessive, they can easily "disappear" in otherwise legal trade (a $20,000 "mistake" in a $1–2 million trade is unlikely to raise eyebrows). Others may mix IFTS with tourist business, wire transfer services, grocery, music or video stores, antiquity trade, farm exports or jewelry shops, for example. In other cases, "payments" are made for goods that are not delivered, mislabeled in the invoice, or returned after delivery is recorded. The payment does not appear to be connected to any unusual or suspicious deal. In South Asia, gold movement across national borders is frequently linked to *hawala* either as a method of balancing accounts or as a reason for *hawala* transfers.

Detecting and proving criminal offenses and intent is more difficult when such co-mingling takes place. Even trained professionals find it hard to detect an IFTS operation. So, for businesses operating with a lot of cash or high turnover rates, it is very easy to hide *hawala*-like deals amongst other transfers.

Smart targeting and avoidance of unnecessary harm to innocent parties

A related challenge is how to prevent and target illegal acts perpetrated through IFTS without affecting the numerous innocent customers who remit honest money back home to their family, or unduly disrupting trade or harming legitimate enterprises. Everyone is rightly keen to minimize any "collateral damages" caused by unfocused or unfounded control actions.

Box 8.1 Al Barakaat case: Regulatory overreach and unintended consequences[i]

Somalia's principal export during recent years of crisis has been human labor, and remittance flows from immigrants back to families have been particularly important as the primary sources of hard currency in Somalia. Because there is no banking system, informal money remitters have provided essential services by moving funds inexpensively and reliably. Al Barakaat, an informal money remittance system founded in 1985 and headquartered in the United Arab Emirates, was the largest money remittance system operating in Somalia in 2001, and the primary means that the United Nations used to transmit money for its relief operations there.

On 7 November 2001, the US accused al Barakaat of being the "quartermasters of terror," and of funneling $25 million dollars to Osama bin Laden and al Qaeda.[ii] Reportedly "acting on solid and credible evidence" the Treasury Department raided and closed offices in four states, seized books and records, and blocked the US assets of individuals and organizations connected with al Barakaat, while coordinated action took place in other countries, including the UAE.

The case against al Barakaat was based on previous intelligence reports (some of which had been found to lack credibility), but after 11 September, "all bets were off," and an intensive effort began two weeks after the attacks to prepare a designation package. All Treasury officials had to do was prove that the central company running al Barakaat in the UAE was involved in terrorist financing to shut down and freeze the assets of all al Barakaat entities – there was no need to have evidence or prove a connection between the assets or individual money remitters and terrorist financing. Ignoring concerns specific to the case and general apprehensions by analysts about the probability of false designations made in haste, the US Government decided to designate al Barakaat and its affiliate individuals and businesses.

Amidst great fanfare, President Bush, two Cabinet secretaries, the head of US Customs and numerous other officials announced on 7 November that al Barakaat had raised funds for al Qaeda; managed, invested and distributed those funds; provided terrorist supporters with Internet service, secure telephone communications and other ways of sending messages and sharing information; and even arranged for the shipment of weapons.[iii] Yet more than five years later and "notwithstanding the unprecedented cooperation of the UAE . . . and complete and unfettered access to its financial records, the FBI could not substantiate any links between al Barakaat and terrorism."[iv] No formal indictments or charges related to terrorism have been filed; the only charges (and convictions) in a few US cases relate to transferring funds without a license. The majority of assets frozen in the US (and some assets frozen by other countries under UN resolution) were unfrozen and the money returned after the US-based al Barakaat money remitters filed a lawsuit challenging the action.

The impact of the assets freeze, on the other hand, had severe consequences for individuals, as well as the diaspora community. Money remitters faced the consequences of their businesses being closed down and their assets frozen; customers who had given large amounts of money to be remitted were unhappy with the frozen status, and it was illegal for anyone to engage in financial transactions with individuals listed. One lawyer later commented that his client, who was listed as an individual, " 'couldn't buy a cup of coffee' without violating the OFAC blocking order."[v] Plus the local Somali community lost the most trusted way of getting money to individuals back in Somalia. Rudolf Kent, the

UN humanitarian representative in Somalia, stated that it "is having a very, very serious effect. We are at a point where we have to start anticipating a crisis that could be unique in the modern state system – the collapse of an entire national economy."[vi] A *New York Times* article described the effects of the listing: "an extended family no longer receives remittances from America; an unemployed taxi driver begs from neighbors to feed his children." Al Barakaat was Somalia's largest employer – its biggest bank, biggest phone system, and only water purification plant. The company was forced to lay off 700 employees. Former doctors and lawyers who had found work as al Barakaat cashiers and phone technicians were made jobless. One reported, "I have 20 children by three wives. Now I am jobless. I have no ability to feed them."[vii] Concerns that the action would compound the Somali humanitarian crisis, the impact on the delivery of remittances to families and business was minimized because others, including UNDP and the World Bank stepped in.[viii]

There were also collateral effects on the users of listed entities. The listing of five Somali-related entities associated with al Barakaat in the Minneapolis area reportedly hurt the entire community of Somali, Ethiopian, and Kenyan immigrants who relied on the informal value transfer service to transfer funds to relatives. It took time for them to find alternative sources and as a result, there were holes in the money support system that had consequences, "sometimes involving life or death." Reports stated that "Thousands lost their deposits, and those awaiting money from relatives in Europe and the United States were cut off." Some of the alternative financial services in Somalia began to charge higher percentages on each transfer (from 3 to 5 percent). One World Food Program spokesperson went so far as to attribute malnutrition rates "at very high levels" among children in the southern Gedo region to the abrupt cut-off of al Barakaat remittances, in addition to poor rains, a ban on cattle and camel export, and runaway inflation.[ix]

The al Barakaat financial sanctions also led to difficulties within the UN, since the 1267 Committee added al Barakaat to its list 26 November 2001. Three Swedish citizens of Somali origin filed suit challenging their listing; the case, as well as others, has resulted in significant concerns about the lack of due process and fair procedures in the multilateral sanctions process, and the need for individuals to be able to appeal their listing. (See Chapters 10 and 11 for further discussion of this issue.)

Notes

[i] Information presented is primarily based upon J. Roth, D. Greenberg, and S. Wille, *Monograph on Terrorist Financing* (Staff Report to the Commission), National Commission on Terrorist Attacks Upon the United States, 2004, "Chapter 5: Al-Barakaat Case Study," pp. 67–86. Online. Available HTTP: <http://www.9–11commission.gov/staff_statements/911_TerrFin_Monograph.pdf> (accessed 6 September 2006).

ii   Paul O'Neill, Statement, 7 November 2001. Online. Available HTTP: <http://www.treas.gov/press/releases/po770.htm> (accessed 10 December 2006).
iii "President Announces Crackdown on Terrorist Financial Network," White House Press Release, 7 November 2001. Online. Available HTTP: <http://www.whitehouse.gov/news/releases/2001/11/20011107–4.html> (accessed 7 September 2001).
iv   Roth et al., *Monograph on Terrorist Financing*, p. 84.
v   Roth et al., *Monograph on Terrorist Financing*, p. 81.
vi   Marc Kaufman, "Somalis Said to Feel Impact of US Freeze of al Barakaat," *Washington Post*, 30 November 2001.
vii Donald G. McNeil, Jr., "A Nation Challenged: Sanctions," *New York Times*, 13 April 2002.
viii Nikos Passas, "Fighting Terror with Error: The Counter-productive Regulation of Informal Value Transfers," *Crime, Law and Social Change*, 2006. Online. Available HTTP: <http://dx.doi.org/10.1007/s10611–006–9041–5> (accessed 11 December 2006).
ix   Dee DePass and Lourdes Medrano Leslie, "Somali Businessmen Eager to Get Off List," *Minneapolis Star Tribune*, 23 August 2002.

According to Western Union estimates, the current annual cross-country remittance market is about $249 billion.[7] As the World Bank's Global Development Reports and other publications have repeatedly underscored, immigrant remittances are a growing source of financial flows into developing economies, which is more reliable than foreign direct investment. Regulations should not impose unnecessarily high costs or reduce the range of options available to honest remitters, whose contributions assist in the alleviation of poverty, the encouragement of economic growth and thus a reduction of sources of instability and conflict. Economic, developmental and crime/terrorism control objectives need to be aligned and synchronized. Controls are needed and vulnerabilities must be addressed, but in ways that are evidence-based, measured and proportionate. Regulators must avoid promoting counter-terrorism measures that actually undermine security.

Identifying IFTS

In some cases, IFTS businesses interface with financial institutions; for example, they may have bank or brokerage accounts, bureau de change, offer telephone and fax services, send wires, or engage in real estate deals. This type of interface may multiply the usual difficulties investigators face when they deal with "correspondent" or "pass through" accounts, because it is hard to get information on the true beneficiaries of the transactions. For example, a currency exchange dealer in a given country could possibly send and receive wire transfers for a *hawala* customer via one or possibly two foreign banks. When the funds are booked into correspondent accounts at US banks, identifying the parties to a given transaction is an onerous or even impossible task. The same type of challenge arises when accounts are held either by IFTS operators or their clients in private banking departments.[8]

In such cases it is important for bank officials, credit card companies, brokerages, money exchanges, transmitters, etc. to be familiar with IFTS patterns, recognize them and report them as suspicious. However, such professionals are frequently unaware of such patterns or indicators of illegal IFTS operations. They therefore do not detect or report suspicious transactions for authorities to investigate.

By lending itself to the laundering and hiding of the proceeds of criminal activities, such as gold smuggling, human traffic, illegal drugs and arms trade, terrorism, fraud, tax evasion, and corruption, IFTS raise hurdles in the efforts of law enforcement to identify the beneficiaries of amounts that are being transferred and to follow the money trail to the ultimate destination.

Policy and risk assessment

How can we tell whether policies are working and having a substantial impact? To the extent that the primary concern is about the funding of terrorism or facilitation of other crimes, appearances may be deceptive. For instance, if some IFTS activity is declining, as has been reported,[9] this may not necessarily be good news. That is, former IFTS dealers may be switching to alternatives (for example, commodity-based value transfers and other IVTMs) with which law enforcement agents are likely to be even less familiar. They may be aware of under- and over-invoicing practices, but private investigators and law enforcement agents have also encountered more sophisticated schemes, whereby the perpetrators engage in no eyebrow-raising activities (for example, trade diversion, which may involve the transfer of value without the physical movement of money or goods; for more information, see Chapter 7 by deKieffer).

Indeed, some of the risks entailed by policies that are not well thought-out include the following:

*   Reduction of the positive economic impact of labor remittances at the regional and national level.
*   Criminalization of otherwise legitimate actors.
*   Higher human costs (e.g. families of immigrants not receiving desperately needed income).
*   Alienation of large segments of a population from the government or those perceived as driving the national and international regulatory efforts.
*   Shift to IVTMs, such as mis-invoicing or trade diversion.

Authorities are currently attempting to regulate and render IFTS more transparent (under whatever terms they use; e.g. money service business or MSB).[10] To the extent these efforts are not carefully thought through and accepted by the participants, the intended shift from informal to formal institutions may not occur. Rather a shift towards the use of IVTMs may result. Policy-makers run the risk of not just leaving the door open for more sophisticated value transfer methods that come with a higher capacity for voluminous amounts, but also providing incentives for operators and legitimate users to turn to shady financiers. The additional risk in such a case is that policymakers know even less about IVTM vulnerabilities and serious criminal abuse. In other words, insensitive or unsuccessful regulatory frameworks can result in a criminalizing effect for people and funds that are absolutely legitimate. Instead of increasing transparency of fund transfers and reducing crime, policy-makers may in fact be encouraging the opposite result.

Moreover, from a preventive point of view, reducing the number of IFTS operations may mean far fewer opportunities to monitor suspicious activities and gather valuable intelligence about planned crimes. To the extent the media-reported nexus of *hawala* with terrorist funding is accurate, finding the right balance between the goal of intelligence gathering and that of shutting down *hawala* operations is no easy task.

As noted earlier, despite some claims made in the press about the methods used by the 11 September hijackers to transfer their funds, all available evidence points to their use of banks, wire services, credit card accounts and other regulated remitters. So, while the funding of terrorism may well occur through IFTS, there is little empirical ground to support the belief that militants generally prefer to use this method or that IFTS are more vulnerable than the regulated sector. Arguments have been made to this effect, but evidence generally shows the opposite.[11]

Designing and developing an international regulatory framework

The task of introducing effective regulation, therefore, is more complicated than one might think. In order to achieve the desired goals and avoid unintended consequences, regulation must be the end-result of a long process involving fact-finding, understanding of local cultures and specificities and consensus building. Some measures introduced and considered as positive by bodies such as the United Nations and the FATF are as follows.

Licensing and registration

The central debate in the recent literature focuses on whether to require registration or licensing. Some of the literature requires both and advocates that "all jurisdictions should introduce a system of registration and licensing of alternative remittance providers, including agents of principal providers."[12]

The definition adopted for regulatory purposes has a huge impact on the decision to license or register. In June 2003, the FATF issued a Best Practices Paper for combating the abuse of alternative remittance systems, which adopted a broad definition of a money or value transfer service (MVT service) as:

> A financial service that accepts cash, checks, other monetary instruments or other stores of value in one location and pays a corresponding sum in cash or other form to a beneficiary in another location by means of a communication, message, transfer or through a clearing network to which the MVT service belongs. Transactions performed by such services can involve one or more intermediaries and a third party final payment.[13]

In a deliberate attempt to be as inclusive as possible, the paper also noted that a MVT service may be provided by "persons (natural or legal) formally through the regulated financial system or informally through entities that operate outside the regulated system," that in some jurisdictions, "informal systems are frequently referred to as alternative remittance services or underground (or parallel) banking systems," and that often these systems have ties to particular geographic regions and are therefore described using a variety of specific terms which include *hawala*, *hundi*, *fei-chien*, and the black market peso exchange.

As policy-makers search for a global minimum standard, a good way forward may be to develop a system that requires registration and encourages licensing in order to fully comply with the other recommendations proposed in the implementation package.

There are notable differences in what licensing actually involves in various jurisdictions. In some, it entails nominal or no cost to licensees, while in others it comes with the requirement to pay a substantial bond or fee. For many traditional and small-size or family-run IFTS operations, this constitutes an unbearable burden. It may be wise to either remove the cost of licensing or reduce it and scale it to the volume of IFTS business to be licensed.[14]

Reporting requirements

In line with the above debate, there has also been a tendency for regulators to call for countries to require transaction reports in line with their existing reporting requirements for formal financial institutions. This approach amounts to an attempt to make formal institutions out of informal and traditional networks.[15] We need to bear in mind that we are dealing with a different financial creature. Is it possible to design reporting requirements that are tailored to their operating characteristics?

The US Financial Crimes Enforcement Network (FinCEN) conducted a systematic study to develop a more complete picture of the networks and mechanics of IVTS, assess their potential for abuse and to recommend appropriate measures. The US approach has been to require the registration of IFTS at the federal level (with FinCEN) and licenses at the state level.

Failure to get a state license, where it is required, constitutes a federal felony with heavy sanctions provided. Under current laws IFTS also must employ customer identification procedures for certain transactions, maintain financial records for some time, and are required to file Currency Transaction Reports (CTRs) and Suspicious Activity Reports (SARs).

According to a 2002 US Treasury report to Congress, the Bank Secrecy Act and the Patriot Act provisions are sufficient for the regulatory tasks relative to IVTS for the time being.[16] The report emphasized the need to continue monitoring the situation in order to see whether adjustments are necessary with respect to IVTS. FinCEN and the US Treasury Department recognized also the need for a more complete understanding of all types and mechanisms of IVTS by controllers and lawmakers.

However, there has been no systematic assessment to date of the compliance rate with the new regulations. As has been pointed out, the lack of coordination between the federal and the state levels has led to significant difficulties facing legitimate companies. Following unclear signals from federal supervisory authorities (such as OCC, FDIC and FinCEN) on due diligence and know your customer rules, many US banks decided to close all MSB accounts or refused to open new ones, because they regard them as a high risk to be avoided.[17] Even when they can afford the high cost of full compliance with all rules, hundreds of MSBs, which include IFTS, have lost their bank accounts.

In any event, scores of cases generated by law enforcement actions indicate the continuing operation of unlicensed informal remitters. Given the record-keeping and customer identification practices of IFTS operators, it is to be expected that at least some have not registered. In addition, ledgers or notes maintained by such operators in code or shorthand that make them impossible to decipher, gaps in kept records, or service to customers with no questions asked about their true identity, the origin of their money, or the reason for the transfer would all constitute violations of US regulations.

Similarly to most countries with formal rules about IFTS and despite calls for outreach and attempts to do so with various communities, US efforts have been primarily directed at communicating to remitters their duties and obligations – that is, after the rules were put in place.

This is precisely why a consultation process is necessary; trust is the core element of IFTS operations. How and under what circumstances can they be expected to violate this element and provide information on their clients to the authorities? Attempting to guess the answer or simply applying IFTS standards originally tailored for formal institutions is not the most appropriate way of constructing and implementing effective policy measures. Genuine outreach, better understanding of how IFTS mechanics may have shifted in the aftermath of new regulatory and law enforcement practices, and insights into how IFTS operators can enhance traceability of transactions in innovative ways are in order.

Effective implementation of an international regulatory framework

While some of the literature on IFTS discusses the context or the conditions under which policy recommendations can or ought to be implemented, there has been insufficient discussion of the pre-conditions necessary for the effective implementation of rules.

In its examination of recent and on-going regulatory practices, an IMF–World Bank study[18] noted that for purposes of achieving long-term financial sector development and minimizing the potential risks of financial abuse and criminal activity, a two-pronged approach is required. In countries where an informal *hawala* system exists alongside a well-functioning conventional banking sector, it is recommended that *hawala* dealers be registered and keep adequate records in line with the FATF recommendations. Efforts should be made to improve the level of transparency in these systems by bringing them closer to the formal financial sector without altering their specific nature. In conflict-ridden countries without a functioning banking system, requirements beyond basic registration may not be feasible because of inadequate supervisory capacity.

Simultaneously, the regulatory response should address weaknesses that may exist in the formal sector. The formal and informal financial systems tend to benefit from each other's deficiencies. Policy-makers should address economic and structural weaknesses that encourage transactions outside the formal financial systems, as well as the weaknesses in the formal financial sector itself.

Prescribing regulations alone will not ensure compliance. Regulators need to possess the appropriate supervisory capacity to enforce the regulations, and they need to provide incentives towards compliance with the regulations.[19] Compliance is likely to be weaker where there are major restrictions on transactions through the formal financial system.

The IMF–World Bank study also cautioned that the application of international standards needs to pay due regard to specific domestic circumstances and legal systems and concluded that policy-makers should acknowledge the existence of practical reasons, from the customer's point of view, to resort to informal methods rather than use banks for international payment purposes.[20] There can be instances of legitimate difficulties in applying the FATF recommendations without major adjustment; see, for example, the experience in South Africa, where such efforts resulted in the de facto exclusion of more than half the population from financial services. As long as such drivers exist, the *hawala* and other IFT systems will continue to exist, and thus addressing IFTS will require a broader response, including well-conceived economic policies and financial reforms, a well-developed and efficient payment system, and effective regulatory and supervisory frameworks.

The June 2003 FATF Best Practices Paper (see note 13) outlined several guiding principles for the implementation of Special Recommendation VI which recognize the complexity of the task facing regulators, namely:

- *In certain jurisdictions, informal MVT services provide a legitimate and efficient service.* Their services are particularly relevant where access to the formal financial sector is difficult or prohibitively expensive. Informal MVT services are available outside the normal banking business hours. Furthermore, money can be sent to and from locations where the formal banking system does not operate.

- *Informal MVT services are more entrenched in some regions than others for cultural and other reasons.* Underground banking is a long-standing tradition in many countries and predates the spread of Western banking systems in the nineteenth and twentieth centuries. These services operate primarily to provide transfer facilities to neighboring jurisdictions for expatriate workers repatriating funds. However, the staging posts of underground banking are no longer confined to those regions where they have their historical roots. Accordingly, informal MVT services are no longer used solely by persons from specific ethnic or cultural backgrounds.

- *MVT services can take on a variety of forms, which, in addition to the adoption of a risk-based approach to the problem, points to the need to take a functional, rather than a legalistic definition.* Accordingly the FATF has developed suggested practices that would best aid authorities to reduce the likelihood that MVT services will be misused or exploited by money launderers and the financiers of terrorism.

- *Government oversight should be flexible, effective, and proportional to the risk of abuse.* Mechanisms should minimize the compliance burden, without creating loopholes for money launderers and terrorist financiers and without being so burdensome that it in effect causes MVT services to go "underground" making them even harder to detect should be given due consideration.

- *It is acknowledged that in some jurisdictions informal MVT services have been banned.* Special Recommendation VI does not seek legitimization of informal MVT services in those jurisdictions. The identification and awareness-raising issues noted may, however, be of use for competent authorities involved in identifying informal MVT services and for sanctioning those who operate illegally.

These principles were largely influenced by extensive research that was undertaken by the Asia Pacific Group, FinCEN, the International Monetary Fund and the World Bank. In the months leading up to the Interpretive Note and the Best Practices Paper, these institutions were engaged in various policy research papers on various aspects of IFTS.

Conclusion

IFTS is neither the only nor the most important financial vehicle used by terrorists nor the most vulnerable to abuse.[21]

As detailed above, we recommend a multi-faceted approach towards addressing the abuse of IVTS. In countries where informal systems exist alongside a well-functioning conventional banking sector, *hawala* dealers should be registered and keep adequate records in line with FATF recommendations. Efforts should be made to improve the level of transparency in these systems by bringing them closer to the formal financial sector without altering their specific nature. In conflict- and poverty-afflicted countries with no functioning banking system requirements beyond basic registration may not be feasible because of lack of supervisory capacity (e.g. Afghanistan).

Experience also suggests that regulation is most effective when those subject to it participate in its formulation and/or regard it as appropriate and legitimate. Efforts should also be made to engage IFTS operators and their clients in a consultation process conducive to reaching a consensus on what measures and steps are desirable and necessary. It is essential to seek a two-way dialogue, as is the practice quite frequently with formal businesses and sectors. It is important to emphasize that for these consensus-building campaigns to work, it is essential to recognize the following:

- Their focus should be on identifying and, if necessary, creating positive incentives for the operators to become active participants in the implementation of a regulatory and supervisory framework.
- In some cases, the operators are highly trained and well-educated individuals. Some are former bankers and well aware of the concerns that are shared by regulatory and law enforcement agencies.
- Although operators are often geographically dispersed and engaged in a variety of businesses, they tend to be aware of their competitors. In some cases, like Afghanistan, they might even have an informal association or recognized leadership. Generally this may be someone who has been in the business in the area the longest, or they may provide wholesale settlement services. Awareness campaigns are best advised to seek out such informal bodies and to work with them in each community or area.

Once a consensus-building consultation is complete and before establishing a regulatory framework, it is essential that each jurisdiction undertake a comprehensive awareness-raising campaign. If the jurisdiction adopts the FATF special recommendations, the target institutions must be involved in a dialogue that accommodates their interests, concerns, and specific institutional characteristics. Although terrorist financing concerns are of great importance given the obvious consequences that they present, awareness campaigns ought not to focus on this risk *exclusively*. Doing so risks creating a level of unease or discomfort that may discourage operators from working with regulators.

In conclusion, we wish to draw attention to wider public and other policy implications. Because the IFTS serve millions of legitimate and mostly poor recipients of remittances in the global South, it is vital that authorities

- explore ways of offering additional channels for fund transfers;
- assist financial institutions;
- ensure continuation of vital services and minimum disruption;
- improve institutional or official methods offering similar services; and
- reduce economic and other structural problems (which are the root causes for both IFTS and terrorism).[22]

Once those policies are implemented, cracking down on criminal IFTS uses will become an easier task.

Notes

1 See Asia Pacific Group, *Report for the APG Money Laundering Methods and Typologies Workshop*, Singapore, 17–18 October 2001; Financial Action Task Force, *Report on Money Laundering Typologies, 1996–1997*, Paris: FATF, OECD, 1997; Financial Action Task Force, *Report on Money Laundering Typologies, 1998–1999*, Paris: FATF, OECD, 1999; Financial Action Task Force, *Report on Money Laundering Typologies, 2000–2001*, Paris: FATF, OECD, 2001; Financial Action Task Force, "Report on Money Laundering Typologies," (appendixes to FATF *Annual Reports*), Paris: FATF, OECD, various years; *Forex Association of Pakistan*, Press release, 6 January 2002; United Arab Emirates Central Bank, *Abu Dhabi Declaration on Hawala*, Abu Dhabi: UAE Central Bank, 16 May 2002.
2 Financial Action Task Force, Special Recommendation VI Alternative Remittances. Online. Available HTTP: <http://www.fatf-gafi.org/document/9/0,2340, en_32250379_32236920_34032073_1_1_1_1,00.html> (accessed 22 August 2006).
3 N. Passas, *Informal Value Transfer Systems, Money Laundering and Terrorism*, Washington, DC: Report to the National Institute of Justice (NIJ) and Financial Crimes Enforcement Network (FINCEN), 2003.
4 See M. El Qorchi, S. Maimbo, and J.F. Wilson, *Informal Fund Transfer Systems: An Analysis of the Informal Hawala System*, Washington, DC: International Monetary Fund, 2003.
5 N. Passas, *Informal Value Transfer Systems, Money Laundering and Terrorism*, Report to the National Institute of Justice (NIJ) and Financial Crimes Enforcement Network (FINCEN), Washington DC, 2003. Online. Available HTTP: <http://www.ncjrs.gov/pdffiles1/nij/grants/208301.pdf> (accessed 22 August 2006).
6 This section draws on N. Passas, *Informal Value Transfer Systems, Money Laundering and Terrorism* and US Department of Treasury, *A Report to the Congress in Accordance with Section 359 of the Uniting and Strengthening America by Providing Appropriate Tools Required to Intercept and Obstruct Terrorism Act of 2001*, November 2002. Online. Available HTTP: <http://www.fincen.gov/hawalarptfinal11222002.pdf> (accessed 22 August 2006).
7 "Sending Greenbacks Back to the Old Country: Immigrant Experience," *St. Louis Post-Dispatch*, 3 December 2005.
8 Concerted regulation and supervision of wire transfers in the formal sector is a

recent phenomenon; so, to the general IFTS control difficulties, are added problems with regulating correspondent accounts, private banking, commodities trade, online payments, etc.

9 For example, the spectacular rise in recorded remittances to Pakistan has been interpreted as a corresponding reduction of the *hawala/hundi* market share for that country.

10 See, for example, rules in the US under the Patriot Act and Bank Secrecy Act on MSBs enforced by the Internal Revenue Service, OCC, Federal Deposit Insurance Corporation, FinCEN at the federal level; there are many rules at the state level intended to regulate MSBs; see a discussion of such efforts in N. Passas, "Fighting Terror with Error: The Counter-productive Regulation of Informal Value Transfers," Crime, *Law and Social Change*, 2006 Online. Available HTTP: <http://dx.doi.org/10.1007/s10611–006–9041–5> (accessed 11 December 2006).

11 For instance, barter deals and ordinary banks were used by the Madrid bombers who interestingly used *hawala* to send money to their families in North Africa (Passas, "Fighting Terror with Error").

12 2001 Asia Pacific Group (APG) Working Group Recommendation 1. Online. Available HTTP: <http://www.ustreas.gov/offices/enforcement/key-issues/hawala/ARUBS-WG–2003.pdf> (accessed 22 August 2006).

13 Financial Action Task Force, *Combating the Abuse of Alternative Remittance Systems: International Best Practices*, 2003. Online. Available HTTP: <http://www.fatf-gafi.org/dataoecd/39/17/34033713.pdfarch=%22Combating%20the%20Abuse%20of%20Alternative%20Remittance%20Systems%3A%20International%20Best%20Practices%22> (accessed 22 August 2006).

14 N. Passas, *Informal Value Transfer Systems*.

15 N. Passas, "Formalizing the Informal? Problems in the National and International Regulation of Hawala," in *Regulating Hawala and other Informal Funds Transfer Systems*, Washington, DC: International Monetary Fund, 2005.

16 US Department of Treasury, *A Report to the Congress in Accordance with Section 359 of the Uniting and Strengthening America by Providing Appropriate Tools Required to Intercept and Obstruct Terrorism Act of 2001*, November 2002. Online. Available HTTP: <http://www.fincen.gov/hawalarptfinal11222002.pdf> (accessed 22 August 2006).

17 For a discussion of this crisis, see N. Passas, "Fighting Terror with Error"; see also statements made at public hearing on "Bank Secrecy Act's Impact on Money Services Businesses" held by the United States House of Representatives Committee on Financial Services Subcommittee on Financial Institutions and Consumer Credit, June 21, 2006. Online. Available HTTP: <http://financialservices.house.gov/hearings.asp?formmode=detail&hearing=482&comm=3> (accessed 22 August 2006).

18 The study examined the (i) historical and socioeconomic context within which *hawala* has evolved; (ii) operational features that make the system attractive for both legitimate and illegitimate purposes; (iii) fiscal and monetary implications for informal *hawala*-remitting and *hawala*-recipient countries; and (iv) current regulatory and supervisory responses. M. El Qorchi, S. Maimbo, and J.F. Wilson, *Informal Fund Transfer Systems: An Analysis of the Informal Hawala System*, International Monetary Fund, 2003.

19 The State Bank of Pakistan, for example, given the large number of expatriates in Saudi Arabia, implemented a subsidy of 25 Saudi rials paid to currency companies and banks per recorded transaction.

20 The State Bank of Pakistan, for example, has introduced a system of subsidies paid to financial institutions for inward remittances that follow the formal/regulated path.

21 See S.M. Maimbo, *The Money Exchange Dealers of Kabul: A Study of the Hawala*

System in Afghanistan, Washington, DC: World Bank, 2003; N. Passas, *Informal Value Transfer Systems and Criminal Organizations; A Study into So-Called Underground Banking Networks*, The Hague: Ministry of Justice, 1999. Online. Available HTTP: <http://www.wodc.nl/images/on1999–4_Full%20text_tcm11–5548.pdf> (accessed 22 August 2006); N. Passas, "Facts and Myths About 'Underground Banking,' " in P.C. van Duyne, V. Ruggiero, M. Scheinost and W. Valkenburg (eds.) *Cross-Border Crime in a Changing Europe*, Tilburg and Prague: Tilburg University and Prague Institute of Criminology and Social Prevention, 2000; N. Passas, "Financial Controls of Terrorism and Informal Value Transfer Methods," in H. van de Bunt, D. Siegel, and D. Zaitch (eds.) *Transnational Organized Crime, Current Developments*, Dordrecht: Kluwer, 2003; N. Passas, "Hawala and Other Informal Value Transfer Systems: How to Regulate Them?" *Journal of Risk Management*, 2003, pp. 39–49; Passas, *Informal Value Transfer Systems*; Passas,"Formalizing the Informal?"; Passas, "Fighting Terror with Error."

22 Passas, *Informal Value Transfer Systems*.

9 Al Qaeda and the gemstone trade

Douglas Farah

There is strong documentary and interview evidence to suggest that commodities such as gold, diamonds, and tanzanite have played an important role in terrorist financing at different times and places. Diamonds, in particular, appear to have been used to raise money, launder funds, and store financial value. Gold, for a variety of cultural and logistical reasons, has been used primarily as a way to hold and transfer value. It is my contention, as detailed in this chapter, that commodities, and more specifically gemstones, thus are not tangential to the financial structure of terrorism, but are a central part of it and represent a continuing challenge to efforts to combat the financing of global terrorism.[1]

Gemstones and al Qaeda

Since the mid-1990s, terrorist groups have used diamonds and tanzanite for both financing terrorist activities and helping terrorists move their money outside the formal financial sector.[2] Gemstones are ideal for several reasons: they hold their value over time, they are easy to transport, they do not set off metal detectors in airports, and they can be easily converted back to cash when necessary. This is especially true of "blood diamonds," or diamonds mined by non-state armed groups, mostly in sub-Saharan Africa, in order to finance their wars. Diamonds are mined in areas outside government control, where illicit trade has flourished for years and where it is easy for clandestine structures to operate while drawing little attention from the law enforcement or intelligence communities.

Al Qaeda sought to exploit vulnerable aspects of the diamond businesses in West Africa, East Africa, and Europe almost since its inception in the early 1990s. The Taliban and the Northern Alliance exploited Afghanistan's emerald fields to finance their activities throughout the Afghan war of the 1980s, so gemstones were not an unknown revenue source.[3]

African connections

Strong documentary, interview, and circumstantial evidence ties al Qaeda to the African diamond trade. Despite the reluctance of some in the US intelligence community to acknowledge the links, others, particularly in the military intelligence community and some in the Treasury Department, have found them to be credible. In June 2005 a former CIA station chief in West Africa for the first time publicly acknowledged that the substance of the reporting on the al Qaeda presence in Liberia and Sierra Leone was accurate. "They [al Qaeda operatives] were there during the period in question," said Mike Shanklin, referring to the period of 1998–2001. "And clearly they were involved in some sort of a diamond business. That's a fact."[4]

The evidence points to two distinct phases in al Qaeda's diamond activities. The first phase started sometime before 1996, when bin Laden lived in the Sudan, and was aimed at helping finance the organization. This phase is well documented, including al Qaeda's exploration of diamond deals in Liberia prior to 1998 and the creation of two diamond mining ventures in East Africa.[5] This phase, documented in court cases and al Qaeda's own writings, lasted until about the end of 1998. The latter years overlap with the large-scale, al Qaeda-dominated purchase of tanzanite in East Africa.

The second phase began in late 1998 and lasted at least until late 2001, when the stones appear to have been used primarily to store value for al Qaeda, rather than to raise money. Initial evidence of al Qaeda's interest in diamonds and other gemstones came from the testimony of al Qaeda members convicted of the 1998 US embassy bombings in East Africa.[6]

Information on the second phase of the activities, primarily in Liberia, came to light during investigations in West Africa; first published in the *Washington Post*, investigations by the London-based NGO Global Witness, the UN-backed Special Court for Sierra Leone, European intelligence investigations, and others followed.

Most of this information came from eyewitness accounts of the activities of several senior al Qaeda operatives, both in Sierra Leone and Liberia.[7] Given the nature of the illicit trade, there is little documentary evidence. What little there is – including telephone records of calls to Afghanistan, airplane tickets for some of the suspected intermediaries, hotel registrations for some of the same individuals, and bank records – supports the thesis of al Qaeda's involvement in the diamond trade in Liberia and Sierra Leone.

The first phase

Some of the most compelling testimony on al Qaeda's early interest in gemstones came in the 2001 trial of Wadih el Hage, a naturalized US citizen who worked for several years as bin Laden's personal secretary. During the trial, witnesses repeatedly referred to diamond deals, and el Hage's personal file of business cards, telephone directories, and notebooks are full of references to gemstone deals, including diamonds. There is even a page in a notebook where he wrote "Liberia," followed by a list of four names and telephone numbers.[8]

Additionally, buyers were listed in Antwerp, London, the United States, and Cyprus. Transcripts from the trial show that in early 1993 a senior al Qaeda operative and al Qaeda co-founder, Abu Ubadiah al Banshiri, established a diamond and gold mining company called Taheer Ltd., in Tanzania. El Hage sold diamonds through Taheer and, in 1994, set up another gemstone company in Tanzania called Tanzanite King.[9] Al Qaeda developed a strong interest in tanzanite and, in the aftermath of the 11 September attacks, sought to exploit the tanzanite trade for financial benefit.[10]

The court transcript also paints a picture of al Qaeda engaging or attempting to engage in a variety of other economic activities. But a measure of the importance of the gemstones is that this venture accounted for el Hage's trips to Antwerp, London, San Francisco, Los Angeles, Cyprus, and elsewhere. None of the other ventures did. It is unlikely bin Laden's personal secretary would travel that extensively and spend that much time on something that was not a high priority for the organization. Mamoun Darkanzali, a German charged with supporting al Qaeda, told German authorities he had met el Hage in the early 1990s because el Hage "wanted to make a deal in uncut diamonds." The deal did not go through, he said, because of el Hage's lack of trust in the German buyers.[11]

There are other elements that show al Qaeda's interest in the gemstone trade in this time period, as well as an active interest in Liberia. In November 2003, Shaykh Abdul Qadir Fadlallah Mamour, a radical Senegalese Muslim cleric expelled from Italy back to his native land for supporting al Qaeda, was asked by reporters if he had ever met bin Laden. Yes, Mamour replied, he had met bin Laden three times between 1993 and 1996. The reason, he said, was because bin Laden had capitalized on his diamond business, selling diamonds between Africa and Belgium.[12]

On 21 March 2005, the *al Quds al-Arabi* newspaper printed an interview with Nasir al-Bahari, aka Abu Jandal, a bodyguard of bin Laden. In discussing bin Laden's time in Sudan, al Bahari said that bin Laden was deeply interested in the situation in Liberia and had contact with Liberian combatants. "As for enlarging the scope of al Qaeda in Africa, that is true.... Events took place [in Liberia] and we did not know what was going on," he said. Al Bahari continued:

> But through the al Qaeda movement and some Islamic groups, it became clear that the struggle there was an ethnic–religious struggle between Muslims and Christians in a country where Muslims account for 20 percent of the population. That is why many al Qaeda members wished to move jihad to that country, according to the al Qaeda way and the Afghani way. A leader of the Islamic groups in Liberia told us: "we wished we could have contacted the Arab Afghans, so they would shift the balance of power in that struggle in Liberia." Hence Sheikh Usama's activities in Africa.[13]

The second phase

In late 1998, following the al Qaeda attacks on the US Embassies in Nairobi, Kenya and Dar es Salaam, Tanzania, al Qaeda began to move to the second phase of its diamond operation. The impetus was the Clinton administration's successful freezing of some $240 million in assets belonging to Afghanistan's Taliban government and bin Laden, the rogue regime's guest. The move caught both the Taliban and al Qaeda by surprise because they apparently did not realize the money, mostly held as gold reserves in the United States, could be targeted.[14]

The first known al Qaeda contacts with the Taylor regime and the Revolutionary United Front (RUF), according to eyewitnesses, came in September 1998, just a few weeks after the bombings of the embassies. These contacts continued sporadically for the next two years. It is not clear how many diamonds were purchased in that period, but what is clear is that at least five senior al Qaeda operatives – all involved in the embassy bombings – began appearing in West Africa. The five are Abdullah Ahmed Abdullah, Ahmed Khalfan Ghailani, Fazul Abdullah Mohammed, Sheikh Ahmed Salim Swedan, and Muhammad Atef.[15]

In 2004 and 2005 new information came to light on the second phase of al Qaeda's operations, mostly centered in Liberia and Sierra Leone. It also clarifies the role gemstones have played in the terrorist financial structure.[16] Among these is a series of reports presented to members of the US Congress by the Special Court for Sierra Leone, the UN-backed body investigating crimes against humanity committed in Sierra Leone's brutal civil war.[17] The reports were done at the behest of Court's chief prosecutor, David Crane, and the chief investigator, Alan White. The men worked at the highest level of the US military judicial system and the US law enforcement community.

The Court, through on-the-ground investigations over the course of several years beginning in 2002, documented and reported the presence of about a dozen al Qaeda operatives in Monrovia during the summer of 2001. The sources the Court used were independent of those used by the *Washington Post* and other investigations. Yet the Court established the same timeline, with the same intermediaries and the same sets of meetings with senior Liberian officials and rebel leaders in Sierra Leone.[18] Another source is a Belgian police report on the activities of Lebanese diamond dealers working with Taylor and identified in various investigations as also working with al Qaeda.[19] The report lists "indications of terrorism," including the numerous satellite telephone calls by the diamond dealers to Afghanistan, Iraq and Iran. The last call was made on 10 September 2001.[20]

In a brief presented in court during the 2005 trial in which Aziz Nassour and Samiah Osailly – two diamond merchants involved in aiding al Qaeda in Liberia and Sierra Leone – were convicted of illegal diamond trafficking, Belgian prosecutors wrote, "When we compare the allegations in the *Washington Post* (where they were first published in November 2001) about conflict diamonds serving to lock al Qaeda's assets, with the chronology and combination of the above mentioned conclusions, they appear to coincide remarkably."[21]

Al Qaeda in Liberia

Why would a group like al Qaeda choose West Africa as a place to operate? There are multiple reasons, but one of the most important factors is that in states such as Liberia, Sierra Leone, and most others in the region, governments are weak, corrupt, and exercise little control over much of the national territory. Some states, like Liberia under Charles Taylor, were in essence functioning criminal enterprises that retained only the trappings of a nation-state. There is no indication that Taylor was sympathetic to al Qaeda on any level. It was purely a business transaction. For the right price, Taylor let al Qaeda, Russian organized crime, Ukrainian organized crime, Balkan organized crime, Israeli diamond dealers, and Hezbollah operate under his protection for many years.[22] Yet Taylor's regime could still issue diplomatic passports, register aircraft, issue visas, and enjoy the benefits accorded to a sovereign government.[23]

While al Qaeda had been involved in the diamond trade at least since 1995, its cadres did not stumble blindly into Liberia in the hopes of acquiring diamonds. If they had, they would have been noticed by the traditional buyers on the ground and the merchants in Antwerp. Instead, they used well-known diamond merchants to carry out business on their behalf. Even so, the al Qaeda operatives stood out enough that Liberian police attempted to arrest them in the Boulevard Hotel in late 1998. However, Taylor's special police units intervened at the president's behest to protect them. Instead, the intelligence officers arrested the meddling policemen.[24]

The primary contact was a Senegalese soldier of fortune, Ibrahim Bah, who fought with the mujahideen in Afghanistan in the mid-1980s. He was a graduate of Moamar Gadaffi's terrorist training camps in the early 1980s. After fighting in Afghanistan, Bah returned to Libya and then fought for Hezbollah in Lebanon. He returned to Libya in the late 1980s and became an instructor of the cadre of West African leaders who would wreak havoc on the region: Charles Taylor in Liberia, Foday Sankoh of the RUF, Blaise Compaore in Burkina Faso, and others. In 1998 Bah was a general in the RUF as well as Taylor's chief gatekeeper for diamond dealing. He also often traveled to Antwerp himself to sell stones and had a licensed diamond dealership in Monrovia. Businessmen could only do business in Liberia if they went through Bah or one of Taylor's other two principal gatekeepers. He set up al Qaeda as he did others who could pay the opening price of $50,000 for a piece of the action.[25]

Since the Taylor regime controlled Liberian immigration, al Qaeda operatives were able to come and go unhindered. They were among many who took advantage of Taylor's largesse. Taylor also issued airplane registrations to

Victor Bout, one of the world's largest illegal weapons dealers. By registering his airplanes in Liberia, Bout was able to fly his fleet without any questions being asked or inspections carried out. Bout was later discovered not only to be selling weapons to most sides of most civil wars in Africa, but also to the Taliban and the Northern Alliance in Afghanistan. He often took his payment for his African weapons deliveries in diamonds.[26]

The picture of al Qaeda's activities in West Africa changed dramatically in the latter half of 2000, when senior al Qaeda operatives arrived in Monrovia, Liberia. Having set up an arrangement for the purchase of diamonds through Taylor with the RUF – Taylor's proxy rebel army in neighboring Sierra Leone that controlled the richest diamond areas – al Qaeda buyers went on a spree that lasted from February though August 2001, and perhaps several months more. Here the intention was clearly not to make money, but rather to buy the stones as a way of transferring value from other assets. In order to do this, the al Qaeda operatives were paying a premium over the going rate for uncut stones, leaving regular buyers without any merchandise to purchase. This prompted widespread grumbling in the largely Lebanese diamond-buying community.[27]

The lack of high-quality stones in the local market in Sierra Leone and Liberia was so marked that several local buyers complained to US Ambassador Joseph Melrose that the market was seriously out of balance. While lower-quality stones were available, the better quality ones were not to be found. Melrose, in turn, wrote a cable to the US State Department in July 2001, reporting the lack of diamonds, and that this was due to reports of "bad Lebanese" coming in from Liberia with large amounts of dollars and buying the diamonds at a premium rate.[28]

Law enforcement and intelligence reports have repeatedly claimed that paying this premium made little sense because al Qaeda operatives would then lose money.[29] That, coupled with the drop in the price of diamonds after 11 September, would make such an operation economically illogical. But the premium al Qaeda paid on rough stones in the field does not mean they took that total loss when the stones were sold. Diamonds are sold for only a fraction of their market value in the diamond mines in Sierra Leone and Liberia. Paying a premium on that price is far different from paying a premium on polished stones. And, while the market dropped after 11 September, it was a temporary drop and prices are now above what they were in the summer of 2001.[30]

What is particularly interesting during this time was the collaboration between Sunni and Shi'ite Muslims in this phase of the diamond trade. While al Qaeda operatives on the ground supervised the trade, the middlemen handling the diamonds going to Antwerp initially, and later to Beirut, were part of an organization controlled by Aziz Nassour, a strong backer of both the Amal militia and Hezbollah in Lebanon. Such collaboration was not unusual, but it had been little noticed by the US intelligence community. According to court documents, the al Qaeda collaboration with Hezbollah began when bin Laden was in Sudan and met several times with Imad Mugniyeh, a senior Hezbollah officer.[31]

Bah had turned to Nassour, one of the best-known and best-connected diamond merchants in Africa, to help sell the diamonds in January 2001. Nassour, who later bragged that he was illegally moving $25 million a week in diamonds from Africa to Europe,[32] then visited Monrovia, rented a house for the al Qaeda operatives, sent his established couriers there, and set up his nephew, Samih Osailly, to handle business. The diamonds flowed through ASA Diam, a company in Antwerp controlled by Nassour and owned by his cousin. Therefore, there were no new companies opened to sell the diamonds, companies that could have attracted the attention of authorities or other buyers.[33] Bah's business relationship with Nassour also shows the steps the al Qaeda operatives and their collaborators took to ensure they were not perceived to be new buyers, and that they did not attract undue attention.

The pace of the purchases picked up beginning in January 2001 and lasted until just before 11 September. Telephone records from ASA Diam, the firm handling the diamond sales in Antwerp, show telephone calls to Afghanistan, United Arab Emirates, Iran, and Iraq up to 10 September. A Belgian police report describes al Qaeda purchasing some $19 million worth of RUF diamonds during the 14 months prior to 11 September.[34] The evidence suggests a rapid, large-scale value transfer operation that allowed the terrorist group, perhaps assisted by Hezbollah operatives, to move money out of traceable financial structures into untraceable commodities.[35]

The findings of the 9/11 Commission

The 9/11 Commission examined al Qaeda's use of diamonds in its financial structure and concluded that there is "no basis to dispute" the conclusions of the CIA and FBI that al Qaeda did not use conflict diamonds to fund itself. The *Monograph on Terrorist Financing* (the "Monograph"), reflecting the position of both the CIA and FBI, said it had "evaluated" various reports by journalists, the United Nations, and NGOs of al Qaeda's funding from the West African diamond trade and found them to be "unsubstantiated."[36] This does not reflect the view of the entire intelligence community however, and some military officials have described al Qaeda's continuing presence and renewed interest in Africa.[37]

The Monograph adds that there is "some evidence that specific al Qaeda operatives may have either dabbled in trading precious stones at some point, or expressed an interest in doing so, but that evidence cannot be extrapolated to conclude that al Qaeda has funded itself in that manner."[38] This is the only place in the original 9/11 Commission Report or the Monograph where a distinction is made between activities of "specific al Qaeda operatives" and al Qaeda itself.

While the Monograph is an important document, it is far from a complete map of terrorist financial structures and methods. Its primary methodology, borne out by the footnotes in the document, was to ask the intelligence community to provide any information it had on a specific topic. In this case, the request was for any information on al Qaeda's ties to the diamond trade from 1998 to 2001. During this time, the intelligence community had gathered no information on this activity, in part because it had no agents on the ground in Liberia and Sierra Leone. Therefore, there was no information in the files to report.[39]

This methodology is particularly problematic in this case because the report itself acknowledges that "Terrorist financing was not a priority for either domestic or foreign intelligence collection. As a result, intelligence reporting on the issue was episodic, insufficient and often inaccurate."[40] The Monograph is harshly critical of both the FBI[41] and the CIA for largely failing to "comprehend al Qaeda's methods of raising, moving and storing money"[42] prior to the 11 September attacks.

The Monograph states that the CIA's ALEC station, dedicated to tracking bin Laden, did "everything but terrorist financing. Any intelligence it had on terrorist financing appeared to have been collected collaterally, as a consequence of gathering other intelligence."[43] It further adds that "there was almost no intersection between those who understood financial issues and those who understood terrorism."[44]

The Monograph states that al Qaeda did not use diamonds to fund its activities. It does not address the fundamental contention of most of the reporting on the matter, including my own, which is that the diamond purchases were not primarily revenue-generating efforts. Rather, in the 10 months prior to 11 September, al Qaeda sought to move financial assets out of traceable institutions and holdings into untraceable commodities, such as diamonds.

Given the 9/11 Commission's reliance on the information of an intelligence community that knew little about terrorist finance prior to 11 September, and the nature of the FBI's subsequent investigations into the diamond trade, the conclusions reached are not surprising. However, they reflect a lack of appreciation of the lengthy field investigations carried out by others, and an over-reliance on classified information from an intelligence community that had little new field research information.

Lessons to learn and the road ahead

There are several lessons that can be learned about the use of commodities like diamonds for the financing of terrorism. One is that groups using terrorism are sophisticated in their exploitation of "gray areas" where states are weak, corruption is rampant, and the rule of law nonexistent. It appears that they have used areas like West Africa for many years to finance their activities. Al Qaeda correctly calculated that Western intelligence services did not have the capacity, resources, or interest to track their activities there. To take advantage of these areas meant exploiting the natural resources available for their own purposes.

A second lesson is that groups using terrorism in these areas learn from their own mistakes, as well as from each other. They are adaptable in ways that make them extremely difficult to combat. Hezbollah has been using diamonds from West Africa to finance its activities for at least 20 years, perfecting smuggling routes to Europe and Lebanon, developing a network of middlemen, and successfully embedding its financial structure within the diamond trade. In the late 1990s, al Qaeda operatives plugged into the same network.

A third lesson is that small clues and critical analysis matter in tracing terrorist funding and the use of commodities, but there was limited understanding of the financial structure of al Qaeda before 11 September. The intelligence community never carried out a comprehensive look at al Qaeda's financial structure until 1999. The 9/11 Commission found the same to be true for the entire intelligence community in looking at al Qaeda's organizational structure in its entirety. Rather than understanding the complex web of commodities, charities, and individual donors that filled al Qaeda's coffers, the conventional wisdom in the intelligence community was that bin Laden was using his personal wealth to finance his organization's operations.[45]

A fourth lesson is that there may be a connection between terrorist networks and criminal networks, in which their activities overlap in the environments of failed states, like that of Liberia. Commodities like diamonds are the coin of choice as the different groups provide different services to governments or rebel groups. The goods and services are provided in exchange for cheap access to commodities that are easy to transport. In 2000, criminal and terrorist elements operating simultaneously in Liberia under Charles Taylor included senior al Qaeda operatives; Victor Bout, the arms merchant who registered more than 50 aircraft in Liberia; Lenoid Menin, a Ukranian–Israeli drug dealer and arms merchant; South African mercenaries; and Aziz Nassour, the one-time bagman for Mobuto Sese Seko in Zaire and then-middleman for both al Qaeda and Hezbollah.

There are several steps that should be taken to begin to combat the use of commodities by terrorists. The weapon most often brandished, but one that would be the least effective, is to institute new, sweeping regulations on commodity traders. This will simply drive even legitimate businessmen underground or out of business. New regulatory burdens to halt the fraction of illegal activities that benefit terrorists in the diamond industry, gold trade, or *hawala* transactions would hurt millions of people who make their living in these trades or whose families benefit from them. This is especially true of the *hawala* (or informal value transfer) system, discussed more fully in Chapter 8, which primarily benefits millions who live off the remittances sent through this system by family members working in other parts of the world.

Not all regulatory steps are harmful. The Kimberley Process[46] has made getting "blood diamonds" to market more difficult. But even its most ardent supporters acknowledge that it will not ultimately cut off the flow of illicit diamonds. What the process does is add layers of difficulty for those wishing to abuse the system and install some accountability mechanisms to punish those who do not play by the rules. All are useful pieces of a much larger puzzle, but are not a "silver bullet."

The solution that is really needed is also the most difficult and time consuming to carry out: building up intelligence-gathering capabilities on the ground in the "grey areas" or "stateless areas" of the world where the illicit commodity trades flourish and where terrorists have made significant inroads. These areas include parts of West Africa, much of the Democratic Republic of the Congo (DRC), parts of East Africa, and swaths of Central, South, and Southeast Asia. Only specific information gathered at the points of origin in the commodities trade can really help monitor and decipher how the businesses operate.

For example, in Sierra Leone, Liberia, and the DRC, a network of Lebanese diamond traders, related by family and political ties, have traditionally moved the bulk of the "blood diamonds." The kinship networks that are central to this commodity trade need to be mapped and understood as a first step toward defining what action can be taken. It is also essential to understand these groups, which operate in areas of the world where electronic and telephone communication are haphazard at best, and rely on personal contacts, family ties, and couriers for much of their operating structure. High-tech monitoring of communications, while successful against other types of groups, is much less useful in these circumstances.

That such knowledge is lacking is no surprise. At the end of the Cold War, no region of the world suffered more dramatic cuts in the US intelligence architecture than sub-Saharan Africa. More than one third of the CIA stations were eliminated entirely, and those that remained were left with only minimal staffing. Even as the Clinton administration began increasing funding for intelligence in the late 1990s, the region's capabilities and budget remained static.[47]

This means that not only were the commodity trades ignored as collection targets, but they were not well understood. The FBI and CIA, often stuck in the ethnocentricity that has been a traditional hallmark, still focus primarily on bank transactions and wire transfers to track money. Almost no one understands commodities networks. This is slowly changing, especially in the Treasury Department, where some expertise is being husbanded.

To change this collection and analysis pattern will require an investment in time, personnel, and money. It also will require a change in the intelligence culture that is used to focusing on states and state-based challenges rather than amorphous and difficult-to-track commodities in stateless regions. In an era of limited resources, priorities must be set.

There are other steps that can have an important impact. The most urgent is to begin to work seriously with the commodity industries themselves. There is a knowledge base that can be tapped into: many of the important players are concerned about terrorists' potential use of their commodities and they also want to clean up their image. While unwilling to act as government agents, many in these business and NGO communities are willing to share information and ideas on how to clean up and safeguard particular trades. This is important because these groups are relatively small and most members know the major players. Many are anxious to help put the more disreputable elements out of business.

Conclusion

Efforts to deprive terrorists of their funds means, necessarily, depriving them of their safe havens. The new havens are located in parts of the world long ignored: the spreading swaths of stateless territories and rogue regimes. Until we recognize this and begin to understand the true nature of terrorist finance, groups committing acts of terrorism will continue to have access to finance. Commodities, particularly gemstones, have played and may continue to play an important role in terrorist financing, primarily the financial structure of al Qaeda. Given the nature of the transactions, the growing pace of globalization, and the untraceable nature of these transactions, they are likely to remain an important source of terrorist financing for the foreseeable future.

Notes

1 Diamonds have also reportedly been used extensively by Hezbollah through the Lebanese diasporas, but this chapter will focus on the al Qaeda connections. For a fuller discussion of the Lebanese role, including that of Hezbollah and the Amal militia, please see Lansana Gberie, *War and Peace in Sierra Leone: Diamonds, Corruption and the Lebanese Connection*, The Diamond and Human Security Project, Occasional Paper 6, January 2003. Online. Available HTTP: <http://www.pacweb.org/e/images/stories/documents/sierraleone2002_e.pdf> (accessed 11 November 2005); Edward Harris, "Hezbollah Extorting Funds From West Africa's Diamond Merchants," Associated Press, 29 June 2004. This chapter is based, in large part, on D. Farah, *Blood from Stones: the Secret Financial Network of Terror*, New York: Broadway Books, 2004.

2 For a fuller discussion of al Qaeda's ties to the tanzanite trade, see R.Block and D. Pearl, "Underground Trade: Much Smuggled Gem Called Tanzanite Helps bin Laden Supporters," *Wall Street Journal*, 16 November 2001, A1. For a description of al Qaeda's ties to the diamond trade, see D. Farah, "Report Says Africans Harbored al Qaeda," *Washington Post*, 30 December 2002, A1. Online. Available HTTP: <http://www.washingtonpost.com/ac2/wp-dyn/A48929-2002Dec28?language=printer> (accessed 11 November 2005); Global Witness, *For a Few Dollars More: How al Qaeda Moved into the Diamond Trade*, London, 2003. Online. Available HTTP: <http://globalwitness.org/reports/show.php/en.00041.html> (accessed 11 November 2005).

3 A.Walizhada, "Afghan Emeralds That Fed War May Now Fund Peace," Reuters News Service, 3 June 2002; S. Coll, *Ghost Wars: The Secret History of the CIA, Afghanistan, and Bin Laden, From the Soviet Invasion to September 10, 2001*, Harmondsworth: Penguin Press, 2004, pp. 344–345.

4 M. Shanklin, Dateline NBC interview, 17 July 2005. Online. Available HTTP: <http://www.msnbc.msn.com/id/8575495/> (accessed 10 November 2005).

5 The accounts of al Qaeda's diamond activity in this period are contained in the testimony of Wadih el Hage, bin Laden's personal secretary, currently serving a life sentence in the United States. His statements and the exhibit materials cited come from *The United States v. Usama bin Laden et al.*, United States District Court, Southern District of New York, before the Hon. Leonard B. Sand, District Judge.

6 Ibid., including the statements of Jamal al Fadl.

7 The eyewitnesses included Cindor Reeves, the son-in-law of Liberian president Charles Taylor; four senior members of the RUF who dealt with al Qaeda operatives; Allie Darwish, who rented the house and lived in it while the al Qaeda operatives were there; diamond miners who sold directly to al Qaeda operatives; and senior Liberian intelligence officials who dealt with the al Qaeda operatives. Although some US intelligence officials have challenged the reliability of Reeves's testimony, British intelligence officials have found him reliable.

8 *United States v. Usama bin Laden*, exhibit 1B117/7E–105.

9 A complete analysis by Global Witness of the documents and the transactions they describe can be found in *For a Few Dollars More*.

10 Block and Pearl, "Underground Trade."

11 M. Darkanzanli, Bundeskriminalamt interview, 15 September 2001. Signed by Schmitz, KHK and Brockmuller, KHK. Provided and translated by the SITE Institute, Washington, DC, 24 February 2004.

12 Al-Sharq al-Awsat website, 30 November 2003. Online. Available HTTP: <http://www.asharqalawsat.com/> (accessed 10 November 2005).

13 "Bin Laden 'Bodyguard' Details Al-Qa'ida's Time in Sudan, Move to Afghanistan," *Al Quds al-Arabi*, 21 March 2005, p. 19.

14 D. Benjamin and S. Simon, *The Age of Sacred Terror*, New York: Random House, 2002, p. 289.

15 "Independent Source Findings of the Special Court of Sierra Leone," Office of the Prosecutor, June 2004, obtained by author.

16 The most comprehensive analysis of the possible ongoing al Qaeda activities in West Africa is provided by the Special Court for Sierra Leone, "Charles Taylor's Influence and Destabilization in West Africa: Guinea, January 2005," marked "extremely sensitive." The allegations have been repeated publicly numerous times by Court officials, including on Dateline NBC.

17 "Charles Taylor's Influence;" Special Court for Sierra Leone, Office of the Prosecutor, 29 October 2004, "Memorandum for the Record," marked "extremely sensitive."

18 "Memorandum for the Record."

19 "Case LIBI," prepared by the Federal Police, GDA Antwerp-Diamond Section, marked "For Police Use Only." Online. Available HTTP: <http://www.douglasfarah.com/pdfs/stonesbelgiumpp.pdf> (accessed 11 April 2007).

20 G. Simpson, "U.N. Ties al Qaeda Figure to Diamonds," *The Wall Street Journal*, 28 June 2004, A3. See also Farah, *Blood from Stones*. Belgian investigators said they were unable to obtain US cooperation in tracing the telephone numbers in Afghanistan. They noted, however, that the calls were made when the Taliban and its allies in al Qaeda controlled 95 percent of Afghanistan's national territory and all the known satellite phones that could be reached by dialing the Afghanistan country code (931). They also said that satellite telephones were only accessible to the elites of the Taliban and al Qaeda in Afghanistan, and that the Northern Alliance did not use satellite telephones with the Afghan country code. They surmised that, given Afghanistan's lack of any type of jewelry trade under Taliban rule, the calls were made relating to the sale of diamonds being handled by Aziz Nassour, the person making the calls.

21 Unofficial translation of Public Prosecutor File 1/2002, Subsection General Examining Magistrate, Antwerp, "Conclusion 5: Information Regarding Washington Post Article Dated 2.11.2001," p. 39.
22 These ties are documented in a number of reports to the United Nations Security Council by the Panel of Experts for Liberia, issued every six months from December 2000 until December 2004. The reports trace the different criminal activities and weapons sales under the Taylor regime. Based on these reports, all senior Liberian officials were placed on the UN travel ban list, and many have had their assets seized. Included on the list of those under travel ban, still in force, are diamond dealers who dealt with al Qaeda.
23 Farah, *Blood from Stones.*
24 Dateline NBC.
25 Numerous eyewitnesses told of Bah's role, independently offering some of the same details. He is described in a numerous reports to the UN Security Council as a member of Taylor's inner circle and the gatekeeper on diamond deals. The reports note Bah uses different passports and is often known by the name "Ibrahima Balde."
26 Farah, *Blood from Stones*, pp. 42–43.
27 This information comes from interviews with diamond dealers on the ground in Sierra Leone and Liberia during the Summer of 2001 and afterwards.
28 Interviews with US Ambassador Joseph Melrose, Summer 2002.
29 The FBI and CIA have released to Congress several reports on their investigation that contain this and other critiques of the diamond ties to al Qaeda. The most comprehensive is the FBI "Letterhead Memorandum," dated 18 July 2003, obtained by the author.
30 Author interviews with diamond dealers in Antwerp in July 2005.
31 Testimony of Jamal al-Fadl, *United States v. Usama bin Laden et al.*
32 BBC Documentary, "Blood Diamonds," *The Third Degree*, BBC Three, 10 February 2003.
33 For full details, see Unofficial translation of Public Prosecutor File 1/2002, Subsection General Examining Magistrate, Antwerp; *Farah, Blood from Stones*, pp. 71–99.
34 Public Prosecutor File 1/2002, "Case LIBI." Online. Available HTTP: <http://www.douglasfarah.com/pdfs/stonesbelgiumpp.pdf> (accessed 11 November 2005).
35 Farah, *Blood from Stones.*
36 J. Roth, D. Greenberg, and S. Wille, *Monograph on Terrorist Financing* (Staff Report to the Commission), National Commission on Terrorist Attacks Upon the United States, 2004, p. 23. Online. Available HTTP: <http://www.9–11 commission.gov/staff_statements/911_TerrFin_Monograph.pdf> (accessed 11 November 2005).
37 T. Pitman, "U.S.: Al-Qaida Thought to be Looking at Africa as Haven, Training Site," Associated Press, 6 March 2004. Online. Available HTTP: <http://www.azstarnet.com/dailystar/relatedarticles/12756.php> (accessed 11 November 2005).
38 Ibid.
39 Author interview with 9/11 Commission staff, October 2004, and with CIA and DIA officials active in West Africa.
40 Roth et al., *Monograph on Terrorist Financing*, p. 4.
41 Ibid., p. 5.
42 Ibid., pp. 5–6, 36.
43 Ibid.
44 Ibid., pp. 36.
45 Ibid., p. 4.

46 The Kimberley Process is an international certification scheme regulating trade in rough diamonds. Comprised of states and regional economic organizations, and working in cooperation with the international diamond industry and civil society, the Kimberley Process is intended to stem the flow of conflict diamonds and therefore, the use of the diamonds to fund armed conflict. For more information, see The Kimberley Process Certification Scheme website. Online. Available HTTP: <http://kimberleyprocess.com/site> (accessed 16 April 2007).
47 Author interviews with intelligence officials. Also, Farah, *Blood from Stones*.

Part III

Responses to the terrorist financing challenge

10 The US regulatory approach to terrorist financing

Sue E. Eckert [1]

The events of 11 September precipitated a sea change in the manner with which regulators and financial institutions approached the issue of terrorist financing. Existing tools of financial sanctions and regulatory measures to fight misuses of the US financial system were immediately redeployed to combat the financing of terrorism, while new initiatives were developed in the United States and internationally to launch the "financial war against terrorism." Overall, the post-11 September period has been characterized by the expansion of institutional mandates to include countering the financing of terrorism (CFT) efforts, enhanced international cooperation and coordination, and a new awareness of the importance of denying financial support to terrorist organizations and terrorist-supporting countries. This chapter discusses the evolution of the United States' CFT regulatory policies, identifies ongoing challenges, and provides recommendations to improve the regulatory approach to combating terrorist financing.

Regulatory environment before 11 September 2001

Prior to the events of 11 September, little public attention was focused on terrorist financing. Only a few regulatory programs addressed the issue, and the topic was considered arcane, within the purview of a handful of experts. The 9/11 Commission *Monograph on Terrorist Financing* (the "Monograph") characterized the prevailing attitude towards CFT: "Terrorist financing was not a priority ... and there was little interagency strategic planning or coordination. ... Most fundamentally, the domestic strategy for combating terrorist financing within the United States never had any sense of urgency." [2]

The two programs relevant to countering the financing of terrorism in place before 11 September were administered by the Department of Treasury: the Financial Crimes Enforcement Network's implementation of Bank Secrecy Act measures to fight money laundering, and the Office of Foreign Assets Control's program of economic sanctions against designated countries (including those determined to be state sponsors of terrorism) and groups (including terrorist groups and individuals). [3] While neither of these programs was initially developed specifically to counter the financing of terrorism, by late 2001 both had expanded to target the finances of individuals and organizations involved in or supporting acts of terrorism.

FinCEN and the Bank Secrecy Act

For more than 35 years, the Bank Secrecy Act (BSA) has been a cornerstone of US anti-money laundering (AML) efforts and anchored the broader initiative to curb the abuse of financial institutions – including (especially since 2001) by those who support acts of terrorism. While BSA regulations prior to 11 September had positive spillover effects for countering the financing of terrorism, the act primarily focused on the suspicious movement of large sums of money, with terrorist financing remaining a peripheral issue. This changed following 11 September, and in 2001 the BSA was augmented to better serve CFT efforts.

Congress enacted the BSA in 1970 to ensure that cash transactions of more than $10,000 were identified and reported to the government. At the time, there were reports of hundreds of thousands of dollars being carried into banks in grocery bags and suitcases from drug proceeds, yet there were no requirements for banks to inform federal authorities about large cash transactions. The BSA-imposed reporting requirements were intended to prevent the exploitation of the financial sector by a fast-growing "underground economy" through increased transparency of cash transactions. As such, the passage of the BSA represented a normative shift in financial sector regulation, whereby the need for "transparency, accountability, and traceability of financial transactions, regardless of their provenance, destination, or the mechanics of their movement" became widely accepted.[4]

The BSA functions in two ways. First, the Act makes information relevant to the detection, prevention, deterrence, and investigation of financial crime available to the government through a system of required recordkeeping and reporting. Second, the Act, as amended over the years, ensures that financial institutions create policies, procedures, and systems (including proper identification of customers and detection of suspicious financial activity) to make the financial system more transparent and to help protect financial institutions – and therefore the financial system – from being unwitting participants and conduits for financial crime.[5] The Financial Crimes Enforcement Network (FinCEN) was created in the early 1990s to serve as a focal point and repository for government-wide collection of information concerning financial crimes, and to administer the BSA, with authority to impose civil penalties for reporting violations.

Over the years, the BSA has been amended numerous times to both expand the transaction reporting requirements beyond banks to other types of more broadly defined financial institutions and improve efforts to combat drug-trafficking and money laundering. In 1992, Congress required the maintenance of records regarding both domestic and international funds transfers. Then, in 1994, the BSA was strengthened through the Money

Laundering Suppression Act which increased reporting requirements of banks, and mandated that banks devise more effective measures to prevent money laundering. Beginning in 1996, FinCEN required banks to file Suspicious Activity Reports (SARs) in addition to Currency Transaction Reports (CTRs).

Despite the steady strengthening of the BSA since its passage, a number of initiatives failed to find sufficient support until after 11 September when focus shifted to CFT efforts. For example, beginning in 1994, Congress raised concerns regarding vulnerabilities posed by money service business (MSB);[6] check cashers, money remitters, and other businesses involved in wiring money (e.g. informal value transfer systems, or *hawala*) were unregulated. Congress encouraged the Department of Treasury to regulate these businesses, but regulations were not implemented until after 11 September.[7] Only after the terrorist attacks were the CTR and SAR requirements expanded to cover the full range of the financial services industry, focusing on the use of such information to thwart the financing of terrorism. The primary focus of FinCEN and the US enforcement community before 11 September, thus, was on finding and disrupting large sums of money generated through drug-trafficking and other financial crime. There was little attention paid specifically to terrorist financing.[8]

International efforts paralleled those enhancing the US regulatory environment. Throughout the 1990s, multilateral initiatives to address money laundering, in particular, gained momentum with the adoption of the Financial Action Task Force (FATF) 40 Special Recommendations (1990);[9] the European Union's First Money Laundering Directive (1991); initiatives of the the Basel Committee on Banking Supervision, the Egmont Group of financial regulators (1995), and the G7's Financial Stability Forum (1998); the United Nations Convention to Combat Transnational Organized Crime (1998), and ultimately, the United Nations Convention on the Suppression of the Financing of Terrorism (1999).

OFAC and economic sanctions

The other US initiative relevant to using financial authorities to counter terrorism prior to 11 September concerned economic sanctions administered by the Office of Foreign Assets Control (OFAC). The International Emergency Economic Powers Act (IEEPA) provides broad authority for the President to impose economic sanctions on countries, groups, and individuals who pose a threat to the national security, foreign policy, or economy of the United States.[10] OFAC's mission historically has been to implement sanctions against foreign governments whose policies are inimical to US foreign policy and national security interests. Acting under general Presidential wartime and national emergency power, as well as specific legislation, OFAC prohibits transactions and freezes (or "blocks") assets subject to US jurisdiction. The objective of economic sanctions is to deprive targets of the use of their assets and to deny access to the US financial system and the benefits of trade, transactions and services involving US markets, businesses and individuals.[11]

The origins of OFAC's involvement in the fight against terrorism stem from the initial conception of terrorism as state-sponsored.[12] Acting under the broad authority of IEEPA and pursuant to Presidential order, OFAC's focus in the realm of terrorist finance was to compile available evidence establishing that certain foreign entities or individuals were owned or controlled by, or acting on behalf of, a foreign government subject to an economic sanctions program. Historically, such entities became, in OFAC parlance, "Specially Designated National" – (SDN) – and subject to the same sanctions as the governments to which they were related.[13] Generally, US policy from the late 1970s through mid-1990s focused on deterring and punishing state sponsors as opposed to terrorist groups themselves.

In a significant policy shift in January 1995, President Clinton invoked IEEPA authorities to deal with the threat posed by terrorists seeking to disrupt the Middle East Peace Process, thereby marking the beginning of sanctions to target terrorists, terrorist groups, and their fundraising. This action of naming "Specially Designated Terrorists" (SDT), implemented under Executive Order 12947, opened the door to new programs and expanded the use of economic sanctions against non-state actors. (These programs later grew that year to include targeting of narcotic trafficking cartels in Columbia.[14]) The Anti-Terrorism and Effective Death Penalty Act of 1996 likewise embraced the designation process, requiring the Departments of State, Justice, and Treasury to identify, on a biennial basis, foreign terrorist organizations (FTO) and to prohibit their fundraising efforts, including freezing their funds in the United States.[15]

In the wake of the 1998 embassy bombings in Nairobi and Dar es Salaam, Osama bin Laden and al Qaeda were named as SDTs, and a White House-led counter-terrorism initiative began focusing on terrorist financing. Initially, US Government agencies had little information about the sources of financing that maintained bin Laden's growing terrorist network, especially informal value transfer systems such as *hawala*. According to counterterrorism czar Richard A. Clarke, "the departments were doing a lousy job of tracking and disrupting international criminals' financial networks and had done little or nothing against terrorist financing."[16] It became clear, however, that al Qaeda received substantial funds from Islamic charities and non-governmental organizations, many from Saudi Arabia. In 1999–2000, the Clinton Administration initiated bilateral discussions with Saudi officials, and developed multilateral approaches to identify money laundering havens, charities, deep-pocket donors, and other entities providing financial services to terrorists.[17]

The United States multilateralized sanctions on al Qaeda through the adoption of United Nations Security Council Resolutions (UNSCR) 1267 (1999) and 1333 (2000) imposing targeted financial sanctions against the Taliban, Osama bin Laden and al Qaeda.[18] Chapter 11 of this volume describes the limited nature of the 1267 Committee sanctions against al Qaeda before 11 September. Prior to that time, however, they were the only international requirements for countries to prohibit the financing of terrorists such as al Qaeda, or to ensure that their national financial systems were not being used for terrorist purposes.

Financial community concerns

By the late 1990s, with the new focus on regulation of the financial services industry – both nationally under the BSA and internationally – a backlash was developing from the financial sector. The US domestic business climate was increasingly unsympathetic to additional regulation, with some even advocating the rolling back of controls established under the BSA. The growing interest in targeting financial controls was itself, in part, a reaction to the steady flow of new sweeping regulatory requirements, the blunt nature and severe economic consequences that comprehensive sanctions were having on Iraq, and the ever-increasing use of sanctions as a tool of foreign policy by the US Congress and the Administration.[19]

In December 1998, the Board of Governors of the Federal Reserve System (joined by the Federal Deposit Insurance Corporation, the Office of the Comptroller of the Currency, and the Office of Thrift Supervision) proposed new rules that would have required banking organizations to establish "Know Your Customer" (KYC) policies and procedures, requiring basic common identifier information about banks' customers to better identify potentially illegal or suspicious activity. In Congressional testimony a year after the rules were first proposed, Richard A. Small, Assistant Director of the Division of Banking Supervision and Regulation, noted the "unprecedented" resistance to the regulations, despite the fact that "[f]or the majority of customers, we assumed that banks would find that they posed no or minimal risk" to privacy, and the KYC programs "would be nothing more than formalizing existing procedures for identifying customers and following existing suspicious activity reporting requirements."[20] The proposed rules were ultimately withdrawn as a result of industry resistance.

Anti-regulatory concerns persisted, and in 2000, legislation was introduced to weaken aspects of the BSA by making the filing of SARs permissive rather than mandatory. Notwithstanding efforts by the Clinton Administration to toughen illicit financing standards, the drumbeat to weigh the costs of new anti-money laundering requirements against their benefits gained momentum. Those concerns found sympathy in the new administration of President George W. Bush in early 2001. The President's economic advisors opposed the strengthening of anti-money laundering laws, and Secretary of the Treasury Paul O'Neill even questioned the USG's investment in multilateral efforts aimed at tax evasion and anti-money laundering regulatory efforts.[21] The initiatives that had been taken by the Clinton Administration to pursue al Qaeda's financing went dormant.

Thus, immediately prior to the attacks of 11 September, an anti-regulatory wave seemed to sweep the United States. While some officials questioned the constitutionality of the US anti-money laundering regime, others articulated skepticism and concern about the multilateral initiatives of the FATF and OECD. With the attacks on New York and Washington, however, efforts to counter money laundering – thereafter inextricably tied to the targeting of terrorist finances – found almost universal support. As Sidney Weintraub wrote: "The events of September 11 have obviously made a difference in the tone of this debate. No one cares much anymore about a cost-benefit analysis of preventing money laundering."[22]

US response to 11 September [23]

Within two weeks of the attacks, President Bush "launched a strike on the financial foundation of the global terror network."[24] Harnessing existing authorities and programs, the terrorist designations and asset freezes that had been previously a little known and understood tool of policy-makers, moved center-stage to become the highly touted first front of the Administration's "war against terrorism."

Freezing terrorist assets

On 24 September 2001, President Bush announced Executive Order 13224, "Blocking Property and Prohibiting Transactions with Persons Who Commit, Threaten to Commit, or Support Terrorism," declaring "that grave acts of terrorism and the threats of terrorism committed by foreign terrorists . . . constitute an unusual and extraordinary threat to the national security, foreign policy, and economy of the United States."[25] Under IEEPA authority, the order implemented UNSCR 1333, after a delay of more than nine months, and enhanced the Department of Treasury's ability to designate individuals and entities as terrorists, target their financing, and strategically block their assets and access to the international financial system. The two goals were "to follow the money as a trail to the terrorists, and to freeze the money to disrupt their actions."[26]

Under Executive Order 13224, US persons are prohibited from transacting or dealing with individuals and entities owned or controlled by, acting for or on behalf of, assisting or supporting, or otherwise associated with al Qaeda, bin Laden, and associated groups. The 27 individuals and organizations listed became "Specially Designated Global Terrorists" (SDGTs).[27] The Executive Order also blocked all property and interests in property of designated persons. Additional designations were made on 12 October, 2 November, 7 November, 4 December and 20 December, so that by the end of 2001, the US had designated 158 individuals and organizations pursuant to Executive Order 13224.[28] The Administration expanded the sanctions beyond al Qaeda and the Taliban to include Hamas, Hezbollah, the FARC, the Real

IRA and others, and by doing so, the "war on terrorist financing" was globalized.

The pressure to launch this first phase of the "war on terrorism" was intense and hurried. Within weeks of the attacks, a new interagency process to identify and freeze assets was established. According to Secretary of the Treasury Paul O'Neill's account:

> Now all there was to do was seize some assets, and quickly. The President was to announce the new executive order on September 24, launching the war on terrorism. He needed some assets to point to. "It was almost comical," [David] Aufhauser said. "We just listed out as many of the usual suspects as we could and said, Let's go freeze some of their assets."[29]

The Monograph describes the post-11 September designation and asset freeze process as "chaos":

> The goal set at the policy levels of the White House and Treasury was to conduct a public and aggressive series of designations to show the world community and our allies that the United States was serious about pursuing the financial targets. It entailed a major designation every four weeks, accompanied by derivative designations throughout the month. As a result, [some] Treasury officials acknowledged that some of the evidentiary foundations for the early designations were quite weak.... The rush to designate came primarily from the NSC and gave pause to many in the government.[30]

In what became known as the "Rose Garden strategy" of regular Presidential announcements about the freezing of assets of terrorist-related organizations and individuals,[31] an extraordinary process ensued that departed from the usual procedures to compile and verify evidentiary information about those listed.[32] With many new political players in the process, a new emphasis was placed on the speed of designation, number of designations, and amount of money blocked.

With much of the first phase of the "war on terrorism" dominated by public designations and the blocking of bank accounts, the number of assets frozen worldwide was used as an early indicator of progress. Media reports regularly touted money frozen or seized, with officials claiming ultimately that as much as $147 million worth of terrorist assets have been blocked or frozen worldwide.[33] There have been questions about the significance of these figures, however, as many funds associated with the Taliban were frozen in 2000. Moreover, as discussed in Chapter 1, the accounting of funds frozen by the US has differed from that maintained by the 1267 Committee. But more importantly, measuring the success of a sanctions program, especially a list-based program that targets terrorists and their support networks, by the amount of money blocked in many ways conveys a fundamental misunderstanding about the purpose and intended effect of the program.[34] Whatever the amount of terrorist assets frozen internationally, the volume is not an appropriate measure of success. Rather, the greater value of the program lies in publicly identifying, and thereby financially isolating those who support and contribute to terrorist organizations, thereby deterring others. While public designations continue as an important part of the fight against terrorism, subsequent attention has been focused on other regulatory responses, and in particular, the gathering and analysis of financial information as a tool to understand better terrorist networks.[35]

USA Patriot Act

In addition to freezing terrorist assets, the other significant change in the US regulatory landscape was the adoption of the USA PATRIOT Act (Patriot Act) on 26 October 2001, providing powerful new authorities to combat terrorist financing and expanding the responsibilities of financial institutions.[36] The unprecedented political will prompted by the attacks prompted Congress to pass with little debate sweeping new regulatory measures that had been long-opposed by financial institutions and privacy advocates as too costly or invasive.[37] Most significantly, the Patriot Act strengthened extant anti-money laundering measures as a framework for CFT regulations. In particular, Title III of the Act (known as the International Money Laundering Abatement and Anti-Terrorist Financing Act of 2001) introduced new regulatory measures to *inter alia*: (1) expand BSA requirements to all financial institutions, as defined under the Bank Secrecy Act, including MSBs;[38] (2) authorize countermeasures against jurisdictions or foreign financial institutions for failure to take steps to stop money laundering activity; (3) prohibit correspondent accounts with certain money laundering financial institutions; (4) enhance information-sharing; and (5) require greater customer identification. These extraordinarily powerful new measures are outlined below:

- Section 311 of the Patriot Act authorizes the Treasury Department to impose graduated, proportionate measures against foreign money laundering and terrorist financing entities. As such, Section 311 is a heavy hammer to punish non-cooperative foreign entities, and has been used to apparent effect in sanctions imposed on the Macau-based Banco Delta Asia (BDA) for involvement in North Korean money laundering activities.[39]
- Sections 313 and 319(b) of the Act strengthen the protection of the gateway to the financial system – correspondent accounts – by requiring US financial institutions to terminate such accounts maintained by foreign "shell banks" and to take reasonable steps to ensure that they do not indirectly provide banking services to foreign shell banks.
- The Patriot Act also facilitates the sharing of certain financial information about individuals among law enforcement and financial institutions;

among regulators, law enforcement, and the intelligence community; and among financial institutions themselves.[40] Section 314 of the Act permits FinCEN to share this information with banks regarding possible terrorist or money laundering activity.

- Section 326 enhances the financial footprint of transactions by requiring financial institutions to identify and verify the identity of new customers. Subsequent regulations establish minimum due diligence procedures for customer identification programs, which play an important role in creating audit trails that law enforcement officials can use to investigate cases of money laundering or terrorist financing.

- The Patriot Act also expands OFAC's authority to block financial transactions by clarifying that OFAC can freeze assets of suspect entities before a formal designation in "aid of an investigation." This far-reaching authority is designed to prevent the flight of assets and prevent targets from engaging in potentially damaging behavior or transactions.[41]

In addition to Executive Order 13224 to freeze terrorists' assets and new AML/CFT authorities under the Patriot Act, the US has also expanded the use of financial measures to counter related threats of weapons of mass destruction (WMD) proliferation. Executive Order 13382, issued by President Bush in June 2005, authorizes financial sanctions against proliferation networks and denies designated persons or entities access to US markets and financial system. As of April 2007, 35 entities and two individuals, including some from Iran, North Korea and Syria had been designated. Financial sanctions against Bank Sepah, the fifth largest Iranian state-owned financial institution, for services to the Iranian missile industry were multilateralized through UNSCR 1747.[42]

Ongoing challenges

More than five years after 11 September, important changes have taken place in the regulatory environment to combat the financing of terrorism. Within the United States, the BSA and Patriot Act have expanded the responsibilities of a wide array of entities and increased the power of investigatory and regulatory bodies. Internationally, between UNSCR 1373 and action by the FATF to tailor its 40 AML measures and adopt new CFT recommendations, the US has *de facto* exported its regulatory model and established international terrorist financing standards and norms. (See Chapter 11 for a detailed discussion on international initiatives to address terrorist financing.) Despite these regulatory advances, significant challenges remain.

Limitations of AML Measures for CFT

In the rush to action following the terrorist attacks, existing AML measures were extended, largely unmodified, to address terrorist financing. While it is understandable why AML standards and practices were "taken off the shelf," there is a need to examine whether the initial response was appropriate, and whether these measures are the most effective in combating the financing of terrorism.

Money laundering and terrorist financing often are grouped together and discussed as challenges that are the same. While clearly related, terrorist financing and money laundering are two very different problems that require different techniques to detect and investigate them.[43] Money laundering generally involves a "forensic" exercise – a crime has been committed, and the criminal activity has produced a significant amount of "illicit" proceeds, which involves the effort to hide or clean those illicit proceeds so they can be reinvested into legitimate businesses or other financial activities, or back into the criminal organization. Efforts to detect or investigate money laundering are aimed at ripping away the profit – and thereby the motive – from crime.

Terrorist financing, on the other hand, involves the movement or use of often small amounts of money intended to fund an entity or operation. Unlike money laundering, which tries to hide dirty money, terrorist financing often involves clean money being used for illegal purposes. The source of the money is often legitimate, as in the case of charitable donations or profits from front businesses diverted from their ostensible uses, and the ultimate goal is not usually acquiring more funds. Thus, the objective of efforts to counter terrorist financing is often to better understand terrorists, terrorist organizations, and their support structure in order to disrupt and prevent operations.[44]

In testimony before the Senate Committee on Banking and Urban Affairs, Treasury Under Secretary Stuart Levey explained:

> In the money laundering field, investigators look through a telescope trying to detect the movement of large amounts of dirty cash. When investigating terrorist financing, investigators use a microscope in order to track the movement of relatively small amounts of often "clean" money, intended to support a nefarious purpose. Financial experts in the private sector have developed a set of typologies to detect money laundering activity; terrorist financing transactions, by contrast, may bear no inherent identifying trademarks whatsoever.[45]

While both AML and CFT efforts seek to increase the traceability of funds and to establish greater knowledge of sources, significant differences remain, raising questions as to whether such differences demand specialized regulatory approaches. The application of AML strategies, especially to non-bank institutions, poses unique challenges, and in some cases AML measures have not yielded the intended result, as discussed below in the context of MSBs. There has been little serious questioning of the current approach, however, and a fundamental reexamination is in order, as it may be necessary for regulatory requirements to be modified. The financial industry has consistently requested practical guidance from the government in detecting terrorist financing. Development of terrorist financing indicators, as has been done with money laundering, is important in order to elicit appropriate financial information from the industry.

Utility of financial intelligence

Financial information represents some of the best evidence in efforts to identify, reconstruct, disrupt, and dismantle the financing of terrorism. Money is the "Achilles' heel of a terrorist," that leaves a signature, "which, once discovered, has proven to be the best single means of identification, prevention and capture."[46] Moreover, financial intelligence is uniquely reliable:

> Much of the intelligence of war is, in fact, suspect – the product of treachery, deceit, custodial interrogation, bribery, and encrypted talk. But audit trails do not lie. They are diaries of terror, and they reveal the secrets necessary to stem tithes intended to underwrite acts of terror.[47]

The Patriot Act advances the sharing of financial information at multiple levels, but especially among regulators and financial institutions. BSA anti-money laundering systems are intended to enhance the paper trail through KYC and due diligence policies and record-keeping, and are designed to identify large amounts of currency injected into the system.

The question remains as to whether the current use of SARs, CTRs and other reporting requirements primarily aimed at financial institutions are the most effective means of eliciting CFT information. SARs are required for suspicious transactions above $5,000 in cases in which the suspect can be identified, and suspicious transactions above $25,000 if the financial institution cannot identify the suspect. CTRs are required for cash deposits of $10,000 or more. However, simply breaking large transfers of funds into smaller increments, while proscribed, remains a means of circumventing CTRs and SARs.

There has also been a rapid increase in the volume of information submitted by financial institutions, generating new challenges and raising questions as to the government's ability to utilize the data obtained.[48] SARs related to terrorism have increased dramatically – in the five years before the terrorist attacks, banks filed 32 reports connected to potential terrorism; in the six months following 12 September, over 1,600 SARs citing suspected links to terrorism were filed – 250 times the average number in previous years.[49] In 2006, more than 1 million SARs were filed; yet, consistently, less than 1 percent of the SARs relate to terrorist financing. In fact, in 2005, only 0.19 percent of suspicious activity reports were attributed to terrorist finance.[50] Compounding this problem, FinCEN, the recipient of the reported information, does not have a centralized and systematic program to review and exploit the data.[51]

Moreover, there is reason to question the value of data resulting from increased reporting. With palpable fear among financial institutions that a BSA reporting or an OFAC compliance mistake today will subject them to scrutiny and potential criminal and/or civil action in the future, many institutions are now filing suspicious activity reports "defensively." A "when in doubt, file" syndrome has become commonplace to stave off criticism or second guessing by regulators, some of whom have seemingly linked the number of SAR filings with the adequacy of a SAR program.[52] Financial institutions, from the smallest community banks and credit unions to the largest money center banks, are telling regulators that they would rather file now than face criticism later.

Such defensive filing results in the database becoming populated with inappropriate reports, diluting the value of the information, implicating privacy concerns, and putting the quality of the body of reported information at risk. Left unaddressed, consumers of the data – law enforcement, regulatory agencies and intelligence agencies who rely on such information to identify trends and patterns of illicit activity, as well as compliance-related deficiencies – will suffer. While the most sophisticated analytical tools and data warehouses allow users to exploit the data more efficiently, no system can reasonably and effectively cull defensively filed reports. As financial institutions spend more time and resources on increased filing, the quality of reporting on truly suspicious activity will degrade.

Public–private collaboration and information sharing

The success of CFT efforts depends on coordination of the public and private sectors. As Robert Werner, former Director of FinCEN, testified:

> The success of this regime depends upon the government and financial institutions acting in true partnership – each committed to the goal of taking reasonable steps to ensure that the financial system is protected from criminals and terrorists to the greatest extent possible through the development of appropriate programs and the sharing and dissemination of information.[53]

Partnership demands commitment on both sides. For the private sector this means developing and implementing reasonable, risk-based programs to address potential financial crime posed by business lines and customers, which should result in the reporting of suspicious activity and other relevant information to the government when appropriate. The government, in turn, must inform the private sector about the risk and, most important, be willing to share sensitive information with the private sector so they can develop their programs to address the risks associated with their business and customers. Moreover, government needs to protect the confidentiality of financial information and safeguard the privacy rights of US citizens, concerns which reportedly have led to increasing doubts about the utility of CFT reporting.[54]

To counter terrorist financing most effectively, new ways of sharing information with the financial community should be explored. The strategy thus far, of increased reporting requirements for banks and some MSBs, and the extension of AML regulations to informal value transfer systems, has focused on increasing the flow of data from the financial sector to the US Government. Enhancing the flow of communication in *both* directions, however, is essential for effective measures in the financial sector. Notwithstanding the considerable challenge of determining the accuracy and usefulness of relevant information, the government must do a better job of providing the private sector with sensitive information – not only regarding trends and patterns, but also about specific threats associated with terrorist financing. Recent initiatives by the UK Government to further sharing of intelligence-related information with the private sector could be instructive, and new ways of monitoring suspected accounts (short of freezing them) may be appropriate.[55]

Sharing relevant sensitive information with the financial sector in new, more effective ways necessarily breaks old, deeply entrenched paradigms and brings the financial sector into a more collaborative relationship with the government. The twentieth-century model of governments alone protecting their citizens from outside threats is no longer valid in a post-11 September world. Now more than ever, the effectiveness of CFT efforts depends directly on the cooperation of the private sector, as bank officials – not federal regulators – take the actual steps to identify and report suspicious activity and to block specific transactions.

Industry concerns: compliance costs and high risk banking

Financial institutions as well as governments are spending increased amounts of financial and human capital ensuring compliance with the AML/CFT regime. The major burden of cutting off terrorist financing is borne by banks and other financial institutions, and industry representatives have voiced concern about compliance costs. For many large financial institutions, the additional costs of CFT measures beyond those required for AML compliance are likely to be comparatively minimal and far easier to implement. For newly covered non-bank institutions, however (especially small MSBs such as cash checkers and remittance services) the cost of compliance with enhanced reporting requirements can be much more financially significant. Moreover, compliance with the growing number of international and regional CFT conventions, recommendations, and rules of the last few years can pose a daunting challenge to both governments and private companies.

There is no precise estimate as to the cost of AML/CFT compliance (especially distinguishing it from other bank compliance requirements concerning safety and soundness requirements). In noting the substantial compliance costs, *The Economist* quoted KPMG consultants estimating that it costs each mid-tier bank in Britain £3m–4m ($5m–6m) to implement a global screening programme that involves regularly checking customer names – and those of third parties involved in their transactions – against United Nations embargo and American sanctions lists for possible terrorist matches. Multinational banks are estimated to spend another £2m–3m ($3m–5m) per year to oversee implementation in worldwide operations. In addition, tens of millions of pounds are spent each year in London alone on data storage and retrieval to satisfy a requirement that banks' client and transaction data be kept for five to seven years. Similar rules exist in America, Singapore and other European countries.[56]

Whatever the costs of compliance may be, accurately assessing them is extraordinarily difficult and not likely to be overwhelmingly compelling when compared to the security benefits of preventing terrorist attacks or degrading terrorist networks. It is, however, important to understand regulatory costs and to take steps to mitigate them when possible.

In addition to compliance costs, there have been growing concerns within the financial sector regarding the ability of money service businesses to establish and maintain banking services. Banks have increasingly exited existing relationships with MSBs because of regulatory confusion and lack of guidance.[57] Cautious about the reputational risk associated with BSA violations, financial institutions have reassessed the risks associated with MSBs, leading many to terminate so-called "risky" account relationships. Customers in the money services businesses sector, embassy banking, and certain correspondent banking relationships have suffered widespread termination of banking services, resulting in a labeling by some of MSBs as "unbankable."[58]

As with defensive SARs, decisions to terminate account relationships may be based on a misperception of the level of risk, but the result can seriously restrict banking services to an entire sector. The risk of MSBs' relationships being terminated on a widespread basis could cause these businesses to go "underground." Such a loss of transparency would damage efforts to protect the US financial system from misuse, including terrorist financing. Steps have already been taken, including a March 2005 statement to clarify that the BSA does not require banking institutions to serve as *de facto* regulators of the money services business industry.[59] While such guidance is a step forward in addressing access of MSBs to banking services, the problem persists, and the "MSB-bank environment needs radical change."[60]

Repercussions of early designations

The freezing of assets, used sparingly, was a powerful tool even before 11 September, but Presidential designations that began within weeks of the attacks became a frequent and prominent feature of the US public campaign against terrorism. The United Nations, for the most part, promptly multilateralized US designations in late 2001 through the addition of most names to the list maintained by the 1267 Committee. As noted previously, however, this forward-leaning approach to financial sanctions created a number of problems that subsequently have complicated the use of the instrument.

As the Monograph noted, the pressure on OFAC to proceed rapidly with designations was substantial. The analysts wanted more time to make their evidentiary packages more complete and robust, but were told that they could not have it, evidently due to "external demands."

> Some believed that the government's haste in this area, and its preference for IEEPA sanctions, might result in a high level of false designations that would ultimately jeopardize the United States' ability to persuade other countries to designate groups as terrorist organizations. Ultimately, as we discuss later, this proved to be the case with the al-Barakaat designations, mainly because they relied on a derivative designation theory, in which no direct proof of culpability was needed.[61]

In the rush to respond and demonstrate progress, the US made some designations on the basis of a lower threshold of evidence – one that might not necessarily stand up in court. Several legal challenges have been filed in foreign courts and even in the US to designations made in the months immediately after 11 September.[62] While no national or regional court to date ultimately has invalidated national measures giving effect to sanctions, the challenges have complicated the use of the financial sanctions instrument. Chapter 11 discusses the due process concerns and perceptions of unfairness associated with multilateral financial sanctions in greater detail. While improvements in listing requirements and statements of case seemingly have reduced cases of wrongful listing and subsequent challenges, they underscore the importance of reliable information for the continued efficacy of multilateral financial sanctions.

Recommendations

Successes and challenges notwithstanding, there is clearly a need to reassess and refine the US regulatory approach to AML/CFT.

Clarify regulatory guidance and adjust policies to changed circumstances

Establishing clear guidance for suspicious activity reporting, combined with consistency in the application across agencies, is important in addressing the defensive filing phenomenon. FinCEN has begun to clarify requirements through a compliance manual to promote consistent applications of standards in examining compliance, but greater guidance, especially on suspicious activity reporting and terrorist financing indicators, is necessary.

The fundamental approach to CFT has not changed much since 11 September, as it continues to be focused on formal sector regulatory requirements, notwithstanding the fact that the role of financial institutions in the financing of terrorism appears to have been greatly diminished. There is a need, therefore, to constantly reassess policies, especially in light of how terrorists fund activities. Terrorists are adaptive, but national regulatory policy changes more slowly. If particular regulatory requirements are not working to achieve CFT goals, the burden should be relieved. Likewise, policy-makers need to be open to different ways of achieving objectives. In this regard, enhanced cooperation between financial regulators and those on the ground (the military, for example, in Iraq and Afghanistan) could lead to a better understanding of how terrorists raise and move money and more flexible responses to counter it.

Focus on vulnerable sectors and means, but tailor approaches

MSBs are a huge industry segment providing financial services, often to the unbanked population in overwhelming need of such services.[63] As noted in Chapter 8, while MSBs are vulnerable to moving terrorist funds, it is unlikely that subjecting them to the same AML/CFT requirements as depository institutions will be fully effective. "Although the potential (ab)use of informal financial networks for terrorist support must be considered, current practices make it less likely that controllers will be able to detect them."[64] *A one size regulatory approach does not fit all sectors or situations*; differentiated regulatory and outreach measures are necessary to elicit compliance and cooperation of MSBs. Failure to do so is likely to drive this substantial sector even further underground.

Greater attention also should be focused on specific methods used by terrorists to finance themselves, which is less through formal sector financial institutions, and more through cash, trade-based money laundering, shell companies and charitable donations. In particular, large movements of cash require differentiated responses and enhanced multilateral cooperation among customs and other enforcement officials.

Maintain sound basis for financial sanctions and focus on enforcement

The freezing of assets is a powerful tool in the "war on terrorism." Decisions regarding terrorist designations and asset freezes must be based on thorough evidentiary criteria that can be shared and sustained in multilateral discussions. For the continued utility of the instrument, it is critically important that the designation process be accurate, objective, and based on sound information, thoroughly vetted. Mistakes made in the immediate aftermath of 11 September have been costly in terms of credibility with European allies. As noted in Chapter 11, due process and human rights concerns that have grown in recent years should be addressed through revision of UN procedures for listing and de-listing.[65]

Furthermore, greater focus must be placed on implementation and enforcement of financial sanctions, including evaluating the record of terrorist financing prosecutions. The limited number of successful terrorist financing criminal convictions to date should prompt an evaluation of the factors leading to such results with a view toward determining whether a reassessment of strategy is appropriate.[66]

Provide information and incentives for industry compliance

To safeguard the financial system from abuse, government and the private sector must act in true partnership. While no industry relishes regulation, with the proper relationship and more robust lines of communication, regulation can be more collaborative to benefit both parties in terms of being more effective and more efficient. The US financial industry and MSBs play the central role in implementing CFT policies; the effectiveness of CFT efforts depends directly on the cooperation of the private sector. New ways of sharing information with the financial community are needed, including novel means of sharing intelligence that allow financial accounts to be monitored rather than merely closed down, thereby depriving the government of useful information about terrorist networks.

To ease the regulatory burden on those companies with good compliance programs, incentives should be developed to streamline reporting requirements and permit demonstrated compliance efforts to constitute a mitigating factor for inadvertent regulatory violations.[67]

Have realistic expectations but refine financial instruments

With vast amounts of money moving internationally and especially through informal channels, it is unrealistic to think that CFT initiatives by themselves will stop terrorism, or even successfully cut off the flow of money to terrorists. While important progress has been made in blocking terrorists' funds, al Qaeda and other groups utilizing terrorism continue to have access to financial resources. Financial measures are but one part of the larger counter-terrorism strategy, of which military, intelligence and law enforcement factors play a more significant role.

Yet, the financial sanctions instrument for CFT purposes is a relatively new tool that needs to be explored and refined. The complications associated with modifying the sanctions on the Macau-based Banco Delta Asia (BDA) for involvement in North Korean money laundering activities is instructive. While financial sanctions are indeed powerful, they are also complex and can have unintended and possibly far-reaching consequences. Likewise, recent efforts by the US to "leverage market forces" and use moral suasion to urge multinational companies to divest from countries such as Iran, North Korea or Sudan, while innovative, may have drawbacks which are yet to be realized. The increasing movement to divest from Iran, which has been championed by the Missouri Treasurer in the State's pension fund, and the push toward "terror-free investment funds," while on its face appears voluntary, could devolve into mandatory measures with an extraterritorial reach.[68] It is useful to recall the contentious experiences from the early 1980s over the Soviet pipeline with European allies, and seek to prevent major diplomatic disagreements among allies. Diverting attention away from critical multilateral counter-terrorism cooperation will not enhance our mutual security.

Conclusion

There is no denying that the regulatory system built to ensure financial transparency, much of which is aimed at money laundering stemming from the drug trade, has costs associated with it – both for governments and especially for the private sector. The question remains: Are these systems necessary and appropriate? Do they sufficiently provide governments with critical information needed to vigorously detect, investigate, and disrupt terrorist financing?

In an October 2005 article, *The Economist* posited:

> The best test of a regulation is that its constraints work cost effectively against the problem it was introduced to solve. Alas, on that simple measure the elaborate efforts . . . to curb terrorism by stopping the flows of money that sustain it, must be judged a failure. Complex and unwieldy regulations have been imposed, but are not working, indeed arguably were always misguided. They should be scrapped and resources concentrated more productively elsewhere. . . . However, loading down the world's financial system with a heavy new regulatory burden makes little sense.[69]

So, has the CFT regulatory regime been for naught? Has it resulted in unduly burdensome regulation without a commensurate enhancement of security?

The answer is a qualified "No." Financial sanctions have increased the associated risks of doing business with terrorist-supporting entities, and made it costlier and more difficult for terrorist groups to raise and move funds. AML/CFT procedures have enhanced due diligence and reporting of suspicious activities, making it more difficult for terrorists to use the formal financial system to move money.

Yet, terrorist acts persist, and funds remain available. The insurgency in Iraq appears by all accounts to be well-financed, whether through smuggling of cash, extortion, or otherwise. Equating effects of regulatory efforts to combat terrorist financing with effectiveness, therefore, is problematic and misleading. Administration officials admit that measuring the impact and effectiveness of financial sanctions is extremely difficult, as "such information can be fragmentary and highly classified."[70] Regulatory instruments are blunt at best, and counterproductive at worst. The consequences of regulatory programs that miss the mark, or even worse, make the objective more difficult to achieve, drive terrorist financing networks underground and alienate the very groups whose cooperation is needed in being able to monitor and detect such transactions.[71]

While it is impossible to know with certainty how effective CFT efforts truly are, regulatory approaches to counter terrorist financing will remain an important part of the overall US counter-terrorism strategy. In light of changing tactics of groups using terrorism and unintended consequences, however, CFT policies must be continually reevaluated. A serious rethinking and assessment of CFT policies to date has not been done systematically. The collective challenge is to attempt to evaluate the costs and benefits of such measures, and to modify and tailor the regulatory regime when required.[72]

Notes

1 The author wishes to thank Richard Newcomb and William Langford for their generous time in discussing these issues during formulation of this chapter. None of the statements, characterizations or errors contained therein, however, should be attributed to anyone other than the author. In addition, Kate Roll is acknowledged gratefully for her substantial assistance in the research and writing of this chapter. Her willingness to help, wherever she was in the world at the time, is greatly appreciated.

2 J. Roth, D. Greenberg, and S. Wille, *Monograph on Terrorist Financing* (Staff Report to the Commission), National Commission on Terrorist Attacks Upon the United States, 2004. Online. Available HTTP: <http://www.9-11commission. gov/staff_statements/911_TerrFin_Monograph.pdf#search=%229%2F11%20 commission%20monograph%22> (accessed 7 September 2006), pp. 4, 34.

3 This chapter focuses on the regulatory programs within the Department of Treasury and does not address the initiatives to track and prosecute terrorist financing cases in the Department of Justice and the intelligence community. Similarly, however, there was no infrastructure in place to analyze terrorist financing within the FBI prior to 11 September. See J. S. Pistole, Federal Bureau of Investigation, "Testimony before the Senate Committee on Governmental Affairs," 31 July 2003. Online. Available HTTP: <http://www.fbi.gov/congress03/ pistole073103.htm> (accessed 6 September 2006).

4 J. Winer, "Globalization, Terrorist Finance, and Global Conflict – Time for a White List?" in Mark Peith (ed.) *Financing Terrorism*, Boston, MA: Kluwer Academic Publishers, 2002, p. 27.

5 These measures include suspicious activity monitoring and reporting, customer identification and due diligence obligations. See W. J. Fox, Remarks at the 23rd Cambridge International Symposium on Economic Crime, 5 September 2005. Online. Available HTTP: <http://www.fincen.gov/director_speech_ cambridge.pdf> (accessed 21 November 2005).

6 Money service businesses (MSBs) are a special category of non-bank financial institutions that include businesses dealing with money orders, travelers checks, money transmission, check cashing, currency exchange, and stored value. Before 11 September, the scope of the BSA was limited primarily to depository

institutions, casinos, and some money services businesses. It was not, however, until after 11 September that the BSA and its requirements were extended to cover currency dealers and exchangers, and the scope has been gradually expanded. In June 2005, dealers in precious metals, stones, or jewels were required to establish anti-money laundering programs. On 31 October 2005, FinCEN extended the requirements to establish anti-money laundering programs, including filing of suspicious activity reports, to insurance companies.

7 In Summer 2001, Treasury announced a six month delay in registration of MSBs which was scheduled for 31 December 2001; following the 11 September attacks, Treasury decided to maintain the original implementation date. Roth et al., p. 39.

8 Ibid., p. 38.

9 After 11 September, the original FATF 40 recommendations were enhanced with eight specific additional recommendations to target terrorist financing. These are discussed in greater detail in Chapters 8 and 11.

10 50 USC 1701, et seq.

11 R. R. Newcomb, Director, Office of Foreign Assets Control, US Department of the Treasury, "Testimony before the House Financial Services Subcommittee on Oversight and Investigation", 16 June 2004. Online. Available HTTP: <https://www.ustreas.gov/press/releases/js1729.htm> (accessed 7 September 2006). Sanctions imposed by Congress include the Iran/Libya Sanctions Act, the Cuba Democracy Act, the Antiterrorism and Effective Death Penalty Act, the Helms-Burton Act, the Trade Sections Reform Act, and the Narcotics Kingpin Act.

12 To this end, OFAC has or has had economic sanctions programs targeting in various ways all countries that the US regards as state sponsors of terrorism – Iran, Iraq, Libya, Syria, Sudan, Cuba, and North Korea.

13 R. R. Newcomb, Director, Office of Foreign Assets Control, US Department of the Treasury, "Testimony before the Senate Governmental Affairs Committee," 31 July 2003, Online. Available HTTP: http://www.senate.gov/~govt-aff/index.cfm?Fuseaction=Hearings.Testimony&HearingID=106&WitnessID=367 (accessed 7 September 2006).

14 At the 50th anniversary celebration of the founding of the United Nations in New York in October 1995, President Clinton announced that he was taking new extraordinary measures to target groups and individuals involved in trafficking narcotics into the US. To this end, he named the leaders of several drug cartels based in Cali, Columbia, and in so doing, prohibited transactions of any nature with them by US persons wherever located in the world. He also conferred upon the Treasury Department the authority to designate additional parties, thereby prohibiting transactions with such persons or other corporate entities acting for or on their behalf.

15 P.L. 104–132, which also explicitly prohibited fund-raising for groups supporting terrorist organizations, also contained numerous other provisions that allowed for the prosecution of terrorism-related crimes. See Daniel Benjamin and Steven Simon, *The Age of Sacred Terror*, New York: Random House, 2002.

16 R. A. Clarke, *Against All Enemies: Inside America's War on Terror*, New York: Free Press, 2004, pp. 190–191.

17 Ibid., pp. 191–196.

18 Successive United Nations Security Council Resolutions since 1267 have been adopted altering the list of entities to which multilateral sanctions apply and the monitoring of sanctions – 1333, 1363, 1388, 1390, 1455, 1526, and 1617. See Chapter 11 for a more detailed description of UN initiatives to counter terrorist financing.

19 R. R. Newcomb, "Session 2: Canada and U.S. Approaches to Trade Sanctions – U.S. Speaker," *Canada–United States Law Journal*, 2005, vol. 31,

p. 50. For more information on the evolution of targeted financial sanctions, see the Targeted Sanctions Project at the Watson Institute for International Studies, Brown University, at <http://www.watsoninstitute.org/project_detail.cfm?id=4>.

20 R. A. Small, "Proposed 'Know Your Customer' Regulation," Testimony before the Subcommittee on Commercial and Administrative Law, Committee on the Judiciary, US House of Representatives, Washington, DC, 4 March 1999. Online. Available HTTP: <http://www.federalreserve.gov/BOARDDOCS/TESTIMONY/1999/19990304.htm> (accessed 10 December 2006).

21 See Clarke, *Against All Enemies*, p. 196; W. F. Wechsler, "Follow the Money," *Foreign Affairs*, July/August 2001; and "Wrong Signal on Money Laundering," *New York Times*, 28 June 2001. Online. Available HTTP: <http://www.nytimes.com/2001/06/28/opinion/28THU3.html?ex=1131512400&en==faf3c0be70cc34d9&ei=5070> (accessed 7 November 2005).

22 S. Weintraub, "Tools to Combat Terrorism: Disrupting the Financing of Terrorism," *The Washington Quarterly*, Winter 2002, vol. 24, no. 1, p. 57.

23 Following 11 September, the Treasury Department also developed guidelines to prevent terrorist abuse of the charitable sector. The Anti-Terrorist Financing Guidelines are not formal regulations but rather voluntary guidance for non-profitmaking organizations that have been criticized as too onerous and vague. See "US Department of the Treasury Anti-Terrorist Guidelines: Voluntary Best Practices for US-based Charities," September 2006. Online. Available HTTP: <http://www.treas.gov/press/releases/reports/0929%20finalrevised.pdf> (accessed 24 April 2007); and S. Beatty, *Wall Street Journal*, 13 October 2006, W2.

24 "President Freezes Terrorists' Assets," Remarks by the President, Secretary of the Treasury O'Neill and Secretary of State Powell on Executive Order, 24 September 2001. Online. Available HTTP: <http://www.whitehouse.gov/news/releases/2001/09/20010924-4.html> (accessed 6 September 2006). See also R. Suskind, *The Price of Loyalty*, New York: Simon & Schuster, 2004, p. 192.

25 Executive Order 13224, "Executive Order on Terrorist Financing Blocking Property and Prohibiting Transactions With Persons Who Commit, Threaten to Commit, or Support Terrorism," 24 September 2001. Online. Available HTTP: <http://www.whitehouse.gov/news/releases/2001/09/20010924-1.html.> (accessed 7 September 2006). See also Newcomb "Testimony before the House Financial Services Subcommittee on Oversight and Investigation."

26 "President Freezes Terrorists' Assets," Remarks by the President, Secretary of the Treasury O'Neill and Secretary of State Powell on Executive Order, 24 September 2001.

27 Initially, 27 individuals and groups were designated as SDGT – 13 terrorist groups, 11 individuals, and three charities, including measures to disrupt the financing operations of an international *hawala* network, traditional banking networks, and activities of several NGOs supplying financing and other services to al Qaeda. The list has gradually expanded (with some deletions) so that as of September 2006, a total of 460 individuals and entities have been designated under EO 13224.

28 See US Treasury Department, "Terrorist Financing Fact Sheet," 20 December 2001. Online. Available HTTP: http://www.treas.gov/press/releases/po886.htm (accessed 6 September 2006). As of 31 December 2005, 42 FTOs were listed. US Treasury Department, "Terrorist Assets Report, Calendar Year 2005," Online. Available HTTP: <http://www.ustreas.gov/offices/enforcement/ofac/reports/tar2005.pdf> (accessed 7 September 2006).

29 Suskin, *The Price of Loyalty*, p. 193.

30 Bracketed text is the authors' clarification. Roth, et al. *Monograph on Terrorist Financing*, p. 79.

31 R. Suskind, *The One Percent Doctrine*, New York: Simon & Schuster, 2006, p. 142.

Following the first announcement on 24 September 2001, subsequent announcement of terrorist designations and asset freezes took place on 11 October, 2 and 7 November, and 4 and 20 December 2001.

32 In fact, the unusual political involvement in the designation process led to unique circumstances. Whereas OFAC has traditionally been delegated authority to make designations (and therefore to alter them) when the President announced the first Executive Order, a list of names was annexed to the Order, making it difficult for sanctions to be changed without subsequent Presidential action.

33 "UN Sanctions 'Hitting al-Qaeda,'" *BBC News*, 11 January 2005. Online. Available HTTP: <http://news.bbc.co.uk/2/hi/americas/4164631.stm> (accessed 6 September 2006). According to State Department officials, approximately $142 million was frozen and $65 million seized in countries around the globe, including the United States. Online. Available HTTP: <http://www.state.gov/e/eb/rls/rm/39719.htm> (accessed 7 September 2006).

34 Perhaps when evaluating sanctions against oil-rich nations like Iran, Iraq, or Libya with significant previous US economic relations, this may be one of many factors to look to in measuring success. But even then, it has not proven to be the determinative measure in the success of the program.

35 K. W. Dam, Deputy Secretary of the Treasury, "The Financial Front of the War on Terrorism – The Next Phase," Remarks Delivered to the Council on Foreign Relations, 8 June 2002. Online. Available HTTP: <http://www.treas.gov/press/releases/po3163.htm> (accessed 7 September 2006).

36 US Patriot Act, enacted on 26 October 2001 and renewed March 2006, is an acronym for the "United and Strengthening America by Providing Appropriate Tools Required to Interrupt and Obstruct Terrorism." "Patriot Act," P.L. 107–56.

37 J. Milligan, "Regulatory Avalanche: Tide of New Regulations is Forcing Banks to Build a True Compliance Culture," *Banking Strategies*, vol. 80, no. II, March/April 2004. Industry characterized most of the provisions of Title III of the Patriot Act as "unsuccessful legislative vehicles from previous Congresses." See J. J. Bryne and M. D. Kelsey, "US PATRIOT ACT Three Years Later (What a Long Strange Trip It's Been, Part 1)," *ABA Banking Compliance*, September/October 2004.

38 The Patriot Act expanded the term "financial institution" to include "any other person who engages as a business in the transmission of funds, including any person who engages as a business in an informal money transfer system or any network of people who engage as a business in facilitating the transfer of money domestically or internationally outside the conventional financial institution system." *FinCEN Advisory: IVTSs*, March 2003, no. 33. Additional institutions covered by the new requirements included securities brokers or dealers, money transmitters, travel agencies, credit card operators, insurance companies, currency exchangers, dealers in precious metals, stones, or jewels, and casinos and gambling establishments.

39 Since the Patriot Act's adoption, the Treasury Department has used 311 authorities to designate three foreign jurisdictions (Ukraine, Nauru and Burma) as countries of primary money laundering concern. Such designations prompted major legislative reforms in Ukraine, allowing for its removal. In the case of Nauru, Section 311 facilitated a coordinated AML response by US financial institutions. In addition, eight foreign financial institutions have been designated, including two Burmese banks, Latvian financial institutions, the Commercial Bank of Syria for laundering illicit proceeds of Iraqi oil and supporting terrorism, and the Macau-based Banco Delta Asia (BDA) for involvement in North Korean money laundering activities. The BDA case, in particular, has been highly touted by the Bush Administration as evidence of the success of financial sanctions, as dozens

of financial institutions have curtailed business with North Korea. Unforeseen problems in resolving the BDA sanctions as part of a comprehensive deal with North Korea over its nuclear activities, however, demonstrate that financial sanctions are powerful but complicated instruments, the implications of which should be fully considered before imposition. See D. Glaser and A. Szubin, "Joint Testimony before the Committees on Foreign Affairs and Financial Services," 18 April 2007. Online. Available HTTP: <http://www.ustreas.gov/press/releases/hp361.htm> (accessed 24 April 2007); S. Weisman, "US Pursues Tactic of Financial Isolation," 16 October 2006, *New York Times*; Statement of Daniel Glaser, Deputy Assistant Secretary (Terrorist Financing and Financial Crimes), US Department of Treasury, before the Senate Banking Committee, 12 September 2006. Online. Available HTTP: <http://www.ustreas.gov/press/releases/hp93.htm> and <http://www.treas.gov/offices/enforcement/311_actions.shtml> (accessed 6 September 2006); and "Prepared Remarks of Stuart Levey Before the 5th Annual Conference on Trade, Treasury and Cash Management in the Middle East," 7 March 2007. Online. Available HTTP: <http://www.ustreas.gov/press/releases/hp297.htm.> (accessed 25 April 2007)

40 K. W. Dam, "Testimony before the Senate Banking Committee," 29 January 2002. Online. Available HTTP: <http://www.treas.gov/press/releases/po3295.htm> (accessed 29 May 2007).

41 Before passage of the Patriot Act, OFAC was wary of relying on classified information under IEEPA programs, because, unlike the Antiterrorism and Effective Death Penalty Act of 1996, IEEPA did not contain a provision explicitly authorizing submission of classified information to a court, in camera and ex parte, upon a legal challenge to a designation. The Patriot Act greatly enhanced OFAC's ability to make and defend designations by clarifying that OFAC may use classified information in making designations without turning the material over to an entity or individual that challenges its designation.

42 P. McNerney, "Combatting WMD Proliferation Support Networks: Financial and Economic Sanctions," Testimony before the House Committees on Foreign Affairs and Financial Services, 18 April 2007. Online. Available HTTP: <http://www.internationalrelations.house.gov/110mcn041807.htm> (accessed 24 April 2007). Administration officials' successful characterization of the measures have been bolstered by announcements by major European banks voluntarily scaling back their investments and dealings in Iran.

43 W. J. Fox, Remarks to ABA Money Laundering Enforcement Seminar, 31 October 2005. Online. Available HTTP: <http://www.fincen.gov/aba_aba_seminar.pdf> (accessed 21 November 2005).

44 D. Aufhauser, "Testimony before Senate Judiciary Committee," 26 June 2003. Online. Available HTTP: <http://kyl.senate.gov/legis_center/subdocs/sc062603_aufhaus.pdf> (accessed 21 November 2005).

45 S. A. Levey, "Testimony before the Senate Committee on Banking and Urban Affairs" 29 September 2004. Online. Available HTTP: <http://www.treas.gov/press/releases/js1965.htm> (accessed 7 September 2006)

46 Aufhauser, "Testimony before Senate Judiciary Committee."

47 D. Aufhauser, "Terrorist Financing: Foxes Run to Ground," *Journal of Money Laundering Control*, 2003, vol. 6 no 4, pp. 301–305.

48 Some officials have indicated that new provisions of the Patriot Act prompting the range of IVTS to register have resulted in a flood of information which the US Government has had neither the time nor the resources to analyze.

49 Financial Crimes Enforcement Network, "The SAR Activity Review: Trends, Tips and Issues," no. 8, April 2005. Online. Available HTTP: <http://www.fincen.gov/sarreviewissue8.pdf> (accessed 23 August 2006).

50 Out of 535,663 reports in 2005, there were 991 reports which were characterized

as suspicion of terrorist finance. Financial Crimes Enforcement Network, "The SAR Activity Review: By the Numbers," Issue 6, May 2006. Online. Available HTTP: <http://www.fincen.gov/sar_review_by_the_numbers_issue6.pdf> (accessed 23 August 2006).

51 J. A. Cassara, *Hide & Seek: Intelligence, Law Enforcement, and the Stalled War on Terrorist Finance*, Washington, DC: Potomac Books, 2006, p. 237.

52 Financial Crimes Enforcement Network, "The SAR Activity Review: Trends, Tips and Issues," issue 8, April 2005. Online. Available HTTP: <http://www.fincen.gov/sarreviewissue8.pdf> (accessed 21 November 2005), and "The SAR Activity Report: By the Numbers," Issue 6, May 2006. Online. Available HTTP: <http://www.fincen.gov/sar_review_by_the_numbers_issue6.pdf> (accessed 5 September 2006).

53 R. W. Werner, Director of FinCEN, "Testimony before the Senate Banking Committee," 12 September 2006. Online. Available HTTP: <http://www.fincen.gov/werner_statement_09122006.html> (accessed 20 September 2006).

54 The controversy regarding US Government arrangements for access to information generated through the Society for Worldwide Interbank Financial Telecommunication (SWIFT) has raised concerns regarding the confidentiality of financial information, especially regarding the EU Privacy Directive. Online. Available HTTP: <http://www.swift.com/index.cfm?item_id=60275> (accessed 6 September 2006), and "German Concerns at Swift Disclosure," *Financial Times*, 6 September 2006.

55 H.M. Treasury, "Launch of Anti-money Laundering and Counter-Terrorist Finance Strategy," 28 February 2007. Online. Available HTTP: <http://www.hm-treasury.gov.uk/newsroom_and_speeches/press/2007/press_23_07.cfm> (accessed 26 April 2007).

56 "Financing Terrorism: Looking in the Wrong Places," *The Economist*, 20 October 2005.Online. Available HTTP: <http://economist.com/displaystory.cfm?story_id=5053373> (accessed 21 November 2005).

57 J. J. Byrne, "Testimony before a Joint Hearing of the House Financial Services Oversight and Investigations Subcommittee and the House International Relations International Terrorism and Nonproliferation Subcommittee," 4 May 2005. Online. Available HTTP: <http://www.aba.com/NR/rdonlyres/222CE044–577A–11D5-AB84–00508B95258D/44048/JByrneTestimony05042005.pdf> (accessed 21 November 2005).

58 Werner, "Testimony before the Senate Banking Committee."

59 Statement of William J. Fox, Statement at Hearing before the Committee on Financial Services, US House of Representatives, 26 May 2005. Online. Available HTTP: <http://www.fincen.gov/foxtestimony052605.pdf> (accessed 21 November 2005).

60 Byrne, "Testimony before a Joint Hearing."

61 Roth, et al. *Monograph on Terrorist Financing*, p. 79. [0]

62 In late 2006, a US district court judge challenged the legality of Executive Order 13224, designating SDGTs, as "unconstitutionally vague on its face and overly broad." See *United States District Court, Central District of California Humanitarian Law Project, et al. Plaintiffs, v. United States Department of Treasury, et al.* Case No.: CV 05–8047 ABC (RMCx). Online. Available HTTP: <http://www.cacd.uscourts.gov/CACD/RecentPubOp.nsf/bb61c530eab0911c882567cf005ac6f9/7d5c944cb7f546168825723500599af7/$FILE/CV05–8407ABC.pdf> (accessed 28 November 2006).

63 Data concerning the number of MSBs vary. There were 26,951 registered MSBs (as of August 2006). Online. Available HTTP: <http://www.msb.gov/pdf/msb_registration_list.pdf> (accessed 5 September 2006). However, "estimates of the number of MSBs run into the hundreds of thousands, ranging from Fortune

500 companies with numerous outlets worldwide, to independent convenience stores offering check-cashing services." See Julie Williams, Statement Before the US Senate Committee on Banking, Housing, and Urban Affairs, 26 April 2005. Online. Available HTTP: <http://www.occ.treas.gov/ftp/release/2005–41a.pdfnsarch=%22estimate%20unregistered%20msbs%22> (accessed 5 September 2006).

64 N. Passas, "Fighting Terror with Error: The Counter-productive Regulation of Informal Value Transfers" in *Crime, Law and Social Change*, 2006, vol. 45, nos. 4–5, p. 335.

65 T. J. Biersteker and S. E. Eckert, *Strengthening Targeted Sanctions through Fair and Clear Procedures*, Targeted Sanctions Project, Watson Institute for International Studies, Brown University, New York: United Nations, A/60/887 S/2006/331, June 2006. Online. Available HTTP: <http://watsoninstitute.org/pub/Strengthening_Targeted_Sanctions.pdf> (accessed 5 September 2006). The White Paper contains recommendations to enhance current UN listing and de-listing procedures.

66 Transactional Records Access Clearinghouse (TRAC), Syracuse University, "Criminal Terrorism Enforcement in the United States During the Five Years Since the 9/11/01 Attacks." Online. Available HTTP: <http://trac.syr.edu/tracreports/terrorism/169/> (accessed 21 November 2006). According to the report, of the 1,078 terrorism financing-related referrals for prosecution, only 98 were convicted.

67 B. E. Rock, "Testimony before the Committee on Financial Services, Subcommittee on Financial Institutions and Consumer Credit, United States House of Representatives," 18 May 2006. Online. Available HTTP: <http://www.aba.com/NR/rdonlyres/222CE044–577A–11D5-AB84–00508B95258D/44029/BRockTestimony05182006.pdf> (accessed 9 September 2006).

68 For example, see legislative efforts in the 110th Congress to remove Presidential wavier authority from the Iran Sanctions Act to require mandatory sanctions against foreign companies investing in the Iranian oil sector.

69 "The Lost Trail – Efforts to Combat the Financing of Terrorism are Costly and Ineffective," *The Economist*, 22 October 2005. Online. Available HTTP: <http://www.belt.es/articulos/articulo.asp?id=3161> (accessed 10 December 2006), and "Looking in the Wrong Places," *The Economist*, 22 October 2005. Online. Available HTTP: <http://economist.com/displaystory.cfm?story_id=5053373> (accessed 10 December 2006). "What we are seeing is terror done on the cheap and yet all the regulations to monitor financial transactions and crack down on this are looking for larger sums." G. Hosein, "Why Terror Financing is so Tough to Track Down," *Christian Science Monitor*, 8 March 2006. Online. Available HTTP <http://www.csmonitor.com/2006/0308/p04s01-woeu.html> (accessed 10 December 2006).

70 Glaser and Szubin "Joint Testimony before the Committees on Foreign Affairs and Financial Services."

71 Passas, "Fighting Terror with Error."

72 W. J. Fox, Statement before the House Subcommittee on Financial Institutions and Consumer Credit, 22 September 2005. Online. Available HTTP: <http://www.fincen.gov/foxstatement092205.pdf> (accessed 6 September 2006).

11 International initiatives to combat the financing of terrorism

Thomas J. Biersteker, Sue E. Eckert, and Peter Romaniuk

Since the attacks of 11 September, there have been a number of international initiatives to counter terrorist financing. International cooperation has given rise to a web of institutions and multilateral initiatives to suppress the financing of terrorism. This institutionalization has had tangible effects at the national level, especially when measured by the establishment or enhancement of national legal frameworks, the creation or strengthening of administrative infrastructure, the introduction and use of a variety of different regulatory measures, and evidence of enforcement.

Even with this progress, however, more than five years into the "war on terrorism," a number of challenges to the advancement of initiatives countering the financing of terrorism (CFT) have emerged. Among these, limitations of state capacity, competing perceptions about the salience of CFT measures, and concerns regarding human rights are well known. Emerging challenges include private sector concerns regarding the costs of implementation, Member State fatigue in reporting to United Nations' bodies, and institutional lethargy and bureaucratic delay within the UN.

This chapter describes and analyzes international initiatives to suppress terrorist financing in three sections. First, we document the breadth and depth of international cooperation on terrorist financing in the post-11 September period, illustrating the web of institutions and initiatives now mobilized around the issue. Second, we briefly elaborate an analytical framework for assessing the impact of international cooperation in this area. While multilateral initiatives have been relatively effective in inducing change at the national level, we identify existing and emerging challenges in the implementation of CFT initiatives. Finally, we address key questions for consolidating existing gains in the effort to suppress terrorist financing: (1) how to ensure parallel implementation, (2) how to address human rights concerns in CFT initiatives, and (3) the future role for UN organs in CFT.

CFT efforts prior to 11 September

Prior to the attacks of 11 September, there was no coordinated, global effort to constrain the financing of acts of terrorism, and "existing prescriptions were woefully inadequate in dealing with the multi-dimensional nature of the challenge."[1] Following the attacks, the previously limited efforts to combat terrorist financing by intergovernmental organizations and private sector organizations gained new levels of support, participation, and relevance.

The UN's effort to target financial measures against terrorists originated in October 1999, with the adoption of United Nations Security Council Resolution (UNSCR) 1267 directed at al Qaeda and its supporters in the Taliban regime of Afghanistan. The sanctions committee formed to oversee and implement the resolution designated the individuals and entities subject to financial sanctions and gathered identifying information. As with all sanctions regimes at the time, however, the enforcement of the financial measures was limited. To help strengthen the instrument of targeted financial sanctions, the Swiss government launched the "Interlaken Process" (1998–2001), the results of which demonstrated that effective financial sanctions were technically feasible, if political will and harmonization of national practices could be achieved.[2] Throughout this period, the instrument of targeted financial sanctions gradually matured.[3]

Since 11 September 2001, the al Qaeda/Taliban Sanctions Committee, or the 1267 Committee as it is more generally known, has been at the forefront of the operational aspects of implementation activities, maintaining the global list of individuals and groups designated as supporting or engaging in acts of terrorism. Over time, the list of terrorist entities against which all Member States are required to restrict financing has broadened to include groups "associated with" al Qaeda, Osama bin Laden and the Taliban. Likewise, the quality of identifying information provided to Member States on designated individuals, groups, and their financial supporters has improved. The Committee has also taken steps to address human rights and due process concerns regarding the informational bases for listing, and developed procedures for the de-listing individuals.

Shortly after the passage of UNSCR 1267, the United Nations General Assembly in December 1999 adopted the International Convention on the Suppression of the Financing of Terrorism. Proposed following the August 1998 bombings of the US embassies in Nairobi, Kenya, and Dar es Salaam, Tanzania, the Convention calls on all states to criminalize the financing of terrorism, cooperate in CFT investigations, and freeze terrorist assets. As of September 2001, however, only four countries had ratified the Convention. Subsequently, the number of parties to accede to the Convention has increased to 158[4] (see Figure 11.1 on p. 240). The Convention is part of the 12 universal conventions and protocols against terrorism.[5] Prior to the attacks of September 2001, fewer than a dozen states had signed all 12 existing conventions on international terrorism. By June 2006, that number had grown, but only to 43.

Other multilateral initiatives, primarily concerned with transnational crime and money laundering activities, were underway involving actors in both the public and the private sector, prior to UNSCR 1267 and the Terrorist

Financing Convention. Established in 1989 at a G7 meeting, the Financial Action Task Force (FATF) developed its "forty recommendations" or best practices for combating money laundering, subsequently updated in 1996 and 2003.[6] First convened in June 1995, the Egmont Group[7] has focused on building an international network of financial intelligence units (FIUs). The Egmont Group continues to bring together financial sector regulators for informal, but regular meetings to compare notes and best practices. The Wolfsberg Group of banks, formed in 2000, performs a similar function for 12 major private-sector financial institutions.

Post 11-September United Nations CFT activities

The international approach to countering the financing of global terrorism changed dramatically after 11 September 2001. One day after the attacks, the Council acted decisively and adopted Resolution 1368, establishing a legal basis for action against global terrorism. The resolution invoked Article 51 of the United Nations Charter, recognizing the inherent right of self-defense, essentially legitimating subsequent US-led military action in Afghanistan against the Taliban. A little more than two weeks later, on 28 September 2001, the Security Council unanimously adopted UNSCR 1373 directly addressing the financing of terrorism. Adopted under Chapter VII of the Charter, UNSCR 1373 requires all 191 Member States to suppress the financing of terrorism. Specifically, UNSCR 1373 required states to criminalize active or passive support for terrorists prior to an act of terrorism, freeze funds expeditiously, share operational information, and provide technical assistance to enhance multilateral cooperation in the area.

UNSCR 1373 also established the Counter-Terrorism Committee (CTC) to implement its operative provisions. Under the leadership of its first chairman, United Kingdom Permanent Representative Ambassador Sir Jeremy Greenstock, the committee introduced innovative procedures, notably, its mandatory reporting process and interactive dialogue with States. All Member States were required to report to the CTC on the national measures taken to implement the resolution. Once reports were submitted and translated, the CTC made the reports publicly available on its website. The Committee also provided explicit guidelines to facilitate Member States' preparation of reports, which provided an important threshold for substantive reporting, and helped to establish a basis for subsequent iterative dialogue with States regarding implementation.

In stark contrast to experience with previous sanctions resolutions, all 191 UN Member States filed at least an initial report with the CTC. Most states filed more than one report, with the majority of reports following the detailed guidelines laid out by the committee. While the frequency of reporting has diminished over time, as of March 2007, more than 700 reports had been received, with 67 Member States having submitted their fifth reports, and more than half (or 112) having filed at least four reports to the CTC.[8]

Beyond the simple process of iterated reporting, the CTC periodically invited ambassadors or representatives of Member States to meet with members of the Committee or its designated experts to elaborate or answer specific questions about the implementation of policy measures described in their reports. Thus the Committee established an *interactive* process of reporting and monitoring, with responses to specific questions posed by the Committee reflected in subsequent reporting to the body. Reading successive reports posted on the UN website, it is possible to gain a glimpse into the dynamics of the iterative process.

There is evidence that both the quality of reporting and progress on criminalizing terrorist finance have improved over time. In the first round of reports submitted to the CTC in late 2001 and early 2002, many Member States argued that existing anti-money laundering legislative authority sufficiently met their obligation to criminalize terrorist financing. Reviews of second round reports to the CTC by the end of 2002 suggest that as the dialogue between Member States and the CTC proceeded, States began to move beyond reliance on anti-money laundering statutes and promulgate new laws specific to terrorist financing. The Monitoring Team, established to assist the 1267 Committee, noted in its August 2004 report that a legal basis for freezing assets related to al Qaeda now exists in 188 of the 191 UN Member States.[9]

The CTC, in addition to instituting reporting requirements and establishing CFT standards, has facilitated collaboration among regional organizations. The CTC has convened four special meetings since March 2003, attended by nearly 60 international, regional and subregional organizations to discuss how best to cooperate in the global counter-terrorism effort. Acknowledging the importance of complying with UN counter-terrorism measures and adhering to global standards, especially in the area of terrorist financing, participants share information on best practices and cooperate in facilitating assistance to Member States.[10]

At the outset, the CTC focused on establishing a legal basis in all Member States to criminalize the provision of financing to groups committing acts of terrorism. It emphasized the importance of setting up administrative mechanisms in Member States to freeze funds expeditiously and to extend CFT measures beyond the formal financial sector, to include the operations of charitable organizations and the activities of informal value transfer systems, commonly known as *hawalas*. Beyond focusing attention on the financing of terrorism, UNSCR 1373 also called upon Member States to address the provision of arms and other means of logistical support to groups using terrorism (including monitoring travel and preventing movement across national boundaries).

It was quickly apparent to the CTC that many states lacked the capacity to implement important aspects of the ambitious new counter-terrorism agenda. Indeed, most of the States that have filed only a single report to the committee are among the poorest countries of sub-Saharan Africa or small island states in the Caribbean and the Indian Ocean. The UN Security Council passed Resolution 1377 in November 2001, calling upon Member States with technical capacity to assist those lacking the capacity to implement the terms of the preceding counter-terrorism resolutions. Shortly after the passage of this resolution, the CTC began a technical assistance program that concentrated on coordinating bilateral offers of assistance – as well as offers of technical assistance from international, regional, and sub-regional organizations – with the needs of Member States requesting assistance for their counter-terrorism efforts.

Ambassador Curtis Ward, former Advisor on Technical Assistance to the CTC, reported "over fifty States indicated in their first reports that they needed assistance to implement resolution."[11] By the end of 2003, more than 160 States had requested or received capacity-building assistance through the CTC. The number grew as more states apparently reached a clearer understanding of what was expected of them. According to Ward, the greatest needs for assistance appear to have been in drafting anti-terrorism law and in developing banking and financial law and regulations.[12] Since the passage of UNSCR 1377 in November 2001, the CTC has facilitated assistance in legislative drafting, support to banking supervisory bodies, and establishment of financial intelligence units in almost 60 countries. A total of 89 countries have participated in CTC-sponsored workshops, and training in countering terrorist financing has been provided to 71 countries. In a parallel effort to provide technical assistance, the World Bank reported receiving more than 100 requests from countries to help build capacity to fight money laundering and terrorist financing.[13]

After the second and third rounds of reports submitted to the Counter-Terrorism Committee, the momentum of the process began to slow. In an effort to "revitalize" the CTC and the UN's ongoing engagement with the global counter-terrorism effort, the UN Security Council passed Resolution 1535 in March of 2004. The Chair of the Committee had by this time passed from the UK to Spain, and the revitalization effort both retained the CTC as the primary mechanism to assist States in combating terrorism and created the Counter-Terrorism Executive Directorate (CTED). Established as a special political mission, the CTED monitors the implementation of UNSCR 1373. The CTED has an initial term that extends through to the end of 2007.

During 2003 and 2004, the 1267 Committee increased its oversight and monitoring of Member States' implementation and enforcement efforts with regard to actions against specific individuals and groups. The 1267 Committee modeled its newly introduced reporting and evaluation procedures after those used by the CTC. The two committees work in concert. The CTC concentrates on the medium to long-term strategic, legal, and institutional aspects of countering terrorism, and it promotes changes in legislation and the strengthening of administrative institutions and enforcement mechanisms. The 1267 Committee focuses on the short to intermediate term tactical and operational aspects of the issue, maintaining the list of specifically designated individuals and groups, and monitoring the actions by Member States to block specific transactions.

The 1267 Committee has been somewhat less successful than the CTC in securing compliance with its reporting requirements. As of September 2006, 147 Member States had submitted a report to the 1267 Committee in accordance with UNSCR 1455 (2003), which leaves 44 non-reporting States of which 31 are common non-reporting or late-reporting States to the 1267 Committee, the 1540 Committee and the CTC.[14] There have also been concerns expressed by members of the 1267 Monitoring Group about the quality of some of the reporting by Member States.

Among other UN agencies active in the effort to counter terrorist financing, the United Nations Office on Drugs and Crime (UNODC) has taken measures to integrate its ongoing work – particularly on money laundering – with the CFT efforts of the CTC. The UNODC has provided bilateral assistance to some states in fulfilling their reporting and substantive obligations under resolution 1373, as well as developed technical assistance guides and convened workshops in cooperation with a wide range of regional and sub-regional bodies. While these meetings often discuss issues beyond terrorist financing alone, on at least one occasion UNODC has used the World Bank/IMF/FATF joint methodology for assessing compliance with global counter-terrorist financing standards, discussed further below.[15]

The Financial Action Task Force and other AML/CFT efforts

In addition to the development of a global multilateral framework to combat the financing of terrorism by the United Nations, a second parallel development in multilateral initiatives to suppress terrorist financing has been the deployment of the pre-existing network of anti-money laundering (AML) officials to the task of countering terrorist financing. As noted previously, an expert community of such officials emerged in the late 1980s and grew in strength in the 1990s, reflecting concern among industrialized states about financial crime. The FATF, joined by the Wolfsberg and Egmont Groups, has evolved since the events of 11 September to apply its expertise in AML and institutional capacity-building to CFT efforts.

Acting principally through the Financial Action Task Force (FATF),[16] AML specialists recorded a number of significant achievements, including the elaboration of the initial "Forty Recommendations on Money Laundering" (1990), their subsequent revision (1996 and 2003), a regular exchange of information about money laundering trends and techniques, and the evolution of innovative enforcement measures such as self-evaluations (1991), peer evaluations (1991–1992) and the Non-Cooperative Countries and Territories (NCCT) initiative (2000–2001). Terrorist financing had been discussed in FATF fora prior to September 11,[17] but the attacks prompted a formal expansion of the FATF's mandate in October 2001, resulting in the elaboration of eight – now nine – "Special Recommendations on Terrorist Financing." These recommendations endorsed UN initiatives – specifically, the Terrorist Financing Convention and Security Council Resolutions 1267 and 1373 and their respective successors – and established standards concerning reporting of suspicious transactions related to terrorism and the use of wire transfers, informal value transfer systems, and non-profit organizations to finance terrorism.

The importance of integrating terrorist financing within existing anti-money laundering fora, and especially the FATF, should not be understated. These fora provide an additional institutional framework to develop and oversee counter-terrorist financing measures. Utilizing existing institutions is valuable operationally, as they provide the means to establish global counter-terrorist financing standards (in the form of "recommendations"), the ability to disseminate them (through regular interactions and the FATF-style regional bodies [FSRBs]), mechanisms for advancing their implementation (self-evaluations and peer reviews), and opportunities to share experiences and furnish formal and informal guidance. More specifically, the experts and officials who comprise this network possess technical knowledge that can be beneficially applied to problems of terrorist financing. Adaptation of existing institutions facilitates the political consensus necessary to advance multilateral counter-terrorist financing measures.

In addition to expanding its mandate, the FATF has grown in influence as its own membership, and that of the various FSRBs, have increased. As Figure 11.1 illustrates, membership in the FATF and FSRBs has continued to grow at a steady rate since 11 September. One feature of this growth is that there are now seven FSRBs – on each continent, with new bodies

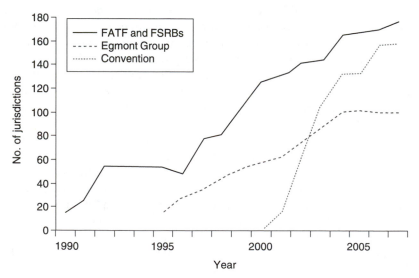

Figure 11.1 Participation in AML/CFT initiatives.

recently created to cover Central Asia and the Middle East and North Africa.[18]

Notwithstanding the importance of the FATF in creating global CFT standards, such efforts to date have relied primarily on "paper compliance" – ensuring that adequate administrative and legal systems exist on paper (be it within a financial institution or a national government) without necessarily focusing on what happens in practice. The FATF process of mutual evaluations largely assess countries' legislative basis for prohibiting terrorist financing, as well as whether a financial intelligence unit (FIU) has been created, but have not been as proactive in monitoring ongoing implementation and enforcement activities.

While not initially concerned with terrorist financing, the Wolfsberg and Egmont Groups, and the networks they established, subsequently contributed to the emergence of a strong basis for multilateral cooperation in countering the financing of terrorism.[19] The Egmont Group of financial intelligence units has also grown significantly since the 11 September attacks from fewer than 20 countries in 1995 to more than 100 in 2006. Similar to FATF meetings, Egmont meetings provide the opportunity for regulators to share experiences in implementing global standards, facilitating more formal aspects of cooperation, such as the exchange of financial intelligence.

In sum, the pre-9/11 anti-money laundering network has a historical comparative advantage in assessing and responding to financial crime. Its substantive and geographical expansion – especially through the FATF – facilitates counter-terrorist financing cooperation operationally and politically. Indeed, anti-money laundering expertise is likely to become even more important as terrorists increasingly utilize crime to raise and move funds.

International CFT standards

Beyond activity within the UN and FATF and related bodies, a third dimension of multilateral cooperation against terrorist financing has been the adoption of international standards developed by relevant international, regional and specialized organizations.

At the international level, the boards of the World Bank (WB) and International Monetary Fund (IMF) developed action plans to enhance efforts to counter money laundering and terrorist financing.[20] In mid-2002, the WB and IMF recognized the FATF's 40+8 (at the time) Recommendations as the relevant international standard for anti-money laundering and countering the financing of terrorism. Later that year, collaborating with the FATF and FSRBs to develop a common methodology for assessment, the Bank and Fund launched a 12-month pilot program to evaluate compliance with the recommendations. With the pilot program judged to be a success, the WB and IMF announced in March 2004 that AML/CFT measures should form part of their permanent activities. Further, the revised FATF 40+9 Recommendations were endorsed by the WB and IMF as the relevant global standard for which Reports on the Observance of Standards and Codes (ROSCs) are prepared. Finally, in light of the revision of the 40+9 Recommendations, the WB and IMF revised and endorsed a common methodology for undertaking anti-money laundering and counter-terrorist financing assessments. According to US Government sources, by the end of 2005 the WB and IMF had conducted more than 50 assessments of member country compliance and had provided technical assistance in over 125 countries.[21]

Regional and sub-regional organizations have also taken on an active role in countering terrorist financing, endorsing UN and FATF measures in the process. While the range of bodies that provide these endorsements is too vast to cover here, organizations on each continent have indicated their support for UN and FATF initiatives. This support has taken in a variety of forms. Most commonly, alongside the growth of FSRBs, regional and sub-regional organizations have issued statements of support for key global counter-terrorist financing initiatives. References to key multilateral AML/CFT initiatives have appeared, or been reproduced, in statements released by the European Union, the African Union, the Gulf Cooperation Council, the South Asian Association for Regional Cooperation, the Association of Southeast Asian Nations and the Pacific Islands Forum, among others.

Other organizations have established formal mechanisms for member countries to report on their implementation of the UN Convention, relevant resolutions, and FATF recommendations. The Asia/Pacific Economic Cooperation group (APEC) established the Counter-Terrorism Action Plan (CTAP) process, which encouraged its 21 member states to identify their CFT needs and offer assistance with capacity-building measures. Regional organizations have been useful as coordinating mechanisms for the provision of technical assistance. Of note is the work of the Inter-American Committee Against Terrorism (CICTE), which itself now provides advice to the Commonwealth of Independent States and the Southeast Europe Cooperation Initiative.[22]

International organizations have also taken actions to institutionalize UN and FATF counter-terrorist financing measures. The G8's Counter-Terrorism Action Group (CTAG), established in 2003, provides counter-terrorism assistance donors with a "forum to identify priority areas of need to implement UNSCR 1373 and to coordinate counter-terrorism capacity-building efforts to maximize impact."[23] CTAG works closely with the CTC, the FATF, and regional organizations to coordinate counter-terrorist financing assistance, and is shifting its regional focus from Africa and the Middle East to Southeast Asia.[24] By mid-2005, CTAG members had provided more than 200 coordinated technical assistance programs to more than 150 countries.[25]

Professional organizations, other than those concerned exclusively with money laundering, have also certified UN and FATF measures as key global standards. For example, each of the peak organizations for regulators in the banking, insurance and securities sectors has taken steps in this direction.[26] Within the critical offshore financial sector, the new and revised FATF recommendations have been "welcomed" by the Offshore Group of Banking Supervisors (OGBS), with a renewed commitment to implementing global standards.[27] Among private sector banks, the Wolfsberg Group adopted a statement supporting the FATF's 8 Special Recommendations and elaborating principles for their implementation by the financial sector.[28]

Overall, international initiatives to counter terrorist financing since 9/11 have extended and expanded existing anti-money laundering cooperation. This has given rise to a web of institutions – led by the UN and the FATF, but joined by the Egmont Group, the Wolfsberg Group, regional bodies, specialized international organizations, and the IMF and World Bank – mobilized around the issue. In many ways, CFT cooperation now constitutes a regime, where the principles (widely held beliefs about the utility of following the movement of money); norms (obligations arising under formal (UN) and informal (FATF) initiatives); rules (the specific regulatory actions to be taken and best practices to be pursued); and decision-making procedures (whether they are manifest in global, regional or specialist organizations) are institutionalized in multiple fora.[29] Beneath this web of institutions are a wide range of bilateral trans-governmental networks on terrorist financing, which have also reinforced and supplemented the regime.

Evaluating the effectiveness of international initiatives to counter terrorist financing

International initiatives can be evaluated by indicators such as increased reporting, the number of requests for assistance, and the number of states that have signed international conventions, created financial intelligence units, or joined international bodies. But the more important measure is the degree to which they have changed domestic policies to be in compliance with the new international standards. Drawing on some of our previous work on targeted financial sanctions,[30] it is useful to differentiate between four aspects of policy implementation when searching for evidence of change at the national level: (1) the establishment of a legal framework; (2) the creation or strengthening of an administrative infrastructure; (3) the introduction and use of a variety of different regulatory compliance measures; and (4) evidence of enforcement.

Regarding legal changes, most countries have shown progress on criminalizing the willful provision of funds for terrorism and for providing a legal basis for the expeditious freezing of the funds of terrorist groups and individuals. New legislation has either been adopted or is formally under review in most countries. As Curtis Ward has argued, *every* State has had to adopt new legislation in order to meet fully all of the requirements of Resolution 1373.[31] While anti-money laundering rules have been tightened, most countries have recognized, in part from the CTC policy dialogues, that anti-money laundering regulations alone are not sufficient to suppress terrorist financing. States also need to be able to identify and freeze terrorist funds quickly, without lengthy formal judicial proceedings. Since this typically requires the decision of competent financial authorities, even if the freeze is a temporary measure, many states need new legal provisions. By 2004, a legal basis to freeze funds expeditiously existed in all but three UN Member States; by 2005, terrorist financing was criminalized in 123 countries.[32]

Most states report changes in administrative infrastructure to deal with terrorist financing, and many for the first time have formed FIUs or other intra-governmental mechanisms to address these issues. It is significant to note the growing number of states that have joined the Egmont Group in recent years (see Figure 11.1). In its effort to support the establishment of administrative infrastructure to implement counter-terrorism measures, the CTC has appointed an assistance team to dispatch information about common standards and best practices. The CTC also created the Directory of Counter-Terrorism Information and Sources of Assistance, an electronic forum for states to offer aid in implementing UNSCR 1373. It is not clear how many states have used this Internet-accessible resource to date, but CTC assistance teams, in bilateral consultations with different states, evaluate gaps in administrative capacity and facilitate assistance from willing donors. Most countries have identified an implementing agency or intra-governmental mechanism for administering controls on terrorist financing, and nearly all have identified central contact points for the CTC.

With regard to regulatory measures, there is evidence that banks and financial institutions have been notified about new regulations relating to the financing of terrorism in most countries. Many countries have introduced new reporting requirements for banks and financial institutions, especially "know your customer" provisions and reports on suspicious transactions. Formal audits have been used less frequently, however. Few states have pursued measures to regulate charities, other than government registration. Saudi Arabia, however, announced an ambitious program for monitoring the activities of all charities operating in the Kingdom. European Union members tend to be the most prone to conduct audits of financial institutions, investigations into charitable organizations, and introduce special measures for high-risk (off-shore) centers under their jurisdiction. There is also some indication that critically placed states, such as Pakistan, have made use of the US list of designated individuals and groups engaged in committing acts of terrorism, rather than relying on the UN list alone.

Until 2002, no state, with the exception of the UAE, had any measures for the regulation of informal money transfer systems such as *hawala* (see Chapter 8 for a discussion of different forms of IVTS). The Saudis claimed in some of their first reports to the CTC that *hawalas* simply did not operate in the country and that every financial institution was under the administrative mandate of the Saudi Monetary Authority. The US federal government has registered well over 16,000 money service businesses under the provisions of the Patriot Act. Australian officials have pursued similar measures, and Hong Kong has been described by Australian regulators as setting the standard in this area.[33] Pakistan and the UAE have also introduced new legislation regarding the operations of *hawalas*.

As an example of enforcement at the national level, US Department of the Treasury officials claimed that $112.2 million was frozen worldwide in the first few months immediately after 11 September 2001. This initial figure includes significant funds of the Taliban regime frozen under UNSCR 1267, going back to October 1999. In November 2003 the US Department of the Treasury reported that more than $136 million in assets had been frozen worldwide and that the US had worked with other governments to seize well over $60 million.[34] US Assistant Treasury Secretary, Juan Zarate stated: "Over 170 countries have taken relevant freezing measures and other steps to ensure that terrorists are deprived of the means and channels of funding."[35] He raised the total figure of assets frozen to $147 million at a briefing for the 1267 Committee in January 2005.[36]

Of the $147 million in assets of terrorist organizations blocked as of January 2005, $36 million have been frozen by the United States and $111 million by other countries (approximately $24m by Switzerland, $11.9m by the UK, $5.5m by Saudi Arabia, and an undisclosed amount by the UAE). The 1267 Committee estimates somewhat lower total amounts frozen than US sources: as of late July 2006, $91.4 million, mainly in the form of bank accounts, had been frozen by 35 Member States under the al Qaeda/Taliban sanctions regime.[37] The total amount affected by these freezing actions came to approximately US $75 million. Pakistan, Saudi Arabia, Switzerland, Turkey and the United States accounted for about $70 million of that amount. A significant part of the assets involved funds attributed to the Taliban, and they have subsequently been returned to the government of Afghanistan.

Eleven of the states reporting to the 1267 Committee that they had detected the presence of al Qaeda-related cells in their countries provided no indication that any assets had been frozen. Some states mentioned investigations being pursued or underway, but few offered new evidence of concrete success. Many states still assert that their financial system is not susceptible to misuse by terrorists.

Prosecutions have been pursued, especially in the US, Germany, Indonesia, and the UK, but few have thus far resulted in the freezing of additional funds. There has been some extraterritorial application of the Patriot Act, specifically against correspondent accounts in Israel, Oman, Taiwan, India, and Belize. These actions have allegedly resulted in the seizure of an additional $2 million, but federal judges have sealed most case records. There is virtually no evidence of the suspension of any banking licenses, but there have been convictions in the US for the provision of "material support." Only the US and the European Union have developed their own lists of groups and individuals legally identified as terrorists, while most other countries rely instead on the lists provided by the 1267 Committee.

There have been important changes in policy introduced at the national level throughout the world. These are important expressions of a global willingness to do something to counter the financing of terrorism, even if material progress to date has been relatively modest. Acts of terrorism such as those committed since 2001 in Indonesia, Turkey, Morocco, Saudi Arabia, Spain, Russia, Egypt, Iraq, and the UK underscore the threat that al Qaeda represents to all states, not just the US. Continuing acts of terrorism tend to propel the global regulatory effort forward. In the final analysis, however, as the 9/11 Commission *Monograph on Terrorist Financing* stated, completely choking off the money to al Qaeda and its affiliated groups has been "essentially impossible."[38]

Challenges to further progress

In spite of some of the successes of multilateral initiatives in inducing national-level change, the period since 11 September has revealed a number of constraints and challenges to further progress in suppressing terrorist financing through multilateral initiatives. While some of these constraints emerged soon after 9/11, others are of more recent origin, and all continue to evolve within the broader global counter-terrorism effort. Here, we address six challenges to the effectiveness and continuation of multilateral counter-terrorist financing cooperation.

First, there are ongoing limitations regarding state capacity to implement global counter-terrorist financing standards. In the immediate post-11 September period, the apparent gap between the requirements of these standards and the existing capability of many states was frequently observed. For example, in the context of UNSCR 1373, the inaugural Chairman of the CTC, Sir Jeremy Greenstock, told the Security Council in January 2002 that the CTC's aim was to "[R]aise the average level of Government performance against terrorism around the globe. This means upgrading the capacity of each nation's legislation and executive machinery to fight terrorism."[39] As indicated above, the capacity-building and assistance initiatives of the CTC and other bodies were designed to address problems of state capacity directly and have enjoyed some successes. However, even where these successes have been recorded – i.e. where the *general* capacity gaps have been reduced – there remain gaps in capacity pertaining to the *specific* requirements of UN and FATF measures. For example, monitors of the Security Council's sanctions against the Taliban, al Qaeda and associated entities have noted gaps relating to the capacity of Member States to implement the specific measures relating to the regulation of charities.[40] Of course, *some* gaps in capacity are inevitable, as existing measures are refined and new standards issued, but these can present opportunities for terrorists to exploit. For this reason, there is a vital need to provide assistance, targeted to specific issues and certain regions.

Second, just as capacity gaps have evolved somewhat from general to specific concerns, so have challenges arising from lack of political will. As the institutionalization of counter-terrorist financing measures (described above) reflects, few states actively resist multilateral initiatives in this area.[41] But, even as states have come to accept global standards *per se*, they may lack the political will to implement them, in whole or in part. This is especially the case of the poor countries striving to meet basic human needs which simply have other priorities and view themselves unlikely to be central players in the financing of terrorism. Also, cases reportedly remain where Member States possess the capacity to implement UN counter-terrorism measures, but fail to do so. Here, the Secretary-General's High Level Panel on Threats, Challenges and Change recommended that the Security Council "devise a schedule of predetermined sanctions for State non-compliance."[42]

   A third constraint on the implementation of multilateral counter-terrorist financing initiatives that arose soon after 11 September relates to the human rights and due process implications of government CFT actions. In particular, some of the designations made by the US in the months immediately following the attacks and adopted by the 1267 Committee have been challenged. The 9/11 Commission detailed the problems with hastily made designations based on a lower threshold of evidence, and the subsequent complications that some of the early designations created for the multilateral designations process.[43] Initially, these concerns emerged in states – such as those in the European Union – where international obligations under UN Security Council resolutions requiring that assets be frozen appeared to come into conflict with the existing rights of citizens as defined in the European Convention on Human Rights (ECHR). For example, in late 2001, Sweden challenged the listing of two of its citizens by the 1267 Committee, citing conflicting obligations under European human rights law which, at the very least, would require that those listed have individual access to procedural protections in the case of asset freezes. The perception of unfairness in the application of financial sanctions has generated public opposition in several countries, and more than 50 Member States have expressed concern about the perceived lack of due process and transparency in the UN listing and de-listing processes. Most important, some Member States have indicated that they are reluctant to propose new listings until an adequate process for the de-listing issue is developed.[44] In response to human rights concerns, in December 2005 the 1267 Committee adopted modest changes to procedures for the listing and de-listing of individuals, but these fall short of permitting listed individuals access to the Committee where they allege wrongful or erroneous listing. Rather, their country of residence or citizenship must make this claim on their behalf.[45] Critics find this approach unsatisfactory, as some states may be unwilling to petition the Committee in individual cases, and more broadly, lack of individual access to the Committee compromises the right to effective remedy, as protected by Article 13 of the European Convention on Human Rights.[46] Although reforms to the Committee's listing procedure – including amendments to allow individuals more direct access to the Committee – have been discussed,[47] until they are adopted legitimate concerns about inadequate notification, accessibility, fair hearing, and effective remedy in current listing and de-listing processes remain unaddressed.[48]

A related concern is the evident gap between the requirements that must be met to designate an individual or entity on one of the lists of global terrorists and the much higher standards of evidence required for legal prosecution. Since the listing process is an administrative one, based on redacted intelligence reports typically provided by a single country, rather than a judicial one, the standards of evidence and concerns for legal due process differ significantly. Within the United States, an interagency process is used to draft the list of targeted individuals and entities, but critics have charged that there is a presumption of guilt based on evidence provided by intelligence agencies and that the US is more interested in adding names to the list as a preventive measure than it is in pursuing a full investigation of their basis. This criticism, based in large part on hasty designations made immediately after 11 September is significant, however, since the US has historically provided most of the names for the UN lists maintained by the 1267 Committee.

Fourth, while state capacity to suppress terrorist financing has improved over time, much of the burden in implementing CFT measures falls on the private sector. As a consequence, variation in the capacity of private sector banks and financial institutions around the world remains a constraint upon the effective implementation of global standards. There is also significant variation within individual countries with regard to capacity of private sector institutions. Larger financial institutions have competitive advantages over smaller institutions when it comes to compliance with reporting on terrorist financing. Immediately prior to 11 September, small and medium-scale regional banks in the US complained about the competitive disadvantages they faced with regard to compliance with anti-money laundering recommendations of the FATF. Larger banks are better able to comply and to manage the additional costs associated with compliance. However, as described in Chapter 10 of this volume, larger financial institutions have called for regulators to revisit currency transaction and suspicious activity reporting requirements in recent years, citing the costs associated with CFT compliance.

Fifth, a particular constraint upon UN-led efforts to suppress terrorist financing concerns the capacity and willingness of Member States to prepare the numerous reports to UN bodies that they are increasingly asked to provide. Given the fact that the CTC, the 1267 Committee, and, beginning in 2004, the 1540 Committee (concerned with the proliferation of chemical, biological, radiological, and nuclear weapons and materials) have all introduced extensive reporting requirements, there is a genuine a problem of mounting "reporting fatigue." Small Member States from the developing world with limited institutional capacity often have great difficulty keeping up with the demands of successive rounds of reporting. If too many demands are placed on reporting alone, the quality of that reporting may begin to decline. Some Member States have indicated that as the reporting demands have increased in recent years, they literally cut and paste portions of one report into another. Others complain that they have difficulty keeping separate the different mandates and concerns of Security Council committees requiring reports. There is also growing evidence of overlap and duplication of effort. The 1267 Monitoring Group reports that some Member States have been confused about the different reporting requirements and believe they have already reported as required, for example, to the CTC.

A final constraint upon the effectiveness of multilateral counter-terrorist financing initiatives, also specific to the UN, concerns institutional lethargy and bureaucratic delay within the organization itself. As discussed above, the political will generated by the 11 September attacks spurred the establishment of the CTC, and also motivated Member States to comply with their initial reporting requirements in an unprecedented manner. However, as time has passed, the dynamism that characterized the post-11 September period has also subsided. By November 2003, when the Chairman of the CTC reported to the Security Council on the challenges encountered in implementing 1373, it was clear that the CTC itself needed to be "revitalized," to permit it to play a more proactive role, especially regarding the coordination of technical assistance.[49]

Perhaps reflecting frustration with the CTC in this regard, G8 states had already signaled their willingness to launch a parallel initiative with regard to technical assistance, creating the CTAG at the Evian Summit in June 2003.[50] The proposed revitalization reforms were subsequently adopted with resolution 1535 (26 March 2004) in which the Security Council decided to establish a Counter-Terrorism Executive Directorate (CTED) to work to the CTC proper.[51] But this decision has proven frustratingly slow to implement, particularly with regard to the UN's cumbersome internal personnel recruiting procedures. There has also been confusion over the scope and domain of the new agency, given the ever-increasing range of UN counter-terrorism activities. Resolution 1566 (8 October 2004) created a Working Group to consider measures to be imposed on terrorists other than those included on the 1267 list, but it is significant to note that the Resolution also requested that the Secretary-General take urgent steps to ensure that the CTED become fully operational. The Secretary-General later did so, providing an assurance that CTED would be fully operational by January 2005.[52] In spite of this, and while CTED was able to participate in a number of field visits, it was not fully staffed until July 2005, creating a backlog of work for the CTC.[53] The travails in establishing the CTED reproduce, rather than resolve, some of the problems that led to the "revitalization" of the CTC. As we discuss below, firmer leadership from the Security Council is an important part of maintaining multilateral support for counter-terrorist financing initiatives.

Recommendations for moving forward

Our discussion raises three key questions as to how to best consolidate the gains from international cooperation on countering the financing of terrorism. In addressing these, we offer several recommendations for the multilateral effort against terrorist financing.

Ensure parallel implementation

As our discussion above implies, remaining gaps in state capacity and political will to implement global counter-terrorist financing standards point to an ongoing problem of parallel implementation. Inconsistent or non-existent implementation may create havens for terrorist funds. The principal international response to this problem – the provision of technical and capacity-building assistance to states in need – has yielded some successes, but needs to be enhanced and extended into the future. In particular, donor states must continue to evaluate and prioritize needs for assistance across the world, and be prepared to provide assistance at the institutional level. As the former President of the FATF, commenting on the importance of mutual evaluation mechanisms, noted:

> Mutual evaluation programmes constitute an enormous challenge for many groups. The FATF itself is struggling with its own limited resources, and other groups may not yet have the full capacity or expertise needed to conduct meaningful mutual evaluations of their members. However, mutual evaluation programmes are essential to our work and to the credibility of our global and regional groups. It is only through mutual evaluations and peer pressure, both at global and regional levels, that we can ensure that the global network against money laundering and terrorist financing exists concretely and is effective in its task. FATF countries are dedicated to making the mutual evaluation process a success, not only within FATF but also within all of the FSRBs. To that goal, the FATF will continue to provide help, as much as needed, to support the FSRBs and contribute to the success of mutual evaluations conducted by regional groups.[54]

In addition to continuing capacity-building and technical assistance initiatives for states, efforts to build private sector capacity can help address problems of parallel implementation. Recent FATF efforts to engage the private sector through the Wolfsberg Group and the International Banking Federation should be replicated at the regional level,[55] and the findings of World Bank/IMF research on best practices in forging public–private partnerships to implement AML/CFT measures should be studied and adopted at the national level.[56]

Finally, emphasizing the positive spillovers of improved financial regulation can encourage consistent implementation of AML/CFT practices. Once established, the improvements in state capacity to suppress terrorist financing can result in other benefits for the governance of the international political and economic systems. For example, effective AML/CFT systems have an enhanced capacity to monitor and limit abuses from potential tax evasion, to pursue funds transferred abroad by corrupt political leaders, to deter money laundering, and to implement future UN targeted financial sanctions. These measures also enhance state institutional capacity in more general terms, contributing to institutional development. Still other positive spillover effects include those resulting from an enhanced reputation for being transparent and non-corrupt, which may extend to attracting future investment.

Integrate human rights concerns in CFT initiatives

The growing gap between what states do in the name of security (and protecting their citizenry) and the means they use to do so (violating the very human rights that many states stand for)[57] plays itself out in the listing process. As discussed above, there have been limited efforts to improve the quality of the information provided on listed individuals and entities and to introduce de-listing procedures by the 1267 Committee. While several examples of successful de-listing exist (both by the 1267 Committee and by some of the UN's other sanctions committees), there remain important criticisms of the process.

First, there is inadequate notification. Member States do not always inform their citizens of their listing. Notification is central to procedural fairness. Individuals should be aware of the reasons for their designation on the lists, as well as the procedures for applying for exemptions and de-listing.

Second, due to the requirement that individuals must gain the backing of a Member State to negotiate their case on a bilateral, state-to-state basis, if states are reluctant to represent the interests of their nationals, or if their petitions are not forwarded to the relevant sanctions committee, the de-listing process is inaccessible and may violate individual rights to direct appeal of their designation.

Third, the right to a fair hearing is denied (prior to a designation of listing), since individuals or corporate entities are never given a chance to defend themselves before the imposition of a sanction (either an asset freeze or a ban on travel). They can be listed with redacted statements of case based on classified intelligence information that is not made available to other Member States. The contents of the statements of case are never made public.

Fourth and finally, the right to an effective remedy is also denied, since if a state of residence or citizenship refuses to take up the case for de-listing, there is no recourse for the individual. There is also no end date to the sanction, and nothing prevents a temporary designation from becoming a permanent, *de facto* confiscation of assets, if no state takes up the case. There is also no periodic review of listings.

Most, but not all, of these concerns could be addressed by reforms to existing practices recommended in *Strengthening Targeted Sanctions through Fair and Clear Procedures*, a White Paper prepared for the governments of Switzerland, Sweden, and Germany by the Watson Institute's Targeted Sanctions Project at Brown University.[58] To the extent possible, there should be a supplemental notification of targets by a UN body, to ensure targets are aware of the measures against them. An administrative focal point within the UN Secretariat should be designated to handle all de-listing and exemption requests. To ensure a fair hearing, norms and general standards should be established for statements of case, the time for review of listing proposals should be extended, a biennial review of listings should be introduced, time limits for review of requests should be established, and clear standards for de-listing promulgated. Finally, some kind of review mechanism should be established that is impartial, has the power to grant appropriate relief, and is accessible – to ensure that the right to effective remedy for a wrongful listing is not denied.

The future role for UN organs

As indicated in this chapter, the web of international initiatives to address terrorist financing has grown beyond the United Nations, to other related international, regional and specialized organizations such as the IMF/World Bank, FATF, Egmont Group, and others. Coupled with the previously noted reporting fatigue resulting from the expansion of UN bodies dealing with various aspects of terrorism – the 1267, 1373, 1540, and 1566 committees, in addition to the Terrorism Prevention branch of the UN Office of Drugs and Crime in Vienna – Member States have expressed concerns about both the duplication of UN efforts and its bureaucratic inefficiencies. These concerns are likely to come into sharper focus as the December 2007 expiration of the CTED's mandate approaches. What role, then, should UN organs play in the multilateral counter-terrorism effort generally, and in terrorist financing in particular?

The first of these questions – concerning the UN role in broader counter-terrorism initiatives globally – has been considered in greater depth elsewhere. Alistair Millar and Eric Rosand argue that a global counter-terrorism body should be created and explore options for doing so.[59] Despite the merits of this proposal, however, other influential actors, including the Secretary-General and the G8,[60] have declined to endorse the creation of a new multilateral organization. Rather, they have taken the position that existing UN counter-terrorism mechanisms should be made to work better, with an emphasis on improved coordination.

Clearly, these broader debates will affect the multilateral effort against terrorist financing, but, given the degree of institutionalization of AML/CFT measures in fora other than the UN, they may do so only at the margins. For the purpose of global action against terrorist financing, the key contribution of the UN has been to establish and maintain the legal basis requiring Member States to prevent the financing of terrorism. No other international or regional group legally mandates that countries take specific actions to freeze assets and prevent the financing of terrorism, as resolutions passed under Chapter VII of the UN Charter require. Moreover, as the effort to counter terrorism is truly a global one, no other international organization has universal membership and application as the United Nations. Initiatives by regional and specialized groups, however instrumental in advancing efforts to counter terrorist financing, cannot replace the central role of the UN in this regard.

Of course, UN organs perform other important functions, such as in compiling the list of persons targeted by financial sanctions pursuant to 1267 and related resolutions. But the key operational tasks of setting AML/CFT standards, monitoring their enforcement and providing technical assistance are, for the most part, undertaken outside of the UN. In other words, the dynamics of international cooperation on AML/CFT issues are distinct – though not entirely separate – from broader debates about the role of the UN on counter-terrorism. For this reason, we predict that the longevity of AML/CFT cooperation will correspond to the strength of expert networks in the area more than UN politics. To the extent that this prediction is borne out, it points to the underlying functional origins of international cooperation.[61] Viewed in this way, the future role for UN organs on counter-terrorism generally may be modest, providing the necessary legal mandate for functional cooperation and coordinating activity across sectors.

Conclusion

In spite of the many limitations, there have been some impressive achievements with regard to international initiatives to suppress terrorist financing since 2001. A new counter-terrorist financing regime has emerged, founded on both horizontal and vertical networks of governments, international organizations, and private sector institutions. Most of the effort and success to date has been with regard to the promulgation of new laws, regulations and controls affecting formal sector transactions. This is a significant achievement, given the fact that $300,000 of the $500,000 estimated to have been used in the attacks of 11 September passed though the US banking system. However, as indicated by other chapters on charities, trade diversion, gemstones, and informal value transfer systems elsewhere in this volume, international efforts to counter the financing of terrorism have only just begun to address a large and complex problem.

As discussed in more detail in Chapter 13 of this volume, as the financing of global terrorism has changed, so too has the need for a change in the nature of the efforts in countering the financing of global terrorism. None-theless, it is important to maintain and strengthen formal sector regulatory efforts, not only because they inhibit the financing of terrorism and enable intelligence into the networks that support terrorist groups, but because they also provide important positive externalities with regard to other transnational concerns, including money laundering, corruption, and tax evasion.

Notes

1 C. A. Ward, "The Role of the United Nations Security Council in Combating International Terrorism," Paper presented at the Oxford Conference – The Changing Face of International Co-operation in Criminal Matters in the 21st Century, Christ Church College, Oxford, UK, 27–30 August 2002, p. 1.
2 Watson Institute for International Studies, *Targeted Financial Sanctions: A Manual for Design and Implementation: Contributions from the Interlaken Process*, 2001. Online. Available HTTP: <http://www.watsoninstitute.org/pub/TFS.pdf> (accessed 4 December 2006).
3 T. J. Biersteker, "Émergence, évolution, effets et défis des sanctions ciblées," *Géoéconomie*, Revue trimestrielle, no. 30, Summer 2004, Table 2. Online. Available HTTP: <http://www.watsoninstitute.org/pub/Biersteker-Targeted_Sanctions.pdf> (accessed 6 December 2006).
4 There were 158 parties as of June 2007. See International Convention for the Suppression of the Financing of Terrorism, United Nations Treaty Collection. Online. Available HTTP: <http://untreaty.un.org/ENGLISH/bible/englishinter-netbible/partI/chapterXVIII/treaty11.asp> (accessed 2 December 2006).
5 The General Assembly adopted a thirteenth counter-terrorism convention, the International Convention for the Suppression of Acts of Nuclear Terrorism, in April 2005.
6 See Financial Action Task Force, *The Forty Recommendations*, Paris: FATF, 2003. Online. Available HTTP: <http://www.fatf-gafi.org/dataoecd/7/40/34849567.PDF> (accessed 4 December 2006).
7 See Egmont Group. Online. Available HTTP: <http://www.egmontgroup.org/> (accessed 7 December 2006).
8 Reports Submitted by Member States pursuant to UNSCR 1373 (2001) and 1624 (2005). Online. Available HTTP: <http://www.un.org/sc/ctc/countryreports/reportA.shtml> (accessed 3 June 2007).
9 1267 Monitoring Group, "First Report of the Analytical Support and Sanctions Monitoring Team appointed pursuant to resolution 1526 (2004) concerning Al-Qaida and the Taliban and associated individuals and entities," 25 August 2004. Online. Available HTTP: <http://www.un.org/sc/committees/1267/monitoringteam.shtml> (accessed 3 June 2006).
10 See United Nations Counter-Terrorism Committee, "Outcome document of the special meeting of the Counter-Terrorism Committee with international, regional and subregional organizations," UN Doc. S/AC.40/2003/SM.1/4, 31 March 2003. Online. Available HTTP: <http://www.un.org/Docs/sc/committees/1373/ctc_meeting.html> (accessed 10 December 2006), and "Follow-up meeting to the United Nations Counter-Terrorism Committee (CTC) Special Meeting of 6 March 2003," UN Doc. S/2004/276, 1 April 2004. Online. Available HTTP: <http://www.un.org/Docs/sc/committees/1373/ctc_meeting.html> (accessed 10 December 2006).
11 C. A. Ward, "Building Capacity to Combat International Terrorism: the Role of

the United Nations Security Council," *Journal of Conflict & Security Law*, 2003, vol. 8, no. 2, p. 302.

12 Personal communication.

13 Although not a direct effect of UN initiatives, there is evidence that bilateral cooperation on the issue independent of the CTC initiatives has also increased in recent years. Bilateral cooperation between the United States and individual countries has risen sharply. Intensive efforts with Saudi Arabia, in the form of enhanced intelligence and law enforcement cooperation, and the UAE on informal transfer systems have strengthened and reinforced capacity to address terrorist financing.

14 United Nations Security Council 1267 Committee Monitoring Group, "Fifth Report of the Analytical Support and Sanctions Monitoring Team appointed pursuant to resolution 1526 (2004) concerning Al-Qaida and the Taliban and associated individuals and entities," 20 September 2006. Online. Available HTTP: <http://www.un.org/Docs/sc/committees/1267/1267mg.htm> (accessed 4 December 2006). "The Team notes that of these 44 States, 24 are from the African group, nine are from the Asian group, 10 are from the Latin American/Caribbean group, and one is from the Eastern European Group."

15 Recent UNODC activity is summarized in United Nations Office of Drugs and Crime, "Strengthening International Cooperation and Technical Assistance in Promoting the Implementation of the Universal Conventions and Protocols Related to Terrorism within the Framework of the Activities of the United Nations Office on Drugs and Crime," UN Doc. E/CN.15/2005/13, 8 April 2005. Online. Available HTTP: <http://www.unodc.org/unodc/en/terrorism.html> (accessed 10 December 2006).

16 The FATF is an inter-governmental body whose purpose is to develop and promote policies, both at national and international levels, to combat money laundering and terrorist financing. The FATF Secretariat is housed at the OECD. The 31 member jurisdictions of the FATF are: Argentina; Australia; Austria; Belgium; Brazil; Canada; Denmark; Finland; France; Germany; Greece; Hong Kong, China; Iceland; Ireland; Italy; Japan; Luxembourg; Mexico; the Kingdom of the Netherlands; New Zealand; Norway; Portugal; the Russian Federation; Singapore; South Africa; Spain; Sweden; Switzerland; Turkey; the United Kingdom; and the United States. The European Commission and the Gulf Co-operation Council are also FATF members. In addition, the People's Republic of China is an observer. The global network that is committed to combating money laundering and terrorist financing includes the seven FATF-style regional bodies: Asia/Pacific Group; the Caribbean Financial Action Task Force; The Eastern and South African Anti Money Laundering Group (ESAAMLG); Eurasian Group (EAG); Grupo de Acción Financiera de Sudamérica – South American Financial Action Group (GAFISUD); Middle East and North Africa Financial Action Task Force (MENAFATF); and Moneyval (Committee of Experts on the Evaluation of Anti-Money Laundering Measures). The Offshore Group of Banking Supervisors is also part of this network. See <http://www.fatf-gafi.org/document/52/ 0,2340,en_32250379_32237295_34027188_1_1_1_1,00.html> (accessed 10 December 2006).

17 For example, see Financial Action Task Force, *Annual Report 2000–2001*, 22 June 2001. Online. Available HTTP: <https://www.oecd.org/dataoecd/13/2/ 34328033.pdf > (accessed 10 December 2006).

18 Financial Action Task Force, *Annual Report 2004–2005*, Paris: FATF, OECD, 10 June 2005, p.10. Online. Available HTTP: <http://www.fatf-gafi.org/dataoecd/ 41/25/34988062.pdf> (accessed 6 December 2006).

19 Taken together, these initiatives constituted a form of "vertical network" of officials from government, the private sector, and international organizations who

gathered together to share information, provide assistance, discuss enforcement, and promote legal and policy harmonization. See A. M. Slaughter, *A New World Order*, Washington, DC: The World Bank and International Monetary Fund,2004 for a discussion of the concept of a vertical network.

20 For an overview of Bank and Fund activities, see P. A. Schott, *Reference Guide to Anti-Money Laundering and Countering the Financing of Terrorism*, 2nd edition, 2004, especially Chapter 10.

21 S. Levey, Under Secretary, Office of Terrorism and Financial Intelligence, US Department of the Treasury, Testimony before the Senate Committee on Banking, Housing and Urban Affairs, 4 April 2006. Online. Available HTTP: <http://www.treas.gov/press/releases/js4155.htm> (accessed 6 December 2006).

22 Most recently, see Inter-American Committee Against Terrorism, "Report on CICTE Activities," OAS Doc. OEA/Ser.L/X.2.5, CICTE/doc.6/05, 17 February 2005.

23 C. B. Realuyo, "G8 Counter-terrorism Action Group Efforts to Combat Terrorist Financing," Presentation to Follow-up Meeting to the United Nations Counter-Terrorism Committee (CTC) Special Meeting of 6 March 2003, 11 March 2004. Online. Available HTTP: <http://www.osce.org/documents/sg/2004/03/3297_en.pdf> (accessed 6 December 2006).

24 G8, "G8 Statement on Counter-terrorism," Gleneagles, July 2005. Online. Available HTTP: <http://www.fco.gov.uk/Files/kfile/PostG8_Gleneagles_CounterTerrorism.pdf> (accessed 6 December 2006).

25 E. A. Wayne, Assistant Secretary for Economic and Business Affairs, US Department of State, Testimony before the Senate Committee on Banking, Housing and Urban Affairs, 4 April 2006. Online. Available HTTP: <http://banking.senate.gov/_files/ACFFE09.pdf> (accessed 6 December 2006).

26 For example, see Joint Forum of the Basel Committee on Banking Supervision (BCBS), the International Organization of Securities Commissions (IOSCO) and the International Association of Insurance Supervisors (IAIS), "Initiatives by the BCBS, IAIS and IOSCO to combat money laundering and the financing of terrorism," IOSCO Public Document No. 146, June 2003.

27 See Offshore Group of Banking Supervisors, "OGBS welcomes Eight Special Recommendations on terrorist financing" (November 2001). Online. Available HTTP: <http://www.ogbs.net/press8specialrecs.htm> (accessed 10 December 2006), and "OGBS welcomes revised FATF Recommendations" (July 2003). Online. Available HTTP: <http://www.ogbs.net/press40recs.htm> (accessed 7 December 2006).

28 Wolfsberg Group, "Wolfsberg Statement on the Suppression of the Financing of Terrorism," January 2002. Online. Available HTTP: <http://www.wolfsberg-principles.com/pdf/ws_on_terrorism.pdf> (accessed 6 December 2006).

29 Stephen Krasner defines regimes as, "sets of implicit or explicit principles, norms, rules and decision making procedures, around which actors' expectations converge in a given area of international relations." See "Structural causes and regime consequences: Regimes as intervening variables," *International Organization*, 1982, vol. 36 no. 2, p. 186.

30 *Targeted Financial Sanctions: A Manual for Design and Implementation, Contributions from the Interlaken Process*, Part 2, Swiss Confederation in cooperation with the UN Secretariat and the Watson Institute for International Studies, Brown University, 2001, pp. 79–112. Online. Available HTTP: <http://www.watsoninstitute.org/pub/TFS.pdf> (accessed 2 December 2006).

31 C.A. Ward, 2003, p. 299.

32 Wayne, Testimony before the Senate Committee on Banking, Housing, and Urban Affairs, 4 April 2006.

33 Interview with senior Australian government official by a member of the Watson Institute Targeting Terrorist Finances Project, January 2003.

34 J. C. Zarate, "Securing the Financial System against Rogue Capital," US Department of Treasury, 10 November 2003. Online. Available HTTP: <http://www.ustreas.gov/press/releases/js984.htm> (accessed 4 December 2006).

35 Ibid.

36 United Nations, "Security Council Committee Meets Senior US Officials to Discuss Implementation of Sanctions against Al-Qaida, Taliban," Press Release, 1 November 2005. Online. Available HTTP: <http://www.un.org/News/Press/docs/2005/sc8288.doc.htm> (accessd 4 December 2006).

37 "Fifth Report of the Analytical Support and Sanctions Monitoring Team appointed pursuant to resolutions 1526 (2004) and 1617 (2005) concerning Al-Qaida and the Taliban and associated individuals and entities," p. 21.

38 J. Roth, D. Greenberg, and S. Wille, *Monograph on Terrorist Financing* (Staff Report to the Commission), National Commission on Terrorist Attacks Upon the United States, 2004. Online. Available HTTP: <http://www. 9–11commission.gov/staff_statements/911_TerrFin_Monograph.pdf> (accessed 7 September 2006).

39 See UN Security Council, transcript of the 4453rd meeting, UN Doc. S/PV.4453, 18 January 2002. Online. Available HTTP: <http://www.un.org/Depts/dhl/resguide/scact2002.htm> (accessed 10 December 2006).

40 1267 Committee Monitoring Group, "Second report of the Analytical Support and Sanctions Monitoring Team appointed pursuant to resolution 1526 (2004) concerning Al-Qaida and the Taliban and associated individuals and entities," UN Doc. S/2005/83, 15 February 2005. Online. Available HTTP: <http://www.un.org/Docs/sc/committees/1267/1267mg.htm> (accessed 10 December 2006).

41 See also "Second Report of the Analytical Support and Sanctions Monitoring Team," p. 8.

42 United Nations High-Level Panel on Threats, Challenges and Change, "A More Secure World: Our Shared Responsibility – Report of the High-Level Panel on Threats, Challenges and Change," UN Doc. A/59/565, 2 December 2004, p. 47. Online. Available HTTP: <http://www.un.org/secureworld/> (accessed 10 December 2006).

43 As the 9/11 Commission *Monograph on Terrorist Financing* noted, the pressure to proceed with designations as rapidly as possible was substantial. While analysts wanted more time to make their evidentiary packages more complete, they were denied it, evidently due to "external demands:" "Some believed that the government's haste in this area, and its preference for IEEPA sanctions, might result in a high level of false designations that would ultimately jeopardize the United States' ability to persuade other countries to designate groups as terrorist organizations. Ultimately, . . . this proved to be the case with the al-Barakaat designations, mainly because they relied on a derivative designation theory, in which no direct proof of culpability was needed." See Roth, et al. *Monograph on Terrorist Financing*, p 79. Thus, in the rush to respond and demonstrate progress, the US made designations on the basis of a lower threshold of evidence – one that might not necessarily stand up in court. See also R. Suskind, *The Price of Loyalty*, New York: Simon & Schuster, 2004, p. 193.

44 T. J. Biersteker and S. E. Eckert, *Strengthening Targeted Sanctions through Fair and Clear Procedures,* Targeted Sanctions Project, Watson Institute for International Studies, Brown University, New York: United Nations, A/60/887 S/2006/331, June 2006. Online. Available HTTP: <http://watsoninstitute.org/pub/Strengthening_Targeted_Sanctions.pdf> (accessed 5 September 2006).

45 See Security Council Committee Established Pursuant to Resolution 1267 (1999),

United Nations Security Council 1267 Committee, "Guidelines of the Committee for the Conduct of its Work," as amended 6 April 2003. Online. Available HTTP: <http://www.un.org/Docs/sc/committees/1267/1267_guidelines.pdf> (accessed 10 December 2006).

46 For example, see I. Cameron, "UN Targeted Sanctions, Legal Safeguards and the European Convention on Human Rights," *Nordic Journal of International Law*, 2003, vol. 72, no. 2, pp. 159–214.

47 The issue, first noted in reports of the 1267 Monitoring Team (see, "Second Report of the Analytical Support and Sanctions Monitoring Team," pp. 17–18), has been under discussion within the 1267 Committee for several years. The de-listing issue was a particular priority in 2006.

48 Biersteker and Eckert, *Strengthening Targeted Sanctions through Fair and Clear Procedures*.

49 See United Nations Counter-Terrorism Committee, "Proposal for the Revitalisation of the Counter-Terrorism Committee," UN Doc. S/2004/124, 19 February 2004. Online. Available HTTP: <http://www.un.org/sc/ctc/cted.shtml> (accessed 10 December 2006).

50 G8, "Building International Political Will and Capacity to Combat Terrorism: A G8 Action Plan," June 2003. Online. Available HTTP: <http://www.g8.fr/evian/english/navigation/2003_g8_summit/summit_documents/building_international_political_will_and_capacity_to_combat_terrorism_-_a_g8_action_plan.html> (accessed 6 December 2006).

51 For a more detailed discussion on this and related points, see D. Cortright, et al., *An Action Agenda for Enhancing the United Nations Program on Counter-Terrorism*, Fourth Freedom Forum/Joan B. Kroc Institute, September 2004. Online. Available HTTP: <http://www.globalct.org/html/Action_Agenda.html> (accessed 6 December 2006).

52 United Nations Secretary-General, "Steps Taken to Make the Counter-Terrorism Committee Executive Directorate Fully Operational: Report of the Secretary-General," UN Doc. S/2004/914, 19 November 2004. Online. Available HTTP: <http://www.un.org/sc/ctc/cted.shtml> (accessed 10 December 2006).

53 E. Løj, Remarks at the 5229th meeting of the Security Council, UN. Doc. S/PV.5229, 20 July 2005. Online. Available HTTP: <http://www.un.org/Depts/dhl/resguide/scact2005.htm> (accessed 10 December 2006).

54 K. Asmal, Remarks at the Asia-Pacific Group on Money Laundering 2005 Annual Meeting, Cairns, Australia, 20 July 2005. Online. Available HTTP: <http://www.apgml.org/about/newsDetail.aspx?newsId=10> (accessed 10 December 2006).

55 Financial Action Task Force, *Annual Report 2004–05*, p.11.

56 World Bank/IMF, "Effective Regimes to Combat Money Laundering and the Financing of Terrorism: Strengthening the Collaborative Process – Lessons Learned," 2004. Online. Available HTTP: <http://siteresources.worldbank.org/EXTAML/Resources/396511–1146581427871/AML.Lessons.Learned.pdf> (accessed 10 December 2006).

57 R. Foot, "Collateral Damage: Human Rights Consequences of Counterterrorist Action in the Asia-Pacific," *International Affairs*, 2003, vol. 81, no. 2, pp. 1–14.

58 Biersteker and Eckert, *Strengthening Targeted Sanctions through Fair and Clear Procedures*.

59 A. Millar and E. Rosand, *Allied Against Terrorism: What's Needed to Strengthen the World Wide Commitment*, New York: Century Foundation Press, 2006.

60 Report of the Secretary General, "Uniting against Terrorism: Recommendations for a Global Counter-terrorism Strategy," UN Doc. A/60/825 (27 April 2006); G8 Statement on "Strengthening the UN's Counter-terrorism Program," 16 July 2006. Online. Available HTTP: <http://www.auswaertiges-amt.de/diplo/

de/Aussenpolitik/FriedenSicherheit/Terrorismusbekaempfung/LinksDownloads/
G8–06-TerrorismusbekaempfungVN.pdf l> (accessed 4 December 2006).
61 R. O. Keohane, *After Hegemony: Cooperation and Discord in the World Political
Economy*, Princeton, NJ: Princeton University Press, 1984.

12 Lessons for countering terrorist financing from the war on serious and organized crime

Michael Levi

An understanding of the similarities and differences between terrorism and organized crime, beyond the fact that there is a metaphorical "war" on both, is essential if we wish to shed further light on the way that terrorists acquire their resources. Against precisely what – in both cases – is one waging a war and claiming battle victories? How will we know whether or not we are winning, and what criteria will the public use when deciding whether or not they accept official claims of success? Improved analysis of organized crime will greatly improve our understanding of terrorist groups' financial efforts because the methods of one often support the activities of the other. While few people with legitimate jobs knowingly invest in criminal enterprises (other than thrill-seekers or those who reply to "419 letter" offers to move the proceeds of corruption abroad), the financing of terror from legal sources is commonplace. Criminal funds, irrespective of whether or not they are accrued by "organized crime," are nevertheless a financial component of terrorism, the more so if or when legal sources are cut off – for example, by measures against charitable and other donations.

Parsing what we have learned from the experience of combating both terrorism and organized crime is more difficult than it might appear. As a blanket term, "organized crime" obscures the myriad levels of criminality (frauds, drugs, and traffic in illegal migrants, to name just a few) and forms of organization (hierarchical "gangs," loose networks, etc.) that it encompasses. Additionally, despite the billions spent annually on domestic and international enforcement, there has been a remarkable lack of analysis of the impact of control measures on organized crime. Rather, analysis tends to focus on law enforcement and other supply-side activity indicators. An oblique indicator of this lack of evidence is the complete absence of discussion of organized (or white-collar) crime in the report *What Works*,[1] the influential review of crime prevention strategies commissioned in 1996 by the United States Congress. Subsequent efforts by Sherman et al. and by Wilson and Petersilia also failed to address the etiology of these sorts of offenses while examining their selection of crime issues of concern to the American people.[2]

The terms "organized crime" and "terrorism" both carry metaphorical baggage that can trap us within the constraints of common terminology that we assume everyone understands. Many use the term "organized crime" as if it were a coherent, common noun describing a well-understood set of arrangements to commit crime. However, criminal organizations are variously represented as taking any of a number of forms:

1   A hierarchical organization dominating global activity (an analogy in the legitimate sphere would be Microsoft);
2   A set of giant firms competing but acting more or less in tandem (analogous to the Seven Sisters of the oil industry);
3   A series of networks of varied size, stability, and mutual exclusivity;
4   Possibly, a combination of (1) or (2) with (3), since there is no reason to believe that even a dominant criminal organization would control all crimes.[3]

There is no adequately verified evidence that any criminal organization in the world falls into the first category, and the second is ill-populated, if populated at all over the long term. Note that to satisfy the criteria for classification as a criminal organization under the UN Transnational Organized Crime Convention 2000, a group needs only three or more people committing crime for gain over a period of time with an element of cross-border activity in some part of their criminality (including financing and laundering). This is not a very high threshold.

Models of terrorist groups may differ in some respects, but the forms listed above generally apply. Noting the analogous models and structures of terrorist and criminal organizations challenges current assumptions and disparate approaches to fighting terrorism and organized crime. If there is indeed an array of terrorist organizations varying in size and structure, sometimes cooperating but also sometimes competing[4] – a network or series of unconnected networks[5] rather than a single organization – then is it analytically sensible to speak of a unitary "terrorism"? Why should we refer to "organized crime" or, for that matter, to "al Qaeda" as if "it" were an organization whose accountability structure, management chart, and field of operations are reliably known, allowing us to know when we have or have not defeated "it"? The language we use – though marvelous for creating a comprehensible imagery for the general public – gets in the way of clear thinking about both crime and terrorist finance. It interferes with efforts to devise sensible control strategies, assuming (as I do) that the latter are indeed our aim.[6]

In a sense, it is easier to tell whether terrorism has been stopped than whether organized crime has been stopped: in the case of terrorism, the cessation of attacks after a given period may suffice, whereas in the case of organized crime, the absence of signs might indeed be (mis)taken as an indicator that "it" is under control. The continued use of drugs and vice is not evidence of the types of criminal (or terrorist) organizations that supply them. There is now widespread acceptance – at least in principle – that the "new terrorist" warfare is asymmetric; however, a similar understanding of most crime organizations as fractured and non-hierarchical is sometimes elusive. The meaning of the term "networks" is far from obvious when applied either to terrorists or organized criminals, as Dorn, Levi, and King argue in their review of upper-level drug trafficking (see Box 12.1).[7]

This confused usage speaks to a broader need for precise terminology that would allow us to precisely determine the goals of anti-terrorist finance and anti-crime measures. If those goals are more explicitly defined, and if we better understand the natures of the organized crime and terrorist organizations, we then can design anti-terror operations more rationally and – within limits – more effectively. Though some information inevitably must remain secret from the general public, if impact assessment measures are implemented, anti-terror and anti-crime organizations will be held accountable on the basis of their effectiveness and therefore become far more useful to the public than they currently may be. We know from the "war" on organized crime that a lack of decent impact assessment makes it difficult or impossible to know whether anti-crime or anti-terror measures are effective, ineffective, or even counterproductive.

How can the effects of interventions be evaluated?

To learn something analytically about outcomes in the fight against domestic or transnational organized crime, we need an adequate performance evaluation baseline. Yet perhaps excepting anti-drug strategies, in the United States neither a desire for scientific proof of impact nor the willingness to risk falsification of impact has accompanied the decades since (or, for that matter, before) the Organized Crime Control Omnibus Act of the Nixon era that, among other things, ushered in the Racketeer Influenced and Corrupt Organizations (RICO) statute.[8] Whatever measures one might dream up – illicit commodity availability, levels of substance use, number of organized crime groups, extortion, corruption, proceeds of crime confiscation as a proportion of criminal income, etc. – positive progress is difficult to demonstrate except in purely organizational terms such as increased asset forfeitures, arrests, interdictions, and "disruptions" – another elastic though sensible category increasingly used in the UK and some continental European countries.[9] It can be argued reasonably that such evaluation is "just too darn complicated," but it is difficult to sustain rationally the statement that one is "winning" wars (or even battles) on drugs, organized crime, or terrorism if one has no publicly defensible way of showing whether one is winning and is never willing to admit that one might be losing some or all.

We know from the "war" on organized crime that far more detail is available about inputs and outputs – institutions established and actions taken to combat organized crime – than about their impact on criminal behavior. Inputs and outputs, after all, are publicized and readily accessible without the need for agreement on highly contested causal mechanisms.[10] But the fact that practitioners have stretched the label "crime prevention" (or "reduction")

Box 12.1 A note on terminology – networking in the market

Terminology found in the literature is sometimes ambiguous. This is especially so in relation to "network"/"networking" which, whilst popular, seems to mean different things to different people. The overwhelming consensus within the criminological literature is that networks are very important. On inspection, however, it appears that there are at least three common uses of this term:

1   As a way of describing the structure and/or everyday workings of *the market as a whole*, in the sense that the market can be regarded as a complex social network (*singular noun*), within which different participants have to network (*verb*) to carefully seek out and interact with traffickers who may be like or unlike themselves, etc. In other words, through networking, traffickers construct the market.

2   As a way of describing drug markets as made up of *independent small groups or individuals*, sometimes called "disorganized crime," sometimes simply "networks" (*plural*). Doubt is cast upon the existence of larger and/or "harder" criminal organizations operating in the UK or other European contexts, partly because it is posited that LEAs break up larger groups. . . . In other words, in drug trafficking, "small is beautiful."

3   As a way of referring to the durability or otherwise of criminals' organizational and other arrangements, when these are seen as *ever-changing* ("fluid networks" being counterposed to structures of all kinds). In other words, impermanence is the name of the game. (This approach often co-exists with number 2 above, although they are analytically separable.)

For present purposes, within the text of this review, the first meaning – networking within the market – will generally be preferred. This is because, of the three propositions above, the first is not contradicted by any author examined. By contrast, an implication of the second meaning, that upper level drug trafficking lacks larger and/or "harder-edged" organizations, is not well supported by the literature consulted or briefings received. Similarly, regarding the third meaning, although no doubt some traffickers are very much in a state of flux, according to the literature many others are not, persisting more or less in the same forms for years or even decades. Hence, here, "networking" is a term equally applicable to all traffickers, not a type in itself.

Source: Dorn, N., M. Levi and L. King *A Literature Review of Upper Level Drugs Trafficking*, London: Home Office, 2005, p. 9

beyond its normal usage to incorporate what are, in many cases, primarily "repressive" measures complicates this information. Such repressive measures – typically one-off police operations against criminal groups – may have a deterrent or preventative effect, but very little evidence in the course of European research, or from the general literature, has demonstrated any such effect.[11] It is noteworthy that the UK Serious Organised Crime Agency (SOCA) established in 2006 is explicitly a "harm reduction" rather than "law enforcement" body, however there remains much scope for debate about how one can rationally measure "harm." In terrorism, attacks and serious injuries/deaths may look like an obvious measure, but wider harms to communities and the sense/actuality of freedom are more subtle indices, in some ways analogous to organized crime (and crime control) harms.

In short, it remains largely a matter of faith that anti-crime and anti-terror efforts have some impact beyond the immediate operational outcomes (such as arrests, seizures of drugs, or the prevention of chemical precursors being sent to suspected outlets). Such interventions may indeed have a greater impact on reducing terrorist attacks than on limiting the more widely distributed flows of illegal and contraband goods and services which, for a significantly large part, service demands for illicit or tax-evaded products, where the window of opportunity for interventions is generally much longer than it is for measures against terrorism.[12] Both anti-crime and anti-terror prevention strategies might try to focus on potentially and actually motivated offenders, but influencing motivations – "hearts and minds" – is very difficult, even compared with the relatively difficult strategies of situational prevention, target hardening, and generating a fear of infiltration and electronic surveillance to create an incapacitation effect.[13]

Considering these limitations, it would be a major analytical mistake for crime policies to focus only on what is readily measurable; by their nature, some of the most serious and important areas of crime control present the greatest difficulties in generating satisfactory data.[14] Even in the absence of precise measures, analysts should strive for proxy indicators (or a basket of them) of whether or not a particular measure is having an effect in the direction of given strategic objectives.[15] Although networks can be analyzed with quantitative and graphic techniques, the use of solely quantitative replication-type evaluation methods on either organized crime or terrorism is both impractical and inappropriate, involving, as Pawson and Tilley have observed in a more general criminological context, "aiming an unwieldy hammer at an inappropriate sack of nuts."[16]

A number of key difficulties bedevil the measurement of organized crime reduction. These include the following:

1   Use of the nation-state as a unit of offender or victim measurement produces double counting or non-counting where crimes or components of crimes are transnational.

2   Some forms of crime are by their nature less easily counted than others.

Money laundering is an example. With money laundering in particular, multiple counting is possible and arguably legitimate as the same funds go whizzing through various jurisdictions.[17]

3 Separation of the "organized" and "unorganized" components of a particular crime type may prove very problematic. In some respects, separation is easier for crimes with specifiable victims. One might be tempted to suggest, for instance, that all cross-border car theft or fraud could reasonably be counted as organized – unplanned cross-border crime of this kind is presumably quite rare. But at current prices, any one group would have to get up to, say, 50 Mercedes or BMWs per annum to reach the turnover requirement for the former UK National Criminal Intelligence Service (NCIS) – now superseded by SOCA – classification, though not necessarily for the EU classification.[18]

4 Proxies such as drug prices are very unreliable, geographically diverse, and contestable as a measure of the effect of interventions on consensual activities, including not just drug dealing but also most trafficking in human beings – at least in the initial stage.[19]

5 Time scales over which the evaluation process should occur are far more difficult to determine than with most evaluations of efforts to counter crime for gain. This applies especially to operations that involve a build-up of intelligence with previously uncooperative (and still variably cooperative) sectors such as legal banking or formal/informal money remittance services.

6 Any attempt to measure reductions in levels of organization (as opposed to levels of crime) comes up against a host of definitional problems. Even a change from Mafia-type to large but not so monopolistic groups would not count as a reduction in organized crime by EU, Council of Europe, US, or UN definitions.[20]

Hitherto, there has been no obvious move to couch the stated aims of anti-organized crime interventions in terms of specifiable outcomes that are susceptible to some plausible form of measurement: for example, to reduce shootings in Boston, Kabul, or London; to reduce deaths from drugs; to make it harder or more expensive to launder proceeds from drug trafficking; or even to increase the sums actually confiscated or forfeited as a proportion of the sums ordered to be confiscated or forfeited.[21] The following methods might be developed to assess the impact of interventions on specific outputs and outcomes of transnational organized crimes and terrorist finance (from legal and illegal sources):

1 Evaluating the moral climate to test levels of corruption and fear (including the fear of the consequences of not "voluntarily donating" to fundraising efforts);

2 Evaluating commercial responses to regulation by "mystery shopping" to see how easy it would be to circumvent regulations that seek to

regulate organized crime, to protect consumers or the environment, or to stem the financing of terrorism;[22]

3   Evaluating law enforcement techniques such as disruption or sting operations (again, for example, by mystery shopping to see which sorts of transactions would be reported to the regulator) in order to test the operational impact of money laundering regimes;

4   Finding ways to define and measure indirect crime-reduction outcomes and activities that relate less to specific falls in crime and more to reducing the operational and innovative capacities of criminal (and terrorist) organizations or, in other words, to reducing the number of niches available for organized crime to exploit;

5   Finding ways to measure improvements in the capacity of "organized crime and terrorism reducers." This includes improved support and infrastructure for reducing organized crime, such as improvement in crime reducers' operational capacity to work through the stages of the preventive process. Where practitioners must track a constantly changing world of criminal opportunities and criminal methods and scripts, the capacity to amass, analyze, and act on feedback is particularly important. In strategic, future-oriented terms, evaluators should also measure improvements in crime reducers' innovative capacity, because crime reducers may have to out-innovate criminals for crimes to fall in a sustainable way.

6   Reducing harm – the objective of the UK Serious Organized Crime Agency – and finding methods of linking any harm reductions (or increases) to interventions or sets of interventions. To do this properly, there has to be a defensible set of predictions of counterfactuals, i.e. analyses of how crimes might have been expected to change if the measures had not been introduced – a serious empirical and intellectual challenge.

The criminological and "gray" policing literature contains very few examples of evaluated efforts to reduce organized crime or, for that matter, to reduce any sophisticated forms of crime for serious economic gain. Indeed, the most common message from the modest literature that does exist is that such reduction efforts suffer acutely from what conventional project evaluations often refer to as "implementation failure." Much of this literature simply underlines how difficult it is for authorities to act against organized crime in a cross-cutting, interagency way (though such organizational problems may vary significantly between jurisdictions and, perhaps, over time).

Even where authorities have overcome such implementation problems, evaluators have found it difficult to address issues such as "displacement," the substitution of other activities in the place of a disrupted operation, which is more likely to occur and is more difficult to measure in organized criminal groups than among more spatially bounded offenders such as auto thieves, robbers, or burglars. For example, although Levi and Handley illustrate some success in reducing plastic and check fraud through interagency cooperation in the UK and some other jurisdictions,[23] substantial subsequent rises in plastic fraud are ample reminders that at least some criminals search resource-fully for alternative means of income generation, exploit remaining loopholes more intensively, and take advantage of the growth of technological oppor-tunities (for example, by copying card numbers and using them to purchase goods over the internet as well as copying them on to counterfeit physical cards that can be used in retail outlets). This growth in criminal behavior and hard-to-control risk has led to the adoption throughout Europe since 2005 of chip cards that can only be used with personal identification numbers as well as to British card issuers' collective financing, since 2002, of the police Dedicated Cheque and Plastic Crime Unit to deal with these organized eco-nomic crime threats.[24] Most plastic and check frauds are committed for financial gain, but others – for example, some frauds by North Africans and Tamils on cards that are issued or used in the UK – are used to support terrorist activities.

One of the most profound differences between the control of organized crime and that of terrorism is that to stop terrorist finance, one must have much tighter controls than to deter organized crime. First, terrorists need and want less money than do those who seek to maximize economic gains. Second, profit-seeking criminals will usually "come around again" and their indi-vidual crimes will make little impact upon the supply of crime, making patient strategies reasonable when tracing "Mr. Big." By contrast, the aim of anti-terrorist policing is to minimize the chances and consequences of violence (at least against friendly targets) on every possible occasion, so patience is more costly because the harm is greater. However, as already noted, controls on licit sources may have displaced terrorist finance into illegal channels in the first instance. While there may be some absolute prevention of some potential terrorists, tighter controls ultimately reshape rather than resolve the issues.

Unintended consequences and the importance of broader measures

One of the lessons from the general War on Crime that might be applied to the control of terrorist finance is that devising any enforcement strategy runs a substantial risk of unintended consequences.[25] In the area of crime reduc-tion, a classic example is the stimulus President Nixon's anti-marijuana campaign provided to cocaine production in Latin America. A vigorous clampdown on remittances of expatriates in the official or informal sectors might increase both tensions with and within the recipient countries and hostility from the expatriates themselves, even if the measure did reduce the flow of funds to terrorists.[26] Likewise – and more controversially – controls over the expenditures of charities, at least other than those explicitly aimed at supporting the families of suicide bombers and other terrorists, risk a surge in popular hostility towards this policy abroad, even if they were popular (and analytically defensible according to "Western values") at home. The net gains of such measures in terrorist threat reduction are uncertain at present. Explicit public debate on the net benefits of foreign policy pragmatism concerning drugs (and, for that matter, terrorism) has been rare, but defining explicit criteria would nevertheless alter the risks and the game.

More generally, whether at home or abroad, it is often assumed that successfully disrupting organized crime groups or arresting their leaders will reduce overall levels of criminal activity, but this impact is not self-evident. There may be some types of crime that can only be committed with the involvement of organized crime groups, but other types may be committed – perhaps with less efficiency or perhaps with greater efficiency due to less bureaucracy and fewer filters on supply and controls on market entry – by individuals and groups below the modest threshold that qualifies a group as "organized crime."

Furthermore, action against dominant groups of criminals may lead to greater levels of violence, at least in the short run, as competitors seek to take advantage of an opportunity that was formerly regulated by an internal criminal market. This has often been the case with traditional terrorist groups such as the IRA and ETA, when younger radicals replace older leaders who have been killed or imprisoned (e.g. Northern Ireland internment). This is in addition to any retaliatory warfare between groups. Similarly, a larger number of small importers and distributors may move in to replace a concentrated supply of drugs and illegal migrants that has been disrupted. In fact, despite the billions spent on the War on Drugs, there has been almost no upwards pressure on prices (rather the reverse), leaving defenders of the present approach to drug control to argue that prices would have been even lower and consumption higher if controls were not in place.[27] It seems plausible that this modest impact on availability and price also holds for trafficking in people (though until recently, lack of control resources might more plausibly be used to explain it away).

If we are to predict and avoid unintended negative consequences of interventions, we have to develop a dispassionate understanding of the current and plausible positions, functions, and concentrations of different types of criminal activity within criminal (and legitimate) markets. For example, tobacco smuggling to evade excise taxes, with the tolerance if not active complicity of tobacco manufacturers, may in some ways help "the market" and not hurt the profits of the manufacturers.[28] Tobacco counterfeiting, on the other hand, is wholly harmful to corporations and to consumers, especially when the counterfeits are sold at market price, defrauding purchasers. The target of any initiative should be clearly defined: is the target the organization of a criminal activity, the amount of criminal activity, or the level of harm such activity inflicts on individuals, communities, or legitimate businesses?

These considerations are complicated by the transnational dimensions of organized crime: for example, even if the core criminal activities are local, their proceeds may be laundered internationally in jurisdictions where no identified harm is committed.[29] Disciplined targeting of organization, volume, or harm has seldom been found in Europe, at least in the early twenty-first century, and there is little evidence of it elsewhere.[30] Finally, we must learn to see and evaluate the effects of our policies through the eyes of the targeted criminal and potentially criminal audiences rather than through the eyes of policymakers, scholars, or the general public. Realpolitik can get in the way since, in addition to any intended effects on criminality, many control measures are aimed primarily at domestic audiences for political gain or for avoiding political loss.[31]

Evaluating what has been learned from anti-money laundering efforts

The global anti-money laundering (AML) regime has had an indisputable impact on both legislation and institutions, including the criminalization of money laundering activities, the regulation of financial services, and the widespread establishment of Financial Intelligence Units. Nonetheless, the effects of the AML regime on the capacity of criminals to store and move crime proceeds are open to question. Despite individual operational successes, it is difficult to demonstrate any generic reduction in criminal activities as a consequence of "following the money."[32] In practice, the success of vetting the integrity of financial services personnel and of other anti-laundering measures depends not only on the morality and financial circumstances of professionals but also on their perceptions of the risk and the consequence of detection to them personally and to their firms.[33] This in turn depends on the nature of the rules governing behavior and on the loopholes – such as reliance on the due diligence of others further up the line – that exist unintentionally or deliberately, following lobbying or even governmental complicity in reduced compliance.

Cuellar describes lobbying pressures in favor of broad, discretionary legislation that achieves political objectives while later enabling low-visibility downwards negotiation of enforcement policy and resources.[34] The implications of the Second and Third European Money Laundering Directives (2001 and 2005), which extended liability to report money laundering suspicions to accountants, lawyers, and others throughout the extended EU, have yet to work themselves through. Furthermore, later directives are on the way without always knowing or absorbing the impact lessons of earlier ones, either on levels/organization of crimes or, *a fortiori*, on terrorist finance and terrorist acts Levels of visible enforcement of these provisions – prosecutions or de-authorizations of financial and professional intermediaries accused of money laundering or failing to institute proper measures of regulation – have been far from commonplace anywhere in Europe. However, substantial regulatory fines and publicity in countries like Switzerland and the UK have become increasingly significant, serving as symbolic displays of unacceptable practices and generating reputational risk for financial intermediaries.

Here we must take into account that continental jurisdictions such as France, Germany, and Italy practice (at least in theory) the principle of legality (i.e. prosecutions must follow the determination that there is sufficient evidence to convict). By contrast, common-law countries and some civil-law countries such as the Netherlands operate on the principle of opportunity (i.e. there is discretion not to prosecute even where evidence is strong). In practice, however, this distinction may be more apparent than real, since case overloads and skill shortages within scarce resources may prevent financial investigations in legality principle countries from finding sufficient evidence to prosecute.

Australia, Canada, and the United States share a different approach: the treasury and customs departments require all financial institutions and travelers to report all cash deposits, wire transfers, and physical cash exports and imports over a legislatively set limit, which varies from $5,000 to $10,000. It is a criminal offense not to report, and the law is a regular source of prosecutions, though few cases involve "Mr. Bigs" but rather individuals more modestly involved in serious crime networks.[35] These are routine reporting systems, and the intelligence analysis has to be performed by the government agencies – AUSTRAC in Australia, FinCEN in the United States, and FINTRAC in Canada – which seek to review patterns of behavior and to link them with other databases such as those for tax information.[36] In the United States, these analyses have been supplemented by Suspicious Activity Reports (SARs), which require more subjective judgments by reporting institutions and – at least in principle – more urgent responses from law enforcement.[37]

The impact of reports such as SARs on criminal prosecutions, let alone on levels of organization or on crime, remains largely unexplored scientifically,[38] though assertions of the considerable value of reports are commonplace, and both supranational and national bodies exert legal and media pressure to enhance the number and range of reports.[39] New studies of money laundering cases in particular jurisdictions now supplement the individual cases in Financial Action Task Force (FATF), FATF-style regional bodies (FSRBs), and Egmont Group typology exercises intended to give practitioners a better idea of what to look out for.[40] Though improving, the trend analysis in these new studies, however, is primitive and does not take into account the fact that many apparent trends merely represent the product of greater awareness of longer-term patterns. Almost all of the evaluation to date has concerned itself solely with process – especially coordination between different departments, which has generally been found wanting, and with the utility of routine and suspicious activity (or transaction) reports for investigations and prosecutions, which is usually modest in relation to the number of reports made. It is important to evaluate process[41] – of course, lack of coordination and variations in organizational and unit objectives inhibit intelligence collation and operational success – but such process reviews are not the same as evaluating impacts on final objectives.

More generally, it is extremely difficult to achieve any meaningful quantitative measurement in the AML field. One objective of anti-laundering measures might be to reduce the volume of money laundered. However, there exists only the haziest, order-of-magnitude estimation of the volume of money laundering, especially at the global level. At the level of the individual nation-state, one would need to calculate the amount of money generated by and saved from the proceeds of all kinds of crime, then add to it the sums flowing through any given economy that were proceeds of crimes committed overseas. We are nowhere near being able to do that for any country in the world or even for any type of crime, whether it be "predatory" crimes with identifiable victims, like burglary, fraud, and robbery, or "service" crimes like drug trafficking and smuggling illegal migrants. The measurement efforts at the FATF have not yielded anything remotely precise, and certainly nothing with confidence intervals tight enough to be used for evaluating control attempts.[42]

If we add to these difficulties those of measuring how much of the money used to finance terrorist activities originates from legal activities upon which all tax due has been paid, then the problems intensify. There may be substantial arguments about whether money given as charity to the families of suicide bombers or to madrassas from which some terrorists graduated[43] (representing a tiny percentage of all madrassa students) properly ought to count towards this total of "terrorist finance." In short, we have no accurate before-and-after measures of the extent of money laundering in any sphere, whether broken down by type of crime, by place or method, or by organized crime group.

Under such circumstances, it is important to explore less tangible indicators such as the effects of intervention strategies on cultures, groups, and individuals, including financial services personnel. One of the key aims of interventions is to "keep the financial system clean" by increasing the difficulties and costs of laundering. Interviews with bankers and lawyers in Europe and North America in the course of various projects over the past two decades suggest that prior to these measures, bankers, especially in private international banking, saw no reason to turn down business if prospective clients were rich and had no readily known criminal records or major connections to criminal organizations. Now this is no longer true, even in the case of members of political elites, who are known as "Politically Exposed Persons." For example, some major international banks will not accept heads of state from "high risk" countries as their customers because of the political risk from exposure for money laundering. As the 2004 US Senate inquiry into the malpractices at Riggs Bank illustrates, those who do accept such clients may end up regretting it, but presumably only if the authorities both find out and take action.[44] Under the Wolfsberg agreement of November 2000, subsequently revised to take account of terrorist finance, the major international banks set global standards under which all customer identification and transactions are treated the same for anti-money laundering purposes, wherever in the world they take place. Changes have involved imposing tougher processes than required in many member states.

Some interviewees expressed skepticism about whether these changes are real or largely window dressing. Nonetheless, I would consider this alignment of procedures a best practice in organized crime and corruption prevention. Even though these standards were generated as a private sector initiative taken outside the framework of legal regulation, these changes in AML praxis have taken place under the glare of criminal liability and media publicity that create reputational risk by exposing financial institutions to public scrutiny, which should properly be viewed as an important part of the best practice requirements. In other words, when we look at the concept of best practice in this area, we should first decide what our objectives are and then review what we validly know about the political and social preconditions for success – including issues such as institutional autonomy, participation in standards development, political climate, and resources – rather than merely considering the form of the initiative that must underlie the successful implementation of "what works."

The need for impact analysis

Analysis can assist the planning of criminal justice and other responses to offenses by revealing potential weak spots in the criminal "script" (the series of actions and conditions necessary for committing the offenses in question), where interventions can reduce the opportunities and resources open to the offenders and increase the risks they face. While this approach needs to be developed to support analysis at more strategic levels of serious crimes for economic, ideological, political, or religious gain – criminal niches, markets, careers of organizations, etc. – it holds potential in encouraging a sharp focus on key factors in the generation of crime problems.

Developing the capacity of groups pursuing crime and terrorism reduction is a reasonable intermediate goal. Otherwise, at the cost of innovation, one would fund only those few activities that have an immediate behavioral impact on current and potential offenders. However, measures of capacity should not be used as proxies for operational success. One can make sensible "soft" inferences – for example, concerning enhanced anti-money laundering measures – but should exercise caution in so doing. Bolstering intelligence and operational effectiveness, even long-term, is nowhere near the same as reducing the level of undesired behavior, unless the combined motivation and opportunity to commit particular sorts of crimes is quite rare. Given budgetary constraints, capacitation must be linked to demonstrable consequences, though not necessarily on the basis of evidence that can be presented directly to the general public.

In short, despite all the legislative efforts aimed at combating organized crime and money laundering during the 1990s, there have been no major research studies in any key areas that conform to the normal canons of evaluation espoused by, for example, the research arm of the British Home Office or the Campbell Collaboration (though in my view, those particular standards represent an inappropriate hurdle for these forms of criminality).[45] As in law enforcement generally, operational success has typically been measured by the activity indicators of number and quality of arrests and the number of organizations disrupted,[46] perhaps supplemented by large headline figures such as funds seized and accounts frozen in different countries.[47] The lack of systematic before-and-after or comparison-based studies makes it hard to conclude – or even to plausibly expect – that there has been much impact on organized crime levels, however measured.

A review of organized crime reduction best practice for the UK Home Office and European Commission regretfully concluded that only in the area of payment card fraud did sufficiently good data exist to enable a rigorous assessment of the impact being made by law enforcement.[48] Complex strategies in both the fields of counter-terrorism and counter-organized crime need to be evaluated in light of how well particular initiatives further policy objectives. If links between measures and desired outcomes are dubious, then claims that policies are evidence-influenced, let alone evidence-led, are nonsense. Such policies are merely faith-based or reflections of other interests, such as those of the (economic) military–industrial complex or the (understandable) political need to be seen doing something. Reassurance policing and anxiety-enhancing ("awareness raising") media strategies are not the same as crime or risk reduction.

Understanding the financial needs of organized crime and terrorist groups

The amount of money individual criminals and criminal or terrorist networks or organizations "need" depends on a number of factors:

1 Initial capital and human resource assets (including sympathizers);
2 Marginal income (from criminal and legal sources);[49]
3 Fixed and marginal "business costs";
4 "Lifestyle maintenance" costs;[50] and
5 Planned and unplanned longevity of operations and living expenses.

The purposes of an organization whether they are capital accumulation or having fun, religious or explicitly political are unimportant to this model unless they are reflected in the above criteria. However, as with legitimate corporations, the reputation of criminal and political organizations may be important to their community credibility and fundraising capacities.[51] This is one reason for the efforts that go into presentation and propaganda. Genuinely humble and religious (Islamic or non-Islamic) or communist terrorists will need fewer lifestyle expenses unless they are required to maintain a particular cover. But some may be in denial or may be hypocrites, and therefore spend money in ways inconsistent with their professed ideologies.

Reducing the number of state financial sponsors of terrorism including those that also produce illegal drugs can reasonably be expected to make international terrorism harder. However, business costs depend on which operations are planned over what period, on the scale of personnel and weaponry needed, on recruitment costs (which can include ideological indoctrination and team-building, and sometimes long-term financial support for families), and on the competence and corruptibility of the preventative and enforcement forces ranged against the group, all of which vary by type of crime as well as by location. We must be careful that competence of enforcement does not become a tautology ("if they continue, it must be that we are incompetent") or a mere platitude. Potential terrorists and donors may prefer legal-source income, which carries fewer risks from enforcement and, on occasion, provides a legitimate rationale for activities that might otherwise look suspicious. But in some contexts, legal income can shade into extortion (acknowledged or not), where pressure that goes beyond community sentiment and stigma is exerted on existing and potential "donors." This is true of national and transnational organized crime and terrorist networks alike.[52]

The common logic in the shape of the delivery process of many forms of serious crime is as follows:

1   Obtain finance for crime;
2   Find people willing to commit crimes (though finding others may not always be necessary except to the legal definition of transnational organized crime);
3   Obtain equipment and transportation necessary to commit the crimes;
4   Convert, where necessary, products of crime into money or other usable assets;
5   Find people and places willing to store proceeds (and perhaps to transmit and conceal their origin); and
6   Neutralize law enforcement by technical skill, by corruption, or by legal arbitrage, using legal obstacles to enforcement operations and prosecutions that vary between states.

Applying lessons from AML to countering terrorist financing

It is trite to dismiss the value of AML measures to countering terrorist financing by referencing the low operational costs of the Balinese, Kenyan, Spanish, Tanzanian, Turkish, UK, and US bombings. The costs of financing terrorism against hard targets[53] can be much higher, and financing recruitment and the disappearance and reappearance of members of the group and their transportation over long distances to and from secure locations can be very expensive. Particularly in the early stages of a group or network's life cycle, it is clearly an advantage to have access to significant funds, and it is now known fairly well how this was achieved in the case of al Qaeda.[54] If the IRA had not had access to such generous funding from US sympathizers via Noraid, largely without interference from the US Government and judiciary, it is hard to believe that they could have sustained their activities in Ireland and on the British mainland for so long – even despite the widespread crime that they (and Protestant paramilitaries) engaged in and continue to engage in, including armed robbery, counterfeiting, drug trafficking, extortion (e.g. over gaming machines and taxi cabs), fuel oil smuggling, and bankruptcy and tax frauds.[55] Likewise, irrespective of events in Israel and Iraq, if militants had not had such generous funding from the West in Afghanistan and in similar struggles against communism or, in the Islamic case, funds from Saudi Arabia (and elsewhere in the Middle East) and logistical support from Pakistan, then the scale of terrorist jihadism might well have been different. However, we are where we are now, not where we might have been had those factors not occurred and had measures against terrorist and potential terrorist finance been introduced earlier. (Of course, introducing intervention measures earlier would have required more foresight and less tolerance of the risk that those who are presently "our guys" might become "bad guys" in the future than is plausible in the real world. In any case, informal sponsorship carries the risk that proxies will begin "freelancing" and will turn their newfound capacities against their sponsors.)

The international transfer of funds through informal remittance systems challenges both AML policymakers and those concerned with targeting terrorist finances. In the particular case of financial measures against terrorism, the attempt to restrict repatriated funds may generate resentments not normally found in the struggle against organized crime.[56] Poor, primarily Islamic countries are especially dependent on repatriated funds from overseas earnings of expatriate workers. The regulation of money transmission services has at best driven up the price of money transfers. A possible exception is the "light touch" UK regulatory regime that requires underground bankers as well as bureaux de change to register. This system imposes fewer costs or bureaucratic inconveniences. However, it also generates fewer obligations on money transmission businesses and therefore makes it harder to prove that a trader has committed an offense.

Computerized AML software creates particular difficulties. Apart from the automated checking of multiple lists (where name spellings themselves generate many false positives and opportunities for evasion through slight spelling changes), there are no clear models available to predict which funds are likely to be used for criminal or terrorist purposes and which are not. Despite efforts to counter terrorist financing (and their own strategic interest in doing so to protect their own and their customers' assets against the economic consequences of terrorism), international banks have experienced unintended, negative consequences of well-meaning acts such as Executive Order 13338 – Blocking Property of Certain Persons and Prohibiting the Export of Certain Goods to Syria. In this case, foreign banks do not experience the direct application of the executive order, but their associated US banks or corporate enterprises (and US citizens) do, and it becomes legally and politically risky for international banks not to apply the ban worldwide. However, with many exports to Syria going through the Central Bank of Syria, upon which there are European government guarantees, the net effect of stopping trading with Syria is to enable the Central Bank of Syria to claim on those guarantees, generating a large cash gain which could be used to finance terrorism (though the Syrian state already has sufficient resources to finance terrorism if it wishes to do so).

Lessons from fighting terrorism also apply to efforts against organized crime. Containment models of terrorism reduction are as appropriate for the containment of the harmful consequences of organized crime, and both contexts require flexible, responsive, multi-pronged methods. What does it take to have an asset forfeiture system that generates more funds lost to crime than do most current ones? It takes a good piece of legislation, good leadership in organizations with asset forfeiture responsibilities, a good strategy and focus, and a good team of investigators and prosecutors.[57] However, the further effects of taking more money from criminals (or of freezing potential terrorist finances to inhibit their use) remain uncertain. We must also consider in this context the impact of financial intelligence and investigation on the connections between potential offenders and sympathizers who have much to lose from official sanctions, and the social benefits from satisfying the public that those responsible for terrorist outrages have been caught: here the lack of open-source research into investigation outputs does not permit validated claims either of effectiveness or of ineffectiveness. It would be difficult to generate an evaluation that would satisfy skeptics without producing serious counter-intelligence risks.

Conclusion

The application of lessons from the control of transnational organized crime to the control of the financing of terror has proved to be a difficult task, especially when warfare is as asymmetric as the recent "Islamic terrorism" has been. When approaching either organized crime or terrorism, we need to spend our time not only on fine-tuning legislation, but also on understanding the cultural, organizational, structural, and human relations issues that need attention in order to make criminal or terrorist control systems more efficient and effective. Some inroads were made against the financing of the IRA and Protestant paramilitaries by reducing their criminal opportunities, but their needs for arms as well as explosives were substantial, and many "soldiers" with little legitimate income had to be supported over lengthy periods of time.

In the wider sphere of the financing of extremist religious, hate, political or animal rights groups that advocate the use of violence in particular contexts, reductions in funding may have an impact on the broader conditions that increase the pool of potential terrorists: one example would be the deregistration or official listing of self-proclaimed charities that incite intolerant versions of Islam or are specifically dedicated to supporting financially the families of "martyrs." However, in the narrower tactical sphere of financing smaller "non-spectaculars," suicide bombers have fewer long-term needs and it is not reliably known how far their willingness to die would be reduced if their families had less financial support.[58] It should be self-evident that restricting terrorist finances limits the scale of damage that terrorist groups can generate. Nevertheless, the immediate financial needs of many terrorist operations are so modest that it would be very difficult to restrict their criminal opportunities to such a limiting extent (e.g. ten average size credit card frauds would have been sufficient to finance the Madrid bombings; the London bombings cost significantly less),[59] though forcing would-be terrorists into crime commission might enhance their risks of discovery. However, in neither transnational organized crime nor terrorism is it conceivable that monitoring and criminal and civil justice methods alone will eliminate risks. It would be a serious error to believe or pretend otherwise.

Terrorist groups can finance activities in a number of ways, including the following:

1   Distribute funds from a central point, though this means exposure of the "bankers" via regular contacts, making them vulnerable to the exposure of any one contact;
2   Receive start-up finance, following which they are expected to fend for themselves; or
3   Function like a web without a central point, but with connections to some external and otherwise independent groups.

Bell argues that while cash forfeiture at entry and exit points may be worthwhile as a disruptive strategy, "it has little long-term value unless the cash can be tracked back to its origin and becomes useful in detecting a terrorist funding source and those who rely upon it."[60] Freezing the funds of named individuals and other entities alone can generate, once and for all, deprivations of funds, and it may not matter in incapacitation terms whether or not the funds are finally confiscated or forfeited, but this strategy cannot readily apply to assets held by others. The UK Asset Recovery Agency and Irish Criminal Assets Bureau can use their powers to tax funds from an unknown source in a targeted way against suspected terrorist fund-raisers.[61] Other countries' taxation or civil investigation authorities may do likewise and, if the funds have not been declared on tax returns already due, penalties can be imposed leading to the forfeiture of almost the entire sums. (Once taxed, the remaining sum is thereby legitimized and laundered, though this does not grant the beneficial owners or intermediaries relief from any criminal charges that might otherwise be brought for involvement in crimes.)

The difficulty of demonstrating impact is not a recipe for inaction, either operationally or analytically. Sophisticated work needs to be done to measure impacts both on organized crime and terrorist finance.[62] In both cases, these measures will probably have to form part of a basket of measures including precursor chemicals (conventional and nuclear), weaponry, and the decline of net impact attacks. As with crime reduction measures generally, part of the danger lies in the overselling of predicted impact in order to get the "juice" deemed politically necessary for control measures to be passed,[63] which can generate cynicism at a later date. Indeed, whatever is done about organized crime and terrorism prevention, there will be some who argue that the reduction is not real because the threat was less than was asserted to begin with: true or false, this is a significant difficulty for governments whose publics are distrustful. There is currently immense goodwill from most of the international banking community over efforts to combat the financing of terror,[64] that risks dissipation as disillusionment in many countries with the impact of Suspicious Activity Reports (SARs) kicks in. The national and global management of AML and asset freezing and forfeiture/recovery regimes has proven to be a difficult though dynamic process, whose impact on levels and organization of crime remains to be reviewed more fully than has occurred to date.

In reality, the best that can probably be achieved by "follow-the-money" methods in countering terrorist finance is some intelligence that allows for interventions to make arrests, permit physical observations, and prevent particular individuals and groups from obtaining the funds for particular projects beyond the trivial amounts needed for suicide bombings at the local level – or make them run higher risks in the search for funding. At some stage, we might benefit from greater clarity in our assessment of the utility of financial intelligence. At least currently, financial records are most likely to be useful in connecting up relationships after the fact that otherwise might not emerge or be denied: this may have implications for the time over which records should be kept. It is uncertain whether such records (and SARs) can ever produce little enough "noise" to be useful to detecting and preventing future terrorist acts other than in the case of nominal "hits." Past and potential sources of major finance may also be deterred from funding larger attacks and/or larger numbers of attacks by fear of publicity and by financial and penal sanctions. This gives countering terrorist finance a more modest place in the panoply of counter-terrorist controls than some might assert or wish, but sober assessment may be better than faith.

Alternatively, if we adopt a broader construct of the financing of terror, a much more ambitious program of cutting off all funds that might support "anti-Western" (i.e. anti-consumer capitalist) activities would involve a serious attack upon the funding of churches, mosques, synagogues and sects that encourage violence. This would provoke a serious conflict with some Islamic countries (and Islamic and non-Islamic "extremist" groups within the West) and is beyond current political doctrine: given oil-dependence and the vast sums invested by Saudi Arabia, for example, in the West, it would involve major systemic risks for the world economy.

The implications of these conclusions for resource allocation for terrorist finance are more difficult to assess. The methodology by which one might work out the optimal level of expenditure and powers in combating serious crimes for gain and terrorism, within the constraints of scarce social resources overall, is too heavy a task for this chapter and for the current knowledge of this author. That is a job for politicians. It is hoped that this review will assist them and citizens in making and judging these difficult decisions. What is clear is that the role of financial intelligence and financial investigation goes well beyond the issue of getting more Suspicious Activity Reports or freezing the accounts of designated persons. How far one wants to extend it depends on whether one sees the boundaries of the subject as being the tactical one of making it more difficult for would-be terrorists to get hold of the materiel they want to kill or injure citizens, or the strategic/geopolitical one of preventing the encouragement of "violent extremism." There will undoubtedly be no easy consensus on what behavior, emanating from which countries, falls into the latter category.

Notes

1 L. W. Sherman, D. Gottfredson, D. MacKenzie, J. Eck, P. Reuter, and S. Bushway, *Preventing Crime: What Works, What Doesn't, What's Promising*, Washington, DC: National Institute of Justice, grant no. 96MUMU0019, 1997.
2 L. W. Sherman, D. P. Farrington, B. C. Welsh, and D. L. MacKenzie, *Evidence-Based Crime Prevention*, London: Routledge, 2002; J. Q. Wilson and J. Petersilia, *Crime*, San Francisco: ICS Press, 1995; R. MacCoun and P. Reuter, *Drug War Heresies: Learning from Other Vices, Times and Places*, New York: Cambridge University Press, 2001; P. Reuter and A. Stevens, *An Analysis of UK Drug Policy*, London: The Stationery Office, April 2007. Online. Available HTTP: <http://www.ukdpc.org.uk/docs/UKDPC%20drug%20policy%20review.pdf> (accessed 25 April 2007). Drug issues – for some purposes a sub-set of organized crime – do receive some attention in both sets of works. Sherman et al. acknowledged that at that time there had been no adequate impact evaluation on drug enforcement either. (Though see MacCoun and Reuter, *Drug War Heresies*, for some acute analysis of drug enforcement.) Neither work mentions terrorism or any other transnational issues. Even before the 11 September and subsequent attacks that have scarred the Western (particularly American) psyche and generated so much collateral damage, the perception that organized crime and terrorism were less amenable to the statistical experimental manipulations and replication methods advanced in those texts may have been a factor (though there is plenty of war gaming potential in both). However, given that both Sherman and Reuter had previously done important work on corruption and the organization of illicit markets, the apparent placement of white-collar and organized crime in the "too difficult" pile is all the more intriguing, perhaps because neither variety of crime lends itself to the easy definitions and less difficult (for Congress) politics of the subjects Sherman and Reuter did tackle. Given the subsequent Enron and Wall Street scandals, some of them linked to money laundering for crimes elsewhere, perhaps this inattention to the problems business poses for crime is unfortunate.
3 Some paramilitary-style organizations such as the IRA or UVF might have sought to do so in parts of Ireland, at least while they still had illicit political rather than criminal ambitions. They aimed partly to legitimate themselves in the local

community as more effective controllers of household and street crimes committed by wild youths than could the official police, while benefiting from the crimes
for gain they commit and from "taxing" the crimes of others against "permissible
targets." There is a tension between the financial needs of "the organization", the
persons working for themselves as well as it, and the need not to alienate community support (whose own values may shift over time, for example over crimes
against business). It is one thing to make money from selling decent quality
counterfeits on street markets or from robberies of unpopular firms; it is another
to sell drugs in the community or to cause such a high rate of crime against
business that there are no local services and less employment. In the latter cases,
people may remain silent out of fear, but this drains positive support for the
group.

4   Though as Caulkins, Kleiman, and Reuter note, terrorist networks and organiza-
tions have less incentive to inform for competitive benefit than do drug networks.
J. Caulkins, M. Kleiman, and P. Reuter, "Lessons of the 'War' on Drugs for the
'War' on Terrorism" in A. Howitt and R. Pangi (eds.) *Preparing for Domestic
Terrorism*, Cambridge: MIT Press, 2003.

5   As in the phrase that a group was "al Qaeda-inspired" rather than being part of
"al Qaeda." The epistemology of how we would rationally decide how to allocate
these terms to particular circumstances lies outside the scope of this essay.

6   It would be wrong to argue that governments are not actually seeking to reduce
terrorism against their citizens, but it would also be naïve to ignore the importance of political (with a large or small "p") considerations in front of domestic
audiences as determinants of crime control policies in any system: the question is
whether evidence-based or even evidence-inspired models have any real impact on
anti-organized crime and anti-terrorist finance policy-making and, if so, under
what conditions. One of the advantages of the "war" metaphor is to generate
greater "fishing" powers for financial information as well as to excuse errors and
abuses. Cuellar (*Tenuous Relationship*) suggests that bureaucratic and political
advantage may be the main policy aims, and the avoidance of being labeled "soft
on crime" certainly is a key factor molding responses to all crimes, especially
including terrorism. However, the amount of space for alternative perspectives
can differ over time and between countries, though the development of the European Union's Freedom, Security and Justice remit plus groupthink produces more
centripetal force for commonality than would otherwise have occurred between
what are now the 27 countries of the EU. This requires more elaborate policy
analysis than was possible in van Duyne and Levi (*Drugs and Money*), which
sacrificed the complex reality of the interests involved in policy-making in favor
of a slightly misleading clarity. See also Elvins (*Anti-Drug Policies*) for a good
insight into the EU, though EU–US as well as internal EU crime and security
policy-making has altered substantially since 11 September. M. F. Cuellar, "The
Tenuous Relationship Between the Fight Against Money Laundering and the
Disruption of Criminal Finance," *Journal of Criminal Law and Criminology*, Win-
ter/Spring 2003, vol. 93 nos 2–3, pp. 311–466; P. C. van Duyne and M. Levi, *Drugs
and Money: Managing the Drugs Trade and Crime-Money in Europe*, London:
Routledge, 2005; M. Elvins, *Anti-Drug Policies of the European Union*, London:
Palgrave Macmillan, 2003.

7   N. Dorn, M. Levi, and L. King, *Literature Review on Upper Level Drug Trafficking*, Home Office RDS On-Line Reports 22/05, 24 February 2005, p. 9.

8   For a discussion of some of these issues in an American context, see National
Research Council, *Transnational Organized Crime: Summary of a Workshop*,
Washington, DC: National Research Council, 1999. In Europe, especially Belgium, the Netherlands, Sweden and the UK, there is greater interest in critical
analysis of patterns of criminal organization. See, for a general review, M. Levi,

"Organised Crime and Terrorism", in M. Maguire, R. Morgan and R. Reiner (eds.) *The Oxford Handbook of Criminology*, 4th edn, Oxford: Oxford University Press, 2007.

9 There is a lack of consistency in the application of concepts such as "disruptions" of operations and, especially, of organizations: the closer we move towards network analysis and away from "criminal organizations," the more difficult it is to audit such claims. We must question what it is that one is disrupting, for how long, and the proportion of the market that is thus affected, especially given the time lag and the existence of stocks (rather than just flows) of drugs, weapons, illegal migrants, etc. Some factors may be researchable – e.g. the flows of "new girls" in the sex industry – but others are more difficult to track.

10 Outputs may include high-profile raids and arrests, irrespective of whether this leads to any subsequent criminal justice action.

11 For a review, see M. Levi and M. Maguire, "Reducing and Preventing Organized Crime: an Evidence-Based Approach," *Crime, Law and Social Change*, June 2004, vol. 41, no. 5, pp. 397–469.

12 Moreover, it may well be the case that suppliers of illegal goods and services will come round again, whereas this might not be the case for "front line" terrorists, especially (obviously) suicide bombers.

13 There are similarities in the difficulties of infiltrating ethnic minorities for transnational organized crime and terrorism.

14 A criticism often made of police performance measures developed, for example, by the UK Home Office Police Standards Unit, though there are some signs of an appreciation of the need to shift towards qualitative measures. An unintended consequence of this is to prioritize short-term over longer-term strategic approaches.

15 This is true *a fortiori* where the serious harm is not demonstrably present: it is an ambitious task indeed to estimate or measure the reduction in a hypothetical future level and form of criminal organization.

16 R. Pawson and N. Tilley, "Caring Communities, Paradigm Polemics, Design Debates," *Evaluation*, 1998, vol. 4, no. 1, pp. 73–90.

17 From the viewpoint of the joint and several jurisdictions, it makes perfect sense to discuss the flows entering and leaving each and to try to review the amount of laundering that goes on in each jurisdiction, consisting of proceeds of crimes "earned" there plus funds laundered from crimes elsewhere. What we must then avoid doing is adding up all these jurisdiction-based data separately as if they were a global total of "proceeds of crime," because that would involve double counting and would lead to an exaggerated "dirty money" total. As Reuter and Truman (*Chasing Dirty Money*) and Levi and Reuter ("Money Laundering") note, even for drug expenditures, financial data are poor outside the United States. As UK studies by Gold and Levi (*Money-Laundering in the UK*), Levi and Osofsky ("Investigating, Seizing and Confiscating"), and Dorn, Levi, and King (*Literature Review*) observe, we know far too little about the savings ratios of serious offenders to produce accurate data about how much of their criminal income they launder. P. Reuter and E. Truman, *Chasing Dirty Money*, Washington, DC: Institute for International Economics, 2004; M. Levi and P. Reuter, "Money Laundering" in M. Tonry (ed.) *Crime and Justice: A Review of Research*, vol. 34, Chicago, IL: Chicago University Press, 2006, pp. 289–375; M. Gold and M. Levi, *Money-Laundering in the UK: an Appraisal of Suspicion-Based Reporting*, London: Police Foundation, 1994; M. Levi and L. Osofsky, "Investigating, Seizing and Confiscating the Proceeds of Crime," in B. Webb (ed.) *Police Research Group Crime Detection and Prevention Series: Paper No. 61*, London: Home Office Police Department, 1995; Dorn et al., *Literature Review*.

18 If a group split up its operations so that fewer than 50 car thefts happened in

each country, and if there were no intelligence collation across the different EU member states, then in practice this group might not be defined as "organized crime."

19 This is plainly a major area of controversy, but there is little *a priori* reason to believe that, other than political asylum-seekers, many illegal migrants, even sex workers, are other than voluntary economic migrants, though they are commonly mistreated and exploited when they reach their destinations (both in terms of local standards and – arguably to a far lesser extent – standards in their home countries). Aside from this economic issue, an unreliably known but probably large percentage of sex workers was not told that sex work would be their income source when they were trafficked out. One has to ask whether the supply of willing economic emigrants – even sex workers – would be so large if families back home seldom heard from emigrants again or seldom received repatriated funds (often from informal value transfers, aka underground banking) as a return on their investments.

20 Partly for this reason, counting the number of organized crime groups – a difficult task in itself (Gregory, "Classify, Report and Measure") since it is unclear how many network members reasonably should be counted in one or more particular groups – does not seem illuminating unless one knows what proportion of the varied criminal markets the groups account for. More criminal organizations could be a positive rather than a negative sign if it indicates less concentrated social and economic power. Other questions relate to the need to establish a way to evaluate "success" using business measures such as turnover, profit, growth, and investment. F. Gregory, "Classify, Report and Measure: the UK Organised Crime Notification Scheme," in A. Edwards and P. Gill (eds.) *Transnational Organized Crime: Perspectives on Global Security*, London: Routledge, 2003. "The most directive positive effect of the change to Europol's mandate is that it is no longer bound to the restriction that an organised criminal structure must be involved before Europol can act." See Commission of the European Communities, "Commission Staff Working Document Accompanying the Proposal for a Council Decision establishing the European Police Office (EUROPOL) Impact Assessment" {COM(2006) 817 final}{SEC(2006) 1683}, Brussels: Commission of the European Communities, 20 December 2006. Online. Available HTTP: <http://ec.europa.eu/dgs/justice_home/doc/sec_2006_1682_en.pdf> (accessed 25 April 2007).

21 In most countries outside the United States, amounts of money or substitute assets ordered to be given to the state after criminal proceedings are termed "confiscations," forfeitures relating to the instrumentalities of crime or sometimes to moneys seized by customs officers and taken away by administrative procedures. In the United States, the generic term "forfeitures" typically is used both for instrumentalities of crime and for proceeds. This, not surprisingly, is the source of much confusion. See also Reuter and Truman, *Chasing Dirty Money*.

22 It would be a serious mistake to assume that regulations that have an impact on organized crime are intended primarily for that purpose. It is desirable to review the positive and negative impact a variety of regulations have on crime opportunities. For a review of the analytical and practical possibilities of such anticipatory crime cost-benefit analysis on behalf of the European Commission, see double thematic issue on Proofing EU Legislation against Crime, *European Journal on Criminal Policy and Research*, December 2006, vol. 12, nos. 3–4.

23 M. Levi and J. Handley, *The Prevention of Plastic and Cheque Fraud Revisited*, London: Home Office Research Study 182, 1998; M. Levi, *The Prevention of Plastic and Cheque Fraud: a Briefing Paper*, London: Home Office, 2000.

24 US card issuers are not currently planning to implement these measures, which may increase their liability to fraud, especially overseas where merchants will still

be obliged to accept US magnetic stripe cards, creating for criminals opportunities and incentives that are denied to them on, say, European-issued cards.

25 One should not abandon the attempt to regulate simply because there are some negative consequences, intended or unintended: the issue is whether the *net* effect is positive or negative compared with the alternative(s). For a more general discussion of counterproductive crime prevention and regulation, see P. N. Grabosky, "Counterproductive Regulation," *International Journal of the Sociology of Law*, December 1995, vol. 23, pp. 347–369; and P. N. Grabosky, "Unintended Consequences of Crime Prevention," in R. Homel (ed.) *The Politics and Practice of Situational Crime Prevention*, Mounsey, NY: Criminal Justice Press, 1996.

26 The importance of "hearts and minds" in reducing terrorism is a contentious issue, since it is the hinterland of support services rather than "hardened" core terrorists that are likely to be affected thereby.

27 This is subject to the continued illegality of drug use. Excluding general cultural sympathizers, the rates of active terrorism are far lower than the rates of active drug-taking. See Reuter and Stevens, *An Analysis of UK Drug Policy*; MacCoun and Reuter, *Drug War Heresies*; and R. MacCoun and P. Reuter, "The Varieties of Drug Control at the Dawn of the Twenty-First Century," *The Annals of the American Academy of Political and Social Science*, July 2002, vol. 582, pp. 7–19.

28 If customs authorities are unable to get taxes either out of the genuine products or counterfeits, then manufacturer complicity is arguably tax-neutral, whatever this says about the morality of the suppliers.

29 In reality, even where financial intermediaries (e.g. bankers) in other jurisdictions are aware that funds come from crimes elsewhere, few feel sufficient empathy to treat such conduct as seriously as proceeds of domestic crimes, whether they are Caribbean bankers laundering the proceeds of US drugs sales or American and European bankers laundering the proceeds of transnational bribery. As regards the formal sector, my interviews suggest that in those cases where they suspect specific criminal acts or purposes, bankers and other intermediaries are more likely to appreciate the importance of helping the fight against terrorism than the fight against drugs or other crimes, except perhaps for the fight against banking frauds.

30 Levi and Maguire, "Reducing and Preventing Organised Crime." This is not to deny that there have been periods of Italian history when severe measures have been directed against "the Mafia."

31 This applies to the War on Terror as well as the War on Organized Crime or on Drugs. The audience-directed nature of public statements is a constant problem for those who interpret politicians' and others' public statements as a reflection of their aims. Some might argue that actual effects on criminality are irrelevant to politicians and even law enforcement agencies, but though this may sometimes be true, it is not a position adopted here.

32 Gold and Levi, *Money-Laundering in the UK*; W. Wechsler, "Follow the Money," *Foreign Affairs*, July/August 2001, vol. 80, no. 4, pp. 40–57.

33 There is evidence, though of a rather anecdotal character, that professionals as well as businesspeople are more willing to engage in criminal behavior if faced with failure of their livelihoods (M. Levi, *The Phantom Capitalists*, 2nd edn., Aldershot: Ashgate, forthcoming; M. Sutton, *Handling Stolen Goods and Theft: a Market Reduction Approach*, Home Office Research Study 178, London: Home Office, 1998; S. Simpson, *Corporate Crime, Law and Social Control*, Cambridge: Cambridge University Press, 2002; D. Middleton and M. Levi, "The Role of Solicitors in Facilitating 'Organized Crime': Situational Crime Opportunities and Their Regulation," *Crime, Law and Social Change*, 2005, vol. 42 nos 2–3, pp. 123–161). Most of this evidence relates to individuals and small firms, but it is plausible that it applies to larger companies and to financial institutions such as banks. It

also might be encouraged by the growing role of performance-related bonuses and short-term employment, which combined form a disincentive for honesty and for rejecting potentially suspicious customers. In complex organizations, however, there may be checks and electronic controls on employee deviance, at least where the values of the organization are opposed to it.

34 Cuellar, "Tenuous Relationship."

35 Mark Motivans notes that between 1994 and 2001 "about 18,500 defendants were charged in US district court with money laundering as any charge" with sentences for those convicted averaging four years. Moreover, in 2001, "the 22 commercial defendants charged with money laundering included auto dealerships, grocery stores, banks, furniture stores, construction firms, and beauty shops. They represented a small fraction of money laundering defendants." M. Motivans, "Money Laundering Offenders, 1994–2001," Bureau of Justice Statistics, 2003. Online. Available HTTP: <www.ojp.usdoj.gov/bjs/abstract/mlo01.htm> (accessed 3 October 2005).

36 The role of tax collection in the background to money laundering is much disputed. In Canada, for example, FINTRAC can disclose where there are "reasonable grounds to suspect the information would be relevant to the investigation of money laundering, the financing of terrorism or a threat to the security of Canada." For FINTRAC to disclose on a tax-related matter, it is required to meet a double threshold: the above as well as reasonable grounds for pertinent offenses under relevant tax legislation. The legislated requirement for a double threshold makes it clear from a policy and operational standpoint that tax issues are a distant secondary focus, at least in the Canadian context. By contrast, though they receive far fewer reports, the UK tax and social security authorities can plug into suspicious transaction reports.

37 See *FinCEN's 314(a) Fact Sheet*, US Treasury, 26 October 2004, 15 March 2005; FinCEN *Annual Report 2004*, US Treasury, 2005.

38 For exceptions, see P. C. van Duyne and H. de Miranda, "The Emperor's Clothes of Disclosure: Hot Money and Suspect Disclosures," *Crime, Law and Social Change*, September 1999, vol. 31, no. 3, pp. 245–271; M. Fleming, *UK Law Enforcement Agency Use and Management of Suspicious Activity Reports: Towards Determining the Value of the Regime*, 2005. Online. Available HTTP: http:// www.jdi.ucl.ac.uk/downloads/publications/research_reports/Fleming_LEA_Use_ and_Mgmt_of_SARs_June2005.pdf (accessed 10 April 2007).; GAO, "Investigating Money Laundering and Terrorist Financing: Federal Law Enforcement Agencies Face Continuing Coordination Challenges," 11 May testimony to the House of Representatives, Washington, DC: General Accounting Office, GAO–04–710T, 2004; Gold and Levi, *Money-Laundering*; and KPMG, *Money Laundering: Review of the Reporting System*, London: KPMG, 2003; Cuellar, "Tenuous Relationship."

39 Hitherto, the pressure on the inter-bank transfer system SWIFT to mandate the completion of the originating account details in every electronic transfer has not been successful, but it is not known what the effects on laundering capacities of such a change would be. Plainly, apart from pure prevention and deflection, the impact of money laundering reporting depends on enforcement follow-up of those reports, and there are no systems of which our survey has been made aware that measure enforcement inputs in a realistic way and relate them either to outputs or to outcomes. For example, sensitizing talks to the private sector aimed at reminding them of their responsibilities and training them in how to spot some forms of money laundering may raise the level of reports – an intermediate efficiency measure – and even make it impossible for some criminals to launder the proceeds of some crimes altogether. However, to contrast two countries with a relatively low and a relatively high reporting rate, Switzerland and the UK or Netherlands, it is arguable that the Swiss do more with their reports both in efficiency and in

effectiveness terms. The temptation to use high suspicious transaction reporting rates as a performance indicator should be resisted unless it is accompanied by some further justification for improved effects.

40 For example, see S. Schneider, *Money Laundering in Canada: an Analysis of RCMP Cases*, Toronto: Nathanson Center, 2004.

41 For a good example of a process review, see S. Lander, *Review of Suspicious Activity Reports Regime*, London: The Stationery Office, March 2006. Online. Available HTTP: <http://www.soca.gov.uk/downloads/SOCAtheSARsReview_FINAL_Web.pdf> (accessed 25 April 2007).

42 P. Reuter, "Assessing Alternative Methodologies for Estimating Revenues from Illicit Drugs," unpublished paper, 2000; Levi and Reuter, "Money Laundering: A Review of Current Controls and their Consequences"; J. Walker, *Estimates of the Extent of Money Laundering in and through Australia*, Queanbeyan, NSW: AUS-TRAC/J. Walker Consulting Services, 1995; J. Walker, "Introduction," *International Journal of Comparative Criminology*, 2001, vol. 1, no. 2, pp. 1–7. Indeed, to the extent that a literal reading of the laundering legislation would include not just money but also property conversion and concealment, it is hard to know how one might precisely work out the laundering parameters.

43 But almost none of those involved to date in suicide bombings in the West.

44 US Senate Minority Staff of the Permanent Subcommittee on Investigations, *Money Laundering and Foreign Corruption: Enforcement and Effectiveness of the Patriot Act. Case Study Involving Riggs Bank*, Washington, DC, 15 July 2004. There are, however, major difficulties in identifying their associates and even some family members, despite the availability, for a fee, of well-researched, competitive, private-sector databases such as Factiva, Momenta Compliance Services, World-Check, and World Compliance that review such relationships. Riggs Bank was only one of a long chain of banks that have accepted money – invariably, they claim, unknowingly – from corrupt Politically Exposed Persons or from other sorts of criminals.

45 Home Office Crime Reduction College, *Passport to Evaluation*, London: Home Office, 2002. See also K. Pease, "Crime Prevention," in M. Maguire, R. Morgan, and R. Reiner (eds.) *The Oxford Handbook of Criminology*, 3rd edn, Oxford: Clarendon Press, 2002; and The Campbell Collaboration. Online. Available HTTP: <http://www.campbellcollaboration.org> (accessed 16 September 2005). The latter aims to sustain a concept of "valid science" by only accepting those studies that meet the sampling and replication standards of medical trials: quite apart from other criticisms, this has the unintended effect of marginalizing any studies in the area of organized, terrorist, and white-collar crimes, since they are not amenable to such experimental techniques.

46 NCS, *National Crime Squad: Corporate Plan 2002–2005*, London: National Crime Squad, 2002; Department of Justice, *FY 2002 Performance Report/FY 2003 Revised Final Performance Plan/FY 2004 Performance Plan*, Washington, DC: Department of Justice, 2003. The UK Serious and Organised Crime Agency (which commenced operations 2006) and the Home Office are seeking to develop more sophisticated performance criteria, but this is a far from easy task. SOCA's Annual Plan states (pp. 8–9):

> The Home Secretary's letter sets out more immediate ways to assess progress. In the order in which they should appear as SOCA develops, they are:
>
> - growth in SOCA's own capacity to make a difference, with particular focus on the quality of understanding of organised crime;
> - performance against asset recovery targets; and

- evidence of dislocation of criminal markets, including evidence that criminal groups are finding the UK a less attractive market;

and then goes on to set out the criteria in more (but not unambiguous) detail. See United Kingdom Serious Organised Crime Agency (SOCA), *Annual Plan 2007/08*, London: The Stationery Office, 2007. Online. Available HTTP: http:// www.soca.gov.uk/assessPublications/downloads/SOCAAnnualPlan2007_8.pdf (accessed 25 April 2007).

47 As Levi and Osofsky (1995), the PIU (*Recovering the Proceeds of Crime*), Assets Recovery Agency (*Annual Report 2005–2006*), and National Audit Office (*The Assets Recovery Agency*) reports indicate, the subsequent confiscations tend to be much smaller, though the attrition between seizure and actual confiscation may be less in the UK than in many parts of continental Europe, where assets are frozen automatically for a short period following the making of a suspicious transaction report (see Kilchling, "Die Praxis der Gewinnabschöpfung"; Vettori, *Tough on Criminal Wealth*). This is a large issue in Australia also (see Freiberg and Fox, "Evaluating the Effectiveness of Australia's Confiscation Laws").

> Levi and Osofsky, "Investigating, Seizing and Confiscating"; PIU, *Recovering the Proceeds of Crime*, London: Performance and Innovation Unit, Cabinet Office, 2000; M. Kilchling, "Die Praxis der Gewinnabschöpfung in Europa," *Kriminologische Forschungsberichte aus dem Max-Planck-Institut für ausländisches und internationales Strafrecht*, vol. 99, Freiburg in Breisgau: Max Planck, 2002; United Kingdom Assets Recovery Agency *Annual Report 2005–06*, London: The Stationery Office, June 2006. Online. Available HTTP: <http://www.assetsrecovery.gov.uk/NR/rdonlyres/8D8413B8-B0FE-4A9F-AA02-2E2A9771A809/0/ARAAnnualReport06_new.pdf> (accessed 25 April 2007); B. Vettori, *Tough on Criminal Wealth: Exploring the Practice of Proceeds from Crime Confiscation in the EU*, Dordrecht, Netherlands: Kluwer, 2006; United Kingdom National Audit Office, *The Assets Recovery Agency*, London: The Stationery Office, February 2007. Online. Available HTTP: http://www.nao.org.uk/publications/nao_reports/ 06–07/0607253.pdf (accessed 25 April 2007); A. Freiberg and R. Fox, "Evaluating the Effectiveness of Australia's Confiscation Laws," *Australia and New Zealand Journal of Criminology*, 2000, vol. 33, no. 3, pp. 239–265.

48 Levi and Maguire, "Reducing and Preventing Organized Crime."

49 Though an otherwise legal source can be made into a criminal source by banning the purpose or cause for which it is collected or transmitted. Compare the non-criminalization of Noraid (for the Republican cause in Northern Ireland) with the ready criminalization of funds for Islamic charities deemed (on only partly justiciable evidence and intelligence) to support terrorist organizations. This does not resolve issues of "primary purpose" nor does it determine what proportion of the funds are required to go to terrorist purposes before the organization is deemed a terrorist organization.

50 Some poor terrorists in the Third World may be motivated by the wish to generate economic benefits to their families via post-suicide bomb charitable support. However, this is unlikely to be common in all countries where terrorism occurs, and Gunning in Chapter 5, critically analyzes such claims in publications available at the time of writing. Quite apart from issue of principle to Islamic charities, the empirical issue of how much terrorism would be reduced if subsequent support for families were cut off remains a topic of contention.

51 Though not always in the manner intended by the Great Powers. What constitutes a good reputation in the eyes of the Great Powers (e.g. moderation and active hostility to the use of terror by rebel groups) may make them unattractive to

potential donors or sympathizers in their own reference group on the grounds that they are "compromised."

52 Of course, it is part of ideological campaigns to represent donations as either extortion or voluntary gifts, and it may not be easy for outsiders or even, sometimes, the terrorists themselves, to judge.

53 A term that must be identified independent of whether or not an attack was successful, if it is not to be tautological.

54 J. Roth, D. Greenberg, and S. Wille, *Monograph on Terrorist Financing* (Staff Report to the Commission), National Commission on Terrorist Attacks Upon the United States, 2004. Online. Available HTTP: <http://www.9–11commission. gov/staff_statements/911_TerrFin_Monograph.pdf#search=%229%2F11%20 commission%20monograph%22>; Council for Foreign Relations, *Terrorist Finance: Report of an Independent Task Force Sponsored by the Council on Foreign Relations*, Washington, DC: Council for Foreign Relations, 2002; Council for Foreign Relations, *Update on the Global Campaign against Terrorist Financing: Second Report of an Independent Task Force Sponsored by the Council on Foreign Relations*, Washington, DC: Council for Foreign Relations, 2004; GAO, "Investigating Money Laundering."

55 The transformation (especially post-conflict) of ideological terrorist groups into criminal racketeers for gain, and the impact of strategies to combat this, lies outside the scope of this review. See Independent Monitoring Commission, *Third Report*, HC1218, London: The Stationery Office, 2004 and bi-annually through Independent Monitoring Commission, *Fourteenth Report*, London: The Stationery Office, 12 March 2007. Online. Available HTTP: http:// www.independentmonitoringcommission.org/documents/uploads/14th_IM-C_Report.pdf (accessed 25 April 2007); Northern Ireland Affairs Committee, *The Financing of Terrorism in Northern Ireland*, Fourth Report of Session 2001–02, HC978–1, London: The Stationery Office, 2002; Northern Ireland Affairs Committee, *The Impact in Northern Ireland of Cross-Border Road Fuel Price Differentials: Three Years On*, First Report of Session 2002–03, HC 105–1, London: The Stationery Office, 2002; Northern Ireland Office, *Government Response to Goldstock Report*, Belfast: Northern Ireland Office, 2004; Northern Ireland Task Force, *Threat Assessment 2003: Serious and Organised Crime in Northern Ireland*, Belfast: Northern Ireland Office, 2004 (and annually thereafter).

56 In the UK and some other jurisdictions, rigid customer identification requirements generate substantial resentment, not just among international businesspeople but among the elderly, married women whose accounts for proof of identity may be held solely in the name of their husband, and other segments of the population that attract sympathy in the popular press. This has led to some discussion in regulatory circles of trying to get the financial institutions to adopt a more context-sensitive approach, which is anyway more consistent with the notion that "Know Your Customer" is an ongoing risk-based process. The principle of this is now accepted by the Financial Services Authority and the UK Treasury, though risk-based approaches to terrorist finance remain problematic to formulate and assess.

57 For some excellent insights into knowledge management in proceeds of crime and organized crime reduction, see E. Bell, "Knowledge Management in the Proceeds of Crime Community," *Journal of Financial Crime*, 2001, vol. 8 no. 3, pp. 207–217; and E. Bell, "Sex Trafficking: a Financial Crime Perspective," *Journal of Financial Crime*, 2001, vol. 9, no. 2, pp. 165–178.

58 Doubtless the existence of welfare for the families of suicide bombers makes them more comfortable in their choice of action, but such welfare may not be a necessary condition for terrorism.

59 The London bombings cost less than $2,500 according to law enforcement

estimates. However, though the origins of the funds are unknown, the fact that one bomber who worked in a fish and chip shop reportedly left over $210,000 net (at historic conversion rates) in his estate suggests that more spectaculars could have been afforded. See Sophie Goodchild, "The Mystery of the London Bomber and his Secret Wealth" *The Independent*, 8 January 2006. Online. Available HTTP: http://news.independent.co.uk/uk/crime/article337244.ece (accessed 10 April 2007). This might raise the question of why those funds were not passed on to fund further terrorism if the bomber knew he was going to die.

60 E. Bell, "The Confiscation, Forfeiture and Disruption of Terrorist Finances," *Journal of Money Laundering Control*, 2003, vol. 7, no. 2, p. 114.

61 Independent Monitoring Commission, *Third Report*, Northern Ireland Office, *Government Response to Goldstock*.

62 Some such work on organized crime harm measurement is being undertaken by and on behalf of the UK Home Office.

63 There are, of course, bigger issues that relate to the cultures of response to threats. See W. Rees and R. Aldrich, "Contending Cultures of Counterterrorism: Transatlantic Divergence or Convergence?" *International Affairs*, 2005, vol. 81, no. 5, p. 905.

64 With the exception, it may be argued, of some banks that are highly dependent on the Saudis or other "extreme" versions of Islam, which may be ambiguous in their views about controlling proselytizing funds that might fall within the broader category of financing the motivations for terror, in particular the Caliphate.

13 Conclusion

Taking stock of efforts to counter the financing of terrorism and recommendations for the way forward

Thomas J. Biersteker and
Sue E. Eckert

In the more than five years since the attacks of 11 September, much has been said and written about progress in the so-called "war on terrorism." Bush Administration officials cite substantial progress in degrading the al Qaeda network, including killing or capturing most of those responsible for the 11 September attacks. Some Administration officials assert that the absence of terrorist attacks within the United States since 2001 is evidence of success, with the war in Iraq as "in part responsible" for the lack of further attacks.[1] Beyond the military interventions in Iraq and Afghanistan, however, disrupting financial support for terrorism has been a central and highly touted indicator of progress in the "war on terrorism."

> Before 9/11, financiers of terrorism and terrorist financing networks went untouched and largely ignored by the international community. Today, we continue the aggressive worldwide campaign to disrupt terrorist financing, making it harder, costlier, and riskier for al-Qaida and other terrorist groups to raise and move money around the world. . . . Over 400 individuals and entities have been designated under the President's Executive Order . . . effectively blocking their assets and isolating them from the US financial system.[2]

Many independent assessments of US counter-terrorism efforts since 11 September reaffirm the importance, and at least partial effectiveness, of initiatives to target terrorist funds. In noting progress in the designation of terrorist financiers and organizations, the 9/11 Commission recommended that tracking terrorist financing remain front and center in US counter-terrorism efforts (but acknowledged that such efforts are not the primary weapon).[3] The 9/11 Commission's *Monograph on Terrorist Financing* (the "Monograph") further noted:

> While definitive intelligence is lacking, these efforts have had a significant impact on al Qaeda's ability to raise and move funds, on the willingness

of donors to give money indiscriminately, and on the international community's understanding of and sensitivity to the issue. . . . While a perfect end state – the total elimination of money flowing to al Qaeda – is virtually impossible, current government efforts to raise the costs and risks of gathering and moving money are necessary to limit al Qaeda's ability to plan and mount significant mass casualty attacks. We should understand, however, that success in these efforts will not of itself immunize us from future terrorist attacks.[4]

Many contend that the intelligence gathered from financial information has proven to be of great assistance in understanding and disrupting terrorist networks and operations. As former congressman and vice chair of the 9/11 Commission Lee Hamilton summarized:

> The original idea behind tracking and blocking terrorist funding was to starve the beast, and the Treasury Department did develop some very sophisticated tools to identify terrorist funding streams – so much so that they came to see the intelligence gathered in the process as the greatest value.[5]

Financial intelligence is more reliable than other forms of intelligence, and US officials responsible for implementing measures to counter the financing of terrorism contend that although the public only sees the lists of formal designations and total amounts frozen, the intelligence gathered from following the money is often of far-reaching significance. As a result, the 9/11 Public Discourse Project which tracked implementation of the 9/11 Commission's recommendations, has assigned a grade of A– to US Government efforts to combat terrorist financing.[6]

Even a communication among al Qaeda's leadership appears to support the contention that at least some funding has been disrupted. According to a letter between Ayman al-Zawahiri and Abu Musab al-Zarqawi, dated 9 July 2005 (released by the Office of the Director of National Intelligence on 11 October 2005), "many of the lines [of financial support] have been cut off. Because of this, we need a payment while new lines are opened."[7]

Yet, other assessments have not been as favorable, especially concerning the implementation of US Government programs to counter the financing of terrorism (CFT). The General Accountability Office has issued several critical reports, noting that the US does not systematically collect and analyze data on alternative financing mechanisms, that interagency turf battles and lack of cooperation have hindered the effectiveness of enforcement efforts, and well as the provision of technical assistance to other countries, and that the Treasury Department's annual reporting of terrorist assets blocked does not provide sufficient information to assess the Office of Foreign Assets Control's (OFAC) progress.[8] Such reports have provided fodder for political criticism of the Bush Administration CFT efforts that has resulted in the introduction of legislation to end turf wars and to improve the efficiency of US efforts to assist other countries in countering terrorist financing.[9]

Other critiques disparage terrorist financing efforts as part of the broader US "war on terrorism" and the "exaggeration, misinformation, and disinformation that has propelled the effort." Thomas Naylor, in particular, has challenged the existence of "billions of Islamic terrorist dollars" as a fabrication of the US Government and suggested that the counter-terrorist financing effort is not only ineffective, but has converted the world's banking infrastructure into "a global espionage apparatus."[10]

Notwithstanding these critical assessments, there appears to be a fairly broad-based consensus that terrorist financing efforts have worked to some degree, at least relative to other counter-terrorism policies, although not without some real costs. Is this general consensus warranted? What have we learned in the preceding chapters about al Qaeda, the changing nature of terrorist financing, and the effectiveness (or ineffectiveness) of efforts to counter terrorist financing to date?

The changing nature of al Qaeda's structure and financing and the need for an adaptive regulatory response

As Rohan Gunaratna pointed out in Chapter 3, the al Qaeda of today is profoundly different from the organization that engineered the attacks on 11 September. He presents a history of the different organizational forms of al Qaeda, from its formation and emergence as a hierarchical organization, its break-up into a confederation of allied organizations, and its subsequent transformation into a more general jihadi movement. The remnants of the original al Qaeda organization have been more significant as an ideological vanguard, a source of legitimization and justification for acts of global terrorism, than as a source of the planning, detailed direction, financing, and execution of terrorist attacks, but some contend this may be changing.[11] The attacks on the transportation systems of Madrid in 2004 and London in 2005 do not appear to have been directed centrally by Osama bin Laden and his associates hidden in the mountains of Pakistan or Afghanistan, but the attacks were both motivated and subsequently legitimized by al Qaeda. The relationship between the original al Qaeda organization and the attackers in Madrid and London appears to have been a symbiotic one, a relationship between a vanguard and its networked affiliates in a broader and more diffuse jihadi movement. While al Qaeda experienced a resurgence as a territorially based force in Afghanistan in 2007, it appears that many of its affiliates still operate under the banner of al Qaeda in Iraq and northern Africa but are not centrally directed by al Qaeda.[12]

Jessica Stern and Amit Modi argue in Chapter 2 that organizational structure has significant consequences not only for command, control, and mission, but also for the financing of acts of terrorism. To be successful, an effective and surviving terrorist organization needs to be able to change its structure, its message, and even its demands. As al Qaeda has changed over the past 15 years, it has also changed its financing. The mujahideen's anti-Soviet effort in Afghanistan, out of which al Qaeda was formed, financed itself from a variety of sources – charitable giving, direct solicitations, and state support – all with the tacit and direct support of major states (including the United States). After the end of the Afghan conflict in the early 1990s, bin Laden and his associates adapted their strategy to a more diversified set of sources, continuing many of the previous sources (with the important exception of US Government financial and logistical support) and adding legitimate and illegitimate business activities. With its move from the Sudan to Afghanistan in 1996, al Qaeda developed a mutually advantageous relationship with a state sponsor, this time with the Taliban regime. According to Douglas Farah in Chapter 9, following the freezing of its holdings in US formal sector financial institutions after the embassy bombings in 1998, it began to engage in gemstones trade and to operate on the margins of the legitimate world economy.

The information that has emerged to date on the financing of terrorist attacks – from the 2004 Madrid bombings discussed by Phil Williams in Chapter 6 and the 2005 London attacks – suggests that they were financed largely from criminal activities conducted exclusively (at least in the case of the Madrid bombings) within a single state. Formal sector transactions and even the transnational movement of funds are apparently far less significant today than they were in 2001. One way to interpret this development is to credit some success to the extensive international effort to counter the formal sector financing of terrorism globally discussed in Chapter 11.

The jihadi movement of today, a movement that is more inspired by than directed by al Qaeda, is most likely to be self-financed from criminal activities. This is why it is important to better understand some of the mechanisms of trade diversion described by Donald deKieffer in Chapter 7, and the emergence of transactions and tacit alliances with transnational criminal organizations, as discussed by Phil Williams in Chapter 6. There is a great deal for terrorist organizations to learn from the operations of criminal organizations, as Williams points out, particularly as they have moved increasingly into the area of illicit transactions for most of their core financing. He illustrates an example of institutional morphing – a topic also explored by Stern and Modi in Chapter 2 – when he describes how criminal organizations can become terrorist organizations and vice versa. There is much to be learned from previous efforts to combat transnational organized crime, as Michael Levi points out in Chapter 12.

This analysis of the changing structure and financing of al Qaeda is significant, because any effective counter-terrorism strategy must take these changes into consideration. Strategies for countering the financing of terrorism must similarly adapt. As we noted in the introduction and is elaborated

upon in Chapter 10, the initial response to countering the financing of terrorism following the attacks of 11 September was to seize upon existing institutional mechanisms and take policies "off the shelf," some of which had
been pending for years. This is a natural tendency, and it achieved some
concrete results, as the focus on improvements in the regulation and control
of formal sector financial institutions has shown. However, problems with
US designations made in the immediate aftermath of 11 September, in particular, have complicated the use of the financial sanctions instrument, as
discussed in Chapters 10 and 11.

Financial controls and the regulation of formal sector financial institutions
alone is far from sufficient, however, in the broader effort to counter the
financing of terrorism. Much greater attention needs to be paid to multilateral coordination of intelligence and global cooperation to thwart criminal
activities. The threat from al Qaeda is increasingly a criminal one and a
challenge to effective international law enforcement. The problem is that even
(or especially) in the European Union, while the threat is transnational,
the response remains largely contained within individual nation-states.
Al Qaeda has learned to adapt, to transform itself in creative ways, and to
take advantage of globalization in ways that state-sponsored defenses have
not even begun to consider. No state, even the most powerful, can deal with
the transnational threat of terrorism by relying on national means alone.

While there is a compelling need for policy adaptation and innovation,
there is also a need to contain policy over-reaction and regulatory over-reach.
As many of the chapters included in this volume indicate, there remains a
paucity of reliable information about the financing of terrorism. Ignorance
of informal value transfer mechanisms or of the legitimate operations of
the Islamic banking system can lead to sensationalized characterizations and
ill-conceived policy proposals for sweeping regulation that will ultimately do
more harm than good. This is most apparent in the area of informal value
transfer systems (IVTS), as Nikos Passas and Samuel Maimbo argue in
Chapter 8. While the Monograph identified the use of *hawala* for the transfer
of some funds prior to the attacks of 11 September, the overwhelming majority of informal value transfers are perfectly legitimate and IVTS perform an
important social and global developmental role. Inappropriate regulation
resulting in crude attempts to control IVTS could lead to significant
unintended consequences, as we learned from the experience with al Barakaat
in Somalia (see Box 8.1).

Jeroen Gunning in Chapter 5 makes a similar point in his analysis of the
role of charitable giving among the Muslim diaspora communities in contemporary Europe. In the wake of the "home-bred" attacks on the London
underground system in July 2005, this is an extremely important and sensitive
issue, yet Gunning finds little evidence that either charitable giving or the
diversion of funds from charitable organizations is a principal source of
support for contemporary terrorism. While charitable organizations proved
important sources of financial support in the past – especially during the

mujahideen phase of the Afghan struggle and following the departure of the Soviets from Afghanistan – there is little evidence that they are still performing that function to a significant degree. Like IVTS, the overwhelming majority of charitable giving is perfectly legitimate and performs important social and global developmental functions. A move to over-regulate charities could lead to counterproductive results and exacerbate resentment globally.

These general points about the dangers of over-regulation are reinforced in Chapter 10 by Sue Eckert, who argues that important limits exist on the degree to which any regulatory system can cope with excessive amounts of non-essential information. The US experience following the passage of the Patriot Act is illustrative in this regard. The significantly increased volume of suspicious transactions reports, of which few are related to terrorist financing, dilutes and degrades the value of the information provided to regulatory authorities. Processing information is far more important than simply accumulating it, and it is important that regulation be prudently designed with this in mind.

In the final analysis, it is critical to adapt the regulatory response to the real, constantly changing, and most current threats of terrorist financing. Military planners are famous for preparing for the last war, and it is important that those concerned with countering the financing of terrorism not make the same mistake. Al Qaeda has changed. The nature of its fundraising has changed. The ways in which it moves, stores, and uses funds have changed. The significance of transnational movements of funds has apparently diminished (at least for the scale of the operations undertaken in 2004 and 2005). At least this much we know. It is important that CFT efforts proceed from this knowledge, rather than waste resources on countering threats of the past.

Assessing costs and benefits

Ultimately, the assessment of the effectiveness of national and global efforts to counter the financing of terrorism depends on the nature of the threat (the assessment of risk) and on the appropriateness of the response to that threat (i.e. that the benefits of the policy response outweigh the costs of the measures enacted). With regard to the assessment of risk, there is a broad-based consensus in Part I that although al Qaeda is still a threat, it is not the same as it was before 11 September. More recently, a growing literature has emerged that varyingly discusses whether the threat from al Qaeda has been exaggerated,[13] how al Qaeda might end,[14] or whether it is time to declare victory in the war against terrorism and simply move on.[15]

When it comes to an assessment of the benefits and costs of current efforts to counter the financing of global terrorism, there is good evidence to suggest that it is more difficult for terrorists and their key supporters to use the formal financial sector to support their operations today than it was in 2001. Formal financial sector channels for committing acts of terrorism have been effectively closed down for those individuals and corporate entities identified on the lists used by the UN and by national financial regulatory authorities. The capacity of groups to commit acts of terrorism has been degraded – both Madrid and London were financed by extremely modest amounts from petty crime, without trans-border movements of funds. Financial intelligence gathering and analytical capacity appear to have improved globally (at least as indicated by the number of financial intelligence units created since 11 September), and there is evidence to suggest the importance of financial intelligence in tracing the structure and networks of existing terrorist organizations.[16] The ability to reconstruct networks after an attack is an important element of counter-terrorism efforts generally.

Additionally, there are positive institutional externalities associated with the regulatory effort to counter terrorist financing. Although the details vary according to the issue area, the institutional infrastructure established to address terrorist financing (including the use of lists, the creation of financial intelligence units, informing financial institutions of their obligations to block selected transfers, and the creation of new norms that financial institutions should know their customers and report suspicious transactions) could be used for other regulatory efforts. They are useful in initiatives aimed at money laundering, combating transnational criminal organizations, blocking the inappropriate appropriation of public funds for private purposes by corrupt officials (or politically exposed persons), implementing multilateral UN targeted financial sanctions (as in the cases of North Korea and Iran), and even curtailing tax evasion (if the political will existed to make use of the financial infrastructure for these purposes).

At the same time, these benefits do not come without some real costs. They result in increased costs for financial institutions as considered in Chapter 10, many of whom have introduced name recognition software to detect suspicious transactions and developed new internal procedures to know their customers and to train their staff to block or freeze individual transactions. Fears that there would be a decline in charitable contributions to Muslim charities have been realized, at least in the United States,[17] which could have important implications for efforts to address the root causes of terrorism. As we have argued elsewhere, targeted financial sanctions are not as targeted as they might initially appear, and as we saw in the case of al Barakaat, the collateral damage of freezing the assets of the broad group of companies led to severe disruption of fund transfers to a large proportion of the Somali population.[18] There are also significant consequences for individual rights, again as we have written about more extensively elsewhere,[19] concerns that could potentially lead to a reluctance on the part of individual governments to participate in the global effort to maintain the freeze on the assets of listed individuals and groups or to add new names to the lists. These human rights and due process concerns could ultimately undercut state-to-state cooperation on intelligence sharing and other counter-terrorism issues.

On balance, we contend that while the risk remains, the benefits of the regulatory response generally appear at this point to exceed the costs. That is not to suggest, however, that "staying the course" of current policy is an appropriate or effective strategy, particularly given the changing and adapting nature of al Qaeda. Therefore, we conclude with the following policy recommendations.

Recommendations

Keep CFT initiatives in perspective

While CFT initiatives are an important element of a larger counter-terrorism strategy, they are but one of several policies that need to be undertaken in combination to counter global terrorism. As important as the financial component is, intelligence sharing, law enforcement, effective global communication to illustrate the consequences of acts of terrorism, and occasional military intervention will remain primary means of countering terrorism in the near term. Indeed, existing CFT policies, had they been in place and implemented fully on a global scale, would not have prevented the attacks of 11 September. As Levi argues in Chapter 12, this renders the countering of terrorist financing a more modest place in the panoply of counter-terrorist measures. CFT initiatives taken alone will neither stop terrorism, nor even entirely cut off the flow of funds to terrorists, and exaggerated statements (such as "starving the terrorists of funding") ultimately raise expectations about the effort and weaken the tools of assets freezes and designations more generally.

Initiatives to cut off funding of terrorism need to be undertaken in conjunction with enhanced international cooperation and information sharing on intelligence, greater police and judicial cooperation globally, selective military intervention to disrupt known sanctuaries (such as in the case of Afghanistan), more effective communications efforts to counter al Qaeda's messages "in serious ways,"[20] and efforts to address the root causes of terrorism, including both military occupation[21] and the continuing conflicts in the contemporary Middle East, particularly the Israeli–Palestinian conflict. Given that acts of terrorism tend to be committed by actors whose channels of effective political participation are cut off,[22] exploring ways to bring disaffected groups back into legitimate political processes and split them off from al Qaeda should be supported. Ultimately, the development of a global norm against the commitment of acts of terrorism (through the UN General Assembly, among other venues, including the NGO sector) will be necessary to rid the world of acts of terrorism.

Differentiate among groups using terrorism

Beyond considering CFT as just one element of a broader, comprehensive counter-terrorism strategy, it is also important that CFT initiatives distinguish between (and differentiate among) groups committing acts of terrorism. Those acting transnationally on a global scale, like al Qaeda and its affiliates, have different needs, bases, and means of financing themselves, particularly when they are compared to a group acting on a local or sub-national scale. The latter sometimes has access to fixed territorial space from which it can extract resources in ways that approximate a state (i.e. from tariffs or from quasi-taxes on the population). They are also more prone to engage in kidnappings and extortion as means to finance their activities. There are fundamental differences in the goals, the scope of operations, and the ultimate objectives of groups acting globally and groups acting locally or largely contained within a defined territorial space. Extending existing CFT efforts aimed at al Qaeda and its affiliates to every global conflict where acts of terrorism take place not only diffuses the effort, but also ultimately decreases its effectiveness. As James Fallows, drawing on David Kilcullen's widely circulated paper in the *Journal of Strategic Studies*, argued in September 2006: "Western countries should do everything possible to treat terrorist groups individually, rather than 'lumping together all terrorism, all rogue or failed states, and all strategic competitors who might potentially oppose US objectives.' "[23]

Different groups committing acts of terrorism have different means to finance their activities, and these differences need to be taken into consideration when designing a strategy to counter their activities. One size does not fit all.

Drop the "war" metaphor

Finally, it is time to stop using the "war" metaphor and turn the focus to enhanced intelligence sharing and increased police cooperation globally. While it may be useful politically for leaders to characterize the global effort against terrorism as a "war" in an effort to mobilize a population, it is misleading in several respects. First, it inherently privileges military responses and the use of force. As we have argued elsewhere in this volume, military intervention can be an appropriate response in instances where states provide sanctuary to groups committing acts of terrorism in other territories, but it should be considered as only one aspect of a larger, comprehensive strategy and should be used only in exceptional circumstances. Second, the war metaphor legitimizes exceptional measures, such as the suspension of rights, measures that may prove to be unwarranted, given the nature of the threat posed by terrorism. A temporary suspension of rights can be legitimated in exceptional circumstances, but the so-called "war on terrorism" is open-ended. We have no idea how and when it will ever end, and hence a temporary suspension of rights can become, in effect, permanent. Characterizing the effort against al Qaeda as a "war" legitimizes the jihadi movement and ironically works to their advantage in the global competition of ideas by implying their equivalence as adversary. Given the transformation in the nature of al Qaeda, it would be far better for the US to join the rest of the world and begin emphasizing the need for enhanced intelligence sharing and increased police and judicial cooperation, rather than trying to lead a global "war" effort. A global networked threat requires a global networked response.

Undertake a comprehensive assessment of CFT initiatives

To be effective, CFT policies must be recalibrated constantly, especially in light of the adaptive nature of terrorists. The response to terrorist financing has not changed fundamentally since 11 September, nor has there been any comprehensive effort to reassess the policy. The primary focus on the formal financial sector continues, notwithstanding the fact that terrorists have turned to criminal methods and cash smuggling as major methods of raising and moving money. With more than five years of experience, it is time to evaluate critically the results of multilateral CFT policies to date. A comprehensive review should include an assessment of

- the appropriateness of the formal sector focus,
- specific methods terrorists use to finance themselves (cash, trade-based money laundering, shell companies, charitable diversion),
- the continued utility of asset freezes,
- obstacles to private sector compliance and government implementation,
- terrorist financing prosecutions,
- the adequacy of existing CFT institutional mechanisms,
- implementation of CFT standards such as the FATF 40 + 9 recommendations and the UN Convention on the Suppression on the Financing of Terrorism, and
- potential alternatives to achieve CFT objectives.

In addition to these general policy recommendations, we highlight specific recommendations to counter the financing of terrorism, based on the analysis and suggestions of our contributing authors.

Charities

Traditionally, al Qaeda and other groups have utilized charities, NGOs, and mosques to raise funds through direct solicitations and diversion of donations intended for humanitarian purposes. While the risk of abuse of the charitable sector remains real, a differentiated approach, distinguishing between financing humanitarian networks affiliated with resistance groups and financing of terrorism, is needed. Blanket condemnation of groups providing social welfare services alienates Muslim constituencies and prevents aid from reaching those most in need. It also complicates diplomacy, especially the case in the Israeli–Palestinian conflict. Government efforts should focus on assisting charities to be more transparent, clarifying what constitutes financing of terrorism and association, designating independent bodies to regulate and investigate charities, and accrediting charities or developing indicators of trust/approval so that contributors know the group can be trusted to deliver support to appropriate projects.

Zakat contributions are central to the practice of Islam, and a policy that places charitable giving to Islamic organizations under general suspicion contributes to a perception that the effort is directed against the entire Muslim community, rather than a very small segment of that community. Not only is this profoundly unfair, but it will ultimately undercut the effectiveness of other counter-terrorism efforts. Special effort must be taken to reaffirm support for charitable giving through transparent processes.

Informal transfers

Regulation of remittance vehicles is necessary, but should be done in a way that is proportionate to risk and appropriate to particular socio-economic environments. In countries where informal systems exist alongside a well-functioning conventional banking sector, *hawala* or other informal value transfer systems (IVTS) should be registered and required to keep adequate records. In states at risk of institutional collapse or states without functioning formal sector banking systems, requirements beyond registration may not be feasible. Governments should conduct outreach efforts to consult, engage, and build consensus among IVTS operators with regard to the most appropriate measures. Positive incentives should be created for participants in the sector to enhance record-keeping and implement regulatory frameworks. In this regard, greater emphasis should be placed on the traceability of transactions, rather than centralization of data, and measures should be sufficiently flexible so as not to drive IVTS underground.

Trade diversion

With the significant and ever-increasing volume of trade flows, the international trade system is increasingly vulnerable to abuse by terrorists, as well as other criminals, through false invoicing and the use of commodities to move funds, yet relatively little attention has been focused on this mechanism. Governments need to focus more on trade diversion, both to understand better the threat posed by lack of trade transparency and the techniques used, as well as specific efforts to anticipate, detect, and thwart attempts by terrorist groups or their supporters to take advantage of this mechanism. Governments should create trade transparency units to analyze, share, and track international trade data to identify anomalies. Greater cooperation with the private sector victimized by diversion schemes should be explored, and enhanced priority placed on interagency cooperation and prosecution of trade diversion cases.

Commodities

While experts disagree on the extent to which al Qaeda actually utilized commodities such as diamonds to finance operations or move funds before 11 September, it is indisputable that, as with trade diversion, commodities represent a potential vehicle for the financing of terrorism, especially in resource-rich but failing states with weak governance and rampant corruption. Governments should enhance their intelligence-gathering capabilities, particularly financial intelligence capabilities in such states where illicit trade flourishes, devote additional resources to understanding commodity networks, and work with the commodity industries (especially gemstones) and NGOs to share information.

Regulatory measures

Clearer regulatory guidance is needed for the formal financial sector, especially concerning reporting requirements and compliance measures. However, a one-size regulatory policy approach does not fit all sectors, and a tailored approach is necessary for the informal MSB sector. For CFT efforts to be effective, an enhanced partnership between the private sector and government is necessary, and new ways of sharing information and creating incentives for cooperation, such as streamlined reporting should be explored.

Key CFT regulatory tools such as designations and asset freezes must be based on reliable information with appropriate standards of evidence that can be shared and sustained multilaterally. The damage in terms of credibility and multilateral cooperation resulting from the politicization of the designations process in the US has weakened this powerful but essential CFT instrument.

International initiatives

Capacity-building training should be enhanced and efforts undertaken to reinforce the political will to ensure that parallel implementation of CFT measures takes place across national jurisdictions. Rather than simply assessing the presence or absence of legal and regulatory mechanisms, making greater use of the FATF to evaluate implementation and enforcement of national CFT measures could be desirable. It is also important that human rights concerns are addressed through reform of listing and de-listing procedures at the UN and in other institutional settings (the EU and the US Government). Manageable reforms, such as those outlined in *Strengthening Targeted Sanctions through Fair and Clear Procedures*,[24] would accomplish this goal for most constituencies and address a current vulnerability of the financial sanctions instrument. Unless this issue is addressed, several states have indicated that they are reluctant to forward names for designation, and others may have legal difficulties in implementing existing measures.

Finally, efforts should be made to strengthen multilateral coordination among the many international and regional groups involved with counter-terrorism, including cooperation among UN committees dealing with terrorism-related issues.

Future research

Despite what we have learned from our colleagues in this volume, there is still a great deal we do not know about the magnitude and different mechanisms of charities diversion, the use of informal value transfer systems, trade diversion and commodities, and about cash smuggling. Notwithstanding our general knowledge about the broad changes that have taken place in the financing of terrorism, it is humbling to conclude with the admission of how little we know, more than five years after 11 September, about the financing of individual acts of terrorism. As Lee Hamilton notes, "despite all of our sophistication, we have neither starved the beast nor produced very good intelligence on how exactly these organizations continue to finance themselves."[25] There is an urgent need for the further empirical research in this area and the creation of an archive and database of information for subsequent analysis.

As we indicated in the Preface, there is a tendency in much of the first generation of literature about terrorist financing to make broad and sweeping generalizations about the phenomenon from a relatively limited database (either a case study of a group or single illustration of the novel use of a particular financial instrument to support an act of terrorism). This is common during the early stages of research and understanding about any new phenomenon, but it needs to be complemented by a more mature phase of research that differentiates among groups engaged in committing acts of terrorism and begins to identify patterns of change within them over time.

Finally, we need a better understanding of the effectiveness and costs of regulation, considering how "moral panics" can develop at times of perceived crisis and the ways these panics can produce counter-productive or excessive regulatory efforts with unintended consequences. It is important to explore how the effort to find and destroy funding networks in the formal financial sector are forcing groups into riskier conduits such as cash smuggling and crime – the displacement effect – as well as whether this will make it easier or more difficult to detect and control their activities. Realizing that it is impossible to determine with precision the effectiveness of CFT initiatives using quantifiable measures, there is still a need to improve our understanding of the effects of such efforts. It is also important to assess the relative merits of different institutional forms for managing the global counter-terrorist financing effort, from reliance on formal UN agencies to a more informal set of initiatives led by the FATF, regional organizations, and self-regulating groups of financial institutions.

Conclusion

In the final analysis, our goal in this book has been to convene some of the finest minds working on terrorist financing, develop an analytical framework, and identify the most important trends concerning terrorist financing and the global regulatory effort to counter it. We have concluded that the social organization of groups engaged in committing acts of terrorism has profound implications for aspects of their activities, including the financing of terrorism, and that individual groups change over time, in response to regulatory efforts to counter them. There has been an impressive global effort to regulate the trans-border movement of funds through formal sector financial institutions, but groups using terrorism have adapted to this regulatory effort and moved to various forms of crime to continue their activities. This creates ever more difficult regulatory challenges and the potential pitfalls of over-regulation and other negative externalities. For this reason alone, countering of the financing of terrorism needs to be considered within a broader framework of an integrated counter-terrorism strategy that has as its ultimate goal the creation of a global norm against the commitment of all acts of terrorism.

Notes

1 See R. Cheney, "Interview of the Vice President by Sean Hannity," 15 June 2006. Online. Available HTTP: <http://www.whitehouse.gov/news/releases/2006/06/20060615–13.html> (accessed 10 December 2006).
2 "9/11 Five Years Later: Successes and Challenges," September 2006. Online. Available HTTP: <http://www.whitehouse.gov/nsc/waronterror/2006/waronterror0906.pdf> (accessed 10 December 2006).
3 J. Roth, D. Greenberg, and S. Wille, *Monograph on Terrorist Financing* (Staff Report to the Commission), National Commission on Terrorist Attacks Upon the United States, 2004, p. 382. Online. Available HTTP: <http://www.9–11commission.gov/staff_statements/911_TerrFin_Monograph.pdf#search=%229%2F11%20commission%20monograph%22> (accessed 7 September 2006).
4 Ibid., pp. 16–17.
5 T. H. Kean and L. H. Hamilton, *Without Precedent: The Inside Story of the 9/11 Commission*, New York: Knopf, 2006.
6 T. H. Kean, et al., "Final Report on 9/11 Commission Recommendations," 9/11 Discourse Project, 5 December 2005, p. 7. Online. Available HTTP: <http://www.9–11pdp.org/press/2005–12–05_report.pdf> (accessed 10 December 2006). Grades ranged from A– on terrorist financing to F are assessed across the range of recommendations.
7 Translated version of a letter between two senior al Qaeda leaders, Ayman al-Zawahiri and Abu Musab al-Zarqawi, that was obtained during counter-terrorism operations in Iraq. The letter is dated 9 July 2005, but the contents were released by the Office of the Director of National Intelligence on 11 October 2005, only after assurances that no ongoing intelligence or military operations would be affected by making this document public. The relevant paragraph follows: "6–The brothers informed me that you suggested to them sending some assistance. Our situation since Abu al-Faraj is good by the grace of God, but many of the lines have been cut off. Because of this, we need a payment while new lines are being

opened. So, if you're capable of sending a payment of approximately one hundred thousand, we'll be very grateful to you." Online. Available HTTP: <http://www.globalsecurity.org/security/library/report/2005/zawahiri-zarqawi-letter_9jul2005.htm> (accessed 10 December 2006).

8 See US General Accounting Office, *Terrorist Financing: Agencies Should Systematically Assess Terrorists' Use of Alternative Financing Mechanisms*, GAO–04–163, November 2003. Online. Available HTTP: <http://www.gao.gov/new.items/d04163.pdf> (accessed 10 December 2006); US General Accounting Office, *Investigations of Terrorist Financing, Money Laundering, and Other Financial Crimes*, GAO–04–464R Financial Crome Investigations, 20 February 2004. Online. Available HTTP: <http://www.gao.gov/new.items/d04464r.pdf> (accessed 10 December 2006); US General Accounting Office, *Terrorist Financing: Better Strategic Planning Needed to Coordinate U.S. Efforts to Deliver Counter-Terrorism Financing Training and Technical Assistance Abroad*, GAO–06–19, October 2005. Online. Available HTTP: <http://www.gao.gov/new.items/d0619.pdf> (accessed 4 December 2006).

9 See "Reps Moore, Scott and Frank Introduce Counter-Terrorism Financing Coordination Act; *Bill Aims to End Infighting Undercutting Efforts to Stop Terrorist Financing*, 24 April 2007. Online. Available HTTP: <http://www.house.gov/apps/list/press/financialsvcs_dem/press042407.shtml> (accessed 24 April 2007); Text of H.R. 1993, Text of the Counter-Terrorism Financing Coordination Act, Online. Available HTTP: <http://www.house.gov/apps/list/press/financialsvcs_dem/21moorwi_001_xml.pdf> (accessed 24 April 2007); and "Democrats Strive to End Bureaucratic Infighting that Undercuts the Financial War on Terror," 21 September 2006. Online. Available HTTP: <http://www.house.gov/banking-_democrats/pr09212006.html> (accessed 4 December 2006).

10 See R.T. Naylor, *Satanic Purses: Money, Myth and Misinformation in the War on Terror*, Montreal: McGill-Queen's University Press, 2006. Naylor contends that the financial war on terror has been based on gross exaggerations and faulty assumptions, with significant costs, including converting the international financial infrastructure into a tool of governments for global espionage. It is important to note, however, that few credible sources within the US Government contend that there are "billions of Islamic terrorist dollars."

11 According to Bruce Hoffman, "al Qaeda in fact is on the march." See B. Hoffman, "Challenges for the U.S. Special Operations Command Posed by the Global Terrorist Threat: Al Qaeda on the Run or on the March?" Testimony before the House Armed Services Committee, 14 February 2007, Online. Available HTTP: <http://armedservices.house.gov/pdfs/TUTC021407/Benjamin_Testimony021407.pdf?> (accessed 24 April 2007).

12 P. Grier, "Where Does al Qaeda Stand Now?" *Christian Science Monitor* 5 March 2007. Online. Available HTTP: <http://www.csmonitor.com/2007/0305/p01s01-wogi.html> (accessed 24 April 2007).

13 J. Mueller, *Overblown: How Politicians and the Terrorism Industry Inflate National Security Threats, and Why We Believe Them*, New York: The Free Press, 2006.

14 A. Kurth Cronin, "How al-Qaida Ends: The Decline and Demise of Terrorist Groups," *International Security*, Summer 2006, vol. 31, no. 1.

15 J. Fallows, "Declaring Victory," *The Atlantic Monthly*, September 2006.

16 We must admit, however, that we cannot assess this claim directly due to our lack of access to classified intelligence reports.

17 N. MacFarquhar, "Fears of Inquiry Dampen Giving by U.S. Muslims," *The New York Times*, 31 October 2006.

18 T. J. Biersteker, "Émergence, évolution, effets et défis des sanctions ciblées," *Géoéconomie*, Revue trimestrielle, no. 30, Summer 2004. Online. Available HTTP:

<http://www.watsoninstitute.org/pub/Biersteker-Targeted_Sanctions.pdf>
(accessed 6 December 2006).
19 T. J. Biersteker and S. E. Eckert, *Strengthening Targeted Sanctions through Fair and Clear Procedures*, Targeted Sanctions Project, Watson Institute for International Studies, Brown University, New York: United Nations, A/60/887 S/2006/ 331, June 2006. Online. Available HTTP: <http://watsoninstitute.org/pub/ Strengthening_Targeted_Sanctions.pdf> (accessed 5 September 2006).
20 Cronin, "How al-Qaida Ends," p. 44.
21 R. Pape, "The Strategic Logic of Suicide Terrorism" *American Political Science Review*, August 2003. See also, R. Pape, *Dying to Win: The Strategic Logic of Suicide Terrorism*, New York: Random House, 2005.
22 J. Tirman (ed.) *Terror, Insurgency, and the State*, Philadelphia: University of Pennsylvania Press, forthcoming.
23 Fallows, "Declaring Victory," p. 72.
24 Biersteker and Eckert, *Strengthening Targeted Sanctions through Fair and Clear Procedures*.
25 Council of Global Terrorism, "Preliminary Report of the Council on Global Terrorism: State of the Struggle Against Global Terrorism,", September 2006. Online. Available HTTP: <http://councilonglobalterrorism.org/pdf/ A06_265_cgt_report_final.pdf> (accessed 4 December 2006).

Bibliography

"19 Months More in Prison for Professor in Terror Case," *New York Times*, 2 May 2006, A12.

"9/11 Five Years Later: Successes and Challenges," September 2006. Online. Available HTTP: <http://www.whitehouse.gov/nsc/waronterror/2006/waronterror0906.pdf> (accessed 10 December 2006).

"$116 Trillion Lawsuit Filed by 9/11 Families," *CNN.com/LawCenter*, 16 August 2002. Online. Available HTTP: <http://archives.cnn.com/2002/LAW/08/15/attacks.suit/> (accessed 24 November 2004).

"A Banking System Built for Terrorism," *Time*, 5 October 2001. Online. Available HTTP: <http://www.time.com/time/world/printout/0,8816,178227,00.html> (accessed 11 April 2007).

Abbas, H., *Pakistan's Drift into Extremism*, Armonk, NY: M.E. Sharpe, 2004.

Abdel-Halim, M., "Four British Muslims Make It to Parliament," *IslamOnline.net*, Cairo, 6 May 2005. Online. Available HTTP: <http://islamonline.net/English/News/2005-05/06/article03.shtml> (accessed 18 October 2005).

Abocar, A., "Canada Police Say Tamil Gangs Funding Rebels," *Reuters*, 28 March 2000.

Abuza, Z., "Funding Terrorism in Southeast Asia: The Financial Network of Al Qaeda and Jemaah Islamiyah," *NBR Analysis*, vol. 14, no. 5, 2003.

Abuza, Z., *Militant Islam in Southeast Asia: Crucible of Terror*, London: Lynne Rienner, 2003.

Adams, J., *The Financing of Terror*, London: New English Library, 1986.

Adams, J., *The Financing of Terror*, New York: Simon and Schuster, 1986.

"Al-Qaeda Skimming Charity Money," *CBSNews.com*, 7 June 2004. Online. Available HTTP: <http://www.cbsnews.com/stories/2004/06/07/terror/main621621.shtml> (accessed 18 October 2005).

al-Suhaimi, J., "Demystifying Hawala Business," *The Banker*, April 2002, 76–77.

al Zawahiri, A., "The Knights under the Prophets Banner," unpublished manuscript, December 2001.

al Zawahiri, A., "Letter from al-Zawahiri to al-Zaraqawi," *GlobalSecurity.org*, 9 July 2005. Online. Available HTTP: <http://www.globalsecurity.org/security/library/report/2005/zawahiri-zarqawi-letter_9jul2005.htm> (accessed 10 December 2006).

Amidror, Y. and D. Keyes, "Will a Gaza 'Hamas-stan' Become a Future Al-Qaeda Sanctuary?" *Jerusalem Issue Brief*, 8 November 2004, vol. 4, no. 7. Online. Available HTTP: <http://www.jcpa.org/brief/brief004–7.htm> (accessed 17 October 2005).

"An Exploratory Study into the Practice of Proceeds of Crime Confiscation across the EU Member States," unpublished M.Sc. thesis: Cardiff University, 2003.

"An Unforgotten Ransom," *Expatica*, 5 September 2003. Online. Available HTTP: <http://www.expatica.com/source/site_article.asp?subchannel_id=19&story_id =1974> (accessed 19 September 2005).

ANAO, *The Australian Taxation Office's Use of AUSTRAC Data*, Canberra: Australian National Audit Office, 2000.

Andreas, P., *Border Games: Policing the US–Mexico Divide*, New York: Cornell University Press, 2002.

Annals, "The Varieties of Drug Control at the Dawn of the Twenty-First Century," *The Annals of the American Academy of Political and Social Science*, July 2002, vol. 582.

Anthony, A., "Amsterdamned, Part One," *The Observer*, 5 December 2004.

Arquilla, J., D. Ronfeldt and M. Zanini, "Networks, Netwar and Information-Age Terrorism," in I.O. Lesser, B. Hoffman, J. Arquilla, D. Ronfeldt and M. Zanini (eds.) *Countering the New Terrorism*, Washington, DC: Rand Corporation, 1999.

Asia Pacific Group (APG) Working Group Recommendation 1, 2001. Online. Available HTTP: <http://www.ustreas.gov/offices/enforcement/key-issues/hawala/ ARUBS-WG–2003.pdf> (accessed 11 April 2007).

Asia Pacific Group (APG), *Report for the APG Money Laundering Methods and Typologies Workshop*, Singapore, 17–18 October 2001.

Asmal, K., Remarks at the Asia-Pacific Group on Money Laundering 2005 Annual Meeting, Cairns, Australia, 20 July 2005. Online. Available HTTP: <http:// www.apgml.org/about/newsDetail.aspx?newsId=10> (accessed 10 December 2006).

Atran, S., "Mishandling Suicide Terrorism," *The Washington Quarterly*, Summer 2004, vol. 27, no. 3.

Aufhauser, D., Testimony before Senate Judiciary Committee, 26 June 2003. Online. Available HTTP: <http://kyl.senate.gov/legis_center/subdocs/sc062603_aufhaus. pdf> (accessed 21 November 2005).

Ba'asyir, Abu Bakar, Interview, Ngruki, Solo, 11 June 2002.

Baden Intelijen Negara, "Interrogation Report of Omar al-Faruq," Jakarta, June 2002.

Baker, P., "Renewed Militancy Seen in Uzbekistan: Government Crackdown Threatens to Radicalize Previously Non-Violent Groups," *Washington Post*, 27 September 2003.

Bank of England, "Consolidated List of Financial Sanctions Targets in the UK." Online. Available HTTP: <http://www.bankofengland.co.uk/publications/ financialsanctions/current/index.htm> (accessed 17 October 2004).

Basha, Dr. Adnan Khalil, "Largest Islamic Relief Organization Maligned," Letter to the Editor, *Philippine Daily Inquirer*, 22 August 2000.

Basile, M., "Going to the Source: Why Al Qaeda's Financial Network Is Likely to Withstand the Current War on Terrorist Financing," *Studies in Conflict and Terrorism*, 2004, vol. 27, no. 3.

Beam, L., "Leaderless Resistance," *Seditionist*, issue 12, February 1992.

Bekkers, R., "Trust, Accreditation, and Philanthropy in the Netherlands," *Nonprofit and Voluntary Sector Quarterly*, December 2003, vol. 32, no. 4.

Bektiati, B., I. Rosyid and L.N. Idayanie, "Exclusive and Secretive," *Tempo*, 29 January–4 February 2002, no. 21.

Bell, E., "Knowledge Management in the Proceeds of Crime Community," *Journal of Financial Crime*, 2001, vol. 8, no. 3, pp. 207–217.

Bell, E., "Sex Trafficking: a Financial Crime Perspective," *Journal of Financial Crime*, 2001, vol. 9, no. 2, pp. 165–178.

Bell, E., "The Confiscation, Forfeiture and Disruption of Terrorist Finances," *Journal of Money Laundering Control*, vol. 7, no. 2, pp. 105–125, 2003.

Benevolence International Foundation's Bosnia Office, Folder 56, Document 136, 19 March 2002.

Benevolence International Foundation's Bosnia Office, Folder 8, Document 301–47, 19 March 2002.

Benjamin, D. and S. Simon, *The Age of Sacred Terror*, New York: Random House, 2002.

Berdal, M. and M. Serrano (eds.) *Transnational Organized Crime: New Challenges to International Security*, Boulder, CO: Lynne Rienner, 2001.

Biersteker, T.J. "Émergence, évolution, effets et défis des sanctions ciblées," *Géoéconomie*, Revue trimestrielle, N. 30, été 2004, Table 2. Online. Available HTTP: <http://www.watsoninstitute.org/pub/Biersteker-Targeted_Sanctions.pdf> (accessed 6 December 2006).

Biersteker, T.J. and S.E. Eckert, *Strengthening Targeted Sanctions through Fair and Clear Procedures*, Targeted Sanctions Project, Watson Institute for International Studies, Brown University, New York: United Nations, A/60/887 S/2006/331, June 2006. Online. Available HTTP: <http://watsoninstitute.org/pub/Strengthening_Targeted_Sanctions.pdf> (accessed 5 September 2006).

Biersteker, T.J. and S.E. Eckert, *Targeted Financial Sanctions: A Manual for Design and Implementation: Contributions from the Interlaken Process*, Targeted Sanctions Project, Watson Institute for International Studies, Brown University, 2001. Online. Available HTTP: <http://www.seco.admin.ch/imperia/md/content/aussenwirtschaft/sanktionenundembargos/48.pdf> (accessed 11 December 2006).

bin Laden, O., audio tape released 27 December 2004, Foreign Broadcast Information Service (FBIS) Report FEA20041227000762, 27 December 2004.

bin Laden, O., speech, *Al Jazeera*, 4 January 2004. Online. Available HTTP: <http://www.mideastweb.org/log/archives/00000155.htm> (accessed 17 October 2005).

Boim v. Quranic Literacy Institute (291 F.3d 1000).

Borgatti, S.P., "Bureaucracy." Online. Available HTTP: <http://www.analytictech.com/mb021/bureau.htm> (accessed 16 September 2005).

Borgatti, S.P., "The Key Player Problem," *Dynamic Social Network Modeling and Analysis: Workshop Summary and Papers*, National Academy of Sciences Press, 2003.

Borgatti, S.P., "Virtual or Network Organizations." Online. Available HTTP: <http://www.analytictech.com/mb021/virtual.htm> (accessed 16 September 2005).

Borgatti, S.P. and P.C. Foster, "The Network Paradigm in Organizational Research: A Review and Typology," *Journal of Management*, 2003, vol. 29, no. 6.

Bradach, J.L. and R.G. Eccles, "Price Authority and Trust: From Ideal Types to Plural Forms," *American Review of Sociology*, 1989, vol. 15.

Bright, M. and A. Barnett, "IRA linked to Thai share 'Scam,' " *Observer*, 19 August 2001.

Brisard, J.C., *Terrorism Financing*, Report prepared for the President of the UN Security Council, New York, 2002.

Brooke, S., "Outside View: Financing Al-Qaeda 2.0," *United Press International*, 29 June 2004. Online. Available HTTP: <http://washingtontimes.com/upi-breaking/20040629–112719–2610r.htm> (accessed 19 September 2005).

Browne, A., "Hatred Engulfs a Liberal Land," *The Times*, London, 13 November 2004.

Buaras, E.A., "War Costs Labour the Muslim Vote," *Muslim News*, 30 May 2003, issue 169.

Bugg, D., Speech to IAP Conference, 8 December 2003. Online. Available HTTP: <http://www.cdpp.gov.au/Media/Speeches/20030812db.aspx> (accessed 7 September 2006).

Burke, J., *Al-Qaeda: Casting a Shadow of Terror*, London: I.B. Tauris, 2003.

Burke, J., "The Arab Backlash the Militants Didn't Expect," *The Observer*, 20 June 2004.

Burnett, et al. v. al Baraka Investment and Development Corp., et al. Online. Available HTTP: <http://news.findlaw.com/cnn/docs/terrorism/burnettba81502cmp.pdf> (accessed 22 May 2005).

Byrne, J.J., Testimony before a Joint Hearing of the House Financial Services Oversight and Investigations Subcommittee and the House International Relations International Terrorism and Nonproliferation Subcommittee, 4 May 2005. Online. Available HTTP: <http://www.aba.com/NR/rdonlyres/222CE044–577A–11D5–AB84–00508B95258D/44048/JByrneTestimony05042005.pdf> (accessed 21 November 2005).

Bryne, J.J. and M.D. Kelsey, "US PATRIOT ACT Three Years Later (What a Long Strange Trip It's Been, Part 1)," *ABA Banking Compliance*, September/October 2004.

Byman, D., *Deadly Connections: States That Sponsor Terrorism*, Cambridge: Cambridge University Press, 2005.

Cameron, Iain, "UN Targeted Sanctions, Legal Safeguards and the European Convention on Human Rights," *Nordic Journal of International Law*, 2003, vol. 72, no. 2, pp. 159–214.

Canadian High Commission, Malaysia, "RE: Mohammed Mansour Jabarah," 13 May 2002.

Cassara, J.A., *Hide and Seek: Intelligence, Law Enforcement, and the Stalled War on Terrorist Finance*, Washington, DC: Potomac Books, 2006.

Caulkins, J.P., M.A.R. Kleiman and P. Reuter, "Lessons from the 'War' on Drugs for the 'War' on Terrorism," in A. Howitt and R. Pangi (eds.) *Countering Terrorism: Dimensions of Preparedness*, Cambridge, MA: MIT Press, 2003.

Census of England and Wales, 2001: Ethnicity and Religion in England and Wales. Online.   Available   HTTP: <http://www.statistics.gov.uk/census2001/profiles/commentaries/ethnicity.asp#religion> (accessed 11 April 2007).

Cesari, J., "Islam in France: Social Challenge or Challenge of Secularism?" in S. Vertovece and A. Rogers (eds.) *Muslim European Youth – Reproducing Ethnicity, Religion, Culture*, Aldershot: Ashgate, 1998.

Chai, S., "An Organizational Economics Theory of Antigovernment Violence," *Comparative Politics*, October 1993.

Chapman, H., "Lib Dems Delighted at Gaining Britain's Only Muslim MEP," *Muslim News*, 25 June 2004, issue 182.

" 'Charity' and Palestinian Terrorism–Spotlight on the Hamas-run Islamic Al-Tadhamun 'Charitable Society' in Nablus," Intelligence and Terrorism Information Center at the Center for Special Studies, February 2005. Online. Available HTTP: <http://www.intelligence.org.il/eng/sib/3_05/charity_2.htm> (accessed 17 October 2005).

Charity Commission Homepage <http://www.charity-commission.gov.uk/>.

Charity Commission Inquiry Reports. Online. Available HTTP: <http://www.charity-commission.gov.uk/investigations/inquiryreports/inqreps.asp> (accessed 17 October 2005).

Cheney, R., "Interview of the Vice President by Sean Hannity," 15 June 2006. Online. Available HTTP: <http://www.whitehouse.gov/news/releases/2006/06/20060615–13.html> (available 10 December 2006).

Chivers, C.J., "Uzbek Militants Decline Provides Clues to U.S.," *New York Times*, 8 October 2002.

CIA World Factbook. Online. Available HTTP: <http://www.cia.gov/cia/publications/factbook/geos/nl.html#People> (accessed 17 October 2004).

"CIDI vraagt onderzoek naar stichting Al Aqsa Rotterdam," *Rotterdams Dagblad*, 7 August 2002.

CIDI Homepage. Online. Available HTTP: <http://www.cidi.nl> (accessed 17 October 2005).

Clare, P.K., *Racketeering in Northern Ireland: a New Version of the Patriot Game*, Chicago, IL: Office of International Criminal Justice at the University of Illinois at Chicago, 1989.

Clarke, R.A., *Against All Enemies: Inside America's War on Terror*, New York: Free Press, 2004.

Clarke, R.V., *Situational Crime Prevention: Successful Case Studies*, 2nd edn, Albany, NY: Harrow and Heston, 1997.

Clarkson, F., "Journalists or Terrorists?" *Salon*, 31 May 2001.

Club Madrid, "Outcome of 2005 Madrid International Summit on Democracy, Terrorism and Security." Online. Available: <http://media.clubmadrid.org/docs/CdM-Series-on-Terrorism-Vol–2.pdf> (accessed 11 April 2007).

Coalition for Accountability and Integrity, "Opinion Poll on Corruption in the Palestinian Society," 30–31 December 2004. Online. Available HTTP: <http://www.transparency.org/surveys/dnld/palestine_poll.pdf> (accessed 17 October 2005).

Coll, S., *Ghost Wars: The Secret History of the CIA, Afghanistan, bin Laden, From the Soviet Invasion to September 10, 2001*, New York: Penguin Press, 2004.

Commission of the European Communities, "Commission Staff Working Document Accompanying document to the Proposal for a Council Decision establishing the European Police Office (EUROPOL) Impact Assessment" {COM(2006) 817 final}{SEC(2006) 1683}, Brussels: Commission of the European Communities, 20 December 2006. Online. Available HTTP: <http://ec.europa.eu/dgs/justice_home/doc/sec_2006_1682_en.pdf> (accessed 25 April 2007).

Conversations with personnel from UNRWA (Patrick Barbieri), Pharmaciens sans Frontières, Save the Children, and Mennonite Central Committee, Gaza, 1998.

Cooley, J., *Unholy Wars: Afghanistan, America and International Terrorism*, 2nd edn, London: Pluto Press, 2000.

Coolidge, S. and J. Prendergast, "Markets Gouged the Poor, Laundered Money," *The Cincinnati Enquirer*, 3 October 2003.

Cortright, D., et. al., *An Action Agenda for Enhancing the United Nations Program on Counter-Terrorism*, Fourth Freedom Forum/Joan B. Kroc Institute, September 2004. Online. Available HTTP: <http://www.globalct.org/html/Action_Agenda.html> (accessed 6 December 2006).

Council for Foreign Relations, *Terrorist Finance: Report of an Independent Task*

Force Sponsored by the Council on Foreign Relations, Washington, DC: Council for Foreign Relations, 2002.

Council for Foreign Relations, *Update on the Global Campaign against Terrorist Financing: Second Report of an Independent Task Force Sponsored by the Council on Foreign Relations*, Washington, DC: Council for Foreign Relations, 2004.

Council of Global Terrorism, "Preliminary Report of the Council on Global Terrorism: State of the Struggle Against Global Terrorism," September 2006. Online. Available HTTP: <http://councilonglobalterrorism.org/pdf/A06_265_cgt_report_final.pdf> (accessed 4 December 2006).

Crenshaw, M., "An Organizational Approach to the Analysis of Political Terrorism," *Orbis*, Autumn 1985, vol. 29, no. 3.

Crenshaw, M., "The Logic of Terrorism: Terrorist Behavior as a Product of Strategic Choice," in W. Reich (ed.) *Origins of Terrorism: Psychologies, Ideologies, Theologies, States of Mind*, Washington: Wilson Center Press, 1998.

Crenshaw, M., "Theories of Terrorism: Instrumental and Organizational Approaches," in D.C. Rapoport, *Inside Terrorist Organizations*, 2nd edn, Portland, OR: Frank Cass, 2001.

Crenshaw, M., P. Wilkinson, J. Alterman and T. Schaffer, "How Terrorism Ends," Special Report 48, Washington, DC: United States Institute of Peace, 25 May 1999, 3. Online. Available HTTP: <http://www.usip.org/pubs/specialreports/sr990525.pdf> (accessed 16 September 2005).

Cronin, A.K., "How al-Qaida Ends: The Decline and Demise of Terrorist Groups," *International Security*, vo. 31, no. 1, Summer 2006.

Cross-examination of Khertchou. *United States v. Usama Bin Laden, et al.*, Part 1, Book 3, pp. 1409–1492.

Cuellar, M., "The Tenuous Relationship Between the Fight Against Money Laundering and the Disruption of Criminal Finance," *Journal of Criminal Law and Criminology*, vol. 93, no. 2–3, pp. 311–466, Winter/Spring 2003.

Cullison, A., "Inside al-Qaeda's Hard Drive," *Atlantic Monthly*, September 2004.

Dam, K.W., Deputy Secretary of the Treasury, "The Financial Front of the War on Terrorism – The Next Phase," Remarks Delivered to the Council on Foreign Relations, 8 June 2002. Online. Available HTTP: <http://www.treas.gov/press/releases/po3163.htm> (accessed 7 September 2006).

Damask, J.A., "Cigarette Smuggling: Financing Terrorism?" Mackinac Center for Public Policy, 1 July 2002. Online. Available HTTP: <http://www.mackinac.org/article.asp?ID=4461> (accessed 19 September 2005).

de Vreij, H., "Behind the Dutch Terror Threat," *Radio Netherlands*, 22 July 2004. Online. Available HTTP: <http://www2.rnw.nl/rnw/en/currentaffairs/region/netherlands/ned040722.html> (accessed 17 October 2005).

de Vreij, H., "Dutch Link in Madrid Bomb Plot?" *Radio Netherlands*, 21 October 2004. Online. Available HTTP: <http://www2.rnw.nl/rnw/en/currentaffairs/region/westerneurope/10610251> (accessed 17 October 2005).

Dean, P., "Pirate Videos Fund IRA Terrorism, U.K. Government Says," *Billboard*, 6 August 1994.

della Porta, D., "Left-Wing Terrorism in Italy," in M. Crenshaw (ed.) *Terrorism in Context*, University Park, PA: Pennsylvania State University Press, 1995.

"Democrats Strive to End Bureaucratic Infighting that Undercuts the Financial War on Terror," 21 September 2006. Online. Available HTTP: <http://www.house.gov/banking_democrats/pr09212006.html> (accessed 4 December 2006).

Department of Justice, *FY 2002 Performance Report/FY 2003 Revised Final Perform-ance Plan/FY 2004 Performance Plan*, Washington, DC: Department of Justice, 2003.

Department of Trade and Industry, *Review of Company Law*, London: Department of Trade and Industry, 2002.

DePass, D. and L.M. Leslie, "Somali Businessmen Eager to Get Off List," *Minneapolis Star Tribune*, August 23, 2002.

der Derian, J., "911: Before, After and In Between," in C.J. Calhoun, P. Price and A. Timmer (eds.) *Understanding September 11*, New York: W.W. Norton & Company, 2002.

Dey, J., "Sources Say Mumbai Remains Key Conduit of Lashkar-I-Taiyibah Funds," New Delhi, *Indian Express*, 13 June 2002.

Dorn, N., "Proteiform Criminalities: the Formation of Organized Crime as Organisers' Responses to Developments in Four Fields of Control," in A. Edwards and P. Gill (eds.) *Transnational Organized Crime: Perspectives on Global Security*, London: Routledge, 2003.

Dorn, N., M. Levi and L. King *A Literature Review of Upper Level Drugs Trafficking*, London: Home Office, 2005.

Dudkevitch, M., "Army Seals Offices of Hamas Charity Organizations," *Jerusalem Post*, 8 July 2004.

Dutch Intelligence and Security Services (AIVD), "Antwoorden op kamervragen over financieringen vanuit Saoedi-Arabië," 31 December 2002. Online. HTTP: <http://www.aivd.nl> (accessed 1 July 2004).

Dutch Intelligence and Security Services (AIVD), "Antwoorden op kamervragen over de mogelijke financiering van de Al-Tawheed moskee in Amsterdam," 2 March 2004.

Dutch Intelligence and Security Services (AIVD), "Antwoorden op kamervragen over de organisatie Al-waqf Al-islaami die in de Al Furqaan moskee in Eindhoven opleidingen verzorgt tot strijder in de heilige oorlog," 24 June 2003.

Dutch Intelligence and Security Services (AIVD), "Antwoorden op kamervragen over onderzoek naar een mogelijke tijdelijke sluiting van de Al-Fourqaan moskee in Eindhoven," 24 June 2003.

Dutch Intelligence and Security Services (AIVD), "Brief aan de Tweede Kamer over de stichting Al Waqf al-Islami," 25 April 2003.

Dutch Intelligence and Security Services (AIVD), "Recruitment for the Jihad in the Netherlands." Online. Available HTTP: <http://www.aivd.nl/contents/pages/2285/recruitmentbw.pdf> (accessed 17 October 2005).

Dutch Intelligence and Security Services (AIVD), "Saoedische invloeden in Neder-land. Verbanden tuseen salafistische missie, radicaliseringsprocessen en islamitisch terrorisme," AIVD report, 9 June 2004. Online. Available HTTP: <http://www.aivd.nl/contents/pages/8931/rapportsaoedischeinvloeden.pdf> (accessed 18 October 2005).

Dutch Intelligence and Security Services (AIVD), "Tegoeden Al-Aqsa bevroren na onderzoek AIVD," AIVD Press Release, 9 April 2003, Online. Available HTTP: <http://www.aivd.nl/algemene_onderdelen/tegoeden_al-aqsa> (accessed 17 October 2005).

Duyne, P.C. van and H. de Miranda, "The Emperor's Clothes of Disclosure: Hot Money and Suspect Disclosures," *Crime, Law and Social Change*, 1999, vol., 31 no. 3, pp. 245–71.

Duyne, P.C. van and M. Levi, *Drugs and Money: Managing the Drugs Trade and Crime-Money in Europe*, London: Routledge, 2005.

Dwikarna, Agus, "I Don't Have a History of Violence," interview, *Tempo*, 6 January 2003.

Dyer, C., "Charity Sues Jewish Board over Hamas Claim," *The Guardian*, London, 20 October 2003.

Eberhart, D., "Hamas Touts Untouchable 'Secret' Funding Sources," *NewsMax.com*, 5 December 2001. Online. Available HTTP: <http://www.newsmax.com/archives/articles/2001/12/4/175008.shtml> (accessed 17 October 2005).

Elangovan, A.R. and D.L. Shapiro, "Betrayal of Trust in Organizations," *Academy of Management Review*, vol. 23, no. 3, 1998.

Elegant, S., "The Terrorist Talks," *Time Asian Edition*, 5 October 2003.

Elegant, S. and J. Tedjaskmana, "The Jihadis' Tale," *Time Asian Edition*, 27 January 2002.

El Qorchi, M., S.M. Autmainbo and J.F. Wilson, *Informal Fund Transfer Systems: An Analysis of the Informal Hawala System*, International Monetary Fund, 2003.

Elvins, M., *Anti-Drug Policies of the European Union*, London: Palgrave Macmillan, 2003.

Erickson, B., "Secret Societies and Social Structure," *Social Forces*, vol. 60, no. 1, September 1998.

Esman, A., "The Arabian Panther," *Foundation for the Defense of Democracies*, 14 June 2004. Online. Available HTTP: <http://www.defenddemocracy.org/research_topics/research_topics_show.htm?doc_id=228652> (accessed 18 October 2005).

European Union, "List of Persons and Entities Subject to Financial Sanctions." Online. Available HTTP: <http://europa.eu.int/comm/external_relations/cfsp/sanctions/list/version4/global/e_ctlview.html#en845> (accessed 17 October 2005).

Fallows, J., "Declaring Victory," *The Atlantic Monthly*, September 2006.

Farah, D., *Blood from Stones: the Secret Financial Network of Terror*, New York: Broadway Books, 2004.

Fearon, J. and D. Laitin, "Ethnicity, Insurgency, and Civil War," *American Political Science Review*, February 2003, vol. 97, no. 1.

Federal Research Division, Library of Congress, *Terrorist And Organized Crime Groups In The Tri-Border Area (TBA) Of South America*, July 2003.

Federal Research Division, Library of Congress, *The Nexus Among Terrorists, Narcotics Traffickers, Weapons Proliferators, and Organized Crime Networks in Western Europe*, December 2002. Online. Available HTTP: <http://www.loc.gov/rr/frd/pdf-files/WestEurope_NEXUS.pdf> (accessed 19 September 2005).

Fielding, N., "How al Qaeda Utilises Family Networks?," Presentation at Watson Institute, Workshop on the Financial and Transnational Dynamics of Terrorism, Providence, RI, 24–25 October 2003.

Financial Action Task Force, *Annual Report 2000–2001*, Paris: FATF, OECD, 22 June 2001. Online. Available HTTP: <http://www.fatf-gafi.org/dataoecd/36/21/35689876.pdf> (accessed 6 December 2006).

Financial Action Task Force, *Annual Report 2004–2005*, 10 June 2005, p.10. Online. Available HTTP: <http://www.fatf-gafi.org/dataoecd/41/25/34988062.pdf> (accessed 6 December 2006).

Financial Action Task Force, *Combating the Abuse of Alternative Remittance Systems: International Best Practices*, 2003. Online. Available HTTP: <http://www1.oecd.org/fatf/pdf/SR6-BPP_en.pdf>.

Financial Action Task Force, *Interpretative Notes to the Forty Recommendations, 1990–1995*, Paris: FATF, 1995.

Financial Action Task Force, *Money Laundering Typologies*, Paris: FATF, 2004. Online. Available HTTP: <http://www.fatf-gafi.org/dataoecd/19/11/33624379.PDF> (accessed 4 October 2005).

Financial Action Task Force, *The Forty Recommendations*, Paris: FATF, 1990.

Financial Action Task Force, *The Forty Recommendations*, Paris: FATF, 2003. Online. Available HTTP: <http://www.fatf-gafi.org/dataoecd/7/40/34849567.PDF> (accessed 4 October 2005).

Financial Action Task Force, *Report on Money Laundering Typologies, 1996–1997*, Paris: FATF, OECD, 1997.

Financial Action Task Force, *Report on Money Laundering Typologies, 1998–1999*, Paris: FATF, OECD, 1999.

Financial Action Task Force, *Report on Money Laundering Typologies, 2000–2001*, Paris: FATF, OECD, 2001.

Financial Action Task Force, *Report on Money Laundering Typologies, 2002–2003*, Paris: FATF, OECD, 2003.

Financial Action Task Force, "Report on Money Laundering Typologies," various years (appendixes to FATF Annual Reports), Paris: FATF, OECD, "Forex Association of Pakistan," Press Release, 6 January 2002.

Financial Action Task Force, *Special Recommendation VI Alternative Remittances.* Online. Available HTTP: <http://www.fatf-gafi.org/document/9/0,2340,en_32250379_32236920_34032073_1_1_1_1,00.html#VIAR> (accessed 10 December 2006).

Financial Crimes Enforcement Network, "The SAR Activity Review: By the Numbers," May 2006, issue 6. Online. Available HTTP: <http://www.fincen.gov/sar_review_by_the_numbers_issue6.pdf> (accessed 23 August 2006).

Financial Crimes Enforcement Network, "The SAR Activity Review: Trends, Tips and Issues," April 2005, issue 8. Online. Available HTTP: <http://www.fincen.gov/sarreviewissue8.pdf> (accessed 21 November 2005).

"Financing Terrorism: Looking in the Wrong Places," *The Economist*, 20 October 2005.Online. Available HTTP: <http://economist.com/displaystory.cfm?story_id=5053373> (accessed 21 November 2005).

First Report of the Analytical Support and Sanctions Monitoring Team appointed pursuant to resolution 1526 (2004) concerning Al-Qaida and the Taliban and associated individual and entities, S/2004/679/, 25 August 2004. Online. Available HTTP: <http://www.un.org/sc/committees/1267/monitoringteam.shtml> (accessed 6 September 2006).

Fleming, M., *UK Law Enforcement Agency Use and Management of Suspicious Activity Reports: Towards Determining the Value of the Regime*, 2005. Online. Available HTTP: <http://www.jdi.ucl.ac.uk/downloads/publications/research_reports/Fleming_LEA_Use_and_Mgmt_of_SARs_June2005.pdf> (accessed 10 April 2007).

Florida Department of Law Enforcement Press Release, 21 July 2003. Online. Available HTTP: <http://www.fdle.state.fl.us/press_releases/expired/2003/20030721_Adulterated_Drugs.html> (accessed 12 October 2005).

Food and Drug Administration, "Combating Counterfeit Drugs: a Report of the Food and Drug Administration, Annual Update," Rockville, MD: US Department of Health and Human Services, 18 May 2005. Online. Available HTTP: <http://www.fda.gov/oc/initiatives/counterfeit/update2005.html> (accessed 12 October 2005).

Foot, R., "Collateral Damage: Human Rights Consequences of Counterterrorist Action in the Asia-Pacific," *International Affairs*, 2003, vol. 81, no. 2, pp. 1–14.

Forego, J., "Columbia Arrests 3 as IRA Bomb Experts," *New York Times*, 15 August 2001.

Fox, W.J., Remarks at the 23rd Cambridge International Symposium on Economic Crime, 5 September 2005. Online. Available HTTP: <http://www.fincen.gov/director_speech_cambridge.pdf> (accessed 21 November 2005).

Fox, W.J., Remarks to ABA Money Laundering Enforcement Seminar, 31 October 2005. Online. Available HTTP: <http://www.fincen.gov/aba_aba_seminar.pdf> (accessed 21 November 2005).

Fox, W.J., Statement at Hearing before the Committee on Financial Services, US House of Representatives, 26 May 2005. Online. Available HTTP: <http://www.fincen.gov/foxtestimony052605.pdf> (accessed 21 November 2005).

Fox, W.J., Statement before the House Subcommittee on Financial Institutions and Consumer Credit, 22 September 2005. Online. Available HTTP: <http://www.fincen.gov/foxstatement092205.pdf> (accessed 21 November 2005).

Frantz, D., "Front Companies Said to Keep Financing Terrorists," *New York Times*, 19 September 2002.

Freeh, L., Statement Before the United States Senate Committee on Appropriations, Subcommittee for the Departments of Commerce, Justice, and State, the Judiciary, and Related Agencies, 4 February 1999. Online. Available HTTP: <http://www.fas.org/irp/congress/1999_hr/990204-freehct2.htm> (accessed 5 September 2006).

Freiberg, A. and R. Fox, "Evaluating the Effectiveness of Australia's Confiscation Laws," *Australia and New Zealand Journal of Criminology*, 2000, vol. 33, no. 3, pp. 239–65.

Friman, R. and P. Andreas (eds.) *The Illicit Global Economy and State Power*, Lanham, MD: Rowman and Littlefield, 1999.

Frumkin, P., *On Being Nonprofit: A Conceptual and Policy Primer*, Cambridge, MA: Harvard University Press, 2002.

GAO, *Investigating Money Laundering and Terrorist Financing: Federal Law Enforcement Agencies Face Continuing Coordination Challenges*, May 11 testimony to House of Representatives, GAO–04–710T, Washington, DC: General Accounting Office, 2004.

Geneva Convention Relative to the Protection of Civilian Persons in Time of War, 12 August 1949. Online. Available HTTP: <http://www.unhchr.ch/html/menu3/b/92.htm> (accessed 17 October 2005).

"German Concern at Swift Disclosure," *Financial Times*, 6 September 2006.

Gerth, J. and J. Miller, "Threats and Responses: the Money Trail," *New York Times*, 17 October 2002.

Glaser, D.L., "Who Pays the Iraqi Insurgents?" testimony of Daniel L. Glaser, Acting Assistant Secretary for the Office of Terrorist Financing and Financial Crimes, US Department of the Treasury before the House Financial Services Subcommittee on Oversight and Investigations and the House Armed Services Subcommittee on Terrorism, 28 July 2005. Online. Available HTTP: <http://financialservices.house.gov/media/pdf/072805dg.pdf> (accessed 21 October 2005).

Glaser, D. L., Testimony before the Senate Banking Committee, 12 September 2006. Online. Available HTTP:<http://www.ustreas.gov/press/releases/hp93.htm> and <http://www.treas.gov/offices/enforcement/311_actions.shtml> (accessed 6 September 2006).

Glaser, D.L., and A. Szubin, "Joint Testimony before the Committees on Foreign Affairs and Financial Services," 18 April 2007. Online. Available HTTP: <http://www.ustreas.gov/press/releases/hp361.htm> (accessed 24 April 2007).

GlobalOptions, Inc., *An Analysis of Terrorist Threats to America's Medicine Supply*, Signature Book Printing, Inc., 2003.

Glover, T., "A Continent of Crooks: Fraud in the European Community," *EuroBusiness*, February 1995, vol. 2, no. 9.

Godson, R. and P. Williams, *Strengthening Cooperation against Transnational Crime: Elements of a Strategic Approach*, Paper presented at the International Conference on Responding to the Challenges of Transnational Crime, Courmayeur: United Nations, 1998.

Godson, R., *Trends in Organized Crime*, Spring 1999, vol. 4, no. 3, pp. 1–7.

Gold, M. and M. Levi, *Money-Laundering in the UK: an Appraisal of Suspicion-Based Reporting*, London: Police Foundation, 1994.

Gonnerman, J., "The Terrorist Campaign Against Abortion," *Village Voice*, 9 November 1998.

Grabosky, P.N., "Counterproductive Regulation," *International Journal of the Sociology of Law*, December 1995, vol. 23, pp. 347–369.

Grabosky, P.N., "Unintended Consequences of Crime Prevention," in R. Homel (ed.) *The Politics and Practice of Situational Crime Prevention*, Mounsey, NY: Criminal Justice Press, 1996.

Greenberg, M., W. William and L. Wolosky, *Terrorist Financing: Report of an Independent Task Force Sponsored by the Council on Foreign Relations*, New York: Council on Foreign Relations, 2002.

Gregory, F., "Classify, Report and Measure: the UK Organised Crime Notification Scheme," in A. Edwards and P. Gill (eds.) *Transnational Organized Crime: Perspectives on Global Security*, London: Routledge, 2003.

Gruen, M., "Hizb ut-Tahrir," unpublished report, 30 January 2004.

G8, "Building International Political Will and Capacity to Combat Terrorism: A G8 Action Plan," June 2003. Online. Available HTTP: <http://www.g8.fr/evian/english/navigation/2003_g8_summit/summit_documents/building_international_political_will_and_capacity_to_combat_terrorism_-_a_g8_action_plan.html> (accessed 6 December 2006).

G8, "G8 Statement on Counter-terrorism," Gleneagles, July 2005. Online. Available HTTP: <http://www.fco.gov.uk/Files/kfile/PostG8_Gleneagles_CounterTerrorism.pdf> (accessed 6 December 2006).

G10 Committee on Banking Regulations and Supervisory Practices, "Prevention of Criminal Use of the Banking System for the Purpose of Money Laundering," Basel Statement of Principles, 1988.

Gufron (Mukhlas), A., *Jihad Bom Bali*, unpublished manuscript, April 2003.

Gunaratna, R., "The Lifeblood of Terrorist Organisations: Evolving Terrorist Financing Strategies," in A. Schmid (ed.) *Countering Terrorism Through International Cooperation*, International Scientific and Professional Advisory Council of the UN Cooperation and the UN Terrorism Prevention Branch, 2001.

Gunaratna, R., "The Post-Madrid Face of Al Qaeda," *The Washington Quarterly*, Summer 2004, vol. 27, no. 3.

Gunaratna, R., *Inside Al Qaeda*, New York: Berkeley Books, pp. 81–93, 2002.

Gunaratna, R., *Inside al Qaeda: Global Network of Terror*, New York: Columbia University Press, 2002.

Gunning, J., "Hamas, Socialisation and the Logic of Compromise," in J. Tirman and M. Heiberg (eds.) *Turning the Tables on Terrorism*, Philadelphia: University of Pennsylvania Press, 2005.

Gunning, J., "Making Sense of al-Qaeda in Europe," Oxford-Princeton Conference on Muslims in Europe post 9/11, Oxford, 26 April 2003. Online. Available HTTP: <http://www.sant.ox.ac.uk/princeton/gunning-full.pdf> (accessed 23 May 2005).

Gunning, J., "Peace with Hamas? The Transforming Potential of Political Participation," *International Affairs*, 2004, vol. 80, no. 2.

Gunning, J., monograph on Hamas, Cambridge: Cambridge University Press, forthcoming.

Gunning, J., *Re-Thinking Western Constructs of Islamism: Pluralism, Democracy and the Theory and Praxis of the Islamic Movement in the Gaza Strip*, doctoral thesis, Durham: Centre for Middle Eastern and Islamic Studies, 2000.

Harik, J.P., *Hezbollah: The Changing Face of Terrorism*, London: I.B. Tauris, 2004.

Harmonized Tariff System of the United States, 19 CFR 1–199; HTSUS 9801.00.

Heiberg, M., B. O'Leary and J. Tirman *Terror, Insurgency, and the State*, Philadelphia: University of Pennsylvania Press, 2007.

Herrera, C., "Bin Laden Funds Abu Sayyaf Through Muslim Relief Group," *Philippine Daily Inquirer*, 9 August 2000.

"Hezbollah and the West African Diamond Trade," *Middle East Intelligence Bulletin*, June/July 2004, vol. 6, no. 6–7. Online. Available HTTP: <http://www.meib.org/articles/0407_l2.htm> (accessed 19 September 2005).

Hoffman, B., *Inside Terrorism*, New York: Columbia University Press, 1998.

Hoffman, B., "The Use of the Internet by Islamic Extremists," Testimony before the House Permanent Select Committee on Intelligence, 4 May 2006. Online. Available HTTP: <http://www.rand.org/pubs/testimonies/2006/RAND_CT262–1.pdf> (accessed 31 May 2007).

Hoffman, B., "Challenges for the U.S. Special Operations Command Posed by the Global Terrorist Threat: Al Qaeda on the Run or on the March?" Testimony before the House Armed Services Committee, 14 February 2007. Online. Available HTTP: <http://armedservices.house.gov/pdfs/TUTC021407/Hoffman_Testimony021407.pdf> (accessed 31 May 2007).

Home Office Crime Reduction College, *Passport to Evaluation*, London: Home Office, 2002.

Horgan, J., "The Provisional IRA in 2005: the Final Moments of an Increasingly Irrelevant Movement?" Paper prepared for International Workshop on Global Terror and the Imagination, University of Pittsburgh, 24–27 March 2005.

Horgan, J. and M. Taylor, "Playing the 'Green Card': Financing the Provisional IRA: Part 1," *Terrorism and Political Violence*, Summer 1999, vol. 11, no. 2.

Horsley, N., "The Nuremberg Files." Online. Available HTTP: <http://www.christiangallery.com/atrocity/> (accessed 25 August 2002).

Hosein, G., "Why Terror Financing is so Tough to Track Down," *Christian Science Monitor*, 8 March 2006. Online. Available HTTP: <http://www.csmonitor.com/2006/0308/p04s01-woeu.html> (accessed 10 December 2006).

House of Commons, The Stationery Office, *Report of the Official Account on the Bombings in London on 7th July 2005*, HC 1087, 11 May 2006. Online. Available HTTP: <http://www.official-documents.gov.uk/document/hc0506/hc10/1087/1087 .pdf> (accessed 6 September 2006).

Hudson, R., "Terrorist and Organized Crime Groups in the Tri-Border Area (TBA) of South America," Report prepared by the Federal Research Division, Washington, DC: Library of Congress, July 2003.

Hudson, R., *The Psychology and Sociology of Terrorism*, Library of Congress Federal Research Division, 2000. Online. Available HTTP: <http://web.archive.org/web/ 20021209181134/http://www.loc.gov/rr/frd/Sociology-Psychology+of+Terrorism.htm> (accessed 9 December 2002).

Huysmans, J., "The European Union and the Securitization of Migration," *Journal of Common Market Studies*, vol. 38, no. 5, December 2000.

International Crisis Group (ICG), "Jemaah Islamiyah in South East Asia: Damaged But Still Dangerous," ICG Asia Report no. 63, 26 August 2003.

Ihsane, El Kadi, "In the Heartland of the GSPC," *Algeria Interface*, 16 December 2002. Online. Available HTTP: <http://www.algeria-interface.com/new/ article.php?article_id=657&lng=e> (accessed 15 May 2004).

Independent Monitoring Commission, Third Report, HC1218, London: The Stationery Office, 2004.

Independent Monitoring Commission, *Fourteenth Report*, London: The Stationery Office, 12 March 2007. Online. Available HTTP: <http://www.independent monitoringcommission.org/documents/uploads/14th_IMC_Report.pdf> (accessed 25 April 2007).

Indonesian National Police, "Interrogation of Mohammad Nasir bin Abbas," Jakarta, 18 April 2003.

Inter-American Committee Against Terrorism, "Report on CICTE Activities," OAS Doc. OEA/Ser.L/X.2.5, CICTE/doc.6/05, 17 February 2005.

International Convention for the Suppression of the Financing of Terrorism, 1999.

International Crisis Group, *Indonesia Backgrounder: Jihad in Central Sulawesi*, 3 February 2004.

International Crisis Group, *Jemaah Islamiyah in Southeast Asia: Damaged but Still Dangerous*, ICG Asia Report No. 63, August 2003.

International Convention for the Suppression of the Financing of Terrorism, United Nations Treaty Collection. Online. Available HTTP: <http://untreaty.un.org/ ENGLISH/bible/englishinternetbible/partI/chapterXVIII/treaty11.asp> (accessed 2 December 2006).

International Monetary Fund, "Financial System Abuse, Financial Crime, and Money Laundering-Background Paper." IMF Background Paper, Washington, DC: IMF, 12 February 2001.

Jacobs, J., *Gotham Unbound*, New York: New York University Press, 1999.

"Jakarta Asks Manila to Clarify Arrests," *Philippine Daily Inquirer*, 17 March 2002.

Jayanegara, Dr.H. Asep R., Secretary, Komite Penanggulangan Krisis, Dewan Dakwah Islam Indonesia, Interview, Jakarta, 8 January 2003.

Johnson, E.L., *The History of YMCA Physical Education*, Association Press, 1979.

Joint Forum of the Basel Committee on Banking Supervision, the International Organization of Securities Commissions and the International Association of Insurance Supervisors, "Initiatives by the BCBS, IAIS and IOSCO to Combat

Money Laundering and the Financing of Terrorism," IOSCO Public Document No. 146, June 2003.

Jones, C., W. Hesterly and S. Borgatti, "A General Theory of Network Governance," *The Academy of Management Review*, October 1997, vol. 22, no. 4.

Kafala, T., "Palestinians Suffer as Charities Close," *BBC News Online*, 30 January 2002. Online. Available HTTP: <http://news.bbc.co.uk/1/hi/world/middle_east/1789093.stm> (accessed 18 October 2005).

Kaplan, D., "The Saudi Connection," *U.S. News and World Report*, Washington, DC, 15 December 2003.

Kaplow, L., "Backgrounder: Israel's Adversaries: Hamas: Back-seat Driver to Arafat Group," *Atlanta Journal-Constitution*, 24 January 2002.

Kaufman, M., "Somalis Said to Feel Impact of US Freeze of al Barakaat," *Washington Post*, 30 November 2001.

Kean, T.H. and Lee H. Hamilton, *Without Precedent: The Inside Story of the 9/11 Commission*, New York: Knopf, 2006.

Kean, T.H., et. al., "Final Report on 9/11 Commission Recommendations," 9/11 Discourse Project, 5 December 2005, p. 7. Online. Available HTTP: <http://www.9-11pdp.org/press/2005-12-05_report.pdf> (accessed 10 December 2006).

Keats, A., "In the Spotlight: the Salafist Group for Call and Combat (GSPC)," Center for Defense Information, 14 January 2003. Online. Available HTTP: <http://www.cdi.org/terrorism/gspc-pr.cfm> (accessed 19 September 2005).

Keohane, R.O., *After Hegemony: Cooperation and Discord in the World Political Economy*, Princeton, NJ: Princeton University Press, 1984.

Kepel, G., *Allah in the West*, Stanford, CA: Stanford University Press, 1997.

Kepel, G., *Jihad: the Trail of Political Islam*, London: I.B. Tauris, 2000.

Kepel, G., *The Prophet and Pharaoh: Muslim Extremism in Egypt*, London: Al Saqi Books, 1985.

Kilchling, M., "Die Praxis der Gewinnabschöpfung in Europa," *Kriminologische Forschungsberichte aus dem Max-Planck-Institut für ausländisches und internationales Strafrecht*, vol. 99, Freiburg in Breisgau: Max Planck, 2002.

Kingstone, J., "Clear Evidence of Links between Tamil gangs and LTTE," *CanTYD Media*, 2003.

KPMG, *Money Laundering: Review of the Reporting System*, London: KPMG, 2003.

Krasner, S., "Structural Causes and Regime Consequences: Regimes as Intervening Variables," *International Organization*, 1982, vol. 36, no. 2, pp. 185–205.

Kupperman, R.H., "A Dangerous Future," *Harvard International Review*, Summer 1995, vol. 17, no. 3.

Lander, S., *Review of Suspicious Activity Reports Regime*, London: The Stationery Office, March 2006. Online. Available HTTP: <http://www.soca.gov.uk/downloads/SOCAtheSARsReview_FINAL_Web.pdf> (accessed 25 April 2007).

Lankhorst, F. and H. Nelen, "Professional Services and Organised Crime in the Netherlands," *Crime, Law and Social Change*, January 2005, vol. 42, no. 2–3.

Leiken, R., "Immigration: Is Integration Failing?" panel discussion, International Summit on Democracy, Terrorism, and Security, Madrid, 9 March 2005. Online. Available HTTP: <http://english.safe-democracy.org/keynotes/immigration-is-integration-failing.html> (accessed 17 October 2005).

Lerner, S., "The Nuremberg Menace," *Village Voice*, 10 April 2001. Online. Available HTTP: <http://www.villagevoice.com/issues/0114/lerner.php> (accessed 16 September 2005).

Levey, S., Under Secretary, Office of Terrorism and Financial Intelligence, US Department of the Treasury, Testimony before the Senate Committee on Banking, Housing and Urban Affairs, 4 April 2006. Online. Available HTTP: <http://www.treas.gov/press/releases/js4155.htm> (accessed 6 December 2006).

Levey, S., Under Secretary, Office of Terrorism and Financial Intelligence, US Department of the Treasury, Prepared Remarks before the 5th Annual Conference on Trade, Treasury and Cash Management in the Middle East, 7 March 2007. Online. Available HTTP: <http://www.ustreas.gov/press/releases/hp297.htm> (accessed April 2007).

Levi, M., "The Prevention of Plastic and Cheque Fraud: A Briefing Paper," London: Home Office, 2000.

Levi, M., "Organised Crime and Terrorism", in M. Maguire, R. Morgan and R. Reiner (eds) *The Oxford Handbook of Criminology*, Fourth Edition, Oxford: Oxford University Press, 2007.

Levi, M. and J. Handley, *The Prevention of Plastic and Cheque Fraud Revisited*, London: Home Office, Research Study 182, 1998.

Levi, M. and A. Smith, *A Comparative Analysis of Organized Crime Conspiracy Legislation and Practice and Their Relevance to England and Wales*, London: Home Office OLR 17/02, 2002.

Levi, M. and M. Maguire, "Reducing and Preventing Organized Crime: an Evidence-Based Approach," *Crime, Law and Social Change*, June 2004, vol. 41, no. 5, pp. 397–469.

Levi, M. and Reuter, P., "Money Laundering" in M. Tonry (ed) *Crime and Justice: A Review of Research*, vol.34, Chicago: Chicago University Press, 2006, 289–375.

Levi, M., H. Nelen and F. Lankhorst, "Lawyers as Crime Facilitators in Europe: an Introduction and Overview," *Crime, Law and Social Change*, January 2005, vol. 42, no. 2–3.

Levitt, M., "Combating Terrorist Financing, Despite the Saudis," Washington Institute for Near East Policy, *Policy Watch* #673, 1 November 2002.

Levitt, M., "Islamic Extremism in Europe: Beyond al-Qaeda: Hamas and Hezbollah in Europe," Testimony to the Joint Hearing of the Committee on International Relations, Subcommittee on Europe and Emerging Threats, United States House of Representatives, 27 April 2005.

Levitt, M., "Saudi Financial Counter-Terrorism Measures (Part II): Smokescreen or Substance," Washington Institute for Near East Policy, *Policy Watch* #687, 10 December 2002.

Levitt, M., "The Political Economy of Middle East Terrorism," *MERIA Journal*, December 2002, vol. 6, no. 4.

Løj, E., Remarks at the 5229th meeting of the Security Council, UN Doc. S/PV.5229, 20 July 2005. Online. Available HTTP: <http://www.un.org/Depts/dhl/resguide/scact2005.htm> (accessed 10 December 2006).

"Looking in the Wrong Places," *The Economist*, 22 October 2005. Online. Available HTTP: <http://economist.com/displaystory.cfm?story_id=5053373> (accessed 10 December 2006).

Lormel, D., Testimony before the Senate Judiciary Committee, Subcommittee on Technology, Terrorism, and Government Information, 9 October 2002. Online. Available HTTP: <http://corprisk.timberlakepublishing.com/files/10–9.pdf#search=%22Lormel%202002%20testimony%22> (accessed 6 September 2006).

MacCoun, R. and P. Reuter, *Drug War Heresies: Learning from Other Vices, Times and Places*, New York: Cambridge University Press, 2001.

McCormick, G.H., "Terrorist Decision Making," *Annual Review of Political Science*, 2003, vol. 6, pp. 473–507.

MacFarquhar, N., "Fears of Inquiry Dampen Giving by U.S. Muslims," *The New York Times*, 31 October 2006.

McGrory, D. and J. Doran, "Bin Laden Funded by Bogus Charities," *Sunday Times*, 25 September 2001.

Mackenzie Institute, "Funding Terror: The Liberation Tigers of Tamil Eelam and their Criminal Activities in Canada and the Western World," *Mackenzie Briefing Notes*, Toronto: Mackenzie Institute, 1996.

McNeil, D.G., "A Nation Challenged: Sanctions," *New York Times*, 13 April 2002.

McNerney, P., "Combatting WMD Proliferation Support Networks: Financial and Economic Sanctions," Testimony before the House Committees on Foreign Affairs and Financial Services, 18 April 2007. Online. Available HTTP: <http://www.internationalrelations.house.gov/110mcn041807.htm> (accessed 24 April 2007).

Maimbo, S.M., *The Money Exchange Dealers of Kabul: A Study of the Hawala System in Afghanistan*, Washington, DC: World Bank, 2003.

Makarenko, T., "Crime, Terror and the Central Asian Drug Trade," *Harvard Asia Quarterly*, Summer 2002, vol. 6, no. 3. Online. Available HTTP: <http://www.fas.harvard.edu/~asiactr/haq/200203/0203a004.htm> (accessed 19 September 2005).

Makarenko, T., "The Changing Dynamics of Central Asian Terrorism," *Jane's Intelligence Review*, February 2002. Online. Available HTTP: <http://www.janes.com/security/international_security/news/jir/jir020129_1_n.shtml> (accessed 13 April 2007).

March of Dimes, "History of Success." Online. Available HTTP: <http://www.marchofdimes.com/aboutus/789.asp> (accessed 16 September 2005).

Martin, S.T., "Frozen Accounts Jeopardize Learning, Healing in Gaza," *St. Petersburg Times Online*, 15 September 2003. Online. Available HTTP: <http://www.sptimes.com/2003/09/15/Worldandnation/Frozen_accounts_jeopa.shtml> (accessed 18 October 2005).

Melucci, A., *Challenging Codes: Collective Action in the Information Age*, London: Cambridge University Press, 1996.

Merari, A., "The Readiness to Kill and Die: Suicidal Terrorism in the Middle East," in W. Reich (ed.) *Origins of Terrorism: Psychologies, Ideologies, Theologies, States of Mind*, Washington: Wilson Center Press, 1998.

MER-C website. Online. Available HTTP: <http://web.archive.org/web/20041027094523/http://www.mer-c.org/background.htm> (accessed 27 October 2004).

Mesoy, A., *How Does Political Alienation Cause Muslims in London to Engage in Radical Political Behaviour?*, Masters Dissertation, Aberystwyth, 2004.

Metz, S., *The Future of Insurgency*, 10 December 1993. Online. Available HTTP: <http://www.au.af.mil/au/awc/awcgate/ssi/metz.pdf> (accessed 19 September 2005).

Middleton, D. and M. Levi, "The Role of Solicitors in Facilitating 'Organized Crime': Situational Crime Opportunities and Their Regulation," *Crime, Law and Social Change*, January 2005, vol. 42, no. 2–3, pp. 123–161.

Millar, A. and E. Rosand, *Allied Against Terrorism: What's Needed to Strengthen the World Wide Commitment*, New York: Century Foundation Press, 2006.

Milligan, J., "Regulatory Avalanche: Tide of New Regulations is Forcing Banks to Build a True Compliance Culture," *Banking Strategies*, March/April 2004, vol. 80 no. II.

Milton-Edwards, B., *Islamic Politics in Palestine*, London: Tauris Academic Studies, 1996.

Ministry of Home Affairs, "Singapore Government Press Statement on the Detention of 2 Singaporean Members of the Jemaah Islamiyah Karachi Cell," 18 December 2003.

Ministry of Home Affairs, *White Paper: The Jemaah Islamiyah Arrests and the Treat of Terrorism*, Singapore, 2003.

Mueller, J., *Overblown: How Politicians and the Terrorism Industry Inflate National Security Threats, and Why We Believe Them*, New York: The Free Press, 2006.

Munro, C., "Muklas Confessed to Bali, Court Told," *The Age*, 23 July 2003.

Muslim Council of Britain, "Letter to Mosques and Muslim Leaders," *The Guardian*, London, 31 March 2004.

"Muslim Vote Pivotal to General Election Outcome," Press Release, *MABonline.net*, 6 May 2005. Online. Available HTTP: <http://www.mabonline.info/english/modules.php?name=News&file=article&sid=378> (accessed 18 October 2005).

Nadelmann, E., *Cops Across Borders: the Internationalization of U.S. Criminal Law Enforcement*, University Park, PA: Pennsylvania State University Press, 1993.

Nakashima, E., "Indonesian Militants 'Keep Regenerating,'" *Washington Post*, 25 March 2004.

Napoleoni, L., *Modern Jihad: Tracing the Dollars Behind the Terror Networks*, London: Pluto, 2003.

Napoleoni, L., *Terror Incorporated: Tracing the Dollars Behind the Terror Networks*, New York: Seven Stories Press, 2005.

National Commission on Terrorist Attacks, *The 9/11 Commission Report: Final Report of the National Commission on Terrorist Attacks Upon the United States*, New York: W.W. Norton & Company, 2004.

National Research Council, *Transnational Organized Crime: Summary of a Workshop*, Washington, DC: National Research Council, 1999.

Naylor, R.T., *Satanic Purses: Money, Myth and Misinformation in the War on Terror*, Montreal: McGill-Queen's University Press, 2006.

Naylor, R.T., *Wages of Crime*, Ithaca, NY: Cornell University Press, 2002.

NCIS, *Annual Threat Assessment Report 2000*, London: National Criminal Intelligence Service, 2000.

NCIS, *The National Intelligence Model*, London: National Criminal Intelligence Service, 2000.

NCS, *National Crime Squad: Corporate Plan 2002–2005*, London: National Crime Squad, 2002.

NCIS, *Annual Threat Assessment Report 2002*, London: National Criminal Intelligence Service, 2003.

Netherlands Chamber of Commerce Homepage. Online. Available HTTP: <http://www.kvk.nl> (accessed 10 December 2006).

Newcomb, R., "Session 2: Canada and U.S. Approaches to Trade Sanctions – U.S. Speaker," *Canada–United States Law Journal*, 2005, vol. 31.

Newcomb, R., Testimony before the Senate Governmental Affairs Committee,

31 July 2003, Online. Available HTTP: <http://www.senate.gov/~govt-aff/index.cfm?Fuseaction=Hearings.Testimony&HearingID=106&WitnessID=367> (accessed 7 September 2006).

Newcomb, R., Testimony before the House Financial Services Subcommittee on Oversight and Investigation, 16 June 2004. Online. Available HTTP: <https://www.ustreas.gov/press/releases/js1729.htm> (accessed 7 September 2006).

Niksch, L., "Abu Sayyaf: Target of Philippine–U.S. Anti-Terrorism Cooperation," Congressional Research Service, 25 January 2002. Online. Available HTTP: <http://fpc.state.gov/documents/organization/8046.pdf> (accessed 19 September 2005).

Northern Ireland Affairs Committee, The Financing of Terrorism in Northern Ireland, Fourth Report of Session 2001–02, HC978–1, London: The Stationery Office, 2002.

Northern Ireland Affairs Committee, *The Impact in Northern Ireland of Cross-Border Road Fuel Price Differentials: Three Years On*, First Report of Session 2002–03, HC 105–1, London: The Stationery Office, 2002.

Northern Ireland Office, *Government Response to Goldstock Report*, Belfast: Northern Ireland Office, 2004.

Northern Ireland Task Force, *Threat Assessment 2003: Serious and Organised Crime in Northern Ireland*, Belfast: Northern Ireland Office, 2004.

"Not Saying the 'AQ' Word," *Geopolitical Review*, 16 November 2004. Online. Available HTTP: <http://www.geopoliticalreview.com/archives/000500.php> (accessed 17 October 2005).

Offshore Group of Banking Supervisors, "OGBS Welcomes Eight Special Recommendations on Terrorist Financing," November 2001. Online. Available HTTP: <http://www.ogbs.net/press8specialrecs.htm> (accessed 10 December 2006).

Offshore Group of Banking Supervisors, "OGBS Welcomes Revised FATF Recommendations," July 2003. Online. Available HTTP: <http://www.ogbs.net/press40recs.htm> (accessed 7 December 2006).

Olson, M., *The Logic of Collective Action*, Cambridge, MA: Harvard University Press, 1971.

O'Neill, P.Statement, 7 November 2001. Online. Available HTTP: <http://www.treas.gov/press/releases/po770.htm> (accessed 10 December 2006).

O'Neill, S., "British Islam Colleges 'Link to Terrorism,' " *The Times*, London, 29 July 2004.

Page, J., "Muslims Seeking Paradise Turn to Extremism in the Face of Poverty," *The Times*, London, 21 May 2005.

Palestinian Centre for Human Rights, "PCHR Calls upon the Palestinian Authority to Cancel Its Decision to Freeze Funds of Charitable Societies," Press Release, Gaza, 28 August 2003.

Pape, R., *Dying to Win: The Strategic Logic of Suicide Terrorism*, New York: Random House, 2005.

Pape, R., "The Strategic Logic of Suicide Terrorism" *American Political Science Review*, August 2003.

Passas, N., "Facts and Myths About 'Underground Banking,' " in P.C. van Duyne V. Ruggiero, M. Scheinost and W. Valkenburg (eds.) *Cross-Border Crime in a Changing Europe*, Tilburg and Prague: Tilburg University and Prague Institute of Criminology and Social Prevention, 2000.

Passas, N., "Financial Controls of Terrorism and Informal Value Transfer Methods," in H. van de Bunt, D. Siegel and D. Zaitch (eds.) *Transnational Organized Crime, Current Developments*, Dordrecht: Kluwer, 2003.

Passas, N., "Fighting Terror with Error: The Counter-productive Regulation of Informal Value Transfers," Crime, *Law and Social Change*, 2006 Online. Available HTTP: <http://dx.doi.org/10.1007/s10611–006–9041–5> (accessed 11 December 2006).

Passas, N., "Formalizing the Informal? Problems in the National and International Regulation of Hawala," in *Regulating Hawala and other Informal Funds Transfer Systems*, Washington, DC: International Monetary Fund, 2005.

Passas, N., "Hawala and Other Informal Value Transfer Systems: How to Regulate Them?" *Journal of Risk Management*, 2003, pp. 39–49.

Passas, N., *Informal Value Transfer Systems and Criminal Organizations; A Study into So-Called Underground Banking Networks*, The Hague: Ministry of Justice, 1999. Online. Available HTTP: <http://www.wodc.nl/images/on1999–4_Full%20text_tcm11–5548.pdf> (accessed 11 April 2007).

Passas, N., *Informal Value Transfer Systems, Money Laundering and Terrorism, Report to the National Institute of Justice (NIJ) and Financial Crimes Enforcement Network*, Washington, DC: FinCEN, November 2003. Online. Available HTTP: <http://www.ncjrs.gov/pdffiles1/nij/grants/208301.pdf>.

Pathan, D., "Tamil Tiger Foothold Shows Security Flaws," *The Nation*, 31 March 2000.

Pawson, R. and N. Tilley, "Caring Communities, Paradigm Polemics, Design Debates," *Evaluation*, 1998, vol. 4, no. 1, pp. 73–90.

PBS, "A Terrorist's Testimony," *PBS Frontline*. Online. Available HTTP: <http://www.pbs.org/wgbh/pages/frontline/shows/trail/inside/testimony.html> (accessed 19 September 2005).

Pease, K., "Crime Prevention," in M. Maguire, R. Morgan and R. Reiner (eds.) *The Oxford Handbook of Criminology*, 3rd edn, Oxford: Clarendon Press, 2002.

Performance and Innovation Unit (PIU), *Recovering the Proceeds of Crime*, London: Performance and Innovation Unit, Cabinet Office, 2000.

"Periodic Report on the National Emergency with Respect to Persons who Commit, Threaten to Commit, or Support Terrorism, Communication from the President of the United States," US Government Printing Office, 24 September 2002. Online. Available HTTP: <http://www.treasury.gov/offices/enforcement/ofac/presdocs/sdgt902report.pdf#search=%22al%20Barakaat%20delisted%20August%2027%22> (accessed 7 September 2006).

Perlez, J., "Saudis Quietly Promote Strict Islam in Indonesia," *New York Times*, 4 July 2003.

Pieth, M. (ed.), *Financing Terrorism*, Boston, MA: Kluwer Academic Publishers, 2002.

Pipes, D., "A New Way to Fight Terrorism," *Jerusalem Post*, 24 May 2000.

Pistole, J.S., Federal Bureau of Investigation, Testimony before the Senate Committee on Governmental Affairs, 31 July 2003. Online. Available HTTP: <http://www.fbi.gov/congress03/pistole073103.htm> (accessed 6 September 2006).

Post, J., "Terrorist Psycho-Logic," in W. Reich (ed.) *Origins of Terrorism: Psychologies, Ideologies, Theologies, States of Mind*, Washington, DC: Wilson Center Press, 1998.

Powell, W.W., "Neither Market nor Hierarchy: Network Forms of Organization," *Research on Organizational Behavior*, vol. 12, 1990.

"President Announces Crackdown on Terrorist Financial Network," White House

Press Release, 7 November 2001. Online. Available HTTP: <http://www.white house.gov/news/releases/2001/11/20011107–4.html> (accessed 7 September 2001).

"President Freezes Terrorists' Assets," Remarks by the President, Secretary of the Treasury O'Neill and Secretary of State Powell on Executive Order, 24 September 2001 Online. Available HTTP: <http://www.whitehouse.gov/news/releases/2001/09/20010924–4.html> (accessed 6 September 2006).

Ranetunge, D., "British Charities Fund Terrorists," *The Island*, 4 October 2000. Online. Available HTTP: <http://www.priu.gov.lk/news_update/features/20001004British_charities_fund_terrorists%20.htm> (accessed 17 October 2005).

Rapoport, D.C., *Inside Terrorist Organizations*, 2nd edn, Portland, OR: Frank Cass, 2001.

Rapportage werkgroep/Terrorismefinanciering en terrorismebestrijding, 8 July 2003. Online. Available HTTP: <http://www.fecinfo.nl> (accessed 24 June 2004).

Rashid, A., *Jihad: the Rise of Militant Islam in Central Asia*, New Haven, CT: Yale University Press, 2002.

Rashid, A., "The Taliban: Exporting Extremism," *Foreign Affairs*, November/December 1999.

Ratnesar, R., "Confessions of an Al Qaeda Terrorist," *Time*, 23 September 2003.

"Real IRA Arms Purchasing in Croatia Indicates a Change of Tactics," *Jane's Terrorism and Security Monitor*, 23 August 2000.

"Real Trouble," *The Economist*, 10 March 2001.

Realuyo, C.B., "G8 Counter-terrorism Action Group Efforts to Combat Terrorist Financing," Presentation to Follow-up meeting to the United Nations Counter-terrorism Committee (CTC) Special Meeting of 6 March 2003, 11 March 2004. Online. Available HTTP: <http://www.osce.org/documents/sg/2004/03/3297_en.pdf> (accessed 6 December 2006).

Realuyo, C.B. and S. Stapleton, "Response to Bali: An International Success Story," *eJournal USA*, US State Department, September 2004. Online. Available HTTP: <http://usinfo.state.gov/journals/ites/0904/ijee/stapleton.htm> (accessed 30 August 2006).

Red Cross, "Donate Goods." Online. Available HTTP: <http://www.redcross.org/donate/goods/> (accessed 12 October 2005).

Reference Guide to Anti-Money Laundering and Combating the Financing of Terrorism, Washington, DC: The World Bank and the International Monetary Fund, 2003.

Reinhart, C. and K. Rogoff, "The Modern History of Exchange Rate Arrangements: A Reinterpretation," *NBER Working Paper 8963*, Cambridge, MA: National Bureau of Economic Research, 2002. Online. Available HTTP: <http://papers.nber.org/papers/w8963.pdf> (accessed 11 April 2007).

Report of the Secretary General, "Uniting against terrorism: recommendations for a global counter-terrorism strategy." UN Doc. A/60/825 (27 April 2006). Online. Available HTTP: <http://documents-dds-ny.un.org/doc/UNDOC/GEN/N06/330/88/pdf/N0633088.pdf?OpenElement> (accessed 7 December 2006).

Reuter, P. and E. Truman, *Chasing Dirty Money*, Washington, DC: Institute for International Economics, 2004.

Reuter, P. and Stevens, A., *An Analysis of UK Drug Policy*, London: The Stationery Office, April 2007. Online. Available HTTP: <http://www.ukdpc.org.uk/docs/UKDPC%20drug%20policy%20review.pdf> (accessed 25 April 2007).

Roane, K.R., D.E. Kaplan and C. Ragavan, "Putting Terror Inc. on Trial in New York," *U.S. News and World Report*, 8 January 2001, vol. 130, no. 1.

Robinson, G., "Hamas as Social Movement," in Q. Wiktorowicz (ed.) *Islamic Activism: a Social Movement Theory Approach*, Bloomington: Indiana University Press, 2004.

Rock, B.E., Testimony before the Committee on Financial Services, Subcommittee on Financial Institutions and Consumer Credit, United States House of Representatives, 18 May 2006. Online. Available HTTP: <http://www.aba.com/NR/rdonlyres/222CE044–577A–11D5-AB84–00508B95258D/44029/BRockTestimony05182006.pdf> (accessed 9 September 2006).

Roig-Franzia, M., "Man Convicted of Using Smuggling to Fund Hezbollah," *Washington Post*, 23 June 2002.

Rotella, S., "Jihad's Unlikely Alliance," *Los Angeles Times*, 23 May 2004.

Roth, J., D. Greenberg and S. Wille, *Monograph on Terrorist Financing* (Staff Report to the Commission), National Commission on Terrorist Attacks Upon the United States, 2004. Online. Available HTTP: <http://www.9–11commission.gov/staff_statements/911_TerrFin_Monograph.pdf#search=%229%2F11%20commission%20monograph%22> (accessed 7 September 2006).

Roule, T., "Post-911 Financial Freeze Dries Up Hamas Funding," *Jane's Intelligence Review*, 17–19 May 2002, no. 14.

Rudner, M., "Using Financial Intelligence Against the Funding of Terrorism," *International Journal of Intelligence and Counterintelligence*, 2005, vol. 19, no. 1, pp. 31–58.

Rumsfeld, D., Memo to General Dick Myers, Paul Wolfowitz, etc., 16 October 2003 Online. Available HTTP: <http://www.globalsecurity.org/military/library/policy/dod/rumsfeld-d20031016sdmemo.htm> (accessed 7 September 2006).

Saeed, O., "Labour Has Forfeited the Muslim Vote," *The Guardian*, London, 25 May 2004.

Sageman, M., *Understanding Terror Networks*, Philadelphia: University of Pennsylvania Press, 2004.

Samad, Y., "Imagining a British Muslim Identification," in S. Vertovece and A. Rogers (eds.) *Muslim European Youth: Reproducing Ethnicity, Religion, Culture*, Aldershot: Ashgate, 1998.

Saudi Arabian Monetary Agency, "A Collection of the Monetary and Banking Laws and Regulations," Riyadh: Saudi Arabian Monetary Agency, 1994.

"Saudi Money Transfers to the Hamas and to Extremist Groups Identified with It," Report of the (Israeli) Intelligence and Terrorism Information Center at the Center for Special Studies, February 2003. Online. Available HTTP: <http://www.intelligence.org.il/eng/bu/saudi/saudi.htm> (accessed 17 October 2005).

Schelling, T., *The Strategy of Conflict*, Cambridge, MA: Harvard University Press, 1960.

Schelling, T., *Arms and Influence*, New Haven, NJ: Yale University Press, 1966.

Schelling, T., "What Purposes can 'International Terrorism' Serve?" in R.G. Frey and C.W. Morris (eds.) *Violence, Terrorism, and Justice*, Cambridge: Cambridge University Press, 1991.

Schlosser, E., *Reefer Madness: Sex, Drugs, and Cheap Labor in the American Black Market*, New York: Houghton Mifflin, 2003.

Schmid, A.P., "The Links between Transnational Organized Crime and Terrorist Crimes," *Transnational Organized Crime*, Winter 1996, vol. 2, no. 45, pp. 40–81.

Schneider, S., "Alternative Approaches to Combating Organized Crime: a Conceptual Framework and Empirical Analysis," *International Journal of Comparative Criminology*, 2001, vol. 1, no. 2, pp. 144–179.

Schneider, S., *Money Laundering in Canada: an Analysis of RCMP Cases*, Toronto: Nathanson Center, 2004.

Schott, P.A., *Reference Guide to Anti-Money Laundering and Countering the Financing of Terrorism*, 2nd edn, Washington, DC: International Bank for Reconstruction and Development, the World Bank, and the International Monetary Fund, 2004.

Schwartz, D., *Political Alienation and Political Behavior*, Chicago, IL: Aldine Publishing, 1973.

Scott, W.R., *Organizations: Rational, Natural, and Open Systems*, 2nd edn, Englewood Cliffs, NJ: Prentice-Hall Inc., 1981.

Selznick, P., *The Organizational Weapon: A Study of Bolshevik Strategy and Tactics*, Santa Monica, CA: RAND Corp, 1952.

"Senate Democrats Announce Major Security Legislation: Real Security Act of 2006 Makes Defense of Nation Reflect Lessons of 9/11," 7 September 2006. Online. Available HTTP: <http://democrats.senate.gov/newsroom/record.cfm?id=262588> (accessed 10 December 2006).

"Sending Greenbacks Back to the Old Country: Immigrant Experience," *St. Louis Post-Dispatch*, 3 December 2005.

Shaikh, T., "London to Host Islamic 'Celebration' of Sept 11," *London Telegraph*, 8 September 2002. Online. Available HTTP: <http://news.telegraph.co.uk/news/main.jhtml?xml=/news/2002/09/08/nextre08.xml> (accessed 18 October 2005).

Sharma, R., "LeT Turning Global: Dawood's Links Come to the Fore," *The Tribune*, 19 January 2003. Online. Available HTTP: <http://www.tribuneindia.com/2003/20030119/main1.htm> (accessed 19 September 2005).

Sherman, L.W., D. Gottfredson, D.L. MacKenzie, J. Eck, P. Reuter and S. Bushway, *Preventing Crime: What Works, What Doesn't, What's Promising*, Washington, DC: National Institute of Justice, grant no. 96MUMU0019, 1997.

Sherman, L.W., D.P. Farrington, B.C. Welsh and D.L. MacKenzie, *Evidence-Based Crime Prevention*, London: Routledge, 2002.

Silke, A., "Drinks, Drugs, and Rock'n'Roll: Financing Loyalist Terrorism in Northern Ireland – Part 2," *Studies in Conflict and Terrorism*, 1 April 2000, vol. 23, no. 2.

Simpson, C., "U.S. Seeks Access to Malaysian Al Qaeda Suspect," *Chicago Tribune*, 7 December 2003.

Slaughter, A., *A New World Order*, Princeton, NJ: Princeton University Press, 2004.

Small, R.A., "Proposed 'Know Your Customer' Regulation," Testimony before the Subcommittee on Commercial and Administrative Law, Committee on the Judiciary, US House of Representatives, Washington, DC, 4 March 1999. Online. Available HTTP: <http://www.federalreserve.gov/BOARDDOCS/TESTIMONY/1999/19990304.htm> (accessed 10 December 2006).

Smith, C., "North Africa Feared as Staging Ground for Terror, *New York Times*, 20 February 2007, p. 3. Online. Available HTTP: <http://www.nytimes.com/2007/02/20/world/africa/20tunisia.html?_r=1&th=&emc=th&pag...> (accessed 25 April 2007).

Smith, Paul J., "Transnational Terrorism and the Al Qaeda Model: Confronting New Realities," *Parameters*, 2002, vol. 32.

Society for Worldwide Interbank Financial Telecommunication (SWIFT), "Update and Q&A to SWIFT's 23 June 2006 Statement on Compliance," 25 August 2006. Online. HTTP: <http://www.swift.com/index.cfm?item_id=60275> (accessed 6 September 2006).

Soggot, M., "Conflict Diamonds are Forever," Center for Public Integrity, 8 November 2002. Online. Available HTTP: <http://www.publicintegrity.org/bow/report.aspx?aid=152> (accessed 19 September 2005).

"Special Report: Terror Groups," *The St. Petersburg Times*. Online. Available HTTP: <http://www.sptimes.com/2003/webspecials03/alarian/terror.shtml> (accessed 17 October 2005).

Stark, R., "The Organizational Age," *Sociology*, 3rd edn, Belmont, CA: Wadsworth, 1989.

State Bank of Pakistan, *Annual Report FY 2001*, Karachi: Central Bank, 2002.

Steele, J., "Building Site Thefts Funding Terrorism," *Daily Telegraph*, 9 December 1996.

Stern, J., "The Protean Enemy," *Foreign Affairs*, July–August 2003.

Stern, J., *Terror in the Name of God: Why Religious Militants Kill*, New York: Harper Collins, 2003.

Stork, J., *Erased In a Moment: Suicide Bombing Attacks against Israeli Civilians*, New York: Human Rights Watch, 2002.

Studio MER-C, "Pasir Hitum Teluk Galela" ("The Black Sand of Galela Bay") and "Dan Kesaksian Pun Menangis" ("And the Witnessing Despite the Crying"), video. Online. Available HTTP: <http://web.archive.org/web/20040721081633/http://www.mer-c.org/vcd_01.htm> (accessed 21 July 2004).

Sunier, T., "Islam and Interest Struggle: Religious Collective Action among Turkish Muslims in the Netherlands," in S. Vertovece and A. Rogers (eds.) *Muslim European Youth: Reproducing Ethnicity, Religion, Culture*, Aldershot: Ashgate, 1998.

Superceding Bill of Indictment Docket No 3:00CR 147-MU 03/28/01 *US v. Mohamad Youssef Hammoud et al.*

Suskind, R., *The Price of Loyalty*, New York: Simon & Schuster, 2004.

Suskind, R., *The One Percent Doctrine*, New York: Simon & Schuster, 2006.

"Suspected Terrorists Arrested at NAIA," *Philippine Daily Inquirer*, 15 March 2002.

"Swede Removed from Terror Suspect List," *The Somaliland Times*, 19 August 2006. Online. Available HTTP: <http://www.somalilandtimes.net/sl/2005/239/24.shtml > (accessed 10 December 2006).

Targeted Financial Sanctions: A Manual for Design and Implementation, Contributions from the Interlaken Process, Part 2, published by the Swiss Confederation in cooperation with the UN Secretariat and the Watson Institute for International Studies, Brown University, 2001.

Tenet, G.J., "The Worldwide Threat 2004: Challenges in a Changing Global Context," Testimony of Director of Central Intelligence, George J. Tenet before the Senate Select Committee on Intelligence, 24 February 2004. Online. Available HTTP: <http://www.cia.gov/cia/public_affairs/speeches/2004/dci_speech_02142004.html> (accessed 16 September 2005).

"Terror Suspects Used Donations to Fund Bombings, Train Islamic Extremists," *Associated Press*, 1 January 2003.

"Terrorist Assets Report, Calendar Year 2005," US Department of the Treasury. Online. Available HTTP: <http://www.ustreas.gov/offices/enforcement/ofac/reports/tar2005.pdf> (accessed 7 September 2006).

"The Lost Trail – Efforts to Combat the Financing of Terrorism are Costly and Ineffective," *The Economist*, 22 October 2005. Online. Available HTTP: <http://www.belt.es/articulos/articulo.asp?id=3161> (accessed 10 December 2006).

Tirman (ed.) *Terror, Insurgency, and the State*, Philadelphia: University of Pennsylvania Press, 2007.

Toumpis, S. and A. Goldsmith, "Ad Hoc Network Capacity," Asilomar Conference on Signals, Systems, and Computers, vol. 2, Pacific Grove, CA, October 2000.

Transactional Records Access Clearinghouse (TRAC), Syracuse University, "Criminal Terrorism Enforcement in the United States During the Five Years Since the 9/11/01 Attacks." Online. Available HTTP: <http://trac.syr.edu/tracreports/terrorism/169/> (accessed 21 November 2006).

Traynor, I., "Liberal Culture under Threat in Dutch Religious and Ethnic Crisis," *The Guardian*, London, 12 November 2004.

Tremlett, G., "Karadzic Family 'Arming Real IRA,' " *The Guardian*, 5 April 2001.

United Arab Emirates Central Bank, "Abu Dhabi Declaration on Hawala," Abu Dhabi: UAE Central Bank, 16 May 2002.

United Kingdom Assets Recovery Agency *Annual Report 2005–06*, London: The Stationery Office, June 2006. Online. Available HTTP: <http://www.assets recovery.gov.uk/NR/rdonlyres/8D8413B8-B0FE-4A9F-AA02–2E2A9771A809/ 0/ARAAnnualReport06_new.pdf> (accessed 25 April 2007).

United Kingdom, H.M. Treasury, "Launch of anti-money laundering and counter-terrorist finance strategy," 28 February 2007. Online. Available HTTP: <http:// www.hm-treasury.gov.uk/newsroom_and_speeches/press/2007/press_23_07.cfm> (accessed 26 April 2007).

United Kingdom National Audit Office, *The Assets Recovery Agency*, London: The Stationery Office, February 2007. Online. Available HTTP: <http://www.nao.org.uk/ publications/nao_reports/06–07/0607253.pdf> (accessed 25 April 2007).

United Kingdom Serious Organized Crime Agency (SOCA), *Annual Plan 2007/08*, London: The Stationery Office, 2007. Online. Available HTTP: <http:// www.soca.gov.uk/assessPublications/downloads/SOCAAnnualPlan2007_8.pdf> (accessed 25 April 2007).

"UN Sanctions 'Hitting al-Qaeda,' " *BBC News*, 11 January 2005. Online. Available HTTP: <http://news.bbc.co.uk/2/hi/americas/4164631.stm> (accessed 6 September 2006).

United Nations, "Security Council Committee Meets Senior US Officials to Discuss Implementation of Sanctions against Al-Qaida, Taliban," Press Release, 1 November 2005. Online. Available HTTP: <http://www.un.org/News/Press/docs/ 2005/sc8288.doc.htm> (accessed 4 December 2006).

United Nations Counter-Terrorism Committee, "Follow-up meeting to the United Nations Counter-Terrorism Committee (CTC) Special Meeting of 6 March 2003," UN Doc. S/2004/276, 1 April 2004. Online. Available HTTP: <http://www.un.org/ Docs/sc/committees/1373/ctc_meeting.html> (accessed 10 December 2006).

United Nations Counter-Terrorism Committee, "Proposal for the Revitalisation of the Counter-Terrorism Committee," UN Doc. S/2004/124, 19 February 2004. Online. Available HTTP: <http://www.un.org/sc/ctc/cted.shtml> (accessed 10 December 2006).

United Nations Counter-Terrorism Committee, "Outcome Document of the Special Meeting of the Counter-Terrorism Committee with International, Regional and Subregional Organizations," UN Doc. S/AC.40/2003/SM.1/4, 31 March 2003. Online. Available HTTP: <http://www.un.org/Docs/sc/committees/1373/ ctc_meeting.html> (accessed 10 December 2006).

United Nations General Assembly, *International Convention for the Suppression of the Financing of Terrorism*, 1999. Online. Available HTTP: <http://untreaty.un.org/English/Terrorism/Conv12.pdf> (accessed 17 October 2005).

United Nations High-Level Panel on Threats, Challenges and Change, "A More Secure World: Our Shared Responsibility – Report of the High-Level Panel on Threats, Challenges and Change," UN Doc. A/59/565, 2 December 2004, p. 47. Online. Available HTTP: <http://www.un.org/secureworld/report.pdf > (accessed 7 December 2006).

United Nations Office of Drugs and Crime, "Strengthening International Cooperation and Technical Assistance in Promoting the Implementation of the Universal Conventions and Protocols Related to Terrorism within the Framework of the Activities of the United Nations Office on Drugs and Crime," UN Doc. E/CN.15/2005/13, 8 April 2005. Online. Available HTTP: <http://www.unodc.org/unodc/en/terrorism.html> (accessed 10 December 2006).

United Nations Resolution 1373, 2001. Online. Available HTTP: <http://www.unodc.org/images/resolution%201373.pdf> (accessed 22 May 2005).

United Nations Secretary-General, "Steps Taken to Make the Counter-Terrorism Committee Executive Directorate Fully Operational: Report of the Secretary-General," UN Doc. S/2004/914, 19 November 2004. Online. Available HTTP: <http://www.un.org/sc/ctc/cted.shtml> (accessed 10 December 2006).

United Nations Security Council, transcript of 4453rd meeting, UN Doc. S/PV.4453, 18 January 2002. Online. Available HTTP: <http://www.un.org/Depts/dhl/resguide/scact2002.htm> (accessed 10 December 2006).

United Nations Security Council 1267 Committee Monitoring Group, "First report of the Analytical Support and Sanctions Monitoring Team appointed pursuant to resolution 1526 (2004) concerning Al-Qaida and the Taliban and associated individuals and entities," 25 August 2004. Online. Available HTTP: <http://www.un.org/Docs/sc/committees/1267/1267mg.htm> (accessed 10 December 2006).

United Nations Security Council 1267 Committee Monitoring Group, "Second report of the Analytical Support and Sanctions Monitoring Team appointed pursuant to resolution 1526 (2004) concerning Al-Qaida and the Taliban and associated individuals and entities," UN Doc. S/2005/83, 15 February 2005. Online. Available HTTP: <http://www.un.org/Docs/sc/committees/1267/1267mg.htm> (accessed 10 December 2006).

United Nations Security Council 1267 Committee Monitoring Group, "Fifth report of the Analytical Support and Sanctions Monitoring Team appointed pursuant to resolution 1526 (2004) concerning Al-Qaida and the Taliban and associated individuals and entities," 20 September 2006. Online. Available HTTP: <http://www.un.org/Docs/sc/committees/1267/1267mg.htm> (accessed 4 December 2006).

United Nations Security Council 1267 Committee, "Guidelines of the Committee for the Conduct of its Work," as amended 6 April 2003. Online. Available HTTP: <http://www.un.org/Docs/sc/committees/1267/1267_guidelines.pdf> (accessed 10 December 2006).

United States v. William J. Coleman and Orna Vainstein, Criminal No. 98–71 (SMO), filed 1998.

USA PATRIOT Act of 2001 and ancillary laws, 8 USC 1182, 22 USC 2656, 18 USC 2339.

US Code Title 18, 1001.

US Code Title 18, 1343.

US Code Title 18, 1342.

US Code Title 18, 1956.

US Court of Appeals for the 9th Circuit, *Planned Parenthood of the Columbia/ Willamette Inc.; Portland Feminist Women's Health Center; Robert Crist, M.D.; Warren M. Hern, M.D.; Elizabeth Newhall, M.D.; James Newhall, M.D., Plaintiffs-Appellees, and Karen Sweigert, M.D., Plaintiff, v. American Coalition of Life Activists; Advocates For Life Ministries; Michael Bray; Andrew Burnett; David A. Crane; Timothy Paul Dreste; Michael B. Dodds; Joseph L. Foreman; Charles Roy Mcmillan; Stephen P. Mears; Bruce Evan Murch; Catherine Ramey; Dawn Marie Stover; Charles Wysong, Defendants, and Monica Migliorino Miller; Donald Treshman, Defendants-Appellants*, case no. 99–35320.

US Department of State, *International Narcotics Control Strategy Report 2003*, Bureau for International Narcotics and Law Enforcement Affairs, March 2004.

US Department of State, *International Narcotics Control Strategy Report 2005*, Bureau for International Narcotics and Law Enforcement Affairs, March 2005.

US Department of State, *Patterns of Global Terrorism*, 21 May 2002. Online. Available HTTP: <http://www.state.gov/s/ct/rls/pgtrpt/2001/html/10252.htm#hamas> (accessed 17 October 2005).

US Department of Treasury, A Report to the Congress in Accordance with Section 359 of the Uniting and Strengthening America by Providing Appropriate Tools Required to Intercept and Obstruct Terrorism Act of 2001, 2002. Online. Available HTTP: <http://www.fincen.gov/hawalarptfinal11222002.pdf> (accessed 10 December 2006).

US Department of Treasury, "Terrorist Assets Report, Calendar Year 2005," Online. Available HTTP: <http://www.ustreas.gov/offices/enforcement/ofac/reports/tar2005.pdf> (accessed 7 September 2006).

US Department of Treasury, "Terrorist Financing Fact Sheet," 20 December 2001. Online. Available HTTP: <http://www.treas.gov/press/releases/po886.htm> (accessed 6 September 2006).

United States District Court, Central District of California Humanitarian Law Project, et al. Plaintiffs, v. United States Department Of Treasury, et al. Case No.: CV 05–8047 ABC (RMCx). Online. Available HTTP: <http:// www.cacd.uscourts.gov/CACD/RecentPubOp.nsf/bb61c530eab0911c882567cf 005ac6f9/7d5c944cb7f546168825723500599af7/$FILE/CV05–8407ABC.pdf> (accessed 28 November 2006).

US Executive Order 13224, Executive Order on Terrorist Financing Blocking Property and Prohibiting Transactions With Persons Who Commit, Threaten to Commit, or Support Terrorism,, 24 September 2001. Online. Available HTTP: <http://www.whitehouse.gov/news/releases/2001/09/20010924–1.html.> (accessed 7 September 2006).

US General Accounting Office, *Terrorist Financing: Agencies Should Systematically Assess Terrorists' Use of Alternative Financing Mechanisms*, GAO–04–163, November 2003. Online. Available HTTP: <http://www.gao.gov/new.items/ d04163.pdf> (accessed 10 December 2006).

US General Accounting Office, *Investigations of Terrorist Financing, Money Laundering, and Other Financial Crimes*, GAO–04–464R Financial Crime Investigations, 20 February 2004. Online. Available HTTP: <http://www.gao.gov/new.items/ d04464r.pdf> (accessed 10 December 2006).

US General Accounting Office, *Terrorist Financing: Better Strategic Planning Needed to Coordinate U.S. Efforts to Deliver Counter-Terrorism Financing*

Training and Technical Assistance Abroad, GAO–06–19, October 2005. Online. Available HTTP: <http://www.gao.gov/new.items/d0619.pdf> (accessed 4 December 2006).

US House of Representatives Committee, Financial Services Subcommittee on Financial Institutions and Consumer Credit, "Bank Secrecy Act's Impact on Money Services Businesses," 21 June 2006. Online. Available HTTP: <http://financialservices.house.gov/hearings.asp?formmode=detail&hearing=482&comm= 3>.

"U.S. Indicts British Cleric on 11 Charges," *MSNBC News*, 27 May 2004. Online. Available HTTP: <http://www.msnbc.msn.com/id/5071534> (accessed 17 October 2005).

US Senate, "Money Laundering and Foreign Corruption: Enforcement and Effectiveness of the Patriot Act – Case Study Involving Riggs Bank," Report prepared by the Minority staff of the Permanent Subcommittee on Investigations, Washington, DC: US Senate, 2004.

US v. Hanafy et al. 302 F 3rd 485.

van Natta, D. and T. O'Brien, "Flow of Saudi Cash to Hamas Is under Scrutiny by U.S.," *New York Times*, New York, 17 September 2003.

Vermaat, E., "Bin Laden's Terror Networks in Europe," Toronto: Mackenzie Institute, 2002. Online. Available HTTP: <http://www.mackenzieinstitute.com/2002/2002_Bin_Ladens_Networks.html> (accessed 19 September 2005).

Vettori, B., *Tough on Criminal Wealth: Exploring the Practice of Proceeds from Crime Confiscation in the EU,* Dordrecht, Netherlands: Kluwer, 2006.

Vettori, B., "Tough on Criminal Wealth: Law in the Books, Law in Action," Ph.D. Dissertation, 2004.

Villalon, C., "Cocaine Country," *National Geographic Magazine*, July 2004.

Walker, J., "Introduction," *International Journal of Comparative Criminology*, 2001, vol. 1, no. 2, pp. 1–7.

Walker, J., *Estimates of the Extent of Money Laundering in and through Australia*, Queanbeyan, NSW: AUSTRAC/J. Walker Consulting Services, 1995.

Ward, C.A., "Building Capacity to Combat International Terrorism: the Role of the United Nations Security Council," *Journal of Conflict and Security Law*, 2003, vol. 8, no. 2, pp. 289–305.

Ward, C.A., "The Role of the United Nations Security Council in Combating International Terrorism," Paper presented at the Oxford Conference – The Changing Face of International Co-operation in Criminal Matters in the 21st Century, Christ Church College, Oxford, UK, 27–30 August 2002.

Wazir, B., "Essex Boys Sign up for 'Holy War,' " *The Observer*, London, 24 February 2002.

Wayne, E.A., Assistant Secretary for Economic and Business Affairs, US Department of State, Testimony before the Senate Committee on Banking, Housing and Urban Affairs, 4 April 2006. Online. Available HTTP: <http://banking.senate.gov/_files/ACFFE09.pdf> (accessed 6 December 2006).

Wechsler, W., "Follow the Money," *Foreign Affairs*, vol. 80, no. 4, pp. 40–57, July/August 2001.

Weick, K.E. and K.M. Sutcliffe, *Managing the Unexpected: Assuring High Performance in the Age of Complexity*, San Francisco: Jossey Bass, 2001.

Weintraub, S., "Tools to Combat Terrorism: Disrupting the Financing of Terrorism," *The Washington Quarterly*, Winter 2002, vol. 24, no. 1.

Weisman, S. R. "US Pursues Tactic of Financial Isolation," 16 October 2006, *New*

York Times; Statement of Daniel Glaser, Deputy Assistant Secretary (Terrorist Financing and Financial Crimes), US Department of Treasury, before the Senate Banking Committee, 12 September 2006. Online. Available HTTP:<http://www.ustreas.gov/press/releases/hp93.htm> and <http://www.treas.gov/offices/enforcement/311_actions.shtml> (accessed 6 September 2006).

Weissman, G., *Terror on the Internet: The New Arena, the New Challenges*, Washington: United States Institute of Peace, 2006.

Werner, R.W., Testimony before the Senate Banking Committee, 12 September 2006. Online. Available HTTP: <http://www.fincen.gov/werner_statement_09122006.html> (accessed 20 September 2006).

White, M.J., "The Constitution, Terrorism, and Civil Liberties," 2004 Constitution Address at Dickinson College, 21 September 2004. Online. Available HTTP: <http://www.clarkecenter.org/content/occasionalpapers/Constitution-Civil%20Liberties-White.pdf#search=%22%22every%20dollar%20matters%22%20Mary%20Jo%20White%22> (accessed 30 August 2006).

White, J.R., *Terrorism: An Introduction*, 2nd edn, Belmont, CA: Wadsworth/West, 1998.

Williams, J., Statement Before the US Senate Committee on Banking, Housing, and Urban Affairs, 26 April 2005. Online. Available HTTP: <http://www.occ.treas.gov/ftp/release/2005-41a.pdf#search=%22estimate%20unregistered%20msbs%22> (accessed 5 September 2006).

Williams, P. and R. Godson, "Anticipating Organized and Transnational Crime," *Crime, Law and Social Change*, vol. 37, no. 4, pp. 311–355, 2002.

Wilson, P.Q., *Political Organizations*, Princeton, NJ: Princeton University Press, 1995.

Wolfsberg Group, "Wolfsberg Statement on the Suppression of the Financing of Terrorism," January 2002. Online. Available HTTP: <http://www.wolfsberg-principles.com/pdf/ws_on_terrorism.pdf> (accessed 6 December 2006).

Woodiwiss, M., *Organized Crime and American Power: a History*, Toronto: University of Toronto Press, 2001.

World Bank/IMF, "Effective Regimes to Combat Money Laundering and the Financing of Terrorism: Strengthening the Collaborative Process – Lessons Learned," 2004. Online. Available HTTP: <http://siteresources.worldbank.org/EXTAML/Resources/396511–1146581427871/AML.Lessons.Learned.pdf> (accessed 10 December 2006).

"Wrong Signal on Money Laundering," *New York Times*, 28 June 2001. Online. Available HTTP: <http://www.nytimes.com/2001/06/28/opinion/28THU3.html?ex=1131512400&en=faf3c0be70cc34d9&ei=5070> (accessed 7 November 2005).

"Young Islam: Hardline Youths Fuel Bitter Divide," *The Observer*, London, 4 April 2004.

Zarate, J.C., "Securing the Financial System against Rogue Capital," US Department of Treasury, 10 November 2003. Online. Available HTTP: <http://www.ustreas.gov/press/releases/js984.htm> (accessed 4 December 2006).

Index